In the name of God, the Most

CONFUSED ♡ N ....QUM

"فَإِنَّهَا لا تَعمَى الأبصارُ وَلٰكِن تَعمَى القُلوبُ الَّتي فِي الصُّدورِ"

For indeed, it is not the eyes that grow blind, but it is the hearts within the chests which become blind."

[22:46]

CONFESSIONS OF A LONDON IMAM

PART I – NO TO VIOLENCE IN THE NAME OF GOD

PART II – DECLINE OF MUSLIM NATIONS

By Dr Mohammed Fahim PhD

Dedication

This book and any proceeds from it are fully dedicated to my mosque (Qur'ani Murkuz Trust – South Woodford Islamic Centre – Registered Charity Number: 1081317) in South Woodford, London, England. I have been the Trust's Chairman and Head Imam of the mosque since they were established in 1994. This is a voluntary job and I do not receive any remuneration or financial gain from it. This mosque is known to be a centre of education and for delivering the true moderate and tolerant message of Islam. It empowers women and promotes integration in the West, without losing our faith or diluting our religion. It encourages multi-faith dialogue and respects British values, which in fact, are the same as Islamic values.

Table of Contents

Acknowledgements

At the very outset, I thank God the Al-Mighty for guiding and helping me to write this book.

I would like to express my most sincere thanks to Abdullah Yusuf Ali for his great superlative work, "The Holy Qur'an: Text, Translation and Commentary". I have been studying his work since 1970. It is, by far, the best known, most studied and most respected English translation of The Qur'an. The authenticity of Yusuf Ali's extensive scholarly commentaries and explanatory notes and its distinguishing characteristics have been a great source of inspiration, not only to me, but also to many others. I have referred to many of his comments whilst writing this book. May God reward him abundantly, forgive all his sins and admit him to His Gardens of Bliss.

I would like to thank my fellow trustees at Qur'ani Murkuz Trust (QMT) for their guidance and support whilst writing this book.

Many thanks to the London Metropolitan Police, especially Assistant Commissioner Helen Ball, Commander Mak Chishty and Chief Superintendent Sue Williams for all their support over the years whilst working alongside them in building bridges with the Muslim communities in London. Being the Muslim Chaplain to the Met and a member of the Independent Advisory Group (IAG) helped in improving how the Muslim communities perceive the work of the police. This working relationship had a huge influence in the making of this book.

A great amount of credit is owed to my Personal Assistant (PA) Miss Zainab Abbas for the magnificent work she did in assisting me in checking and revising the text. Credit must also go to Mrs Tallat Bhatti for her tremendous efforts in editing the text.

When it came to publishing the book, we explored many different avenues and concluded that the best way forward was to publish it on Amazon as an e-book and as a hard copy. This responsibility was taken by Mr Bilal Nawaz, whom I thank for his efforts. I also thank my grandson, Ilyas Peters, for the amazing design of this book's cover.

Introduction

In March 2014, I was a speaker at a conference organised by the London Metropolitan Police to address "Ending Violence Against Women and Young Girls". In my speech, I covered the rights given by Islam to women and I spoke against the evil custom and tradition of Female Genital Mutilation (FGM) which is shamelessly practiced in some Muslim countries and even secretly in the UK. I was given a standing ovation.

An incident which occurred at the end of this conference led me to write this book which consists of two parts. **Part I** deals with **"No to Violence in the Name of God"**. Its purpose is to educate people regarding the peaceful teachings of Islam and to deter Muslims from committing any forms of violence in the name of God. Whilst **Part II** addresses the reasons for the **"Decline of Muslim Nations"** and how these nations can become prosperous again and end their current state of humiliation.

But first, let me tell you more on this incident...

When the conference was over, I was approached by two people (who I later learnt were an Iranian father and his daughter). They started verbally abusing me in front of many people. The daughter shouted at me saying, *"You are a liar. Islam never gave any rights to women. Islam condemns and belittles women. Islam favours men over women and permits husbands to beat up their wives"*. I said, *"this is not true; you are taking things out of context"*. The daughter did not even give me a chance to explain and continued shouting. She said, *"Why is the testimony of two women equivalent to one man? Why does a woman get half the inheritance of a man? Why can a Muslim man have four wives and a Muslim woman can only have one husband? Why can a Muslim man marry a Jewish or a Christian woman, but a Muslim woman can only marry a Muslim man? You are talking about an Islam which does not exist"*.

She sounded so angry, but it was clear from her comments that she had no in-depth knowledge of the teachings of Islam. I tried to answer her questions, but without success as she continued shouting and screaming at me. Only God knows what life experiences she had been through for her to think of Islam in this way.

Then her father shouted at me saying, *"Islam is a religion of violence. Muslims kill innocent people in the name of God. They glorify suicide bombers and regard them as martyrs. The Qur'an incites violence against non-Muslims. Tell me, which Islam to follow? Khomeini's Islam (Iranian's Islam) or Taliban's Islam (Afghanistan's Islam) or Wahhabi's Islam (Saudi's Islam)?!"*

I felt extremely sorry for him as his questions and the manner in which he spoke, indicated that he was very confused as well as angry. In his aggressive comments he referred to the city of Qom in Iran, from where many mullahs originated including Ayatollah Khomeini who led the Iranian Islamic revolution in 1978. The father categorically opposed this revolution which in his words forced a militant and bloody Islam on Iranian people, which made him rebel.

I calmly said, *"There is only ONE GOD and ONE Islam. Follow what Prophet Mohammed, peace be upon him (pbuh), brought."* He responded by saying, *"They all claim that they are following Mohammed!"* The man was right but was again showing his confusion. By right I mean that the followers of these different religious sects would actually claim that they are all followers of Mohammed (pbuh).

I replied saying, *"The main reason for your confusion, is that the majority of the Muslims worldwide, do not practice or adhere to God's Commandments in the Qur'an. If you study the Qur'an and reflect on God's Moral Law in it, you will discover God's Islam. You will discover Islamic values which excel any man-made values in the East or the West. Apply these values in the country you live in, whilst respecting the laws of that country and showing gratitude and being loyal as God commands you to be."*

I went on to say, *"Integrate without losing your identity or watering down your religion. Respect the law of the country you live in. Adhere to British values, which do not contradict with Islamic values. If you do all this, you would be applying the Islam in the Qur'an which can suit any time or environment. Call it 'God's Islam', the Islam which God brought to humanity from Adam to Noah to Abraham to Moses to Jesus and to Mohammed, (peace be upon them all). Or call it 'British Islam' if this would make you feel happier."* Then a policewoman escorted me to get me out safely.

The incident above was a very disturbing experience for me. The daughter accused Islam of being hostile and unfair to women. Her father claimed that Islam is a religion of violence, which incites hatred against non-Muslims and justifies their killing. Whilst reflecting on it later and on what is happening in the Muslim World today, if we can call it 'Muslim World', I appreciated the confusion and frustration of the Iranian man and his daughter.

You can see the confusion we are all going through because the **peaceful** religion of Islam has been hijacked by many small factions who claim to be Muslims and who justify the killing and the destruction of each other under a banner, which displays the same message: *"There is no God but Allah, Mohammed is the Messenger of Allah".*

It is sad to mention that a number of mosques in the UK are experiencing militant conduct by some of their worshipers. This has led to the hijacking of several mosques by extremist groups who are distorting the peaceful message of Islam. There are certain Imams who attract individuals from the congregation and create groups, who then revolt against the managing trustees to implement their own agenda for either their own material gains or power, ignoring the spiritual message of the mosque.

I strongly felt that I must dedicate some of my time to respond to the confusion and frustration experienced by many Muslims.

This led me to the writing of this book: "**Confused** ♥️ **Muslims.Qom - Confessions of a London Imam**", ('Qom' is the city in Iran referred to earlier).

In the three chapters of Part I, this book covers topics like jihad, martyrdom, suicide bombers, and counter terrorism. It also explains how Muslims should respond to insults against God and His Messengers, and it refers to Qur'anic guidance in ending violence against women and girls.

In Chapter One of Part II, I detail the impact of God's Moral Law on the formation of the **"Four Jewels of Nation's Prosperity".** In Chapter Two, I refer to the role played by Satan since the creation of Adam to divide and destroy humanity through his human agents. These agents are regarded by God in the Qur'an, as human Satans. They are those who had forsaken God and rejected His Moral Law, denied the Hereafter and pushed people away from His Straight Path. People like that believe themselves to be more superior to others. This is the same superiority complex which led to the expulsion of Satan from God's Grace and excluded him from His Mercy. Satan refused God's Command to prostrate himself to Adam and claimed to be better than Adam because he was created from fire and Adam was created from clay. That was the first ever racist remark to be uttered by one of God's creatures. Unfortunately, this is shared by many people today, who look down on others due to their colour, faith, ethnicity or social status. In Chapter Three, I share my personal experience in inviting all to the Way of God and my involvement with interfaith and multi-faiths activities. All the original letters and emails I refer to within this chapter can be viewed on our Instagram and Facebook links:

http://instagram.com/swic.uk

http://facebook.com/swic.uk

http://twitter.com/ukswic

The work carried out by SWIC (South Woodford Islamic Centre) can be seen on our website and social media channels:

https://swic.uk

In addressing these topics in this book, I relied entirely on the Qur'an and authentic prophetic traditions (hadith) by the Prophet Mohammed (pbuh). There will be those who will disagree with me. However, I am willing to listen to any constructive comments or criticism and I encourage such comments to be sent to me via email to **confused.muslims.qom@gmail.com**

I recommend that this book becomes part of the syllabus of Muslim schools and Mosques' madrasa (schools) to prevent young people being drawn into violence and terrorism. It is also a good read for police officers working with the Muslim communities in the UK.

As mentioned in the Acknowledgments, I have referred to many of the explanations and comments mentioned in the footnotes made by the great Muslim scholar Abdulla Yusuf Ali in his inspiring publication: "The Holy Qur'an: Text, Translation and Commentary". I have always felt that his well-researched comments are like hidden treasures which should be shared with the world. Whenever I refer to any comments, I write FN (footnote) followed by the number and when I refer to any Qur'anic verses, I write the chapter number followed by the verse number.

I hope this book is a source of inspiration to all the readers, especially the young Muslims, who will ascertain from this book, that there is no such thing as radical, militant, or extremist Islam. There is only one Islam, which promotes love, peace, tolerance and justice between all of God's creatures. That is God's Islam.

PART I - NO TO VIOLENCE IN

THE NAME OF GOD

Chapter One -We Can Defeat Terrorism Together

1.1 Introduction

"As for those who strive in Our Cause (do Jihad), We shall surely guide them to Our Ways, Indeed God is with those who do good." – 29:69

Unfortunately, some Muslims as well as non-Muslims, interpret the word "Jihad" as only to mean "fighting a war against non-Muslims". This is incorrect, because firstly the war must be Holy and secondly, participating in a 'Holy War' is one of several forms of "Jihad" as defined by God in the Qur'an and by Prophet Mohammed (pbuh). This misinterpretation of the word "Jihad" arises from misconceptions about terminology, and above all, from distortion by taking quotations from the Qur'an or the Hadith out of context.

For a war to be Holy, it must be fought for a just cause, either in self-defence or in the defence of those who are weak and oppressed, whilst adhering to God's commandments regarding war's conduct. Fighting for name or fame or booty (spoils of war) is not a fight in the Cause of God. Also, a war of aggression is not Holy.

Waging a war to fight an aggressor, irrespective of his religion, is the sole responsibility of the armed forces of any civilised country. This type of fighting is known in Arabic as "Qitaal". It is a form of "Jihad" if it is fought for the Cause of God. If the country becomes occupied, Islam calls upon every citizen, men and women, to rise to fight the occupier and be willing to sacrifice their lives and property to free their country. This is also in accordance with the UN Charter and International Law, which permit fighting the occupier to liberate the country. In modern history, the French resistance against the Nazi occupation in the Second World War was in compliance with this.

Unfortunately, misconception of "Jihad" and "Martyrdom" by some Muslims, led to the formation of militant, radical, and terrorist groups, who took certain verses in the Qur'an out of context, and used them to justify their violence against innocent people. For example, verse 9:29 which says, "*Fight those of the People of the Book, who don't (truly) believe in God nor the Last Day, who don't forbid what God and His Messenger have forbidden nor acknowledge the Religion of Truth, until they pay the Jizya with willing submission, and feel themselves subdued.*", was used by these groups to incite hatred and violence against non-Muslims living in Muslim countries. There is a lot of misunderstanding by Muslims and Non-Muslims regarding the meaning of Jizya.

"*The root meaning of the word Jizya is compensation. The derived meaning, which became the technical meaning, was a poll-tax levied from those who did not accept Islam, but were willing to live under the protection of Islam, and were thus tacitly willing to submit to its ideals being enforced in the Muslim State. There was no amount permanently fixed for it. It was an acknowledgement that those whose religion was tolerated would in their turn not interfere with the preaching and progress of Islam. Imam Al-Shafi suggests one Dinar per year, which would be the Arabian gold Dinar of the Muslim States. The tax varied in amount, and there were exemptions for the poor, females and children (according to Imam Abu-Hanifa), for slaves, and for monks and hermits. Being a tax on able-bodied males of military age, it was in a sense a commutation for military service. The Jizya was thus partly symbolic and partly a commutation for military service, but as the amount was insignificant and the exemptions numerous, its symbolic character predominated.*" FN1281 & FN1282.

Another verse which was taken out of context, is verse 9:123, "*O you who believe! Fight the unbelievers who are near to you and let them find harshness in you. And know that God is with those who fear Him.*" This verse was revealed to address the wars of aggression waged by the idol worshippers in Makkah against the newly formed Muslim community in Madina. When conflict became inevitable, the first thing was to clear the surroundings of all evil, for it is only evil that can rightly be fought.

Unfortunately, The British National Party (BNP), used this verse to incite hatred against Muslims, during their local elections campaign in Loughton and Debden, in Essex, England, in the year 2009. Their leaflet said: "*Do you really want to live next to people who want to kill you?! ... the BNP love Loughton and we'll do all in our power to prevent Islam creeping into our town*"

Verse 9:123 was also used by terrorist groups, like ISIS, Al-Qaeda, Taliban and Bokoharam to justify their crimes against innocent non-Muslims, in the neighbourhoods they controlled.

In the next sections, I will define the meaning of a "Holy War" and the different types of "Jihad" and refer to martyrdom and the punishment and condemnation of terrorism in Islam.

1.2 Different Types of Jihad

A) Jihad as Fighting a Holy War

Fighting only in self-defence or in support of those who are weak and oppressed, whilst observing God's rules and commandments regarding war's conduct on the battlefield, is "Jihad". This has a great reward from God, if the fight is in His Cause.

In 61:10-12, God invites the believers to sacrifice their wealth and their lives in His Cause, in return for the Greatest Salvation: "*O you who believe! Shall I lead you to a bargain that will save you from a grievous chastisement? That you believe in God and His Messenger (Mohammed), and that you strive (your utmost) in the Cause of God, with your wealth and your lives. That is the best for you, if only you knew. He will forgive you your sins, and admit you to Gardens beneath which rivers flow, and to beautiful mansions in Gardens of Eternity, that is indeed the supreme Triumph.*"

What a wonderful bargain! What we are asked to give is so little, but what we are promised in return is so much. There comes God's unbounded Bounty and Munificence.

And in 4:95-96, He says: "*Not equal are those believers who sit (at home), except those who are disabled, and those who strive and fight in the Cause of God with their wealth and their persons. God has granted a grade higher to those who strive and fight with their wealth and persons than those who sit (at home). Unto all (in Faith) God has promised good. But those who strive and fight He has distinguished above those who sit (at home) by a great reward. Ranks specially bestowed by Him and Forgiveness and Mercy. For God is Oft-Forgiving, Most Merciful*"

"*God's goodness is promised to all people of Faith. But there are degrees among men and women of Faith. There are people with natural inertia: they do the minimum that is required of them, but no more. There are people who are weak in will: they are easily frightened. There are people who are so strong in will and so firm in faith that they are determined to conquer every obstacle, whether in their own physical or other infirmities or in the external world around them. In a time of Jihad, when people give their all, and even their lives, for the common cause, they must be accounted more glorious than those who sit at home, even though they have good will to the cause and carry out minor duties in aid. The special reward of such self-sacrifice is special forgiveness and mercy, as proceeding from the direct approbation and love of God.*" FN614.

Cause of God

But what is the meaning of "Cause of God"? I believe that whoever fights to establish the Truth and Justice of God to achieve stable, fair and permanent peace, is fighting for the Cause of God. If the fighting is for fame or name or for material gains or worldly rewards or to occupy a country to rob and enslave its people and demoralise them, then it is not for the Cause of God, and cannot be Holy. Hence, no honourable government should ever initiate a war in any country in the world to promote its arms sales, nor be allies to those who initiate such wars.

It must be made clear that the relationship between people intended by God, as defined in the Qur'an, is one of peace. Islam regards war as a contingency that becomes necessary at certain times and under certain circumstances and conditions, in order to achieve and restore peace, and to stop evil from triumphing in a way that would corrupt the earth. God says in 22:40, "*...For had it not been for God's repelling some people by means of others, monasteries, churches, synagogues, and mosques, in which the name of God is commemorated in abundant measure would assuredly have been pulled down. God will* certainly aid those who aid His (Cause); for verily God is Full of Strength, Exalted in Might (able to enforce His Will)."

War as self-defence

In Islam, there is no justification for war other than self-defence, including pre-empting an imminent attack and the defence of those who are oppressed. God says in 2:190, "*Fight in the Way of God those who fight against you, but don't transgress, as God doesn't love the transgressor.*"

"*So war is permissible in self-defence, and under well- defined limits. When undertaken, it must be pushed with vigour, but not relentlessly, but only to restore peace and freedom for the worship of God. In any case strict limits must not be transgressed: women, children, old and infirm men should not be molested, nor trees and crops cut down, nor peace withheld when the enemy comes to terms.*" FN204.

God reprimands us in verse 4:75, "*And why should you not fight in the Cause of God and of those who, being weak, are ill-treated (and oppressed)? Men, women, and children, whose cry is 'Our Lord! Rescue us from this town, whose people are oppressors, and raise for us from Yourself one who will protect and raise for us from Yourself one who will give us victory'.*"

Therefore, where there is both just cause and righteous intention, war becomes an obligation for self-defence and the defence of those who are oppressed. The fighters should never turn their backs and run away as this is a major sin in Islam as stated in 8:15-16, "*O you who believe! When you face the unbelievers in a battle field, never turn your backs to them. And whoever turns his back to them on such a day, unless it be a stratagem of war, or to retreat to a troop (of his own), he indeed has drawn on himself wrath from God. And his abode is Hell, an evil refuge (indeed).*"

When the believers have been given victory, they should not become triumphant or arrogant or have a sense of being a superpower, because God's help is for those who do not seek to exalt themselves on earth or spread corruption as verse 22:41 says: "*Those who, if We establish them in the land, establish regular prayer and give regular charity, enjoin the right and forbid wrong. With God rests the end (and decision) of (all) affairs.*"

Islam has given instructions for the humane and civilised treatment of prisoners of war and for the relationship with non-Muslims. War is not a means in Islam of converting other people from their religion.

Making peace between warring factions is very highly recommended, as stated in verse 8:61, "*And if they (the enemy) incline to peace, incline you (Mohammed) also to it, and trust in God, for He is the One that hears and knows (all things).*"

This type of "Jihad" which is described above, is known in Arabic as "FardhKefaia", which means, if some people do it, then it is not obligatory on the rest, provided the enemy is not occupying the country. **As previously stated, this role is only to be played by the**

established armed forces of any civilised country.

During the time of Prophet Mohammed (pbuh), over 1400 years ago, the Muslim army was made up of volunteers. If a battle is to be fought, each individual will bring his own means of transport, a camel or a horse or a donkey. They will also bring their own weapons like arrows, spears, swords, and shields. Consequently, they will be entitled to receive a share from the booty, the spoil of war, if they win the battle.

In modern history, no one has the right to form his own army within a country and claim to use it to defend his faith or to protect his people. This would lead to civil unrest and would have disastrous consequences, as it is witnessed in many countries in the world today.

Respecting democratically elected Governments

God commands us in 4:59, to respect the government we democratically elected: *"O you who believe! Obey God and obey the Messenger and those charged with authority (or responsibility or decision, or the settlement of affairs) among you. And if you have a dispute in any matter, refer it to God and the Messenger, if you believe in God and the Last Day. That is better and more beneficial in the end."*

"All ultimate authority rests in God. Prophets of God derive their authority from Him. As Islam makes no sharp division between sacred and secular affairs, it expects governments to be imbued with righteousness. Likewise, Islam expects Muslims to respect the authority of such government for otherwise there can be no order or discipline." FN580.

Fardh Ain – Fight the aggressor as a citizen of the county you reside in

As stated earlier, if the enemy invades a country and occupies it, it becomes obligatory for every citizen, including women, to fight the aggressor. This is known in Arabic as "Fardh Ain". For example, if a country attacks Britain and occupies it, it would be regarded as an aggressor. Hence, it would become mandatory, not only on the British armed forces, but also British civilians, men and women, including British Muslims, irrespective of their origin, to fight the aggressor, even if the aggressor was a Muslim country. This is the justice of Islam, which is not understood by many people whether they are Muslims or non-Muslims. They must all be willing to sacrifice their lives and wealth to liberate Britain.

A stunning biblical example was the fight of young David alongside King Saul, against a tyrant Goliath as stated in the Qur'an 2:251, *"By God's will, they defeated them and David slew Goliath, and God gave him power and wisdom and taught him whatever He willed. And had God not checked one set of people by means of another, the earth would indeed be full of mischief, but God is full of bounty to all the worlds."*

"...When Saul offered his own armour and arms to David, the young hero declined, as he had not tried them, while his shepherd's sling and staff were his well-tried implements. He picked up five smooth pebbles on the spot from the stream and used his sling to such effect that he knocked down Goliath. He then used Goliath's own sword to slay him. There was consternation in the Philistine army. They broke and fled and were cut to pieces." FN286.

Not having the right weapons to fight the occupier is not an excuse to accept any form of oppression. The main lesson is that if we want to preserve our national existence and our faith, it is our duty to fight with courage and firmness. Hence, David became the role model of a "Jihadist". Many young people who fight the occupier emulate what he did. Sadly, to say, that the word "Jihadist" is now used in the media to refer to those who commit terrorist attacks. And those who commit these atrocities claim that they are "Jihadists" fighting a Holy war and justifying the killing of innocent people. This contradicts the teachings of Islam.

Division into warring factions is seen as a punishment, which God brings on people who do wrong. God says in 6:65, "*Say: 'He has power to send calamities (punishment) on you, from above you or from under your feet, or to bewilder you with dissension and make you taste the violence (tyranny) of one another.' See how We explain the Signs that they may understand.*" These wars are not Holy and fighting in them is not "Jihad". Sowing enmity and hatred amongst people is the work of Satan. Therefore, those who listen to Satan will bring God's wrath on themselves by their own actions. War is hateful and there are no winners!

B) Jihad as the Inner Struggle for Self-Refinement

This can be achieved by resisting all forms of temptation by fighting evil within the human soul, inwardly and outwardly, and striving to do good towards all fellow human beings. This is the real battle, which we must all fight, every moment of our lives.

"*As turned out from the creative hand of God, man is innocent, pure, true, free, inclined to right and virtue, and endued with true understanding about his own position in the Universe and about God's goodness, wisdom, and power. That is his true nature, just as the nature of a lamb is to be gentle and of a horse is to be swift. But man is caught in the meshes of customs, superstitions, selfish desires, and false teaching. This may make him pugnacious, (eager to argue, quarrel or fight), unclean, false, slavish by being submissive, hankering after what is wrong or forbidden, and deflected from the love of his fellow-men and the pure worship of the One True God. To cure this crookedness, and to restore human nature to what it should be under the Will of God, man must not ignore God's Moral Law as detailed in His Divine Revelations.*" FN3541.

God says in 91:7-10, "*And by the Soul, and the One Who Perfected it, and inspired it (with conscience of) what is wrong for it and what is right for it. Truly he succeeds who purifies it. And he fails who corrupts it.*"

"*God makes the soul, and gives it order, proportion, and relative perfection, in order to adapt it for the particular circumstances in which it has to live its life. He breathes into it an understanding of what is sin, impiety, wrong-doing and what is piety and right conduct, in the special circumstances in which it may be placed. This is the most precious gift of all to man, the faculty of distinguishing between right and wrong. Man should learn that his success, his prosperity, his salvation depends on himself, on his keeping his soul pure as God made it. And his failure, his decline, his perdition depending on his soiling his soul by choosing evil.*" FN6152

In 6:104, God commanded Prophet Mohammed (pbuh) to say, "*Clear proofs have come to you from your Lord, if any will see, it will be for the good of his own soul, and if any will be blind, it will be to his own loss, and I'm not here to watch over your doings.*"

In the Qur'an, God postulates three states or stages of the development of the human soul:

Unregenerated Soul
Firstly, an unregenerated human soul that seeks its satisfaction in the lower earthly desires. A soul which is not reforming or showing repentance. A soul which incites what is wrong and is prone to corruption, as stated in 12:53, "*...The human soul certainly incites evil, unless my Lord bestow His Mercy. Surely my Lord is Oft-Forgiving, Most Merciful.*"

This soul if not checked and controlled, will lead to perdition. God says in 79:37-39: "*Then as for him who rebelled and transgressed all bounds, and had preferred the life of this world, surely Hell will be his home.*"

"*The abiding Punishment will be for those who had wilfully and persistently rebelled against God, transgressing all bounds, and had given themselves up to the vanities and lusts of this lower life. This punishment will not touch those who had repented and been forgiven, nor those guilty, through human frailty, of minor sins, whose deeds will be weighed in the balance against their good deeds.*" FN5944.

And He says in 95:4-5, "*We have indeed created man in the best of moulds (form, nature). Then We abased him (to be) the lowest of the low. Except those who believe and do righteous deeds, for they shall have a reward unfailing.*"

"*There is no fault in God's creation. To man God gave the purest and best nature, and man's duty is to preserve the pattern on which God has made him. But by making him vicegerent, God exalted him even higher than the angels, for the angels had to make obeisance to him. But man's position as vicegerent also gives him will and discretion, and if he uses them wrongly, he falls even lower than the beasts.*"

"*If man rebels against God, and follows after evil, he will be abased to the lowest possible position. For Judgement is sure. Those who use their faculties aright and follow God's Moral Law will reach the high and noble destiny intended for them. That reward will not be temporary, but unfailing.*" FN6199 and FN6200.

Self-Correcting Soul
Secondly, a self-correcting soul, which feels conscious of sin and resists it. But if it falls into temptation, it immediately regrets it and repents and asks for God's grace and pardon. It tries to amend and hopes to reach salvation. In 75:2 God swears by this soul, "*And I do swear by the self-reproaching soul.*"

When Adam and Eve, fell into temptation and ate from the forbidden tree, they immediately repented and said, "*Our Lord! We have wronged our souls and if You don't forgive us and show mercy to us, we will be among the losers.*" 7:23.

And God, the Most Merciful forgave them, as stated in 2:37, "*Adam received certain words from his Lord, and his Lord accepted his repentance, for He is the Acceptor of repentance, the Most Merciful.*"

When Prophet Moses killed an Egyptian, by mistake, immediately he admitted his wrongdoing and asked for God's forgiveness and at once he was forgiven, as stated in 28:16: "*(Moses) prayed: O my Lord! I have indeed wronged my soul. Please forgive me. So (God) forgave him, for He is the Oft-Forgiving, the Most Merciful.*"

When Prophet Jonah resigned from his job and left his people and ended up in the belly of the whale, he regretted what he did in haste and asked for God's forgiveness and he was forgiven as stated in 21:87-88: "*And remember Zan-Nun (Jonah), when he departed in wrath. He imagined that We had no power over him! But he cried through the depth of darkness: 'There is no God but You. Glory to You. Truly I have wronged my soul.' So, We listened to him and We saved him from his misery (delivered him from distress), and thus We do save (deliver) those who have faith.*"

So, we must learn to say "sorry" whenever we do something wrong, not only to God, but also to the person whom we might have caused any injuries or injustice.

God says in 79:40-41, "*But as for him who had entertained the fear of standing before his Lord (on the Day of Judgement), and restrained his soul from lusts and lower desires, surely the Garden will be (his) home.*"

"*The contrast is complete and parallel. The persistent rebels against God's Moral Law, who preferred the lower life, are to dwell in the Fire of Punishment, while those who humbly feared the punishment of sin and believing in their Lord's warnings restrained their lower desires, will dwell in the Garden of Bliss.*" FN5945

God commands us in 5:105, to guard our own souls, and He confirms that if we follow His guidance, then no harm can come to us from those who stray. Hence, we must first start with our own soul, and strive (do "Jihad") to remain on God's Straight Path.

A Content Soul
Thirdly, a content soul, which has fully submitted itself to its Creator and constantly fights all forms of evilness, as if it has built a fortress around itself, so no evil can penetrate through. It achieved permanent inner-peace. Thus, no external disturbances or trials or tests or calamities would shake its faith. This soul has the highest stage of all, as stated in 89:27-30. To it will be said, at the moment of death and on the Day of Judgement: "*O soul at perfect peace (in complete rest and satisfaction)! Come back to your Lord, fully pleased (with Him) and well-pleasing (Him). Enter among My (Honoured) Devotees and enter My Heaven.*"

"*The climax of the whole is: '**Enter My Heaven!**' People may have imagined all kinds of heaven before, and many types are used in the sacred Word itself. But nothing can express the reality itself better than '**My Heaven**'-God's own Heaven! May we reach it through God's Grace.*" FN6129.

C) Jihad as Commanding What is Right and Forbidding What is Wrong

Commanding what is right and forbidding what is wrong, is a form of "Jihad", only if we have the correct knowledge of God's Moral Law and the authority to do this. God says in 3:104, "*And let there be among you a community inviting to all that is good, and enjoining the doing of what is right, and forbidding the doing of what is wrong; such are they who are successful.*"

We are instructed in 25:52, to wage the biggest "Jihad" of all, with the weapon of God's Revelation, by the Qur'an, not by the sword, "*Therefore do not listen to the unbelievers, but strive against them with the utmost strenuousness, with the Qur'an*". Our striving should be true and sincere. We must be prepared to show it in deeds of charity to our fellowmen. We must be good citizens, supporting social organisations and participating in community work. And our own individual soul must be firm and unshaken in all circumstances.

Imam Ahmad recorded that the Prophet Mohammed (pbuh) said: "*By He in Whose hand is my soul! You will command righteousness and forbid evil, or God will send a punishment on you from Him. Then, you will supplicate to Him, but He will not accept your supplication.*" Also, Imam Muslim recorded that the Prophet (pbuh) said: "*He among you who witnesses an evil, let him change it with his hand, if he can't do that, then by his tongue, if he can't do even that, then with his heart, and this is the weakest faith.*"

God says in 5:78-79, "*Curses were pronounced on those among the Children of Israel who rejected Faith, by the tongue of David and of Jesus the son of Mary, because they disobeyed and used to transgress. Nor did they forbid one another the iniquities which they committed. Evil indeed were the deeds which they did.*"

"*There are bad men in every community, but if leaders connive at the misdeeds of the commonalty, and even worse, if leaders themselves share in the misdeeds, as happened with the Pharisees and Scribes against whom Jesus spoke out, then that community is doomed.*" FN788. The condemnation of evil by David and Jesus was a form of "Jihad" practiced by them both.

D) Jihad as Fighting Injustice by the Pen or the Tongue without Hostility

Fighting injustice by the pen or the tongue, without malice or spite, is a form of "Jihad".

Abu Dawud, Al-Termidhi, and Ibn Majah recorded in their books of Hadith, that the Prophet Mohammed (pbuh) said, "*The best Jihad is a word of truth proclaimed before an unjust tyrant ruler.*" This is because the one who has the courage to denounce injustice, may put himself and his family at great risk. Therefore, admonishing those who practice injustice and supporting those who are weak and oppressed is "Jihad". Ibn Majah also recorded that the Prophet (pbuh) said, "*Behold! Fear from people should not prevent one from saying the truth if he knows it.*"

God, in 11:113, prohibits us from supporting those who are unjust, "*Don't incline to those who do wrong, lest the Fire should touch you, and you have no protectors beside God, then you will not be helped.*"

I will never forget the pain I went through during the war in Bosnia and the massacres and the war-crimes committed against innocent civilians. The entire world was just watching the extermination of the Muslims, from April 1992 to December 1995. The seeming double standards of the West became more apparent as time passed and documented atrocities were recorded and broadcasted globally. Helpless Muslims were exterminated by the Serb forces, as if the Holocaust against the Jews had not taken place previously or had not been heard of. Young Muslim fighters from a number of Muslim countries joined the Bosnian fighters. They regarded this as "Jihad".

My only contribution was to perform "Jihad" by using my pen. I wrote to every single Arab leader, as well as several European leaders. We had no social media at that time, so it was not an easy task to do, but I felt that it was the least I could do.

Covid-19 – A letter to Boris
During the Corona Virus lockdown in 2020, I wrote on 5th May to the Prime Minister, the Rt Hon. Boris Johnson, comparing Covid-19 to the plagues which God sent on the Ancient Egyptians at the time of Prophet Moses:

"Dear Rt Hon Boris Johnson MP

"May God's Peace, Mercy and Blessings be upon you and your family.

"Many congratulations for Wilfred, a Gift from God, and many thanks to God Almighty for healing you after your close brush with the reality of Life and Death.

"I do not doubt that God Almighty has a purpose for you to accomplish. May God Almighty give you strength and resolve to fulfil that.

"I am sure that a person of your stature and in your position must receive varied communications from various perspectives i.e. socio-political, economic and of course faith as well, all offering views and suggestions for making this world a better place to live and learn any lessons we can from history and any adverse situations we are confronted with from time to time.

"Most of the Holy Scriptures, particularly of the three Abrahamic faiths are full of stories and parables, where God Almighty has continued to warn his creation of the consequences if we go astray and transgress.

"The situation the world is facing today with Covid-19 reminds me of the plagues God sent on Pharaoh who persecuted the Children of Israel in Egypt, at the time of Prophet Moses. The plagues included epidemics among men and beasts, locusts, lice, frogs and water turning to blood. These were from among the hidden "Forces of God."

"Pharaoh and his host denied that these calamities were from God and challenged Moses. Eventually, they were all drowned in the sea because they rejected God's Signs and failed to

take heed of the warnings. Pharaoh declared while drowning, "I believe that there is no god except Him Whom the Children of Israel believe in and I'm of those who submit to God's Will." God responded: "too late now, a little while before you were in rebellion and you did mischief and violence! This day We shall save you in the body, that you may be a sign to those who come after you! But verily, many among mankind are heedless of Our Signs." So, Pharaoh became a lesson of history and his mummy is being displayed in the Egyptian Museum in Cairo.

"Most of those countries in the world which promoted wars, sold arms to fighting factions in the Middle East and supported the killing of innocent people including children, ultimately have to pay a hefty price to fight a hidden enemy who can only be seen by an electron microscope. This hidden enemy is one of "God's Forces". We have two choices, either to acknowledge that this plague is retribution from God, hence, to repent and adjust our individual and national conduct or behave as Pharaoh and his Chiefs did and be prepared for the consequences.

"I am sure you are a man of God who believes in the Day of Accountability and Life after Death. The UK government along with others will be held accountable, not only for the huge loss of innocent lives in the Middle East and elsewhere but also the loss of innocent lives and businesses in the UK, because its conduct brought God's Wrath on us all.

"So, please let us all turn to Our Creator in repentance, ask for His forgiveness and amend our national conduct and review our international relations. We should be the Promoters of Peace, as we are now out of EU but we still have an important role through the Commonwealth, which is a forum to be used for promoting peace, cooperation and progress, fairness, justice and protection of human rights. Let us build our nation on these recognised principles.

"I have no doubt that Britain with its glorious past and present standing can still provide that global leadership for a paradigm shift to seek congruence between political rhetoric and political action. The hard-earned precious resources of the West could be constructively spent to develop and educate the poor and powerless of the world instead of destroying them and eliminating them.

"The UK government should never initiate a war in any country in the world to promote its arms sales, nor be allies to those who initiate such wars. We must stop using double standards in our relations. Sooner or later we are all going to leave this world. So, let us leave a good legacy for our future generations and be prepared for "Question Time" on the "Day of Reckoning."

"May God remove His punishment and show Mercy on us all.

"May God save our Queen and our Country. May God's peace prevail.

Kindest regards

Dr Mohammed Fahim

E) Jihad as in Seeking Knowledge

Persevering patiently in seeking knowledge to benefit, not only ourselves, but the whole of humanity, as stated in Chapter 1, of this book, is a form of "Jihad".

F) Jihad as in Performing Religious Rites
Performing religious duties regularly with sincerity and devotion is "Jihad".

Prayers
Keeping up the five daily prayers and waking up every morning before the sunrise to offer the dawn prayer is a form of "Jihad". God commands in 17:78-79, "*Establish regular prayers from the sun's decline till the darkness of the night, and the recital of the Qur'an in the dawn prayer, for the recital of Qur'an at dawn is witnessed (by certain angels)."*

"*The commentators understand here the command for the five daily canonical prayers, that is the four from the declination of the sun from the zenith to the fullest darkness of the night, and the early morning prayer, Fajr (Dawn), which is usually accompanied by a long recitation of the Qur'an. The morning prayer is specially singled out for separate mention because the morning is a 'peaceful hour' and special influences act on the souls awaking from the night's rest. Special testimony is borne to the prayers of this hour by the angelic host.*" FN2275 & FN2276.

God says in 2:238, "*Guard strictly your (habit of) prayers, especially the Middle Prayer, and stand before God in a devout (frame of mind)."*

And He says in 23:1-2 and 23:9, "*Successful indeed are the Believers. Those who humble themselves in their prayers... And those who (strictly) guard their prayers."*

"*In verse 23:2 we were directed to the spirit of humility and earnestness in our prayers. In verse 23:9 we are told how necessary the habit of regular prayer is to our spiritual well-being and development, as it brings us closer to our Creator.*" FN2870.

A man asked the Prophet Mohammed (pbuh): "*O Messenger of Allah, which deed is most beloved to God?*" He replied: "*Prayer at the appointed time*". Then the man said: "*Then what?*" The Prophet replied: "*Kindness to one's parents*". Then the man asked: "*Then what?*" The Prophet said: "*Jihad (fighting) in the Cause of God.*" This Hadith is recorded by Al-Bukhari and Muslim.

Fasting
Fasting (no food, no drink, no sexual fulfilment), from dawn to sunset, requires full control of all desires. This is a form of "Jihad" since it requires a great deal of self-denial and restraint.

Charity

Spending your wealth in the Cause of God to help the poor and the needy, by feeding them or clothing them or educating them or providing medical help or supplying clean water, is also a kind of "Jihad".

Hajj (Pilgrimage to Makkah)

Performing Hajj is "Jihad". Al-Hassan Ibn Ali says that a man came to the Prophet (pbuh) and said, "*I'm a coward and a weak person. Is there anything I can do?*" The Prophet (pbuh) said, "*You may go for a "Jihad" that involves no fighting, that is Hajj.*" This is recorded by Abdur-Razzaq and At-Tabarani. The Prophet (pbuh) accepted the man's limitations without blaming him for them.

In another Hadith, the Prophet (pbuh) said, "*Hajj is the "Jihad" for the old, the weak and the women.*", recorded by Al-Nasai.

Aisha, the wife of the Prophet (pbuh) said that she asked him, "*O Messenger of God! 'Jihad' (fighting in the Cause of God) is the best deed, should we (women) then, not actively participate in it?*" The Prophet (pbuh) replied, "*The best 'Jihad' for you is Hajj Mabrur.*" That is a faultless Hajj accepted by God. Recorded by Al-Bukhari and Muslim.

In another report Aisha said: "*I once asked the Prophet (pbuh): 'O Messenger of God! Should not we (women) actively participate in the 'Jihad' (fighting in the Cause of God) with you?'*"
He replied, '*The best and the most beautiful Jihad for you is Hajj Mabrur.*'"
Aisha commented, "*After hearing that from the Prophet I shall never cease performing Hajj.*"
Recorded by Al-Bukhari and Muslim.

G) Jihad as in Kindness to Parents

Looking after your parents, if they are in need of you, is another form of "Jihad".
A young man came to the Prophet (pbuh) and requested to join him in a battle. The Prophet (pbuh) asked him: "*Have you got parents?*" The man replied: "*Yes.*" The Prophet said: "*Perform Jihad in them.*" Recorded by Al-Bukhari and others.

H) Jihad as in Supporting Your Family

Working hard to earn lawful money to support your family is a form of "Jihad". This is much better than not working and claiming social security benefits when you can afford to work.

The Prophet (pbuh) said, "*If you spent one Dinar in the Cause of God (for a battle), and one Dinar to free a slave, and one Dinar you gave a poor person, and one Dinar on your family, the one which has the highest reward, is the one you spent on your family.*" Recorded by Muslim.

The Prophet (pbuh) also said, "*If a Muslim man spends on his family willingly, to please God, it will be credited to him as a charity.*" Recorded by Al-Bukhari and Muslim.

I) Jihad as in Inviting People to the Way of God

God commands Mohammed (pbuh) to deliver the message in 31:41, *"...Say (O Mohammed): I am commanded to worship God, and not to join partners With Him. Unto Him do I call, and Unto Him is my return".*

"Gods command is universal – to worship and serve Him and refuse to bend the knee to any other; the man of God finds his staff and support in it; but he must invite all to share in its blessings; it came from God, and to God shall we all return" FN1858

God further commands Mohammed (pbuh) in 5:67, *"O Messenger! Proclaim that which has been sent down to you from your Lord, for if you do not then you will not have delivered His message. God will protect you from people (who mean mischief). Surely, God does not guide those who reject faith"*

"Mohammed had many difficulties to contend with, many enemies and dangers to avoid. His mission must be fulfilled. And he must – as he did – go forward and proclaim that Message and fulfil his mission, trusting to God for protection, and unconcerned if people who has lost all sense of right, rejected it or threatened him" FN777

It is the duty of learned Muslims to follow the example of the Prophet Mohammed (pbuh) in inviting all to the way of God. We are messengers of the Messengers (pbut).

I.1) Islamic Model of Religious Preaching and Freedom of Worship

Do not dispute, except in the best way

The Way of God is the only Way that leads to righteousness in this life and salvation in the Hereafter. God in His wisdom directs us in 16:125 to the principles and methodology of religious preaching: *"Invite (all) to the Way of your Lord with wisdom and beautiful preaching, and argue with them in ways that are best and most gracious, for your Lord knows best, who strayed from His Path, and who receive guidance."*

"In this wonderful passage are laid down principles of religious preaching, which are good for all time. But where are the Teachers with such qualifications? We must invite all to the Way of God and expand His Universal Will. We must do it with wisdom and discretion, meeting people on their own ground and convincing them with illustrations from their own knowledge and experience, which may be very narrow, or very wide. Our preaching must be, not dogmatic, not self-regarding, not offensive, but gentle, considerate, and such as would attract their attention. Our manner and our arguments should not be acrimonious, but modelled on the most courteous and most gracious example, so that the hearer may say to himself, 'This man is not dealing merely with dialectics; he is not trying to get a rise out of me; he is sincerely expounding the faith that is in him, and his motive is the love of man and the love of God.'

"It may be that the preacher says to himself, 'What is the use of teaching these people? They have made up their minds, or they are obstinate; or they are only trying to catch me out.' Let him not yield to such a thought. Who knows how the seed of the Word of God may germinate in people's minds? It is not for man to look for results. Man's inner thoughts are known best to God. " FN2161 & FN2162

In 29:46 God directs us to the best way of delivering His Message to the People of the Book, our Jewish and Christian brothers and sisters:

"And don't dispute with the People of the Book, except in the best way, unless it be with those of them who are utterly unjust, but say, 'We believe in the Revelation which has come down to us and in that which came down to you; Our God and your God is One; and we submit ourselves to Him.'"

"Mere disputatious are futile. In order to achieve our purpose as true standard-bearers for God, we shall have to find true common grounds of belief, as stated in the latter part of this verse, and also to show by our urbanity, kindness, sincerity, truth, and genuine anxiety, for the good of others, that we are not cranks or merely seeking selfish or questionable aims.

"Of course, those who are deliberately trying to wrong or injure others will have to be treated firmly, as we are guardians of each other. With them there is little question of finding common ground or exercising patience, until the injury is prevented or stopped."
FN3472 & 3473

Speaking mildly to Pharaoh
When God sent His Messengers, Moses and Aaron to the worst man on earth, a tyrant Pharaoh who claimed to be the only god, He said to them in 20:43-44, *"Go, both of you, to Pharaoh, for he has indeed transgressed all bounds. Speak to him mildly, so that he may take warning or fear (Me)."*

They were both commanded to speak to him a gentle word, no violence or aggression in delivering God's Message. If they were to condemn him or be aggressive or rude in their speech or approach, he would have immediately refused to listen to them. Then, they would have lost every chance to deliver God's guidance to him to permit them to lead the Children of Israel out of Egypt.

A similar command was given to Prophet Mohammed (pbuh) in 3:159, in dealing with his people, *"(O Prophet!) It was God's mercy that you were gentle with them. Had you been rough, hard-hearted, they would surely have scattered away from you. So pardon them, and pray for their forgiveness, and consult them in matters of importance. And when you have taken a decision put your trust in God. Surely God loves those who put their trust (in Him)."*

Any act which lacks mercy is not Islamic
The extremely gentle nature of Prophet Mohammed (pbuh) endeared him to all, and it is reckoned as one of the Mercies of God. One of his titles is "A Mercy to all Creation". So any act which lacks mercy is not Islamic. In spite of the fact that Mohammed (pbuh) was a Messenger of God who received Divine Revelation, he was commanded to take counsel from his people regarding conduct of affairs.

God says in 2:256, *"Let there be no compulsion in religion. Truth stands out clear from Error..."*

"*Compulsion is incompatible with religion: because (1) religion depends upon faith and will, and those would be meaningless if induced by force: (2) Truth and Error have been so clearly shown up by the mercy of God that there should be no doubt in the minds of any persons of goodwill as to the fundamentals of faith; (3) God's protection is continuous, and His Plan is always to lead us from the depth of darkness into the clearest light.*" FN300

In 18:29, God refers to man's free will in choosing whether to believe or not, "*Say (Mohammed): 'The Truth is from your Lord'. Then whosoever wants to believe, let him believe, and whosoever chooses not to believe, let him disbelieve...*". Simply, we are offered the Truth. If we reject it, we must take all the terrible consequences in this life and the Hereafter.

In 4:39 God says to those who reject Faith that there is no burden on them and nothing to fear if they chose to believe, "*What harm would have befallen them if they had believed in God and the Last Day, and spent on charity out of what God had bestowed upon them as sustenance? For God indeed has full knowledge of them.*"

Free will, no compulsion
Even the Messengers of God are not permitted to force people to believe against their will as mentioned in 10:99, "*If it had been your Lord's Will, all who are on earth would have believed! Would you then (Mohammed) compel mankind, against their will, to believe!*"

"*If it had been God's Plan or Will not to grant the limited Free-will that He has granted to man, His omnipotence could have made all mankind alike: all would then have had Faith, but that Faith would have reflected no merit on them. In the actual world as it is, man has been endowed with various faculties and capacities, so that he should strive and explore, and bring himself into harmony with God's Will. Hence Faith becomes a moral achievement, and to resist Faith becomes a sin. As a complementary proposition, men of Faith must not be impatient or angry if they have to contend against Unfaith, and most important of all, they must guard against the temptation of forcing Faith, i.e., imposing it on others by physical compulsion. Forced Faith is no faith. They should strive.*" FN1480

Preaching to remind but not to compel
In 4:80 we are told that by obeying the Prophet (pbuh) we have obeyed God, and the Prophet (pbuh) was not sent to watch over us: "*Whoever obeys the Messenger obeys God. And whoever turns away, We have not sent you (Mohammed) as a warden over them.*"

"*The messenger was sent to preach, guide, instruct, and show the Way, not to drive people to good. That is not God's Plan, which trains the human Will. The Messenger's duty is therefore to convey the Message of God, in all the ways of persuasion that are open to him. If people perversely disobey that Message, they are not disobeying him, but they are disobeying God. In the same way those who obey the Message are obeying God. They are not obliging the Messenger, they are merely doing their duty.*" FN599

God in 88:21-22 refers to the Prophet's (pbuh) responsibility to remind people of the Message without bossing or controlling them, "*Therefore, remind them (of the Message), you are but a reminder. You are not invested with the authority to compel them.*"

"The Prophet is sent to teach and direct people on the way. He is not sent to force their will, or to punish them, except in so far as he may receive authority to do so. Punishment belongs to God alone. And Punishment is certain in the Hereafter, when true values will be restored." FN6170

Examples of my personal involvement in delivering God's message will be presented in Chapter 3, Part II

I.2) Relationship of Muslims with Non-Muslims

Islam established a number of principles governing the relations between Muslims and non-Muslims, as detailed below:

(A) The Universal Brotherhood of Mankind

God says in 4:1, *"O people! Fear your Lord Who created you from a single being (Adam) and out of it created its mate (Eve); and out of the two spread (like seeds) countless men and women. And fear God through whom you demand (your rights) from one another, and (do not sever) the ties of kinship. Surely God is ever watchful over you."*

And He says in 30:22, *"And among His Signs is the creation of the heavens and the earth, and the variations in your languages and your colours. Verily in that are Signs for those who know."*

All mankind were created from a single pair of parents; yet they have spread to different countries and climates and developed different languages and different shades of complexions. And yet their basic unity remains unaltered. They feel in the same way and are all equally under God's care.

God reminds us in 49:13, of this brotherhood, *"O mankind! We created you from a single (pair) of a male and female, and made you into nations and tribes that you may get to know each other (not to despise each other). Verily the most honoured of you in the sight of God is (he who is) the most righteous of you. Surely God has full knowledge and is well acquainted (with all things)."*

This is addressed to all mankind and not only to the Muslim brotherhood. As it is, mankind is descended from one pair of parents. Their tribes, races and nations are convenient labels by which we may know certain differing characteristics. Before God they are all one, and the most honourable are the ones whom are most righteous.

Do not judge others

No one can claim that he is righteous, as it is only God who decides, as stated in 53:32,*"...Therefore, don't claim purity for yourselves, He knows best who guards himself against evil."* In other words, it is absurd for us to justify ourselves, either by pretending that we are better than we are, or by finding excuses for our conduct. None of us has any right to judge the other. God is the only Judge who knows our inmost being.

God commands us in 49:11, not to make fun of others, or to despise them, or to laugh at them. Mutual ridicule ceases to be fun when there is arrogance or selfishness or malice behind it. We may laugh with people, to share in the happiness of life: we must never laugh at people in contempt or ridicule. In many things they may be better than ourselves.

Therefore, we must always remember that we are brothers and sisters in humanity, irrespective of our beliefs, gender, ethnicity or colour. There is no discrimination in Islam, no superiority complex, no inferiority complex, no coconut-syndrome, and no class system. Thus, truly in Islam every human being has dignity and place, as God says in 17:70, *"We have honoured the Children of Adam, provided them with transport on land and sea; given them for sustenance things good and pure; and exalted them above many of Our creatures."*

"The distinction and honour conferred by God on man are recounted in order to enforce the corresponding duties and responsibilities of Man. He is raised to a position of honour above the brute creation: he has been granted talents by which he can transport himself from place to place by land, sea and now by air: all the means for the sustenance and growth of every part of his nature are provided by God; and his spiritual faculties (the greatest gift of God) raised him above the greater part of God's Creation. Should he not then realise his noble destiny and prepare for his real life in the Hereafter?" FN2265

Fair and just dealings
God commands us in 60:8-9, not only to deal fairly and justly with non-Muslims who neither fight Muslims on religious grounds nor drive them out of their homes - that is, those who are neither at war with, nor hostile to, Muslims - but also urges Muslims to be kind to them. The word 'Birr' or 'goodness' which is used in this verse, is a very comprehensive term, signifying that kindness and generosity is over and above justice. It is the same word which is used to describe the Muslim's duty to his parents.

"God doesn't forbid you, with regard to those who don't fight you on account of your religion nor drive you out of your homes, to treat them with goodness and to be just to them; truly, God loves those who are just. Indeed, God forbids you (only) with regard to those who fight you on account of religion and drive you out of your homes, and assist (others) in driving you out, that you turn to them (in friendship); and whoever turns to them (in friendship), they are wrongdoers." 60:8-9

(B) Rights of Non-Muslim Neighbours

"Serve God and do not join any partners with Him; and do good (show kindness) to parents, kinsfolk, orphans, those in need, neighbours who are of kin, neighbours who are strangers, the companion by your side, the wayfarer you meet, and what is your right hand possess: for God does not love the arrogant, the boastful ." This is what God commands in 4:36

"The essence of Islam is to serve God and do good to your fellow creatures. This is wider and more comprehensive than 'Love God and love your neighbour'. For it includes duties to animals as our fellow-creatures and emphasises practical service rather than sentiment.

"Neighbours who are near: that is, physically reside alongside us, as well as intimate relationships, just as neighbours who are strangers includes those whom we do not know or who live away from us.

"The companion by your side maybe your intimate friends and associates, just as the wayfarer you meet maybe a casual acquaintance on your travels. This latter is much wider than the 'stranger within your gate.'

"Real deeds of service and kindness proceed not from showing off or from a superior sort of condescension (cf. 'white Man's Burden'), but from a frank recognition of our own humility and the real claims, before God, of all our fellow-creatures. For in our mutual needs we are equal before God, or perhaps the best of us (as the world sees us) may be worse than the worst of us (from the same point of view). Arrogance is one reason why our deeds of love and kindness do not thrive." FN550-FN554.

The Prophet Mohammed (pbuh) has stated in many authentic Hadith, the rights of our neighbours irrespective of their religion or beliefs.

He commanded us to be good neighbours by practicing the following:
- If your neighbour seeks your help, you help him.
- If he wants to borrow money, you lend it to him.
- If he becomes poor, you become charitable to him.
- If he gets ill, you visit him.
- If he receives good news, you congratulate him.
- If he receives bad news, you give your condolences to him.
- If he dies, you follow his funeral.
- Do not go high in your building, preventing the wind and the light from coming to him, except with his permission. This also applies to planting tall trees in your garden.
- Do not hurt him with the smell of your food without offering him from it.
- If you buy fruits, give him some. If you do not, then hide it before you take it inside your house. And do not allow your children to eat it outside in front of his children.
- Do not disturb him with your noise.
- Do not put any rubbish in front of his house.
- Do not spy on him.
- Do not allow your children to go out to play with things he cannot afford to buy.
- Do not open a window which can overlook him without his consent.

Although we may have different religions, we should continue to be brothers and sisters in humanity. A true Muslim is the one who makes his neighbour feel safe and secure, as stated by Prophet Mohammed (pbuh).

Dr Yusuf Al-Qaradawi, says in His Book "The Lawful and the Prohibited":

"While Islam doesn't prohibit Muslims to be kind and generous to peoples of other religions, even if they are idolaters and polytheists, it looks upon the People of the Book, that is, Jews and Christians, with special regard, whether they reside in a Muslim society or outside it.

"The Qur'an never addresses them without saying, "O People of the Book" or "O You who have been given the Book," indicating that they were originally people of a revealed religion. For this reason there exists a relationship of mercy and spiritual kinship between them and the Muslims, all having in common the principles of the one true religion sent by God through his prophets (peace be on them all), as stated in 42:13, "He has ordained (for the Muslims) the same religion which He enjoined on Noah, and that which We have revealed to you (O Muhammad) and that which We enjoined on Abraham, Moses and Jesus: That you should establish the faith and make no division in it..."

"Muslims are required to believe in all the Books revealed by God and in all the prophets sent by Him; otherwise they are not Believers. God says in 2:136: "Say: We (Muslims) believe in God and in what He has revealed to us, and in what He revealed to Abraham and Ishmael and Isaac and Jacob and the tribes (of Israel), and in what was given to Moses and Jesus, and in what was given to (all) the prophets by their Lord. We make no distinction between any of them, and to Him do we submit."

"Consequently, if the People of the Book read the Qur'an, they will find in it praise for their Books, Messengers, and Prophets.

"If Muslims hold discussions with the People of the Book, they should avoid such approaches as cause bitterness or arouse hostility, as stated in 29:46, "And do not dispute with the People of the Book except by (the way) which is best, unless it be with such of them as transgress, and say, 'We believe in what has been sent down to us and sent down to you, and our God and your God is one, and to Him do we submit"

"Islam permits eating with the People of the Book, sharing the meat they slaughter, and marrying their chaste women, marriage being a relationship of mutual love and mercy. God confirms this in 5:5, "...The food of those who were given the Scripture (before you) is permitted to you and your food is permitted to them. And (lawful to you in marriage are) chaste women from among the Believers and chaste women from among those who were given the Scripture before you..."

1.3 Martyrdom in Islam

Why is it highly desirable in Islam to die as a martyr? Before talking about the reward, let us firstly define who is a martyr?

1.3.1 Who is a Martyr?

Once Prophet Mohammed (pbuh), asked his companions, "Whom would you regard as a martyr?" They replied, "O Prophet of God, whoever is killed on a battle field in the Cause of God is a martyr." The Prophet (pbuh) said: "In this case, the number of martyrs from my followers is small." They asked, "Who are they O Prophet of God?". He replied, "Whoever is killed in the Cause of God is a martyr, and whoever dies in the Cause of God is a martyr, and who ever dies from the plague is a martyr, and the one who is drowned is a martyr." Recorded by Muslim.

The Prophet (pbuh) also said: "*Seven causes of death are considered martyrdom; this is in addition to the one killed in the Cause of God:*
The one who dies from the plague.
The one who drowns.
The one who dies from wounds in his side.
The one who dies as a result of illness in his stomach.
The one who dies from burns.
The one who is crushed under a building.
The woman who dies in childbirth."
This Hadith is recorded by Ahmed, Abu-Dawood and Al-Nasai
In another Hadith, recorded by Ahmed and Al-Termeze, the Prophet (pbuh) said, "Whoever is killed defending his property or defending his life or defending his faith or defending his family is a martyr."

A man came to the Prophet Mohammed (pbuh) and asked him, "*O prophet of God! If someone comes to take my property from me what shall I do?*" The Prophet (pbuh) replied, "*Stop him*". The man asked: "*And if he fights me?*" The Prophet (pbuh) answered, "*Fight back.*" The man asked, "*And if he kills me?*" The Prophet (pbuh) said: "*You die as a martyr*". The man then said, "*And if I kill him?*" The Prophet answered, "*He will be admitted to the Hell Fire.*" A contrast here with current English secular laws on the subject of fighting a burglar!

It is also important to mention that not everyone who is killed on a battlefield is regarded in Islam as a martyr. Abu-Moosa, (one of the Prophet's (pbuh) companions), said, "*A man came to the Prophet (pbuh) and said, "A man may fight for the spoils of war and a man may fight for fame and a man may fight to be known as a courageous warrior. Which of them is fighting for the Cause of God?*". The Prophet (pbuh) replied, "*Whoever fights to make God's Word the highest (i.e. to establish the Truth and Justice of God), he is fighting in the Cause of God.*" So, it is always the intention that counts.

Abu-Dawood and Al-Nasai recorded that a man came to the Prophet (pbuh) and asked him, "*O Prophet of God! What is the reward of a man who fights seeking fame and material gain?*" The Prophet (pbuh) replied, "*He has no reward.*" The man asked the Prophet (pbuh) three times, and the Prophet (pbuh) said, "*No reward for him because God only accepts sincere deeds aimed to please Him.*"

The Prophet (pbuh) said, "*Whoever asks God for martyrdom with great sincerity, God will make him reach the status of a martyr even if he dies in his own bed*". Thus, a man may reach the status of a martyr because of his sincerity, even if he does not die on a battle field.

1.3.2 The Reward of Martyrdom

The Qur'an tells us about the supreme reward promised by God to the believers who are killed whilst fighting in His Cause. For example, verse 9:111 reads: "*God has bought from the believers their lives and their wealth, for theirs (in return) is the Garden (of Paradise). They shall fight in His Cause and shall slay and be slain. It is a promise which is binding on Him in the Torah (the Book to Moses), in the Gospel (the Book to Jesus), and in the Qur'an (the Book to Mohammed); and who fulfils His Covenant better than God? Rejoice then in your bargain that you have made, for that is the supreme triumph.*"

The word 'believers' in this verse refers to those who believed in Moses (pbuh) until the arrival of Jesus (pbuh), then those who believed in Jesus (pbuh) as well as Moses (pbuh) until the message of Mohammed (pbuh), then those who believed in Mohammed, Jesus and Moses (peace be upon them all); those known today as the Muslims, in spite of the fact that all the others are regarded by God, as also Muslims.
Verse 2:154, confirms that the martyrs are alive, "*And don't call those who are slain in the Way of God dead. No, they are living, though you don't perceive it*".

Verses 3:169-171, not only ascertain that the martyrs are alive, but also they are enjoying an excellent reward from God, "*Don't consider those who are slain in God's Way are dead. No, they are living, finding their sustenance in the Presence of their Lord. They rejoice in the Bounty provided by God; and with regard to those left behind, who have not yet joined them (in their bliss). The (Martyrs) glory in the fact that no fear shall come upon them, nor shall they have (cause to) grieve. They glory in the Grace and the Bounty from God, and in the fact that God doesn't waste the reward of the believers.*"

The Prophet (pbuh) said, "*The souls of the Martyrs are inside green birds freely flying in Paradise*" as reported by Muslim. This is, of course, following their death and before the Day of Judgement. He also said, "*The martyr finds the pain of his slaying as painful as you find an insect sting*", as reported by Imaam Ahmed and others.

As you can see from the above, the martyrs are not dead, they live, and in a far higher and deeper sense than in the life they have left. In their case, through the gateway of death, they enter the true real Life, as opposed to its shadow here.

The Martyrs not only rejoice at the bliss they have themselves attained, the dear ones left behind are in their thoughts. It is part of their glory that they have saved their dear ones from fear, sorrow, humiliation, and grief in this life, even before they come to share in the glories of the Hereafter. The dear ones have no cause to grieve at the death of the Martyrs, rather they have cause to rejoice. But we must always remember that it is only God Who decides who should be awarded the status of "Martyrdom".

1.3.3 Examples of Martyrs in the Qur'an

In the following section I have chosen four examples from the Qur'an to refer to those who died as Martyrs. They are namely Abel, the kind and gentle son of Adam, the magicians in Ancient Egypt who were defeated by Moses in the presence of the Pharaoh, John the son of Zakaria and the disciple of Jesus, who volunteered to take Jesus' place on the cross.

A) Abel the Son of Adam

God tells us in 5:27-31, the story of the first act of murder to take place in human history at the time of our father Adam. Adam had two sons Cain and Abel. Cain was the elder, and Abel the younger, the righteous and innocent one. Presuming on the right of the elder, Cain was puffed up with arrogance and jealousy, which led him to hate his younger brother and look down on him.

Cain disputed a decision taken by his father Adam, in favour of Abel. He bitterly argued about it and refused to accept it. So, Adam suggested that each son should present a sacrifice to God, and the one's sacrifice which will be accepted will abide by Adam's decision.

So, God sent a fire which consumed the sacrifice of Abel. This meant that God accepted Abel's sacrifice. Hence, Cain must accept the decision of Adam which was in the favour of Abel. Cane said to Abel, "*Be sure I will kill you...*" Abel replied, "*Surely, God accepts the sacrifice of those who are righteous. If you stretch your hand against me, to kill me, it is not for me to stretch my hand towards you to kill you, for I fear God, the Lord of the Worlds. For me, I intend to let you draw on yourself my sin as well as yours, for you will be among the Companions of the Hell Fire. And that is the reward of those who do wrong.*"

"*Abel's speech is full of meaning. He is innocent and God-fearing. To the threat of death held out by the other, he returns a calm reply, aimed at reforming the other. "Surely," he pleads, "if your sacrifice was not accepted, there was something wrong in you, for God is Just and accepts the sacrifice of the righteous. If this does not deter you, I am not going to retaliate, though there is as much power in me against you as you have against me. I fear my Maker, for I know He cherishes all His Creation. Let me warn you that you are doing wrong. I do not intend even to resist, but do you know what the consequences will be to you? You will be in torment.*" FN733

Unfortunately, the selfish soul of the other led him to the murder of his brother. He murdered him and became himself one of the lost ones.

The innocent unselfish pleading of the younger brother had no effect, for the soul of the other was full of pride, selfishness and jealousy. He committed the murder, but in doing so, ruined his own self. And Abel became the first martyr of the children of Adam, and we all became the descendants of the criminal.

B) The Ancient Egyptian Magicians at the Time of Moses

God mentions in several chapters in the Qur'an, (e.g. 7, 10, 20 and 26) the competition between Moses and the Egyptian magicians, which Pharaoh called for.

When Moses and Aaron arrived in the Palace, they entered on Pharaoh and his Chiefs. Moses said to Pharaoh, *"O Pharaoh! I am a messenger from the Lord of the Worlds. I can only say the truth about God. I have come to you with a clear Sign from your Lord. So, don't inflict any more punishment on the Children of Israel and let them depart along with me."*

Pharaoh said: *"If indeed you have come with a Sign, then show it, if you are telling the truth."*

Then Moses threw his stick, and it became a serpent, which everyone could see. And he drew out his hand from his bosom, and it came out beaming with light.

The Chiefs of the people of Pharaoh said: *"This is indeed a very well-versed magician. His plan is to get you out of your land."*

Did Moses say that? Moses only requested that there be no more torture of the Children of Israel and to allow them to leave Egypt with him.

Pharaoh looked at Moses and said in a very threatening tone, *"Have you come to drive us out of our land with your magic? We can surely produce magic to match yours. So let us agree on a date between us and you."*
Moses said, *"Let us meet on the Day of the Festival, and let the people be assembled when the sun is well up."*

The Chiefs said, *"Keep him and his brother in for a while and send heralds to all the cities in Egypt to bring the best learned magicians."*

The magicians arrived at the assembly point and went straight to Pharaoh, saying, *"Of course we shall have a suitable reward if we win!"* Pharaoh said, *"Yes, indeed, and you shall be of those near to me."* He was so desperate to defeat Moses and crush the Israelites. He put all his hope in his magicians. He could hear the masses of the Egyptians who came to watch the competition saying, *"We may follow the sorcerers if they win!"* All this further added to Pharaoh's arrogance and pride.

The magicians disputed with one another, over their affair, but they kept their talk secret. They said, *"These two are certainly expert magicians. Their object is to drive you out from your land with their magic, and to do away with your most cherished institutions of your ancestral religion and magic. Therefore, concert your plan and unite your efforts. The winner today will have the upper hand in the land."*
They turned towards Moses and said, *"O Moses! Either you throw first, or that we are the first to throw."* Moses said, *"You throw first."* They said, *"By the might of Pharaoh it is we who will certainly win!"* And they threw their ropes and their rods and it seemed to Moses,

on account of their magic, that they moved about like real snakes. They bewitched the eyes of the people, and struck terror into them, and they showed a great feat of magic.

Moses conceived in his mind a sort of fear. God said to him, "*Don't fear. You have indeed the upper hand. Throw which is in your right hand, it will swallow up that which they have faked. What they have faked is but a magician's trick, and the magician neither succeed nor prosper.*"

Moses threw his rod and behold! It swallowed up all the falsehoods which they had faked. Thus, the truth was confirmed. And all that the magicians did was of no effect. So, they were vanquished there and then, and fully humiliated.

The magicians immediately fell down and prostrated themselves, saying, "*We believe in the Lord of the Worlds. The Lord of Moses and Aaron.*" They completely ignored Pharaoh and his Chiefs, who were enraged in anger as they felt their authority in the land had been compromised.

What made the magicians believe in the One True God? It was because Moses' rod turned into a real snake, whilst their rods and robes were made to look like snakes because they bewitched the eyes of the people. The nature of their objects did not change. The magicians, being among the elite scientists in Egypt, could not deny their failure and realised that what Moses brought was not magic, it was a Miracle from God.

But neither Pharaoh nor his Chiefs were happy. Pharaoh screamed at the magicians saying, "*How dare you believe in him before I give you permission? Surely, he must be your leader who taught you magic. This is a trick which you have planned in the City to drive out its people. But soon you will know the consequences.*"

Pharaoh looked at his Chiefs and then turned his angry face towards the magicians, and shouted so loudly to show his authority, "*Be sure I will cut off your hands and your feet on opposite sides, and I will have you crucified on trunks of palm-trees. So, you will know for certain, which of us can give the more severe and the more lasting punishment.*"

The defeat of the magicians by Moses, and for them to denounce Pharaoh's ancestral religion, was a blow for Pharaoh and his Chiefs. So, he decided to take revenge against them and accused them of being traitors and they must suffer the consequences of their treason against the State.

The magicians responded in a very calm tone saying, "*We shall never prefer you to the Clear Signs which have come to us. So decree whatever you desire to decree. For your decision extends only to the life of this world. Surely, we believed in our Lord that He may forgive us our sins, and the magic to which you compelled us to practice. God is Better and Everlasting. Whoever comes guilty to his Lord, on the Day of Judgement, truly for him is Hell. He will neither live in it nor die. But whoever comes to Him as a believer, having done good deeds, for these are high degrees in the Gardens of Eden, beneath which rivers flow, where they will abide forever. That is the reward of those who purify themselves.*" They remembered well what Prophet Joseph, the son of Prophet Jacob, preached in Egypt almost 500 years ago.

What an amazing response by the magicians! At the beginning of the competition they were seeking from Pharaoh material gains, and now they willingly offered their souls to their Creator and preferred to be killed than denounce the One True God, the God of Moses and Aaron. They asked God to pour onto them patience and constancy, and to take their souls as Muslims (those who submitted their will to the Will of God). They were the first Egyptians to die as martyrs, at the time of Moses.

C) John the Baptist the Son of Zakariya

God tells us in 3:38-41, and 19:2-15, that Prophet Zakariya prayed in his very old age for an heir, and God gave him the glad tidings of a righteous son. Zakariya questioned the good news as he was very old, and his wife could not have children. But God confirmed that in spite of that, he will have a noble son and his name will be Yahya (John). The meaning of the word "Yahya" in Arabic is "to live forever", thus indicating that he will die as a martyr.

This was John the Baptist, the forerunner of Jesus. In accordance with his father's prayer he, and Jesus for whom he prepared the way, renewed the Message of God, which had been corrupted and lost among the Israelites. He was given wisdom even as a youth. He was pure and devout and kind to his parents and to all God's creatures. He never used violence, from an attitude of arrogance, nor entertained a spirit of rebellion against Divine Law.

The Qur'an does not mention how John died. But his death is mentioned in Christian theology.

John the Baptist did not live long. He was imprisoned by Herod, the tetrarch (provincial ruler under the Roman Empire), whom he had reproved for his sins, and eventually beheaded at the instigation of the woman with whom Herod was infatuated.

According to the Synoptic Gospels, Herod had imprisoned John the Baptist because he reproved Herod from divorcing his wife (Phasaelis, daughter of King Aretas of Nabataea) and unlawfully taking Herodias, the wife of his brother Herod Philip I.

The beheading of Saint John the Baptist is a biblical event and a holy day observed by various Christian churches that follow liturgical traditions. The day commemorates the martyrdom of Saint John the Baptist, who was beheaded on the orders of Herod Antipas, through the vengeful request of his step-daughter Salome and her mother Herodias.

D) The Double of Jesus

God confirms in the Qur'an 4:157-158, that Jesus was neither killed nor crucified, but it was made to look like that to them. In fact, God saved him from his enemies and raised him unto Himself, in body and soul, and someone else took his place on the cross. So there was crucifixion, but it was not Jesus. In the Prophetic Tradition it is mentioned that a young disciple of Jesus volunteered to be made by God to look like Jesus and to take Jesus' place on the cross. His death was martyrdom. The Gospel of St. Barnabas supported the theory of substitution on the cross.

1.4 Islam Forbids Suicide

To address the issue of suicide, we must remember that God gave man a number of rights, including the right to life. There are many verses in the Qur'an and several hadith in the Prophetic Traditions which confirm this right. This is to ensure the protection of the most valuable gift from the Creator. Consequently, no one has the right to take his own life. God is the only One Who decides when someone will die, in the same way as He decides when someone will be born. God is aware when someone decides to take his own life, but He does not influence him in doing that. If man abuses his free will, then he should neither blame God, nor Satan, he is merely exercising his free will that has been entrusted to him.

God says in 1:195, "...and don't make your own hands contribute to your destruction." And in 4:29-39, He states, "...nor kill (or destroy) yourself for verily God has been most merciful to you. And whoever does this by way of transgression and injustice, We shall surely cast him into the Fire; that indeed is quite easy for God." Hence, we must be careful of our own and other people's lives. We must commit no violence; committing suicide is violence against our own soul and our Creator.

None of us had any choice before coming to this life. None of us know when, or how, or where we will die. I echo what God says in 3:145, "No soul can ever die except with God's permission at a predestined time..." And what He says in 31:34, "...No soul knows what it will earn tomorrow, and no soul knows in what land it will die. Verily God has full knowledge and acquainted (with all things)."
I cannot even push death away if it comes to me or to the nearest and the dearest in my family. The person who commits suicide has no faith in his Creator, and he lost all hope in meeting Him on the Day of Judgement.

God, in 56:83-87, challenges those who don't believe in accountability on the Day of Judgement, to prevent death when it comes to their dearest and nearest, "When the soul of a dying person comes up to his throat, while you gaze on (at him helplessly) and We are nearer to him than you, though you don't see Us. Why if you believe that you will not be judged, do you not restore his soul to him, if you are true (in your claim of independence)?"

"If you disbelieve in Revelation and a future Judgement, and claim to do what you like, including killing yourself, and be independent of God, how is it you can't call back a dying man's soul to his body when all of you congregate round him at his death-bed? But you are not independent of Judgement. There is a Day of Account, when you will have to be judged by your deeds in this life." FN5266.

The state before our present life, or the state after, we can scarcely understand. But our present Life is a test to enable us to strive by good deeds to reach a nobler state, as stated by God in 67:1-2, "Blessed be He in Whose hands is the Dominion (of heavens and earth), and He has power over all things. He Who created Death and Life, that He may test you to determine which of you is best indeed. And He is the Exalted in Might, the Oft-Forgiving." You will fail the test if you decide to end your life by your own hands.

"Death is here put before Life, and it is created. Death is therefore not merely a negative state. In 2:28 we read: 'Seeing that you were without life (literally dead), and He gave you life, then He will cause you to die, and will again bring you to life. And again to Him you will return.' In 53:44, again, Death is put before Life. Death, then, is (1) the state before life began, which may be non-existence or existence in some other form. (2) the state in which Life as we know it ceases, but existence does not cease; a state of Barzakh (23:100), or Barrier or Partition, after our visible Death and before Judgement. After that will be the new Life, which we conceive of under the term Eternity." FN5556.

Whether the dead person has been killed, or had a natural death, or committed suicide, the soul, while leaving the body will experience death in different ways as God tells us in 3:185, *"Every soul will have a taste of death, and only on the Day of Resurrection you will be paid your full recompense..."* And He says in 4:78, that death will find us wherever we may be, *"Wherever you may be, death will overtake you, even if you were in lofty fortified towers..."* So, no one can escape death when his term on this earth comes to an end. When the Angels of death come, they will always be on time as stated in 6:61, *"He (God) is the Irresistible (watching) from above over His servants, and He sets guardians over you. At length, when death approaches one of you, Our angels take his soul, and they never fail in their duty."* And He says in 16:61, *"If God were to (immediately) punish people for wrongdoing, He would not leave, on the (earth), a single living creature. But He gives them respite for a stated Term. When their Term expires, they would not be able to delay (the punishment) for a single hour, just as they would not be able to anticipate it (for a single hour)."*

The Prophet Mohammed (pbuh) described the eternal punishment that will face someone who commits suicide to deter people from doing it. It is recorded by Al-Bukhari and Muslim that the Prophet said, *"Whoever throws himself from a mountain to kill himself, he will eternally be jumping in the Hellfire. And whoever takes a poison to kill himself, his poison will be in his hands, and he will drink it eternally in the Hellfire. And whoever kills himself with a rod, his rod will be in his hands killing himself with it eternally in the Hellfire."*

Al-Bukhari also recorded that the Prophet said: *"Whoever strangles himself, he strangles himself in the Hellfire. And whoever stabs himself, he stabs himself in the Hellfire. And whoever jumps to kill himself, jumps in the Hellfire."*

He also recorded another Hadith, the Prophet said: *"There was before you a man who had a wound, which led him to despair. He had no wish to live, so he took a knife and cut his hand and he bled to death. Then God said: 'My servant went ahead before Me and killed himself. I have prohibited him from Paradise.'"*

As you can see from the above, Islam forbids suicide and also does not permit euthanasia, irrespective of the condition of the patient. The suffering of a believer is regarded as a form of purification and a means of purging sins. One of the best examples in the Qur'an is Prophet Job, who persevered patiently in facing so many calamities as described in the Book of Job in the Old Testament. He did not despair, he held fast to his faith in the One True

God. The Qur'an in 21:83-84, refers, briefly, to his suffering and how did God reward him?: "*And (remember) Job, when he cried to his Lord 'Truly distress has seized me, but You are the Most Merciful of those that are Merciful.' So We listened to him and We removed the distress that was on him, and We restored his people to him, and doubled their number, as a Grace from Ourselves, and a thing for commemoration, for those who serve Us.*" Also in 38:41-44, "*Bring to mind Our Servant Job, behold he cried to his Lord 'Satan has afflicted me with distress and suffering!' (God said to him) 'Strike with your foot, here is (water) to wash, cool and refreshing, and (water) to drink.' And We gave him (back) his people and doubled their number, as a Mercy from Us, and a lesson to all who understand...Truly We found him full of patience and constancy, an excellent servant! He very often turned to Us.*".

Life is the property of God, the Creator, not of man. We had no choice in entering this world and we have no choice to decide when or how or where we should die. It is all in the hands of God.

So, for a terrorist to blow up himself and to kill innocent people, his eternal abode will be the Hellfire, where he will be eternally blowing himself up, again and again.

However, the above doesn't include those who offer their lives willingly in a battlefield in the cause of the Truth, while defending or liberating their country and protecting their honour, and defending those who are oppressed and weak, as previously explained under "Jihad".

1.5 The Punishment and Condemnation of Terrorism in Islam

1.5.1 Islam is Peace

Islam is a religion that covers all aspects of life and there are rules in Islam on war and peace and severe punishment for terrorists.

Unfortunately, some misinformed Muslims as well as non-Muslims justify certain acts of violence and claim that they stem from the Qur'an or the teachings of Islam. In fact, they arise from misconceptions about terminology and distortion of the text by taking it out of context.

In Islam, for any view of any scholar to obtain credibility it must show its textual basis in the Qur'an and authentic Hadith (Hadith is anything Prophet Mohammed (pbuh) said or did or approved, it is referred to in the text as Prophetic Tradition) and must also show that the view is based on sound linguistic understanding of the Arabic text.

The Arabic word 'Islam' is derived from the Arabic verb 'Tasleem' which means peace, submission and obedience. It is also derived from the Arabic noun 'Salam', which means amongst other things, to be at perfect peace. Consequently, the word 'Islam' could be defined as:

'Perfect peace among humanity through absolute submission, resignation and obedience to the Will and the Moral Law of the One and only God, the Creator of the Universe and the Guardian of all that is in the heavens and on earth'.

In other words, absolute submission to God's commandments, tests and trials will lead to the state of a content soul, which will enable man to achieve inner peace. Thus, enabling him to be at one and peace with all the other creatures around him.

The religion of Islam is the complete acceptance of the teachings and guidance of God as revealed to his final and last Prophet Mohammed (pbuh). A Muslim is one who believes in God and strives to structure his life according to God's revealed guidance and the tradition of Prophet Mohammed (pbuh). He also contributes to building human society on this same basis.

The word 'Allah' is the proper name for God in Arabic. It is a unique term because it has no plural or feminine gender. It is a collective word for all the attributes of God and it means among other things 'To Him belongs and to Him returns everything that is in the heavens and the earth'.

One of God's attributes in Arabic is 'Al-Salam', which means 'The Source of Peace'. It is recommended by God that we should greet those whom we know as well as those whom we don't know by saying 'Peace be upon you' and whenever we mention the name of any Prophet of God, we follow it with the saying 'Peace be upon him'.

It is also recommended that a Muslim must always have a smile on his face when he meets people. Also he should not raise his voice when he talks, only to say what is proper or otherwise refrain from talking. Thus, we always have peace among us. Therefore, any act of violence or aggression is regarded as un-Islamic.

Islam is not a new religion. Submission to God and obedience to His commandments was the message preached by ALL of God's Messengers and Prophets from Adam to Noah, to Abraham, to Moses and Jesus, the son of Mary, peace be upon all of them. Hence Islam is in essence the same message and guidance which God revealed to all His Prophets and Messengers. God says in 3:83, "*Say: 'We believe in God and that which has been revealed to us and that which was revealed to Abraham and Ishmael and Isaac and Jacob and the Tribes and that which was given to Moses and Jesus and other Prophets from their Lord. We make no distinction between any of them, and to Him we submit.'*".

However, some details of God's commands varied so as to fit in with the variations in the degree of man's development and comprehension through history. Hence the necessity for the message of Prophet Mohammed (pbuh) who was commanded in 16:123 to restore the religion back to the religion of Abraham. Unfortunately, the use of the word 'Islam' was confused, and gradually lost its broader meaning, thus becoming a reference to certain cultural identities.

1.5.2 Fighting Terrorism

Since 9/11 the whole world has been rushing to debate the definition of terrorism. Islam defines it as an act of war waged against God and His Messengers by openly committing disorders on the earth. Any act of terrorism is severely punishable in Islam as stated in the Qur'an in 5:33-34, "*The punishment of those who wage war against God and His Messenger, and strive with might and main for mischief through the land is: execution, or crucifixion, or the cutting off of hands and feet from opposite sides, or exile from the land. That is their disgrace in this world, and a heavy punishment is theirs in the Hereafter; except for those who repent before they fall into your power, in that case, know that God is Oft-forgiving, Most Merciful.*"

"*For the double crime of treason against the State, combined with treason against God, as shown by overt crimes, four alternative punishments are mentioned, any one of which is to be applied according to the crime committed, viz., execution (cutting off of the head), crucifixion, maiming, or exile. These were features of the Criminal Law then and for centuries afterwards, except that tortures such as 'hanging, drawing, and quartering' in English Law, and piercing of eyes and leaving the unfortunate victim exposed to a tropical sun, which was practised in Arabia, and all such tortures were abolished. In any case sincere repentance before it was too late was recognised as a ground for mercy.*" FN738

Terrorism has no place in Islam
No one who terrorises people has any right to claim that he is a religious person following any religion. No faith would encourage or justify any acts of violence against innocent people irrespective of their beliefs or ethnicity. Prophet Mohammed (pbuh) said: "*Anyone who terrorises people is not among my followers*", reported by Al-Bukhari and Muslim. He also said that no miscreant should be given succour or refuge by any Muslim. In Islam it is a crime to glorify or condone terrorism or even to suggest that suicide bombers killing innocent civilians are martyrs. They are killers waging war against God and His Messengers. The true martyrs are the innocent people they killed.

Killing one innocent soul = killing of all mankind
Of course, no one can wage war against God, as He is the Exalted in Might, the Irresistible. But this emphasises that terrorism is a crime, not just against humanity, but also against God Himself and the teachings of all His Messengers. That is why Islam regards the killing of one innocent soul as equivalent to the killing of all mankind and the saving of one life as equivalent to saving the whole of humanity. Verse 5:32 reads, "*...If anyone slew a person - unless it be for murder or for spreading mischief in the land - it would be as if he slew the whole people: and if anyone saved a life; it would be as if he saved the life of the whole people.*"

Islam is a religion of peace, justice, mercy and tolerance. It is a Divine way that controls all aspects of life including rules governing war and peace. It forbids any aggression against civilian non-combatants. Islam prohibits the killing of children, the elderly, religious people engaged in their worship and non-combatant men and women even on the battlefield. Besides, Islam prohibits poisoning water or destroying crops or animals. Also, those who are not engaged directly in battle should not be harmed. Property that is not used for military purposes, together with such basic resources of life as trees and water, should not be touched. Discrimination and proportionality should be strictly observed. Thus, wars and weapons of mass destruction that destroy civilians and their towns are excluded by the Qur'an and the word and deed of Prophet Mohammed (pbuh). I wonder how many nations who claim to be civilised understand and implement these very highly civilised rules?

The fault lies with man, not his religion
Muslims must understand that Islam is not a headscarf for a woman and a beard and white robe for a man. Islam is above all these trivia. According to Prophet Mohammed (pbuh), God does not judge us by our appearance or our wealth, but He looks at our hearts and our deeds, as reported by Muslim in his book of Hadith. Islam teaches the best values and most sublime morals. It is the misbehaviour of misinformed Muslims due to their misinterpretation of the Qur'an and the Tradition of Prophet Mohammed (pbuh) that provides ammunition to a malicious press, which strives to perpetuate the wrong message about Islam. The fault lies with man not with his religion.

1.5.3 What Religion is Terrorism?

As God is the Most Gracious, the Most Merciful, and the Source of Peace, consequently any act that lacks mercy is not holy and not divine and should not be associated with any religion.

Therefore, terrorists should not be branded with any religion. It would be unfair to Christianity to describe for example:

- Terrorists belonging to the IRA as Catholic terrorists or
- Terrorists belonging to the UDA as Protestant terrorists or
- Terrorists belonging to the ETA as Christian Basque terrorists or
- Hitler who killed millions of Jews and other innocent people as a devout German Christian terrorist or
- The Serb generals who killed over 250,000 Muslims in Bosnia, Kosovo and the rest of the Balkan countries and displaced over 3 million people as devout Christian Orthodox terrorists. In one day, 8,000 Muslim men and boys were killed in Bosnia under the eyes of the UN and no flags were flown at half mast, no tears were shed, and no prayers were said. Why do we always act with double standards? or
- The Corsican terrorist group as Christian French terrorists or
- Timothy McVeigh, the 1995 Oklahoma bomber, who vowed to bring America down before his execution, as an American Christian terrorist or
- The American children who gun down their schoolmates as young American Christian terrorists or
- The ruthless cults who kill their own people as pure Christian terrorists or
- The Swiss man who stormed the Council in Zug in September 2001 and killed and injured many innocent people as a Christian Swiss terrorist or
- The American passenger who cut the throat of the bus driver in September 2001 and caused an accident, which killed many innocent passengers as Christian American terrorist.

The above list may go on and on as there are hundreds of terrorist groups operating worldwide. There is no country in the whole world, which has not suffered from terrorism.

As it is unfair to brand any of the above mentioned terrorist groups as 'Christian terrorists', it is also unjustifiable to call any terrorist group like Al Qaeda or ISIS, 'Muslim terrorists', **because Islam condemns all those atrocities.**

Ahmed Hassan, who tried to blow up a packed tube train at Parsons Green in West London, was jailed in March 2018, to life imprisonment, with a recommendation that he serve a minimum of 34 years. In his sentencing remarks, Mr Justice Haddon-Cave, made the following pertinent and astute observations:

"Finally, Ahmed Hassan, let me say this to you. You will have plenty of time to study the Qur'an in prison in the years to come. You should understand that the Qur'an is a book of peace; Islam is a religion of peace. The Qur'an and Islam forbid anything extreme, including extremism in religion. Islam forbids breaking the 'law of the land' where one is living or is a guest. Islam forbids terrorism (hiraba). The Qur'an and the Sunna provide that the crime of perpetrating terror to "cause corruption in the land" is one of the most severe crimes in Islam. So it is in the law of the United Kingdom. You have, therefore, received the most severe of sentences under the law of this land. You have violated the Qur'an and Islam by your actions, as well as the law of all civilized people. It is to be hoped that you will come to realise this one day."

The Association of Muslim Lawyers in Britain said: *"We as Muslims support and applaud the Learned Judge's insightful and accurate analysis. The despicable act of planning to kill, injure and maim innocent civilians must not go unpunished. The disassociation of any and all acts of terror from the peaceful religion of Islam is vital in redressing the skewed misportrayal perpetrated on a daily basis and is crucial to building the trust lost within our communities."*

1.5.4 Condemnation of Terrorism

I am proud to be a British Muslim of Egyptian origin. I believe "Communities Defeat Terrorism". Every time there is a terrorist attack anywhere in the world, by those criminals who claim to be Muslims, I would immediately issue a "Message of Condemnation". I would share it with members of our congregation at South Woodford mosque in London. I would also share it with the Counter Terrorism team at New Scotland Yard, Metropolitan Police Services, London. If the attack took place in any country in the EU, I would also share my Message of Condemnation with the government of that country.

(1) My Personal Response to 9/11 Terrorist Attacks:

Following the 9/11 terrorist attacks on New York and Washington, I condemned this heinous crime in my Friday sermon, on the first Friday following the attack. A member of my congregation shocked me when she said, "I thought you would condone the attacks!"
I said, "Those who committed these heinous crimes have no faith, morality, decency, or Godliness. What happened will forever remain a horrible scar on the history of Islam and humanity. How can a practicing Muslim support the killing of innocent people? I believe in the sacredness of human life. Not being in agreement with the foreign policy of any country, my religion does not permit me to use violence against innocent people. If a country is

practicing State Terrorism, it is not justifiable for me as a Muslim to retaliate from the innocent people of that country."

I was on holiday in Tunisia when the attacks took place. I came to know about them when I went to a mosque to pray. The people were rejoicing that 'America has been defeated!' as a man in the mosque shouted. Another one said, 'This is the end of America!' People were so jubilant everywhere I turned. When I went to my hotel, I watched the news. It was shocking! A friend of mine said, 'The Muslims are going to have very hard times'. I flew back to London the following day.

No matter how much we condemn it and point to the Qur'an and the Prophetic Tradition to argue that Islam forbids the killing of innocent people, the fact remains that the perpetrators of this crime against humanity have indicated that their actions are sanctioned by Islamic values. The fact that even now several Muslim scholars and thousands of Muslims defend the accused is indicative that not all Muslims believe that the attacks are un-Islamic. This is truly sad and something I have devoted much personal time and research to, to fully understand and attempt to redress, as in this book.

I immediately embarked on a major campaign to condemn the attacks and to educate the public, Muslims and non-Muslims, regarding the true message of Islam, as a religion of Peace, Tolerance and Justice.

On the 19th October 2001, I wrote the following letter to Prime Minister Tony Blair MP:

"Dear Mr Blair,

The indiscriminate accusations made against Islam and Muslims in general, as an immediate reaction to the atrocities in New York and Washington on 11th September 2001, fuelled Islamophobia in this country and other places, which you and Mr Bush attempted to assuage in repeated statements. Nevertheless the melody of Islamophobia remains unabated despite the unequivocal condemnation by Muslim clerics and communities across the world of these acts of terrorism. Every day we receive reports of assaults on Muslims and Muslim places of worship. This centre has been the subject of assault and arson attack in the past and on 8th October 2001, it was once again attacked by extremist groups, who on many occasions terrorised our women and children.

Please find enclosed:

a) A leaflet from the BNP, which reflects the sick minds of the enemies of humanity. It would be an insult to Christianity to brand them as 'Christian Extremists or terrorists'.

b) A statement regarding Islam's condemnation of terrorism and the severe punishment of the perpetrators.

The British Muslims come from many different cultures and races but they are united in two aspects. Firstly, they are British Muslims; secondly, their loyalty is to Britain. In doing this they follow what the Prophet Mohammed (pbuh) said, 'The love of the country is part of the faith".

The British Muslims are in excess of three million and this number comprises a large number from the indigenous population who embraced Islam. The majority of British Muslims are very successful and highly professional law-abiding people. They deserve the full protection of their government against any racist or extremist groups and opportunist politicians. They will not accept any discrimination against them because of their religion. Therefore, in the same way as the Jews and the Sikhs are protected against any discrimination against them based on religious grounds, the law must also be extended to encompass the Muslims to protect them, their properties and their places of worship.

Best regards.

Yours sincerely

Dr Mohammed Fahim
Chairman and Head Imaam of South Woodford Mosque, London"

In the attachment to my letter to the Prime Minister Tony Blair, titled 'Islam Condemns Terrorism', I covered the following points:

1) Islam is Peace
2) Definition and punishment of terrorism in Islam
3) What religion is terrorism?
4) War and Peace in Islam
5) Islam forbids aggression

I received the following response dated 25th October 2001, from Justine Mansell, from the Direct Communications at No 10 Downing Street:

"Dear Dr Fahim

The Prime Minister has asked me to thank you for your recent letter and enclosures.

Mr Blair was pleased to have your comments, which will be carefully considered.

Your sincerely,

Justin Mansell"

In addition to the above, I felt it was so necessary to engage our local MPs in Redbridge as well as all the Councillors. So, I sent the following letter dated 26th October 2001 to all of them:

"Dear ....

Despite the unequivocal condemnation by Muslim clerics and communities across the world of the recent acts of international terrorism, the lingering association of terror with Islam and Muslims persists in many minds.

Please find enclosed a copy of the letter we sent to the Prime Minister along with a statement regarding Islam's condemnation of terrorism and a copy of a recent BNP leaflet for your immediate action.

Many thanks for your help and we look forward to hearing from you.

Best regards

Yours sincerely

Dr M E Fahim"

I give below some of their responses:

A) Letter from Councillor K. E. Axon, Leader of the Opposition, dated 1st November 2001:

"Dear Dr Fahim

Thank you for your letter of the 26th October and for your kindness in forwarding to me a copy of your letter of the 19th October to the Prime Minister, the contents of which I have noted.

I share entirely the views that you expressed to the Prime Minister and as you will know I, together with my two leader colleagues on Redbridge Council plus the religious organisations in the Borough issued a statement immediately after the 11th September making quite clear the points that you make in your letter.

Like you I deplore the publicity from the British National Party and there is nothing I can say that you have not said in your letter regarding their activities within our Borough.

You may rest assured that I will do all that I can as one of the civic leaders to continue with our activities to maintain peace and harmony within the communities in Redbridge.

I'm grateful to you for writing to me and trust that you will be successful in your endeavours with the Prime Minister.

Yours sincerely

Councillor K. E. Axon
Leader of the Opposition"

B) Letter from Councillor Allan Weinberg, Mayor, dated 2nd November 2001:

"Dear Dr Fahim

Thank you very much for sending me a copy of a letter you have sent to the Prime Minister regarding the recent international terrorist acts.

Like you I am under no illusion and I have said it on many occasions that one cannot and must not condemn all Muslims because of the mindless acts of a few.

I assure you of my continued support for the Muslim Community.

Yours sincerely

Councillor Alan Weinberg
Mayor"

C) Letter from Councillor Richard Hoskins, Leader of the Liberal Democrat Group of Councillors, dated 5th November 2001:

"Dear Neighbour

When we meet, we frequently address each other as 'neighbour'. In the Christian faith that has particular meaning from a parable Jesus Christ told about a man who fell among thieves and was cared for not by people of his own sect but by a Samaritan. Though a stranger the Samaritan proved himself a true neighbour.

I would like to think we are true *neighbours and we want to ensure you can share this feeling with your community. There have been points of strain in the recent past. Nevertheless my party totally repudiates all Islamophobia that may now be present locally and internationally.

The BNP and its fascist fellow travellers are abhorrent to Liberal Democrats. We will stand by our Muslim neighbours now and in the future.

Notwithstanding this we can understand the concerns of your members as they see their co-religionists under the massive bombardments they presently undergo. You have also clearly set out the message of the teachings of the Qur'an and the Prophet Mohammed (pbuh). And we know how difficult it is for us to reach those aspirations. But by the grace of our faiths let us try to do so.

I have been thinking further about the needs of all our local communities to be seen working together for the good of our whole Redbridge community. If you feel this would be worth exploring further please give me a ring.

With Best wishes

Richard Hoskins

Leader the Liberal Democrat Group of Councillors"

*The reason we used to call each other 'neighbour', because I had my Care Home, few meters from his house.

On Sunday 11th November 2001, I organised a lecture at our mosque at South Woodford, titled "An Islamic Perspective of Terrorism, Martyrdom, Suicide & Jihad (Striving to do Good)". Muslims as well as non-Muslims were invited to attend. A number of local Councillors, MPs and police officers were also present. It was a great success.

"I hope that we will now rededicate our lives and our institutions to the search for harmony, peace and tolerance. Let us be prepared to suffer injustice rather than commit injustices. After all, it is we who carry the divine burden of Islam and not others. We must be morally better, more forgiving, more sacrificing than others, if you wish to convince the world about the truth of our message. We cannot even be equal to others in virtue; we must excel. It is time for soul-searching. How can the message of Mohammed (pbuh) who was sent as mercy to mankind become a source of horror and fear? How can Islam inspire thousands of youth to dedicate their lives to killing others? We are supposed to invite people to Islam not murder them." - M Khan, Director of International Studies, Adrian College, MI, USA.

(2) My Personal Response to 7/7 Terrorist Attacks:

On Friday 7th July 2006, the anniversary of the London Bombings, I read the following statement to my congregation at South Woodford Mosque, condemning the heinous attacks:

"Today we call to mind the atrocities, which engulfed us all in London last year when many innocent lives were lost and many more were injured. Our hearts go out to all the victims and their families. We pray to God to give them patience and shower His Mercy on all of them..."

After I finished reading my condemnation statement, I asked the congregation to observe one-minute silence to remember and pray for the victims and their families. This might be the first time in history that an Imam in Britain would ask the Friday congregation to do that. But thank God, we have always been the foremost UK mosque in doing this.

(3) My Personal Response to the Brutal Killing of the French Teacher in Oct 2020

On Friday 23rd October 2020, in my Friday sermon I strongly condemned, and without any reservations, the brutal killing of the French teacher Samuel Paty. He was beheaded after showing in class to his students caricatures depicting Prophet Mohammed (pbuh).

President Emmanuel Macron said the attack bore all the hallmarks of an *"Islamist terrorist attack"* and the teacher had been murdered because he *"taught freedom of expression"*.

The murder comes as a trial over the 2015 attack on Charlie Hebdo - a satirical magazine that has published nasty cartoons of the Prophet Mohammed (pbuh) - is under way.

Speaking at a televised memorial service on Wednesday 21st October 2020, Mr Macron told viewers that France *"will not give up our cartoons"*. He added, *"Mr Paty had tried to teach his pupils how to become citizens"*. *"He was killed precisely because he incarnated the Republic"*, Mr Macron said. *"He was killed because the Islamists want our future. They know that with quiet heroes like him, they will never have it."* Further, he sanctioned the projection of the caricatures on the government's buildings.

Freedom of expression or speech is one of the many French values which stem out of its post - revolutionary motto "liberty, equality, fraternity". However, there is no such thing as "absolute freedom of expression or speech", as someone will always be hurt.

On October 2nd, 2020, the French President Emmanuel Macron called Islam "a religion that is in crisis all over the world". He said that he wants "an Islam in France that can be an Islam of the Enlightenment", which will stop "repeated deviations from the values of the republic and which often result in the creation of a counter-society".

Macron's rhetoric about Islam has angered many Muslim leaders and many Muslims worldwide. But it is not the first time the French President has announced his intention to regulate and scrutinise the faith. In 2018, he claimed that Arab States were influencing Muslims in France through the funding of mosques and clerics.

Macron is preparing to introduce a new law in December 2020, which would give the French government powers to monitor and regulate mosques and Islamic communities. He said the law would prevent radicalisation and foster better integration. The law was first introduced on 2nd October but gained support after the teacher's death on October 16th 2020.

In response to Macron's comments, Turkish President Recep Tayyip Erdogan said he believes his French counterpart "needs mental treatment". "What is Macron's problem with Islam? What is his problem with Muslims?" Erdogan added.

France recalled its ambassador to Turkey on Sunday 25th October in response to Erdogan's comments.

"President Erdogan's comments are unacceptable. Excess and rudeness are not a method", an Elysee Palace official told Agence France - Press. *"We demand that Erdogan change the course of his policy because it is dangerous in every respect"*.

I wonder, what happened to the French value "freedom of expression or freedom of speech"? So Charlie Hebdo can produce depicting images of Prophet Mohammed (pbuh), and French teachers can exhibit them in their classrooms and Macron states "will not give up our cartoons", but when Erdogan describes Macron that he is mentally ill because he is attacking the Islamic faith, it becomes an insult and unacceptable and a political row has started by France withdrawing its ambassador to Turkey. Such double standards will not help to eliminate radical Islam from the world. When we make fun of black people we call it racism, and when we mock Jews we call it anti-Semitism, and when we ridicule women we call it sexism, and when we mock Islam we call it freedom of speech.

Every Muslim in the world must condemn, without any reservations, the heinous crime of killing the French teacher, and the three innocent people in the church in Nice on 29th October 2020. But at the same time, the French government must stop practicing double standards. Depictions of the Prophet Mohammed (pbuh) can cause serious offence to Muslims worldwide. The French government is aware of this.

"What else can be said to a head of state who does not understand freedom of belief and who behaves in this way to millions of people living in his country who are member of a different faith?" Mr Erdogan asked.

Pakistan's Prime Minister Imran Khan tweeted on Sunday 25th October 2020 that Mr Macron chose *"to encourage Islamophobia by attacking Islam rather than the terrorists"* and *"to deliberately provoke Muslims, including his own citizens"*.

The response of Mr Macron reminds me of the conduct of Pharaoh at the time of Prophet Moses who persecuted the Children of Israel. They lived in Ancient Egypt for hundreds of years since Prophet Joseph. They were good citizens who contributed to the glory and the prosperity of the country.

In one of his many racist statements Pharaoh said, *"These (Israelites) are but a despised minority, and they are raging furiously against us. But we are a ready host ever on guard"*, 26:53-56.

And in 7:127 the chiefs of Pharaoh's people said, *"Will you leave Moses and his people to spread mischief in the land and to abandon you and your gods?"* Pharaoh said, *"We will slay their sons and save their women. Surely we have irresistible power over them."*

Their persecution was simply because they were Muslims who believed in the One True God and they forsook the Egyptian gods and denounced secularism. At the end, God made the Children of Israel victorious and crushed their enemy and God's enemy and drowned them all in the sea.

Every country has the right to implement counter terrorism policies, but without inciting hatred against innocent and peaceful citizens and causing divisions in societies which can lead to civil unrest. I, as many Muslims, felt saddened that the terror inflicted by the attackers then became synonymous with their purported faith and again, Islam is attacked.

(4) My Personal Messages of Condemnation and Responses Received:

I give below examples of my Messages of Condemnation in my capacity as the Chairman and Head Imam of South Woodford Mosque, London, and responses received.

A) *"ISIS are criminals who hijacked Islam, a religion of peace, tolerance and justice. They are perversion of Islam. Their practices completely contradict all Islamic Values. They are not*

Muslims, even if they are claiming that what they are doing is in response to the wars waged by the West against innocent people, including children, in Afghanistan, Iraq, Syria, Yemen and Libya and the unfair treatment of the Palestinians by the Israelis, and the support of the West of tyrant rulers in the Middle East. This is what ISIS use to promote their rotten ideology and poison the minds of young people.

"Any Muslim who agrees with their ideology or condones their evil practices or join them or sympathises with them in any form is regarded by God in the Qur'an and by Prophet Mohammed (pbuh), as an unbeliever. This means he is not a Muslim. A severe punishment awaits these criminals in this life and in the Hereafter as stated in the Qur'an in verses 4:93 and 5:32-34.

"The murderers who carried out the heinous attacks on innocent people on Westminster Bridge or in Manchester or on London Bridge or anywhere in the world, are nothing but criminals as well as those who supported them. Terrorism has no religion.

"Our hearts and prayers are with the families of the victims. Our sincere condolences to all of them. We feel their pain. May God be with them. May God give them patience and perseverance and reward them for their calamity. May God give those who were injured speedy recovery and re-join them with their families.

"As stated above, Islam is a religion of peace, tolerance and justice. It strongly prohibits and condemns the killing of innocent people anywhere in the world, even on a battle field. Killing one innocent soul is equivalent to killing the whole of humanity and saving one soul is equivalent to saving the entire humanity as stated by God in 5:32.

"We are so proud to be British Muslims. We are an integral part of the British Community. No one can divide us or turn us against each other. This is our Country. We are so grateful and thankful for Her Majesty's Government, the police, the army and all the other services for all they are doing to protect us all.

"Muslims in Britain should not hesitate to report any radical or extremist activities they may witness around themselves to Counter Terrorism/PREVENT. Mosques' Management Committees must be more proactive in discovering radical or extremist conduct or ideologies which might lead to a terrorist attack.

"Unfortunately, following these terrorist attacks, innocent Muslims as well as their mosques, schools and businesses may be targeted by right wing extremists. Mosques' Management Committees must ensure the users are protected at all times. Muslim women and children could be a soft target for these extremist groups. They have to be vigilant and try to avoid walking on their own. All incidents must be reported to the police."

B) In another Condemnation Message sent to Counter Terrorism at New Scotland Yard, London, following terrorist attacks at Barcelona in August 2017, I wrote:

"I feel it is my duty to write to you regarding the recent terrorist attacks at Barcelona. It was so sad to learn that an Imam in a local mosque, few miles away from Barcelona, had radicalised and infected the brains of several young people with his rotten and backward ideology to promote hatred and justify the killing of innocent people.

"So this time it was not only ISIS' propaganda which succeeded in recruiting them, but also a traitor who distorted the true message of Islam and abused his position as a religious leader and masterminded and justified the killing of innocent people.

"These criminals showed no loyalty or gratitude to the country which opened its arms and embraced them and gave them equal rights like its own citizens.

"What lessons should we learn from this awful tragedy?

"We should not deny the fact that there are Imams in Britain who promote radical and extremist ideologies and encourage and justify violence against innocent people.

"Whenever I hear some Muslims criticising the Great Country we live in and calling it "Land of Blasphemy" to justify their unlawful actions, I would immediately say to them, "If you don't like it here, then leave. Go back to where your ancestors came from. Stop using the benefits and the facilities."

"I suggested some time ago that all Imams, Mosques' Management Committees and Trustees, must complete a "Loyalty Declaration Statement" and broadcast it on their mosques' websites. In addition, they must have a "Message of Condemnation" on their websites as well, condemning every terrorist attack anywhere in the world, committed by any terrorist groups like ISIS and others. Hopefully, this would deter people from joining terrorist groups like ISIS or sympathising with them,

"Let us start with the mosques in London. Can Counter Terrorism in the New Scotland Yard carry out the above in a way that the mosques would feel that the police is not interfering in their religious practices? Or is this the responsibility of the Home Office under Prevent? To be practical not many people would really give any attention or notice to Prevent.

"Additionally, we cannot ignore the way some Muslim schools are run or even some State schools. I would also expect that every school will have a "Message of Condemnation" and a "Loyalty Statement" on their websites and school brochures.

"Mosques and schools should promote integration and loyalty to the Great Country we live in. Showing such loyalty is an Islamic virtue. They must promote British Values like democracy, freedom of worship, respecting the views of the others, equal opportunities, freedom of speech, equality, preventing violence against women and young girls, etc... These are values which fully agree with Islamic values. Muslim communities in the UK can and will defeat terrorism, by God's Will."

C) Following the terrorist attacks in Paris and on Father Jacques Hamel, in November 2015, I sent a Message of Condemnation to the French President and Her Majesty The Queen.

I received the following response dated 28th January 2016 from the office of the French President:

"Mr Mohammed Fahim
President and Chief Imam

South Woodford Mosque

10-14 Mulberry Way

South Woodford

London E18 1ED

UK

Paris the 28th January 2016

Mr the President,

The President of the French Republic has been very touched by the terms of your message of support following the terrible attacks that bereaved France on the 13th of November last year. He would like to thank you sincerely.

These horrible attacks have resulted in many casualties. It was the soul of France that these murderers wanted to damage. These are our values of tolerance, peace and freedom, which we will never give up, that they wanted to kill.

Be sure that we will not be impressed by the horror. Far from giving up our resolution, these cowardly and degraded acts reinforce our determination to fight terrorist groups.

In this particularly difficult time, the messages of friendship and solidarity that come to us are a precious help in our fight against hatred and barbarism.

Please agree, Mr the President, the assurance of my distinguishable consideration.

Signed by

Isabella SIMA"

D) And I received the following response from Buckingham Palace dated 17th March 2016:

"Dr Fahim

I have been asked to thank you for your seasonal message of good wishes to The Queen, which was most appreciated, and I apologise for the delay in replying which is due to the amount of mail received recently.

The sympathy and support you express for the victims of the Paris terrorist attacks, and their families, is appreciated, and the views you express regarding those who commit such acts have been duly noted.

I am to thank you for taking the time and trouble to write as you did, and to wish you and the members of South Woodford Mosque my good wishes for the year ahead.

Yours sincerely,

Miss Jennie Vine
Deputy Correspondence Coordinator"

E) Following the terrorist attack on Finsbury Park mosque in London on the evening of 18th June 2017, during the Holy month of Ramadhan and the killing of an innocent worshipper, I received the following response from Counter Terrorism at New Scotland Yard, London:

"Subject: My deepest sympathy

Dear Dr Fahim

Each time there has been a terrorist attack, you have been kind enough to let me and colleagues know how unequivocally you have condemned it.

Let me write this time, to you and your communities, to say how very sorry I am about what happened last night. I saw you at the start of Ramadan with so many of our mutual friends, at what was a joyful Iftar. Since then, the London Bridge attack and now last night's attack have happened. I am deeply sorry that this has happened - at any time, let alone at what should be such a special time for you.

Please may I give you my deepest sympathies.

With kindest regards, Helen

Helen Ball

DAC Metropolitan Police Service"

F) I have been an active member of the London Muslim Community Forum at New Scotland Yard, since 2010. On 2nd June 2017, I received the following letter of appreciation from Commander Mak Chishty, on the day of his retirement:

"Dear Dr Fahim

Assalammoalaikum

London Muslim Community Forum

I just wanted to take this opportunity to express my personal gratitude to you for all the support, advice and friendship you have given me over the past 6 years.

You have always been ready to provide help at any time of the day or night and indeed have turned out on many occasions during some very unsociable hours. I have always valued this enormously and am indebted to you for your selfless efforts in working with the Metropolitan Police Service to keep London safe.

I fully recognise that causes inconvenience to your personal and family life and would like to acknowledge them in also saying thank you to your families as without their support for you it may not have been possible for you to give the commitment that you have always showed.

Your close advice, good council and expert insight of the Muslim communities has proved vital in helping the MPS to develop plans and strategies in response to many critical incidents including the terrible murder investigation of the Syrian Imam in Ealing in April 2015. Your efforts here helped us bring justice to the victim and his family and further helped reassure a very frightened Syrian Community who felt vulnerable and at risk.

In fact, your personal contribution led to building such trust and confidence that members of that community travelled to Manchester at their own expense to support the national Action Counters Terrorism (ACT) Campaign. This has helped reach several thousands of Muslims across the world as a result of which we are now receiving good information to help the national effort to keep us safe from terrorism.

Your advice in relation to many critical issues was extremely helpful in dealing with some difficult operational matters and community confidence, some of these incidents included; the murder of Lee Rigby, Charlie Hebdo, cartoon drawings of the Holy Prophet Mohammed (pbuh) by the far right, terrorist attacks in Paris, Belgium, Nice, Berlin, Orlando, Jo Cox murder, Brexit, Quebec and more recently the Westminster Bridge and the Manchester concert attack.

Your personal reach and influence across all Muslim communities has meant that we were able to make them feel safe and secure at the most vulnerable times.

You have also showed the highest integrity and courage in the face of difficult issues and I'm personally grateful for your support to me when some hard-line Muslim voices were opposing my views.
Your strategic perspective and immense experience across London helped transform the London Muslim Community Forum (LMCF) making it into a nationally recognised forum that is uniquely fully representative of most Muslim denominations and sects. The value of this was seen during our response to the sectarian murder of Mr Asad Shah, when instead of Muslim communities becoming divided on grounds of belief instead, we all stood together on common values of humanity.

I know that you have dedicated enormous personal time and energy for which I and the Metropolitan Police Service (MPS) are extremely grateful. I have had the privilege of leading the responses but could not have done it without your help.
I feel that the challenges we are now facing are even greater than before which will require your continued support and a collective effort to countering violent extremism and building stronger communities.

Although I am saying thank you and farewell for now, I am sure that InshaAllah we will still be crossing paths somewhere along the lines in the future.

Once again - thank you and with my sincerest duas for you, your families and to your communities.

Mak Chishty

1.5.5 Aggressive Islam or Confused Muslims!

In this section I will explain how I managed to deter a young Muslim from joining ISIS and becoming a terrorist.

The Reunion...
In January 2016 I was invited to attend a business meeting in Jeddah, Saudi Arabia. The host was an old Saudi friend, called Adel, who studied in London, but I was much more senior to him in age. I always treated him like a son. He was a very moderate practicing Muslim. He used to come to London in the summer with his young family. We used to go out together visiting parks, touristic sites and do a lot of shopping to take back with them. I really enjoyed their company. Unfortunately, he stopped coming to London for almost five years for personal reasons which I was not aware of.

Adel picked me up from the airport and drove me to my hotel. It was an amazing reunion. He told me that he was having major problems with his only son, Fahd, which had prevented him from coming to London for the last five years. He shared that he had wanted to tell me this face to face. "*My son has become a very fanatic Muslim and he is turning our lives into hell. His mother and his two sisters are really suffering.*" Adel explained. "*I don't want to lose him. That is why we are tolerating his conduct. This is his final year at university, in a few months he will become an engineer, aeronautical engineer like you Dr Fahim.*" Adel added.

The father was in tears. He asked, "*Do you know why we have not been coming to London? Because Fahd regards the West a land of blasphemy. He is the victim of many Imams here who deliver this message every summer from their pulpits telling people not to spend their holidays in lands of blasphemy*", the father went on to explain.

He then begged me to talk to his son. He suggested that I meet with him to help him with his final year project and then try to talk to him.

Such problems were not new to me. I have dealt with many fanatic and extremist Muslims, young and old, men and women, not only in Saudi but also in Egypt and the U.K. Whether they are followers of Wahhabi or Salafi ideology, they would really put you off of Islam, if your belief is so weak. The majority of them are very narrow minded, rude, loud and aggressive and they would consider anyone who criticises them as a Kafir (unbeliever). And they would often justify beheading you, in their perverted and distorted belief of this peaceful religion. Can Islam be so aggressive?

Adel, my friend, said he would pick me up from the hotel in the morning to take me to his office for our business meeting.

That night I could not sleep at all. I knew the boy since a young age. We used to have great times together in London. Last time I saw Fahd, the son, he was 15 or 16 years old. His two sisters were twins, five years younger than him. His mother, Sarah, was a lecturer at the university in Jeddah, a very cultured and educated woman. She was also a much learned Muslim. My family and Adel's family were very close friends.

In the morning, Adel picked me up. It was my 70th birthday, but I didn't want to mention it to him. He apologised for burdening me with his family issues. I reassured him that I would do my best to talk to Fahd. We had a very successful business meeting at his beautiful offices. Adel said, "*I wish if I could have a secretary like yours in London.*" I said, "*You can wish from here to the Day of Judgement! Do you think it will ever happen that you will have a female secretary running your business with all these fanatics everywhere you go?*" I was referring to the religious police who have absolute power to stop any couple and question them if they are married or not and even the power to arrest them if the answer is not satisfactory. I said to Adel, "*You need a young and brave King to bring dramatic changes and to liberate women and give them their rights which were an essential part of Mohammed's message pbuh.*"

A Palace without a Soul...

Adel drove me to his house for a meal. On the way he said, "*We have moved into a new house, I hope you like it. I wish you would have stayed with us, but I know you like to be independent.*"

When we arrived at his house it looked from outside like a palace, so beautifully designed. I congratulated him and wished him all the best. I noticed the house had two entrances, one was designated for women and one for men. I asked Adel, "*Why this segregation? You didn't have this in your previous house!*" He replied, "*It is not me. It is Fahd who insists on this. And I'm so sorry to say you will not be able to see Sarah or the girls, because Fahd imposes full segregation.*" I was so saddened to hear this. The father didn't want to lose his only son so he had submitted fully to his radical views.

We entered through the men's door and I was taken to the lounge to sit. I was overwhelmed by the luxury of the interior design of this beautiful palace. A maid walked in with a tray full of fresh ripe dates and Arabian coffee. While drinking my coffee and chatting to Adel, his son Fahd walked in. "*Salam uncle Fahim, welcome to Jeddah.*" he said. I was so pleased to see him. I got up and we had a big hug. He had a very untidy beard, his hair was down to his ears and his white robe was above his ankle. This is exactly what I had expected to see! It fitted the profile of a radical Muslim as defined by counter terrorism organisations. I noticed he was wearing a very expensive Rolex watch on his right wrist. I knew why the right wrist, but there was no need to comment on it. Radical Muslims misinterpret the recommendation of the Prophet (pbuh) to use the right hand when eating/drinking, shaking hands and only using the left hand in the toilet. this is a matter of hygeine - nothing more.

I gave Adel and Fahd the presents I brought for them from London. I also gave Fahd the gifts my wife gave me for his mother and his sisters to give to them. Fahd looked at his mother's present which was a Chanel No 5 perfume and said, "*Uncle Fahim! Don't you know that it is Haram (unlawful or prohibited) for women to wear perfume?*" I knew what he was talking about, but there was no need at all to start a confrontation, instead I said, "*She will use it at home not when she goes out. Muslim women should smell like garlic and onion when they go out, so they keep the vampire Saudi men away from them!*"

I changed the subject and looked at Adel and said, "*Your walls look very naked! What did happen to the lovely family photos and paintings you had in your previous house?*" Then Fahd answered, "*It is Haram to have them. The Prophet pbuh said no angels would enter a room where there are pictures.*" I have heard this before many times, and I knew the answer which would defeat him fully, but there was no need to alienate him so early. Instead, I said: "*In this case angels of death will never come to take my soul, because I have many photos and paintings everywhere in my house. What the Prophet pbuh prohibited was images of gods or objects worshipped besides the One True God. My family's photos or a painting of a beautiful forest or a sea view are not things to be worshipped.*" Fahd was listening but he didn't comment. His father felt relieved that someone was challenging his son's fanatical views, in a moderate way.

I asked Adel where the piano which he had in the old house was. Fahd answered, "*Music is Haram in Islam.*" I said, "*Are you sure of that? All music? Do you know what did Imam Ibn-Hazm says about music in his book of Fiqh Al-Muhalla?*" He replied, "*I never heard of this Imam.*" I said, "*He was in the Andalusia, South Spain, during the Renaissance of the Muslim Empire. He died almost 1,000 years ago.*"

I looked at Adel and said, "*So you are no longer enjoying your piano!*" "*Dr Fahim! I know you like to listen to me playing it. But you are not strict like my son.*" Adel commented. I responded by saying, "*It is not a matter of being strict or not. When the Prophet pbuh immigrated from Makkah to Madina, he was welcomed on his arrival by people who sang for him and played the drums. Music and singing are not Haram if they are kept within Islamic moral code. There are many authentic Hadith which supports this view. It is not practical just to look at the views of one Mazhab and ignore the others. When the four Mazhabs were formalised, each Imam based his judgment on what collection of Hadith was available to him. Now we have all the Hadith, not only available to us, but also have been verified and revalidated by many imminent scholars. For example, Sheikh Al-Albany examined 14,654 Hadith, and found out that only 8,202 are sound or good whilst the remaining 6,452 are weak or very weak or fabricated. We must understand the difference between the interpretation of a Hadith by Hadith scholars and by Fiqh scholars. It is the interpretation by the Fiqh scholars which matters to us as it explains how the Hadith would affect our lives. The Egyptian Muslim scholar Sheikh Mohammed Al-Ghazaly explained this in his book 'The Prophetic Tradition between the Scholars of Fiqh and Scholars of Hadith. It is a good read.*"

The Last Supper....

Then we were asked to move to the dining room for our meal. Only Adel, Fahd and I sat at the dining table, which sits 12 guests. It was a feast! Unbelievable table spread. We were served by two Indonesian female domestic servants. The china and the cutlery were amazing! Adel said, "*Do you remember? We bought this set from Harrods in the sales five years ago.*" "*Yes, I do remember! I also remember how you haggled with the poor sales woman for almost half an hour to give you more discount. And it was me who convinced her to give you extra discount. So this plate is mine. I will take it with me back to London. Fahd!*

What do you think?" No comment from him. I was just trying to engage with him in any discussion, but he looked so fierce.

Whilst one of the maids was serving the food, she dropped some on the tablecloth. Fahd shouted at her, as if she was a slave, and the girl was trembling and tears were running down her cheeks. Adel said, "*Never mind my dear son, it is washable.*" Fahd filled his plate and did not finish his food. I said, "*Fahd finish your food it is so delicious! I really enjoyed it.*" He said he had enough. I said but it is Haram to throw it in the bin. He responded by saying the servants will eat it. At this moment I could not control myself any longer. I looked at him and said, "*The Prophet pbuh said serve food to your servants before you serve yourself and even let them sit with you. How can you offer them the left over on your plate?*" He, in his ignorance and arrogance, said, "*This left over is a luxury to what they eat in their countries.*" I decided not to comment as I did not want to create a problem for Adel.

One of the maids brought a birthday cake with five candles! Adel said, "*Happy birthday Dr Fahim.*" I was almost in tears. "*O my God! You remembered!*" I exclaimed. Fahd said, "*It is Haram to celebrate birthdays. In Islam we only have two Eid's to celebrate, Eid Al-Fitr (end of the fasting month of Ramadhan) and Eidul-Adha (after Hajj).*" Again, this is not something new I had not heard before. I said, "*My dear son Fahd there is a big difference between the two Arabic words Eid and Yawm. The word Eid refers to the two annual celebrations we have in Islam. However, the word birthday in English should be translated to Yawm Al-Melad not Eid Al-Melad. I want you to read my article on this topic please. It will clarify a lot of misconceptions.*"

I gave my phone to Fahd and I asked him to take a photo of me and his father when I was blowing the candles. He said, "*Taking photos is Haram!*" I asked him if he has a photo in his passport or his driving license or his ID card? He said, "*Yes. But I had no choice. Here I can refuse to take your photo.*" I really felt the pain of his parents. Everything is Haram in the sight of their only son, a fanatic son!

Prayer time was approaching so we got up to get ready. Adel asked me to lead the prayer. Fahd responded by saying, "*I'm going to pray at the mosque. Dr Fahim can't be the Imam, his beard is not a handful.*" I laughed and said, "*Since when did the size of your beard determine who should lead the prayer?*" He left to go to the mosque. And to my surprise his mother and sisters walked in the lounge and welcomed me. I was so pleased to see them. We all prayed together, and they left before Fahd returned.

His Project and my Plan....

Upon Fahd's return from the mosque, I requested to leave with him to go to my hotel in order to discuss his final year project. Adel said Fahd would drive me to the hotel in his new Mercedes. I declined and said we were going to walk to the hotel to digest the lovely food his mother had made. The hotel was about two miles from their house and the weather was so pleasant and I love walking.

Whilst walking together towards the hotel, Fahd mentioned that he was not keen on living in Jeddah because it is a liberal city which permitted women walking without a veil and encourages many non-Muslim expats to congregate along the sea promenade without segregation. "*I prefer Makkah and Madina over Jeddah. I fully support segregation. I mean no mixing between men and women. I'm also in favour of living in a city which prohibits non-Muslims from entering it. I'm willing to join jihadist groups in Syria to fight the infidels*" said Fahd. Mentioning jihadist groups was like a bombshell falling on my head. I was just listening in disbelief! I was aware that these young Muslims are very vulnerable and they are influenced by what they have been taught at school, the religious sermons they have listened to and now what they share on social media. Unfortunately, Saudi promotes its Wahhabi and Salafi ideology through exporting, free of charge, it's very rigid and radical school books to Muslim schools and mosques worldwide, including the UK.

He told me that he supports the Caliphate created by ISIS in Iraq and Syria. I was very saddened to hear that. I informed him that ISIS or ISIL are terrorist groups who have been spreading mischief in the land, killing innocent people and destroying civilisations. Their punishment is mentioned in 5:33-34. I was aware that in June 2014, after making significant territorial gains in Iraq, the group proclaimed the establishment of a Caliphate led by the leader of ISIL, Abu Bakr al-Baghdadi. I said to Fahd if these people are really true Muslims, who have good intentions, God would support them as He says in 22:41, "*(They are) those who, if We establish them in the land, establish regular prayer and give regular charity, enjoin the right and forbid wrong: with God rests the end (and decision) of (all) affairs.*"

"*These people are not doing that. Hence their destruction is eminent. They will perish. God says in 5:32, that killing one innocent soul is equivalent to killing all the peoples of the world and saving one life is as if saving all humanity. Fahd! My dear son! If your parents would hear what you have told me just now, they would drop dead. Please have mercy on them.*" I added.

Suddenly, I saw him stopping in front of a young man, Philipino I thought, who was walking in the opposite direction on the kerb and pushed him on the road. I said to him, "*Excuse me! Why did you do that? This is not a one way kerb! You could have easily allowed him to pass.*" He replied, "*The Prophet pbuh commanded that. The Prophet pbuh said if you see non-Muslims walking on the road narrow their passage.*" I responded very angrily, "*What! Are you telling me that the man who was sent as a Mercy to all creatures (21:107), a man who was the Qur'an walking on earth and had the best sublime manners (68:4), a man who had the most kind heart and God said about him, that if he was harsh and hard-hearted people would have ran away from him (3:159), would command his followers to do what you have just done?*" I continued, "*Even if what you said is in the most authentic books of Hadith, I will not accept it because it contradicts with the spirit of Islam, the teachings of the Qur'an and the great qualities of the Prophet pbuh.*" I stopped him and looked at his face saying, "*These foreigners who are working here are contributing to the development of your country because you don't have enough qualified Saudis to do the job. You will find them everywhere, in hospitals, schools, universities, all industries and even the armed forces. They are also the ones who are cleaning the mess you create, because it is below your dignity as a Saudi to work as a dustman or a cleaner. They are the ones who are cleaning the two most holy shrines in Islam, the Grand Mosque in Makkah and the Prophet's Mosque in Madina. There are no Saudis who are willing even to clean these two sacred sites. The supervisor is a useless Saudi. These foreign cleaners are treated like slaves. They don't have equal rights.*

You should appreciate them and be grateful rather than worrying about the size of my beard or the length of my trousers." He kept quiet.

I continued, "*The Mercedes you drive, the Rolex on your right wrist, your iPhone, your underwear and the robe you are wearing, the shoes on your feet, even the fridge, the freezer and the air condition units you have at your house and the medicine you take are all manufactured by those you call 'infidels'. Almost ninety percent of the goods in the shops in Makkah and Madina are manufactured by Chinese idol worshippers. After all this you are boasting to inform me that you will join ISIS and go to Syria to fight the 'Infidels'. If you want to fight the 'infidels', then boycott all their products. Buy yourself a tent, most probably it will be made in China, and two sheep, imported from Australia, and a camel. Go and live in the desert on your own, and let me know when you will join ISIS!*

"*The Prophet pbuh used an idol worshipper to show him the way when he immigrated from Makkah to Madina on the most important trip in the history of Islam. He pbuh used a Jew in Madina to manufacture his swords, because he was so experienced. And when he pbuh died, his shield was mortgaged with a Jew who didn't charge usury. One of the wives of the Prophet pbuh, was a Jew who embraced Islam and became 'Mother of the Believers', so his in laws were Jews. Verse 5:5 allows Muslim men to marry chaste women from the people of the Book that is Jews and Christians. Our food is lawful to them and their food is lawful to us. These are the people you call infidels and you justify their killing.*"

Eventually we got to the hotel. We sat in the lobby and I asked him to show me his project. He was asked to design the fuel governor of an automatic control system for a jet engine. What is a fuel governor? So when the pilot would switch the auto-pilot on, and sets the speed at, say 900km/hr, the fuel governor would inject more fuel if the speed drops due to any external factors or reduce the fuel if the speed goes over 900km/hr. With a big smile on my face, I said, "*This is so interesting! What a coincidence! Do you know, this was my first job when I joined the aircraft industry in Egypt in 1967? Now we are going to use artificial intelligence in this design.*" He started to relax. We spent two hours going through the work. I told him that I was so pleased with the work he has done so far. I advised him on how to write the table of contents, the introduction, the conclusion and the bibliography. He was so happy.

I asked him if he has read all the books and articles he referred to in the bibliography. He confirmed that he had. I commented by saying also in Islam you must not just rely on one book written by a man to teach you about your religion. You must have an open mind and study different sources and examine various views. We as engineers have a very special logic. People who fly on the planes we design trust us. One of the most interesting topics I learnt at universities in the West was how to critically analyse different views. Fahd was listening to me with love in his eyes. I suggested that we meet in two days' time when his work was ready and in the meantime I would go to Makkah to perform Umra. I suggested to him three Islamic books to read and I promised to buy them from Makkah and give them to him at our next meeting.

The Slave Waiter......

Now I felt it was a good time to talk to him regarding his relationship with his parents. I asked the waiter to come and we ordered two fresh mango juices. When he brought the drinks, I asked him where he is from and he said Bangladesh. *"How long have you been here?"* I asked. *"Three years. I have not been home since I came. We can't afford the tickets. I have very poor parents. My father is blind. My wife gave birth to our third child one month after I left. I have not even seen my newly born daughter. I only earn SR 1,000 (Saudi Riyals) a month, I work six days a week 15 hours a day, from 7am to 10pm. I send all the money to my family. The hotel gives us food and accommodation. But ten people share the same bedroom. If one gets a flu, we all catch it. The best thing is that I will perform my Hajj this year."* I took SR 1,000 out of my wallet, (equivalent to UK £200), and gave it to him. I made sure that Fahd saw me doing that. Then I asked the waiter how many people are working with him. He said nine. I asked him to inform them to come to see me one by one and not to mention anything about the money to them. They came one by one and I gave SR 500 to each one of them. Again, I made sure that Fahd has witnessed this.

When the last waiter left, I said to Fahd, *"this is from my Zakat money. My wife and I do this very often when we come to Makkah and Madina, especially in the month of Ramadhan. These people deserve our Zakat. Can you imagine their hourly rate is about SR 2.5, which is less than UK £0.50. Is this fair? This is slavery. When I give money to these poor people, I remember what God says in 24:33, that the money I give is not mine, it belongs to God. Also you should never expect anything in return or even 'thank you' from them, as God says in 76:9. I was not happy today when you shouted at the maid when she spilt the food on the table cloth. Accidents can happen. I'm sure she works just as hard as these waiters and her payment is almost the same. She must be supporting a poor family back home and maybe she has children who she hasn't seen for a while. If you really love the Prophet pbuh, please try to emulate his character. Be humble, kind, generous and gracious to these extremely poor people who travelled thousands of miles to come to work in your house, to provide you with luxury and comfort. I have known you since you were a baby. You have always been very kind and generous. It is the fanatic views which you have adopted which are turning you to be so harsh and fierce. Would you promise me that you will apologise to her when you go home and ask her to forgive you? Maybe you will give her some money."*
Fahd replied, *"Yes uncle Fahim I will."*
"I love you my dear son" I said.

I asked Fahd how much the Rolex he was wearing was. He answered, *"SR 90,000"*. I asked, *"and your new Mercedes?"* He replied, *"Almost half a million Saudi Riyals."* I asked, *"Who bought these expensive gifts for you?"* he said, *"My parents."* I asked him, *"Would you be willing to sell them and donate the money to the poor and the needy and buy yourself a camel like Prophet Mohammed pbuh? No, you wouldn't. It is easy to grow a beard or to wear a white robe above the ankle or to classify something as Haram without any solid knowledge. The Prophet did not live a luxury life. For days he didn't have proper food to eat, apart from dates and water. He was never harsh to his servants."* Fahd was just listening. I continued, *"The car you are driving is a status car. It is to show off like the Rolex you are wearing. A basic Japanese car and watch would be sufficient for you. God doesn't love those who show off as He says in 31:18 and 57:23. God destroyed Qaroon, who was from the people of Moses, and made the earth to swallow him up with all his treasures, because he was an arrogant boaster, 28:76-83. God doesn't prohibit us from enjoying the favours or the* bounties He bestowed on us, as He says in 28:77, as long as there is no show off or waste and we recognise the rights of the poor and the needy." Fahd said, "I do not show off when I drive my car". I responded by saying, "and your mother when she wears perfume and goes out, her intention is not to attract men to her. Your mother is a very righteous and learned woman. God judges us according to our intentions and what is in our hearts. He knows what we reveal and conceal."

Pocket Money....

"You get a grant from the University and you get monthly pocket money from your parents. How much in total?" I asked. Fahd replied SR 6,000. I questioned him if he donates any amount to the poor and the needy. He said, "not much". I asked, "So you must have a good balance in your bank account! Do you pay any Zakat on it?" He said no because he thought he is still a student and he is not working and earning. I was really shocked regarding his lack of understanding the basic teachings of the religion. I said, "My dear son! You have to pay Zakat on your savings as long as they are more than the minimum exempted amount (Nisab). You have to pay the Zakat, not only for this year, but for all the previous years." Fahd was very happy to do this and said, "Uncle Fahim! Many thanks for your guidance I will do that. Now I know how poor these workers are. I will work out my Zakat money and bring some with me next time when I come to see you to give to these waiters." I praised him and prayed for him.

I told him that during the first two years at university, 1962/1964, my pocket money was one Egyptian Pound a month, which was equivalent to SR10. I would donate every month ten pence to a poor relative cleaner who used to come to help my mother and I would go to the cinema once a week and I would buy refreshments and pay for my transport and I would save 30 pence every month. From the third year and up to the fifth year, we were given a grant of five Egyptian Pounds every month as a reward for studying aeronautical engineering. I would give my father the full amount to help with home expenses and my father would give me back my one Pound pocket money. We were not poor, but we were very content middle-class family. When it came to Islam, we were so rich in our knowledge. We lived the true teachings of Islam.

I said to him that I was not happy regarding the way he treated his parents. Also I'm concerned about his limited knowledge of what is lawful or prohibited in Islam. Fahd was just listening. I continued. "You allow female servants to serve the men. But your own mother can't meet a family friend in the presence of her husband and her son. Who drives your mother and your two sisters everywhere they wish to go to? A sexually frustrated Egyptian male driver who has not been home to see his family for more than five years now. You can clearly see the double standards here. You know well that the Prophet pbuh prohibited a man and a woman of being in a closed place on their own. And a car is a closed place especially with the tinted glass windows. Why can't you or your father drive your mother and your sisters? Because it is impractical for you and your father to do so. You manipulate the religion to suit your own needs. And then you tell me that music is Haram, perfume for women is Haram, photography is Haram, celebrating a birthday is Haram, my beard is not long enough to qualify me to lead prayers, etc... Please my dear son Fahd, or even my grandson, please, please I want you to reflect on what we talked about today." Then his driver arrived to pick him up. We had a big hug and he left on a very happy note.

The Return....

While in Makkah I was communicating with Fahd on a daily basis. He had a few issues with his project and I managed to address these concerns. He told me that he worked out his Zakat money and he apologised to the servant and gave her SR500 from his Zakat money. I was so happy to hear that. I praised him and thanked him. I was also in communication with his parents Adel and Sarah. They were so grateful for my efforts with their beloved son.

Before leaving Makkah I went to a bookshop and bought the books I was going to give Fahd to read. The first book "Fiqh As'sunnah" written by Sheikh As'sayed Sabeq, consisting of two parts. The first part deals with all forms of worship, e.g. Purification, Prayers, Zakat, Fasting, Hajj, Funerals, Inheritance, etc... And the second part addresses Family Law, Criminal Justice, Business Dealings, etc... I have this book in my home library with many other books of Fiqh. I find this one to be the most comprehensive, easy to read and understand and very authentic.

The second book "The Lawful and Prohibited in Islam" written by Sheikh Yusuf Al-Qaradawi deals in a very contemporary manner with many questions facing Muslims worldwide. It covers topics like food, drink, music, dress code, relationships between Muslims and non-Muslims, family issues. These two books are in my home library and my mosque library in South Woodford in London. I have taught from them for many years as they address many misconceptions regarding Islamic teachings and practices.

I also acquired a copy of a book written by Sheikh Mohammed Al-Ghazaly critically analysing how the scholars of Hadith and the scholars of Fiqh have interpreted the Prophetic Tradition.

After praying Isha prayer at the Grand Mosque, in Makkah, I travelled back to my hotel in Jeddah. When I was back in my room I called Fahd to come to me early in the morning to have breakfast together. In a joking manner, I said to him, *"8am means 8am. I want you to stick to Islamic punctuality, not Saudi times."*

When he arrived I was so happy to see him. He gave me a hug and said he had brought his Zakat money with him. I thanked him and went straight to the restaurant to have our breakfast. The waiter was so pleased to see us and welcomed both of us with a beautiful smile. Fahd said he would like to give the money to the waiters as I did last time. I said that will be great. *"How much do you want to give each*?" I asked. He replied, *"SR 100 each."* I told him that is fine, it is about £20. As most of the radicals have no communication skills, he asked me to do it. I said no, you do it. Just fold the note in your hand and put it in his hand without disclosing it. And after that ask the waiter to send the others, one by one. He felt very shy to do that but I prompted him. I sat there watching him doing that. At the beginning he was not confident enough, but eventually he looked very happy and thanked me.

We retired to the lobby. I said we will firstly discuss his project and after that we will have a look at the books I brought.

I was so pleased with the progress he had made and I addressed several points which were still not clear to him. We discussed his work regarding aircraft stability and we read several reports regarding design problems associated with the automatic control system which prevents the plane from stalling. This is when the plane starts to lose altitude and the pilot fails in restoring the plane to normal flight mode. When we were discussing this major design problem, I never thought that in March 2019 the Boeing 737 MAX passenger airliner would be grounded worldwide after two crashes in October 2018 and March 2019 killing 346 passengers due to stalling problems. In January 2021 it was given the all clear to fly again. I was so happy to hear that, because safety comes first.

I turned towards Fahd and said, *"Do you know aircraft stability is like soul stability! There are three types of souls mentioned in the Qur'an. In 12:53 God refers to an evil soul which does and commands evil all the time. Any external small disturbance it may experiences would lead to its perdition. The second one is a self-correcting soul, mentioned in 75:2, God praises it and swears by it. Every time it does something wrong it regrets doing it and makes an effort not to do it again. Very similar to the fuel governor you are designing for your project. Then we have the content soul in 89:27, a soul in complete rest and satisfaction. A soul which will not be affected by any external disturbances, like an aircraft which flies very smoothly in any weather conditions and lands safely by day or night. A soul which is at perfect peace. This is our quest in life."*

I asked the waiter to bring a glass bowl. Fahd asked why I needed it. I said just wait. I placed the bowl on its base on the table and I took a little glass ball out of my key ring. I placed it at the bottom of the bowl and asked him to give the glass ball a little push. The ball oscillated to the left and the right few times and then stopped. I asked him to repeat it but with a bigger push. The ball oscillated again but with wider oscillations, almost reaching the rim of the bowl, then eventually came to a complete standstill. I said to Fahd a pure believing soul is like the glass ball inside the bowl. It will survive any size disturbance it might experience in life and eventually will reach a steady state condition. In engineering terms, in mechanical vibration, we call it damped oscillation. Very similar to what an automatic control system would do to restore the plane to its steady state condition. God confirms in 2:155-157, that we are all going to be tested and tried with something of fear, hunger, loss of wealth and lives and fruits. He also gives glad tidings to those who would persevere patiently and say when hit by a calamity "To God we belong and to Him we return". They are those on whom descend blessings and Mercy from their Lord.

Then I turned the glass bowl upside down, placing it on its rim. Fahd was watching in amazement. I placed the glass ball on the top and asked him to give it a very little push. He said, *"uncle it will run away*!". *"Please just do it"* I said. He did it and the ball went under the next table. This is a parable of a disturbed soul. Any small disturbance would make it suffer, I said. In the same way the plane will go into a spiral and crash, this type of soul will move towards its perdition.

I said, *"are you ok if we go through the books I brought for you to study?".* He said, *"yes please".* I placed the books on the table and just went through the table of contents of each one. He asked me, *"You are an engineer, why do you study religion? There are people who specialise in this."* I responded by saying, *"Studying religion is not a monopoly which only belongs to some Mullahs who act as Muftis who are so narrow minded and they fail in attracting young Muslims and only promote extremism and misguide them to be terrorists.*

The Qur'an commands us to ponder and reflect on God's creation. God expects every Muslim to be a scientist. I have been studying Islam since I moved to London in July 1970. I'm not going to allow such Mullahs to influence me to join terrorist groups and kill innocent people. By studying Islam from the Qur'an and comparing different interpretations and examining various rulings, I became qualified enough as I have produced my own immunity against their false claims."

Confused Muftis.....

I said to Fahd let me share with you some of my bitter experiences I had with your Mullahs who would rush to give Fatwa without solid knowledge. One year my wife and I were attending the Taraweeh prayer in Makkah on the 29th night of Ramadhan. The Imam completed the recitation of the last part of the Qur'an, part 30. We went back to our hotel and switched the TV on to watch the news. Late King Fahd appeared on the TV and announced that due to a mistake made in sighting the moon of Ramadhan, today is the last day of Ramadhan and tomorrow is Eidul-Fitr and people must make up the day they missed. Unfortunately, that year we only fasted 28 days.

Another year we were in Makkah getting ready to perform Hajj in a few days' time. Just three days before the set date, these Mullahs announced that there was a mistake in sighting the moon of Zu-Alhejja and the day of the Hajj will be brought forward by one day. Can you imagine the chaos and the havoc this announcement had made to manage more than two million people coming for Hajj? Trying to be funny, I said , *"imagine on the Day of Judgment if God asks you why you didn't perform Hajj? And you say I did. And God says you came on the wrong day!"*
One year I organised Hajj for a group of friends from London and I was their religious leader. Just one day before the Day of Hajj, a woman informed me that she will have her period soon and she didn't know what to do regarding the final Tawaf around the Kaba, known as Twaful-Ifadha which is a pillar of the rites of the Hajj. I knew the answer but because this was her first Hajj I wanted to make sure that I'm absolutely right.

I went to a special office at the Grand Mosque in Makkah where you can seek religious opinions, Fatwas. There were several queues and I joined one of them. When it was my turn I told the Mufti, who had died his beard with henna and put Kohl in his eyes that we have a woman in our group who would have her period after the Day of Hajj and she couldn't wait until she was clean to perform the Tawaf. He said, *"she must wait until she is pure and then perform the Tawaf"*. I said, *"she will definitely miss her flight back to London and no one is going to wait with her"*. He said in a very commanding tone *"You submit yourself to Hajj. Hajj doesn't submit itself to you"*. I thanked him and left. I saw another long queue which had more women in it. I said to myself maybe they will ask the same question like me, let me join it. While waiting I was reflecting on the whole situation. This problem was experienced by many women since Hajj started from the time of Prophet Ibrahim (pbuh), so there must be a practical solution to deal with it. I waited for a considerable amount of time before entering the office of this Mufti. I told him the problem. He said this is an interesting question and he switched his tape recorder on. Then he asked me: *"Did it happen?"* I said: *"Not yet."* He said: *"When it happens, come back, for there is an appropriate response for every event."* Honestly, if I had any authority I would have sacked both of them. Such were the extremely poor qualities and shallow knowledge of these two Muftis at the most sacred mosque on planet earth. I was so disappointed that after waiting for almost two hours I came out with no answers. This can only reflect the depth of ignorance these Saudi Mullahs have. Being the Custodians of the two most holy shrines in Islam, they promote and try to enforce their radical views of Wahhabism on the rest of the world.

After the sudden jump in the price of oil in the year 1973, when the price of oil went from nine dollars per barrel to 36 dollars, all the Gulf States became so rich. They attracted so many labourers from all over the world. I remember very well that when the Egyptian workers returned home from Saudi Arabia, the majority of them grew an untidy beard, wore a white robe above the ankle, and their women covered their faces with a niqab. That was the version of the Saudi Islam which fuelled many terrorist attacks.

I went back to my hotel. I could not sleep that night so I stayed up and left to perform Fajr prayer in a mosque next to the hotel. The Imam was a young man who did not look Saudi. I approached him after the prayer and asked him where he was from? He told me he is a Jordanian PhD student at the Islamic university in Makkah (Um-Alqura). I was so pleased to hear that. I told him the problem. He immediately and without any hesitation gave me the correct answer, which I was aware of. Then he informed me that this Fatwa was given by the great scholar Ibn-Taimeia, who is followed by the Saudi Mullahs, and I can find it in his book of Fatwas. I went immediately to a bookshop in Makkah, and I bought the book. And while in the bookshop I searched for the Fatwa. It was addressing exactly the same question I was seeking clarification for. And the answer was: "*The woman who has her period and can't wait to be clean to perform Twaful-Ifadha, because the caravan would not wait for her, should wash properly and wear thick pads and perform the Tawaf.*" I was so relieved. I went back to the hotel and I asked my wife to explain to our lady friend what to do.

During the month of Ramadhan, in Makkah and Madina, and for many years, the Witr prayer would be performed every night after the Taraweeh prayer for the entire month and it will also be performed in the last ten nights of the month after Tahajjud prayer. This means having two Witr prayers during the last ten nights of Ramadhan. A few years ago I was in Madina during the last ten nights of Ramadhan. On the night of the 21st of Ramadhan, the first night of the last ten nights, and immediately after the Taraweeh prayer, the Imam, whom I have great respect for, announced that there would be no Witr prayer now as they used to do in previous years. He stated that there would be a Witr prayer only after the Tahajjud prayer. The reason he gave was that there is a Hadith that says there should not be two Witr prayers in the same night. So this Hadith which was there for almost 1400 years has just been discovered by the Saudi Mullahs.

It is also worth mentioning that Saudi Mullahs endorse the stoning to death of a married man or a married woman who committed adultery. Contemporary scholars produced evidences from the Qur'an that the only punishment whether the person who committed adultery is married or not is to be flogged one hundred lashes. In spite of this, these Mullahs use the Hadith and ignore the Qur'an.

The Muftis who claim that you shouldn't travel to 'Land of Blasphemy', ignore the Commands of God mentioned, for example, in 3:137, 6:11, 12:109, 16:36, 22:46, 27:69, 33:42, to travel through the earth and see what was the end of those who rejected the

Truth. And in 29:20 God commands, "*Say (Mohammed): Travel through the earth and see how did God originate creation; so will God produce a later creation; for God has power over all things.*" God also says in 30:9, "*Do they not travel through the earth, and see what was the end of those before them? They were superior to them in strength. They tilled the soil and populated it in greater numbers than these have done. There came to them their messengers with Clear (Signs) (which they rejected, to their own destruction), it was not God, who wronged them, but they wronged their own souls.*" So travelling through the land is a religious duty on every Muslim to reflect on God's creation and ponder on what happened to the previous civilisations when they ignored God's teachings. When Pharaoh at the time of Prophet Moses was drowning, God informed him in 10:92, that his body will be saved and will remain intact to be a Sign to those who come after him. So all tyrant rulers are invited to visit the Egyptian museum in Cairo, Egypt to see the body of the Pharaoh who claimed to be God and persecuted the Children of Israel.

A Surprising Visit...

Suddenly, and to our surprise, we saw Adel, Fahd's father, his mother and his two sisters walking towards us in the hotel lobby. "*What a beautiful surprise!*" I said with a big smile on my face. Adel suggested that we all move to the family section in the restaurant. We had a wonderful time chatting about so many things. Then Fahd said to his father, "*Please ask uncle Fahim to stay little bit longer with us. I enjoy very much the way he explains our religion. He has been helping me with my project. But more importantly he corrected a lot of misconceptions I had. Now I can feel I have been released from my bondage.*" I got up and gave Fahd a big hug and I wept. I reassured him that I will stay for few more days to continue to support him with his project and jointly study the books I brought for him. Thank God everything ended on a very happy note.

1.5.6 The Naïve Muslim

In this section we will hear the story of a young man who was misled by militant Muslims, who in doing so robbed him of the most beautiful days of his life, and he became a victim to their betrayal of Islam. The story is relayed in his own words...

Arrest

It was raining heavily, I was discussing my Islamic dress with my sister explaining I feel protected in wearing the attire for prayer. Suddenly I heard a loud bang at the door. Someone was trying to force their way in so I rushed to the door, but they were in, breaking the front door. I shouted out of fear and shock, "I'll cooperate with you" or something along those lines. It was the Police. About 6 or more policemen rushed in. I was pushed into my front room and kept there. I had no idea where my sister was taken. The only other person in the house was my mum who was upstairs. Mum had no idea what was going on.

I remember looking at the helmet of the Policeman and it said MP, I thought it meant military police but they said it meant Metropolitan Police. I have limited recollection of what was said to me that day. I vaguely remember being told I was under arrest, being held under some act. I was dazed. I had no idea what was going on. I just froze. I do remember odd things, like being cuffed with vertical handcuffs and plastic bags being put onto my hands and feet. What was happening.....and to me. I also remember asking for my glasses which were upstairs. A Policeman went to get my glasses.

I was escorted to a Mazda 6 vehicle accompanied by probably 6 or 4 Police Officers. I think they had on forensic suits, I may have also been put into a forensic suit. As I was being put into the Police car, I remember walking past a man who looked at me with contempt. I assume it may have been some senior officer.

I was put into the back of the Police car, with an officer sitting on either side of me. The car took off suddenly at such a high speed. I was held back when the car was braking heavily due to not having a seatbelt on. I remember saying "I have work from university to finish". I wasn't told what was going on. No one said anything. On arrival at what was a police station I was taken to a cell and my clothes were taken and something was said to me which I do not recall. It was all such a blur.

Interview

I was cautioned by the Police. I didn't understand what that meant. I was then taken to an interview room with a family appointed solicitor. I didn't even understand what my solicitor was saying. I was in shock. I recall having multiple interviews over a couple of weeks where I was shown some pictures of friends and some other disturbing things relating to items which were found in my home. I was confused. Nothing made sense. The solicitor advised me to say "no comment". I didn't understand what was happening to me. I was told that most of the incriminating items were found at my home. I did not understand what was happening. I was able to pray in the dark cell and given food and able to wash for prayer and have a shower. I was also given prayer times as I had asked for the time when prayer was due. I had real difficulties with my prayers. Although I have always prayed. I have been praying since I was 12 years old but with all the stress and uncertainty, I kept forgetting the words to my prayers and had to repeat them to myself again and again.

Charged

I was charged with conspiracy to murder and some other charges. This was a terrorist crime. Me a terrorist? What was the Police saying? I remember saying at the time "I have never conspired with anyone to commit murder". I was a regular somewhat ordinary 24 year old guy at university. I played basketball and watched Ugly Betty. The Police must have the wrong person. It must be a mistake.

I was escorted to court where I was held for a hearing and I specifically remember being restrained as I was escorted from the cell to the courtroom. I felt like I was being pulled apart. Two police officers twisting my arms and escorting me to the courtroom. It felt I was already made to feel guilty.

In short, I was naive and too trusting of a friend who took advantage of me. He left papers and computer equipment in my house and was told not to look at it. It turned out to be terrorist material and this is what resulted in me being convicted. I have paid a very heavy price because ultimately I was foolish and naive.

Time in prison

Being Muslim in prison on what is called a terrorist charge is not exactly a good thing, being in prison for anything generally is not a good thing in itself. You are either drawn into associating with people of the same mind-set or be part of a group for protection. Assumption is what leads people to believe without knowing the reality. For example having been charged for terrorism, it was automatically assumed that I had radical views and my outlook on life is very narrow. I had no choice but to be true to myself and do what I felt was right for me and my faith and my understanding of my religion, which is a religion of peace. This involved having to endure intimidation, aggression and bullying. It's easy to go with the flow and the crowd but more difficult to go against the grain. The only thing which came naturally to me was to associate with whoever I felt comfortable with whether they were Muslim or not, being open with prison staff and being supportive to those in need. In prison everything is magnified from emotion to stress and how you look and understand various things. Similarly you have a range of people you get on with and are drawn towards and others you cannot get on with for whatever reason. I recall befriending someone who was very amusing and funny, whom I got on with and built a rapport with. He was of the Jewish faith. One time I was taken aside by two Muslims who warned me not to associate with my Jewish friend, being told he is the enemy and I may get caught up in something? This really made me want to carry on being true to myself, I chose to do what I felt was right and did not waiver in my resilience. Even though it would not be good for me in the short term. The Jewish guy was my friend. We joked around and spoke about normal everyday life. The Muslim guys had a chip on their shoulders and only spoke to the other Muslims. I didn't relate to that.

The prison imam was a life line for me as I was able to share in confidence my concerns and seek counsel in what Islam teaches in regards to dealing with aggression and extreme behaviour. After some time I noticed phone credit added to my phone account. I was puzzled. I then was told I had a meeting with the psychology team which turned out to be a meeting with two prison governors who wanted me to give information about anything going on inside in exchange for a letter to the parole board confirming my cooperation. This resulted in a different extreme pressure and I started to self-harm with a dismantled razor blade. Unfortunately self harm became quite addictive and I looked for any excuse to cut myself. The reason for this is it gave me a release and a barrier from what was causing me anxiety. The pain and sight of blood was relieving for some reason. I was told by the prison imam that self harm is worse than drinking alcohol. I could end up in a coma. I wouldn't cut myself deep, just enough to feel the pain and have a mark left on my arms. This gave me temporary relief and I used this as a tool to cope. I did however feel guilty afterwards. It was Islamically wrong to harm yourself.

Strip searches and cell searches coupled with dog searching did not sit well with me as cleanliness was a concern. This added to my anxieties and impacted my mental health. I had no street IQ so this meant I was not assertive and confident within myself which I know has something to do with being bullied at school.

Release on Parole

I had my first parole hearing which was a year later than planned. Moving prisons and getting used to another environment had never been an easy thing for me. I found a new solicitor to help me with the Parole hearing. How does one prepare for a parole hearing? I was just myself and my record inside spoke for itself. I was given a chance to explain how I managed to stay true to myself even though pressures from all sides were constantly present. The key for me was to put across my understanding of Islam despite extremist ideology and how I wanted to represent my faith in my understanding and upbringing. A paradox as I'm inside prison doing time for terrorism but I refuse to accept extremist thoughts and beliefs. I chose to act accordingly, it was the only way I knew how to act. Other people eventually began to understand me. I conduct myself in a way that is aligned with my understanding of Islamic principles.

After a while I was given the news that I had been granted release on parole. I had written to friends in previous prisons to share this news and naturally they were very happy for me. It took a while for me to go to a hostel where I would spend some time before being allowed to go home. I was escorted to the hostel by a police team where I was tagged and given a mobile phone to use. There was obviously a list of licence conditions that I had to follow in order to keep my parole. One requirement has to have weekly meetings with probation, charging the Tag and not to leave the premises at certain times. I was told I was not allowed to write to my friends in prison regardless of their Crime. This was a difficult thing for me as I was unable to relate to anyone outside regarding my experiences after 11 years in prison. Even though I was eventually allowed to go home and be with my family I found it very difficult to communicate and relate to them. My family has supported me throughout my time and have suffered tremendously as a result. Naturally they wanted to protect me and there seemed to be tension in the air from my perspective. I resorted to self-harm again and had difficulty with settling in and my mental health was not good. I managed eventually to get through these difficult times but it was never easy.

There is one significant person who has had a profound impact on my life by supporting me in numerous ways. He gave me time from his busy schedule and never judged me. There were times I was really struggling and by the grace of Allah I had a friend and mentor providing invaluable support. It is very rare for a Muslim who is very successful Masha 'Allah, to have taken me under his care and seen my potential and to this day still be there for me. This is all despite any negative impact my past may have had on him, his business and personal life. I pray that Allah rewards him in full in both worlds, and blesses him in every way for his time and sacrifice.

My advice to all especially the youngsters are as follows. Always have a role model or mentor and be as open and honest in your dealings with people. Never to be too trusting of people, and do not allow yourself to be pressured into doing things. When it comes to matters of faith and political matters consult qualified scholars. It is said the scholars are the inheritors of the Prophets. Make sincere Dua for guidance and without a doubt you will be successful. Never lose hope.

When I met my wife through an online App, I did not plan to tell her about my past as previously I had people immediately judging me. However at the end of our first meeting I felt I should tell her. She was surprised but did not immediately reject any further contact. She consulted her Imam whom I met with. We openly discussed who I was, where I am now and where I want to be. Things progressed as there was an open minded approach to things. She met with my mentor to get a greater understanding of me and how far I had come. Families met and we were married after 6 months of our initial meeting. This is due to the blessing of my Creator who is worthy of all praise.

Life today hasn't been easy but with my faith and the support of key individuals, I have managed to secure a good job and have started a family. I still have the occasional bad day from past memories, but on the whole I have managed to put my past behind me and build a good life for myself.

1.6 Conclusion

"As the Prophet is a guide and exemplar among us, so Muslims ought to be exemplars amongst mankind. The best witness to God's Truth are those who show its light in their lives." FN2864.

As stated in the beginning of this Chapter, I explained the different shades of the meaning of the word "Jihad".

"Jihad" as in fighting, was never meant to kill innocent people in the name of God. Even on a battlefield, unless the fight is for self-defence or to defend those who are weak and oppressed, it is not regarded as "Jihad".

We are commanded to fight evil within our own souls to achieve inner-peace in this life and salvation in the Hereafter. We must all practice true and unselfish striving for spiritual good. Restraining anger and concealing others' faults is "Jihad". Resisting the temptations of

drugs, intoxicants, gambling, and unlawful sex is "Jihad". This is the illuminating light of peace and brotherhood that true 'Jihad' surely demands.

We should always support the oppressed and fight tyrant rulers by the pen or the tongue without malice.

We should enjoin what is right and forbid what is wrong, in a peaceful manner, and only if we have the knowledge and the authority to do so. We should invite all courteously to the Way of God, the Straight Way which leads to righteousness, with kind words and wisdom. God says in 29:69, *"And those who strive in Our (Cause), We will certainly guide them to Our Paths, for verily God is with those who do right."*

We should perform our religious duties regularly and devoutly and show kindness to our parents and the poor and the needy.

We should all strive to get to know each other, irrespective of religion, or ethnicity, or creed. We must learn to tolerate each other, accommodate each other, accept each other, and show respect to each other. We must always remember that we are all brothers and sisters in humanity. We have no right to judge each other, or to condemn each other. The only judge is God, Who knows what we conceal and what we reveal. So let us all submit our will to His Will and say, "we hear and we obey".

God says in 29-6, *"And whosoever strives (does "Jihad"), he strives only for his own soul, for God is not in need of (His) creatures".* Consequently, whatever "Jihad" we perform, must be for seeking God's pleasure. This means we should fix our gaze on the love of His creatures and strive to achieve global peace and justice and to denounce violence and our selfishness and greed. Our hearts must be pure from envy, hatred and jealousy. Our minds should only concentrate on fighting evil within our own souls. Thus "Jihad" is to strive for excellence both spiritually and physically, not only for the benefit of our own souls, but also for all of humanity.

Let us all comply with God's commandments in 22:78, *"And strive in the Cause of God as you ought to strive, (with sincerity and under discipline). He has chosen you and has imposed no hardship on you in religion; it is the religion of your father Abraham. It is He (God), Who named you Muslims, both before and in this (Revelation); that the Messenger (Mohammed), may be a witness against you, and you be witnesses against mankind. So, establish regular prayer, give to charity, and hold fast to God. He is your Protector, the best to protect and the best to help."*

It was stated above that not everyone who is killed on a battlefield is regarded in Islam as a martyr. He must be fighting for the cause of God in a holy war to establish the truth and justice of God. Thus, to make God's word the highest.

Also in Islam no one has the right to take his own life. Life belongs to its Creator. Hence, God the Creator is the only One Who decides when someone will die. So, if anyone decides to take his own life by his own hands, he will dwell in the hellfire eternally.

Islam regards terrorism as a major crime against God and His Messengers. A very severe punishment in this life is the recompense of those who strive with might and main for mischief on the earth, and a heavy chastisement is theirs in the Hereafter.

Chapter Two- No To Violence Against God's Mockers

2.1 Introduction

Islam and its followers highly revere the Messengers of God, from Adam to the final seal of all Prophets, Prophet Mohammed (pbuh). Whilst they are not worshipped (as this is forbidden), Muslims respect their names, their lives and their legacies. Therefore, to mock or ridicule the Prophets in any way is not only insulting to Muslims but insults God himself.

Very often, whenever people insult Prophet Mohammed (pbuh) by saying derogatory statements about him or by producing an image to belittle him or making a film to ridicule him, some ill-informed Muslims would react violently. This was unfortunately exemplified when, on 7th January 2015, the offices of the French satirical weekly newspaper Charlie Hebdo in Paris, produced nasty images of Prophet Mohammed (pbuh), and were subsequently attacked by two terrorists who killed 12 innocent people and injured 11 others. The staff of Charlie Hebdo continued with the publication, and the following issue print ran 7.95 million copies in six languages, compared to its typical print run of 60,000 in only French.

In 1988, Salman Rushdie published his book "The Satanic Verses", which was inspired in part by the life of Prophet Mohammed (pbuh). Many Muslims worldwide regarded it as a great insult to the Prophet (pbuh) and Islam. Iran's Ayatollah Khomeini issued a fatwa (Religious Statement), nine days after the publication, accusing Salman Rushdie of blasphemy and sentencing him to death. The author went into hiding and his public appearances became very rare. In addition to the author, the fatwa extended to everyone who had contributed to the publication and distribution of the book, all were accused of blasphemy. The Japanese translator of the work, Hitoshi Igarashi, was stabbed to death in 1991. Italian translator Ettore Capriolo and Norwegian publisher William Nygard were also targeted, surviving the attacks with severe injuries. Many copies of the book were sold, and the author became a great celebrity in the West, although there is still a bounty of four million dollars on his head.

The above information is available on social media in more detail.

So, the violent reaction of these radical Muslims to Charlie Hebdo's weekly newspaper or to Salman Rushdie's book, contributed to making their work more high profile, made the authors known worldwide and they managed to make great financial gains. Thanks to those violent confused Muslims who provided free advertising services! In this Chapter, I refer to insults towards God, His Angels, His Divine Revelations and His Messengers. In 2.6, I will cover how Muslims should respond to such insults.

2.2 Insulting God

Insulting God is not something new. In fact, it started immediately following the creation of Adam and it will continue until the end of this world. It takes different forms, from denying His existence or questioning His power, to associating partners and equals with him in many different forms or accusing Him of committing crimes against humanity and being unfair and unjust. I will give below, from the Qur'an, some examples of those who deliberately insulted God or challenged His power.

A) Satan

In 7:11-18, when Satan refused to prostrate himself to Adam, God asked him, "*What prevented you from prostrating when I commanded you*?" He replied, "*I'm better than him. You created me from fire and created him from clay.*" God condemned him for his racist remark and cursed him. Satan asked for respite to the day of resurrection. And God granted him his request. Satan immediately said, "*Because You have thrown me out of the Way, I will lie in wait for them on Your Straight Way. Then I will assault them from before them and behind them, from their right and their left. Nor will You find, in most of them, gratitude for Your mercies.*"

So, Satan waited till he got the respite, then he broke out into a lie and impertinent defiance. The lie as in suggesting that God had thrown him out of the Way, in other words misled him, whereas his own conduct was responsible for his degradation. The defiance is in his setting snares on the Straight Way to which God directs people.

B) Pharaoh at the Time of Moses

In 28:38, Pharaoh said, "*O Chiefs! No god do I know for you but myself...*" Pharaoh claimed, himself, to be God. Not only one god among many, but the only god.

In 26:29, Pharaoh said to Moses when he came to him with clear signs from the One True God, "*If you take any god other than me, I will certainly put you in prison.*"

And in 79:24, he said, "*I am your Lord, Most High.*"

The ending of the life of Pharaoh is a great lesson to those who put themselves up as rivals or equals to the One True God. He and his host were crushed and drowned in the sea and they will receive humiliating punishment in the Hereafter, and their eternal abode will be the Hell Fire.

C) King Nimrod at the Time of Abraham

Following the destruction of the idols in the temple by the young lad Abraham, the priests decided to burn him alive. They threw him into a furnace and God saved him from the fire. The priests took him to their King, King Nimrod. He was a tyrant ruler who worshipped idols and heavenly bodies. God tells us in 2:258 that Nimrod disputed with Abraham about his Lord, because God had granted him power. He asked Abraham, "*Who is your Lord*?" Abraham replied, "*My Lord is He Who gives life and causes death.*" The King arrogantly replied, "*I can also give life and death. Guards! Free this prisoner who was supposed to be killed and kill the other one who was to be freed. See Abraham, I'm like your Lord*!". As a tyrant ruler he considered his power in sentencing someone to death or sparing someone's life, is equivalent to creating a life and guiding and sustaining it and causing it to die when it's term is reached and bringing it back to life again on the Day of Judgement. This is what Abraham was referring to, the work of the Creator. Abraham took a deep breath and looked at the King who was an authority in astronomy and astrology, and said with great confidence, "*My God is the One Who causes the sun to rise from the east. Can you cause it to rise from the west*?" So, the arrogant King, who rejected faith, was fully defeated and humiliated. He knew well that to cause the sun to rise from the west it means he must reverse the earth's rotation. And before doing that, he must bring the earth to a complete standstill and then to rotate it in the other direction. Surely God does not guide those who are unjust.

D) Doubting God's Power!

D.1) A Man and His Donkey

The story in 2:259, is about a man who was traveling on his donkey and passed by a town which was completely destroyed and razed to the ground. He looked at it in despair and said, "*Can really God bring it back to life after its death*!?". He doubted the power of God when he saw the destruction of a whole community, their city and civilisation. But God can cause resurrection as He has done many times in history, and as He will do at the final Resurrection. Then, God made him die for one hundred years, then raised him up again. God asked him, "*How long have you have been away for*?" He replied, "*I have remained a day or a part of a day!*" God said, "*You have remained for one hundred years. However, look at your food and drink, they remained intact. And look at the bones of your donkey, and that We may make you a Sign for the people. Look further at the bones (of your donkey) to see how We bring them together and clothe them with flesh.*" When this was shown clearly to him, he said, "*I know that God has power over all things.*"

D.2) The Ad People

The Ad people, with their prophet Hud, are mentioned in many places in the Qur'an. Their story belongs to Arabian tradition. Their eponymous ancestor Ad was fourth in generation from Noah, having been a son of Aus, the son of Aram, the son of Sam, the son of Noah. They occupied a large tract of country in Southern Arabia, extending from Umman at the mouth of the Arabian Gulf to Hadhramaut and Yemen at the southern end of the Red Sea. The people were tall in stature and were great builders. They forsook the true God and oppressed their people. They doubted and questioned the power of the One True God. A three years famine visited them, yet they took no warning. They were so arrogant. At length, a terrible blast of wind which lasted for seven nights and eight days destroyed them and their land.

God says in 89:6-8, "*Have you not seen how did your Lord deal with the Ad (people)? Of the (city of) Iram, with lofty pillars, the like of which was not produced in (all) the land?*".
And He says in 41:15-16, "*The Ad people behaved arrogantly through the land, against (all) truth and reason, and said, 'Who is superior to us in strength?' What! Did they not see that God, Who created them, was superior to them in strength? But they continued to reject Our Signs! So We sent against them a furious wind through days of disaster that We might give them a taste of a Chastisement of humiliation in this Life, but the Penalty of the Hereafter will be more humiliating still, and they will find no help.*"

And when they waged wars of aggression against other nations, they did it without any responsibility or consideration for those who came within their power, as stated by God in 26:130, "*And when you strike, you strike like tyrants.*"

Unfortunately, the above does not only apply to the people of Ad. It is also applicable to many arrogant and selfish countries and governments worldwide in our modern history. They divide to rule. They initiate wars in different parts of the world and sell arms to the fighting factions to revive their own economy on the bodies of innocent people including children. Their estimate of their own strength is greater than they can justify by facts. But if they had all the strength which they arrogated to themselves, how could they stand before God, the Creator of everything seen and unseen and the King of the Day of Judgement? How could they protect themselves from the "Forces of God"? Should they not fear God's wrath? Indeed, we are now, in 2020, witnessing a virus (Covid-19) which can only be seen by an electron microscope, which has caused a pandemic and destroyed lives and wealth worldwide.

D.3) The Last Supper – Jesus and His Disciples

God tells us in 5:112-115, the challenge made by the Disciples of Jesus when they questioned the Power of God in sending down from heaven a Table laden with food.
"*Behold! The Disciples said, 'O Jesus the son of Mary! Can your Lord send down to us a Table set (with viands) from Heaven?' Jesus said, 'Fear God, if you have faith.' They said, 'We only wish to eat from it and satisfy our hearts, and to know that you have indeed told us the truth, and that we ourselves may be witnesses to the miracle.' Said Jesus the son of Mary, 'O*

God our Lord! Send down on us from Heaven a Table set (with viands), to be a feast and a solemn festival for us, for the first and the last of us and a Sign from You, and provide sustenance to us for You are the best Sustainer (of our needs).' God said, 'I will send it down on you. But if any of you after that rejects faith, I will punish him with a chastisement such as I have not inflicted on any one among all the peoples.'"

"The request of the Disciples savours a little of (1) want of faith, (2) too much attention to physical food, and (3) a childish desire for miracles or Signs. All these three can be proved from the Canonical Gospels. (1) Simon Peter, quite early in the story, asked Jesus to depart from him, as he (Simon) was a sinful man (Luke v. 8). The same Peter afterwards denied his Master three times shamelessly when the Master was in the power of his enemies. And one of the disciples (Judas) actually betrayed Jesus. (2) Even in the Canonical Gospels, so many of the miracles are concerned with food and drink, e.g. the turning of the water into wine (John, ii. 1-11); the conversion of five loaves and two small fishes into food for 5,000 men (John vi. 5-13), this being the only miracle recorded in all the four Gospels; the miraculous number of fishes caught for food (Luke v. 4-11); the cursing of the fig tree because it had no fruit (Matt. xii. 18-19); the allegory of eating Christ's flesh and drinking his blood (John vi. 53-57). (3) Because the Samaritans would not receive Jesus into their village, the Disciples James and John wanted a fire to come down from heaven and consume them (Luke is. 54)." FN825

D.4) Claiming that God has begotten a Child or He is One of Three

Claiming that God has a child, or He is one of three is regarded by God as blasphemy. There are many verses in the Qur'an which refute claims made by the People of the Book or the pagans that God has begotten a child, a son, or a daughter. I give below a few examples from the Qur'an:

1) For example, God says in 2:116-117, *"They say: 'God has begotten a child.' Glory be to Him. To Him belongs all that is in the heavens and the earth. Everything renders worship to Him. (He is) The Originator of the heavens and the earth. When He decrees a matter, He says to it 'Be', and it is."*

"It is a derogation from the glory of God -in fact it is blasphemy- to say that God begets children, like a man or an animal. The Christian doctrine is here emphatically repudiated. If words have any meaning, it would mean an attribution to God of a material nature, and of the lower animal functions of sex." FN119.

2) In 4:171-173, God commands the People of the Book, not to go beyond the bounds in their religion which would lead to blasphemy, *"O People of the Book! Do not commit excesses in your religion, and do not say anything about God except the truth. The Messiah, Jesus, son of Mary, was (no more than) a Messenger of God, and His Word, which He bestowed on Mary, and a Spirit proceeding from Him. So believe in God and His Messengers. Do not speak of a 'Trinity' - stop (this) that is better for you - for God is only One God. Glory be to Him, He is far above having a child, everything in the heavens and the earth belongs to Him and He is the best one to trust. The Messiah would never disdain to be a servant of God, nor would the Angels who are close to Him. He will gather before Him all those who disdain His worship and are arrogant (to answer). But to those who believe and* do good deeds of righteousness, He will give due rewards and more of His bounty; and to those who are disdainful and arrogant He will give an agonising torment, and they find no one besides God to protect or help them."

"Just as a foolish servant may go wrong by excess of zeal for his master, so in religion people's excesses may lead them to blasphemy or spirit the very opposite of religion. The Jewish excesses in the direction of formalism, racialism, exclusiveness, and rejection of Christ Jesus have been denounced in many places. Here the Christian attitude is condemned, which raises Jesus to an equality with God; in some cases venerates Mary almost to idolatry, attributes a physical son to God and invents the doctrine of the Trinity, opposed to all reason, which according to the Athanasian Creed, unless a man believes, he is doomed to hell forever. Let our Muslims also beware lest they fall into excesses either in doctrine or in formalism." FN675.

"Christ's attributes are mentioned in verse 4:171, above: (1) that he was the son of a woman, Mary and therefore a man; (2) but a messenger, a man with a mission from God, and therefore entitled to honour; (3) a Word bestowed on Mary, for he was created by God's word 'Be', and he was; (4) a spirit proceeding from God, but not God. His life and his mission were more limited than in the case of some other Messengers, though we must pay equal honour to him as a Prophet of God. The doctrines of Trinity, equality with God, and sonship, are repudiated as blasphemies. God is independent of all needs and has no need of a son to manage His affairs. The Gospel of John (whoever wrote it) has put in a great deal of Alexandrian and Gnostic mysticism round the doctrine of the Word (Greek, Logos), but it is simply explained here." FN676.

3) In 5:17, God says, "*They disbelieved indeed those that say that God is Christ the son of Mary. Say, 'Who then has the least power against God, if His Will was to destroy Christ the son of Mary, his mother, and every one that is on the earth?' For to God belongs the dominion of the heavens and the earth, and all that is between. He creates what He pleases. For God has power over all things.*"

"*The most honoured of the prophets of God are but men. All power belongs to God, and not to any man. God's creation may take many forms, but because in any particular form it is different from what we see daily around us, it does not cease to be Creation, or to be subject to the power of God. No creature can be God.*" FN717.

4) And in 5:72-75, God says, "*They certainly disbelieve who say: 'God is Christ the son of Mary.' But Christ, himself, said, 'O Children of Israel! Worship God, my Lord and your Lord. Whoever joins other gods with God, God will forbid him the Garden, and the Fire will be His abode. There will be no one to help the wrong-doers.' They surely disbelieve who say, 'God is one of three (in a Trinity)', for there is no god except One God. If they do not desist from their word (of blasphemy), certainly a grievous punishment will befall the disbelievers among them. Why they do not turn to God and seek His forgiveness? For God is Oft-forgiving, Most Merciful. Christ the son of Mary was no more than a Messenger, many were the messengers that passed away before him. His mother was a woman of truth. They had both to eat their daily food. See how God makes His Signs clear to them, yet see in what ways they are deluded away from the truth!*"

"Mary never claimed that she was a mother of God, or that her son was God. She was a pious virtuous woman. In Mark 12:25 Jesus says, "The first of all the commandments is, Hear O Israel; the Lord our God is One God." In Matt. 4:10, Christ rebukes Satan for desiring the worship of other than God. In John 20:17 Christ says to Mary Magdalene, "Go unto my brethren, and say unto them, I ascend unto my Father and your Father; and to my God and your God." In Luke 18:19 Christ rebukes a certain ruler for calling him Good Master, "Why call me good? None is good, save One, that is, God." FN 782-783.

5) In 6:100-102 God says, *"They made the Jinns equals with God, though it is God Who created the Jinns. And they falsely, having no knowledge, attributed to Him sons and daughters. Praise and Glory be to Him! For He is above what they attribute to Him. (He is the) Wonderful Originator of the heavens and the earth. How can He have a child when He has no consort? He created all things, and He has full knowledge of all things."*

6) And He says in 9:30-31, *"The Jews call Ezra a son of God, and the Christians call Christ the son of God. That is what they say with their mouths. They imitate what the unbelievers of old used to say. God's curse be on them. How they are deluded away from the Truth. They have taken as lords beside God, their rabbis and their monks and Christ the son of Mary, when they were commanded to worship only One God, there is no God but He. Praise and Glory to Him. Far He is from having the partners they associate with Him*."

"Taking men for gods or sons of God was not a new thing. All ancient mythologies have fables of that kind. There was less excuse for such blasphemies after the Prophets of God had clearly explained out true relation to God than in the times of primitive ignorance and superstition." FN1284.

7) In 10:68-70, God warns those who invent lies against Him of a severe punishment in the Hereafter, *"They say, 'God has begotten a child!' Glory be to Him! He is Self-Sufficient! To Him belongs all things in the heavens and on earth. Do you have a warrant for what you are claiming? Do you say about God what you do not know? Those who forge a lie against God will never prosper. A little enjoyment in this world, and then to Us will be their return. Then We shall make them taste the severest chastisement for their disbelief."*

8) God says in 17:111, *"Say: 'Praise be to God, Who did not beget a child, and has no partner in His Kingdom, nor He needs any to protect Him from humiliation.' Magnify Him for His greatness and glory."*

"A first step towards the understanding of God's attributes is to clear our mind from superstitions, such as that God begotten a child, or that He has partners, or that He is dependent upon other beings to protect Him from harm and humiliation. We must realise that He is the One and Peerless. His greatness and glory are above anything we can conceive, but using our highest spiritual ideas, we must declare forth His greatness and glory." FN2324.

9) In 18:1-5, God says: *"Praise be to God, who has sent to His Servant (Mohammed) the Book (the Qur'an), and has not allowed any Crookedness in it. (He has made it) Straight (and*

Clear) in order that He may warn (the godless) of a terrible Punishment from Him, and that He may give Glad Tidings to the Believers who work righteous deeds, that they shall have a goodly Reward. Wherein they shall remain for ever. Further, that He may warn those (also) who say, 'God has begotten a child.' They have no knowledge of such a thing, nor had their fathers. It is a grievous thing that issues from their mouths as a saying. What they say is nothing but falsehood!"

"The warning is not only needed for those who deny God or deny His Message, but also for those whose false ideas of God degrade religion in supposing that God begot a child, for God is One and is High above any ideas of physical reproduction. The attribution of a child 'begotten' to God has no basis in fact or in reason. It is only a 'word' or 'saying' that issues out of their mouths. It is not even a dogma that is reasoned out or can be explained in any way that is consistent with the sublime attributes of God." FN2329-2330

10) The story of the birth of Jesus and him delivering God's Message from the cradle, is given in 19:16-33. God concluded the story by saying in 19:34-45, "Such (was) Jesus the son of Mary, (it is) a statement of truth, about which they (vainly) dispute. It is not befitting to (the majesty of) God that He should beget a child. Glory be to Him! When He determines a matter, He only says to it, 'Be', and it is."

"The disputations about the nature of Jesus Christ were vain, but also persistent and sanguinary. Irrational dogmas should be abandoned altogether. Begetting a child is a physical act depending on the needs of man's animal nature. God Most High is independent of all needs, and it is derogatory to Him to attribute such an act to Him. It is merely a relic of pagan and anthropomorphic materialist superstitions." FN2486-2487.

11) In 19:88-93, God strongly condemns ascribing a child to Him, "They say, 'The Most Gracious has taken a child!' Indeed, you have claimed a thing most monstrous! At it, the skies are about to burst, the earth to split asunder, and the mountains to fall down in utter ruin, that they attributed a child to the Most Gracious. For it is not consonant with the majesty of The Most Gracious that He should beget a child. Not one of the beings in the heavens and the earth but must come to The Most Gracious as a servant."

"The belief in God begetting a child is not a question merely of words or of speculative thought. It is a stupendous blasphemy against the One True God. It lowers God to the level of an animal. If combined with the doctrine of vicarious atonement, it amounts to a negation of God's justice and man's personal responsibility. It is destructive of all moral and spiritual order and is condemned in the strongest possible terms.

"God has no sons or daughters or favourites or parasites, such as we associate with human beings. On the other hand, every creature of His gets His love, and His cherishing care. Every one of them, however humble, is individually marked before His Throne of Justice and Mercy, and will stand before Him on his own deserts." FN2529 & FN2531.

12) In 21:25-27, God says, "We sent no messenger before you (O Mohammed), but We inspired him (saying) 'There is no God but I, so worship and serve Me.' And they say, 'The Most Gracious has taken a child'. Glory be to Him! Those (whom they call children) are *merely honoured servants. They don't speak till He has spoken, and they act (in all things) by His command."*

"This refers both to the Trinitarian superstition that God has begotten a son, and to the Arab superstition that the Angels were daughters of God. All such superstitions are derogatory to the glory of God. The prophets and the angels are no more than servants of God. They are raised high in honour, and therefore they deserve our highest respect, but not our worship. They never say anything before they receive God's command to say it, and their acts similarly conditioned. This is also the teaching of Jesus as reported in the Gospel of St. John (12:49-50), 'For I have not spoken of myself: but the Father which sent me, He gave me a commandment, what I should say, and what I should speak. And I know that His commandment is life everlasting: whatsoever I speak therefore, even as the Father said unto me, so I speak.' If rightly understood, 'Father' has the same meaning as our 'Rabb' in the Qur'an, Sustainer and Cherisher, not Begetter or Progenitor." FN2686-2687.

13) In 23:90-92, God says, *"Indeed We have sent them the Truth, but they indeed are liars. No child did God beget, nor there is any god along with Him; (if there were many gods), behold, each god would have taken away what he had created, and some would certainly have prevailed over others! Glory to God! (He is free) from the (sort of) things they attribute to Him! He knows what is hidden and what is open. Too high He is for the partners they attribute to Him!"*

"The multiplicity of gods is intellectually indefensible, considering the unity of Design and Purpose in the One True God's Wonderful Universe. But if, as polytheists say, there had been subsidiary gods, they would yet have had to submit to the Throne of the Supreme God, and worship Him." FN2931 & FN2228.

14) And God says in 25:1-3, *"Blessed be He Who sent down the Criterion (of right and wrong) (the Qur'an) to His servant (Mohammed), that he may be a Warner to all creatures. He to whom belongs the dominion and sovereignty of the heavens and the earth, no child He has begotten, nor He has a partner in His dominion. It is He Who has created all things and ordered them in due proportions. Yet they have taken, besides Him, gods that can create nothing but are themselves created, that have no control of hurt or good to themselves, nor can they control Death, nor Life, nor Resurrection."*

15) And God says in 39:4, *"Had God wished to take to Himself a child, He could have chosen whom He wanted from what He creates. Glory be to Him! (He is above such things) He is God, the One, the Overpowering."*

"It is blasphemy to say that God begot a child. If that were true, He should have had a wife (6:101), and His child would have been of the same kind as Himself; whereas God is one, with no one else like unto Him (112:4). Begetting is an animal act which goes with sex. How can it be consistent with our conception of One Who is above all creatures? If such a blasphemous thought were possible, as that God wanted someone else to help Him, He could have chosen the best of His creatures instead of lowering Himself to an animal act. But glory to God! He is above such things! His Unity is the first thing that we have to learn about Him. As He is Omnipotent, He requires no creatures to help Him or bring other creatures to Him." FN4246

16) In 72:1-15, God informs us of the reaction of the Jinn when they listened to the recitation of the Qur'an by Prophet Mohammed (pbuh). They said in 72:3, "*And exalted is the Majesty of our Lord, He has taken neither a wife nor a child.*"

"*They abjure paganism and also the doctrine of a child begotten by God, which would also imply a wife of whom he was begotten.*" FN5730.

17) In 112:1-4 God describes His attributes and reveals to us His nature in the most precise and concise manner to eliminate any confusion about Him in our minds, "*Say: 'He is God the One. God the Eternal, Absolute. He begot no one, nor was He begotten. And no one is comparable to Him.'*" This chapter is called in Arabic Al-Ikhlas which means Purity and Sincerity of Faith.

"*The nature of God is here indicated to us in a few words, such as we can understand. The qualities of God are described in numerous places elsewhere in the Qur'an. Here we are specially taught to avoid the pitfalls into which people and nations have fallen at various times in trying to understand God. The first thing we have to note is that His nature is so sublime, so far beyond our limited conceptions, that the best way in which we can realise Him is to feel that He is a Personality, 'He', and not a mere abstract conception of philosophy. He is near us; He cares for us; we owe our existence to Him. Secondly, He is the One and Only God, the Only One to Whom worship is due; all other things or beings that we can think of are His creatures and in no way comparable to Him. Thirdly, He is Eternal, without beginning or end, Absolute, not limited by time or place or circumstances, the Reality. Fourthly, we must not think of Him as having a child or a father, for that would be to import animal qualities into our conception of Him. Fifthly, He is not like any other person or thing that we know or can imagine: His qualities and nature are unique.*" FN6296.

D.5) Claiming that God has Daughters

In 16:57 the Pagan Arabs assign daughters to God, "*And they (the Pagans) assign daughters for God. Glory be to Him. And for themselves (they assign) what they desire.*"

"*Some of the Pagan Arabs called Angels the daughters of God. In their own life they hated to have daughters, as explained in 16:85-86. They practiced female infanticide. In their state of perpetual war, sons were a source of strength to them, but daughters only made them subject to humiliating raids!*" FN2082.

God also responds to their blasphemy in 17:40, "*Has then your Lord, (O Pagans!) preferred for you sons, and taken for Himself daughters among the Angels? Truly you utter a most dreadful saying!*"

And in 37:149-157, God addresses the false claims of the pagans, "*Now ask them (O Mohammed), 'Has your Lord daughters while they have sons? Or did We create the Angels females, in their presence? Behold! It is of their own fabrications that they say, 'God has begotten children'. But most certainly they are liars! Has He preferred daughters to sons?'*"

What is the matter with you? How is it that you judge? Will you not then reflect? Or have you a clear authority? Then bring your book (of authority) if you are truthful!"

"The Pagan Arabs called angels daughters of God. They themselves were ashamed of having daughters, and preferred to have sons, to add to their power and dignity. Yet they invented daughters for God! Any attribution to God of ideas derogatory to His Oneness and His supreme height above all creatures, like claiming that God has begotten a child, is likely to degrade our own conception of God's Universal plan, and is condemned in the strongest terms." FN4129-4130.

D.6) Belittling God: God is Stingy!

God says in 3:181-182, *"God has heard the taunt of those who said: 'Truly God is poor and we are rich.' We shall record what they have said, and the fact of their slaying the Prophets unjustly, and We shall say to them: Taste now the torment of the Fire. That is in recompense for your own deeds, for God never does injustice to people.'"*

"In 2:245 we read: 'Who is he that will loan to God a beautiful loan?' In other places charity or spending in way of God is metaphorically described as giving to God. The Prophet Mohammed (pbuh) often used that expression in appealing for funds to be spent in the Way of God. The scoffers mocked and said: 'So God is indigent, and we are rich!' This blasphemy was of a piece with all their conduct in history, in slaying the Prophets and men of God." FN486.

And in 5:64, He says, *"The Jews say: 'God's hand is tied up.' Let their own hands be tied up and let them be cursed for the blasphemy they uttered. No, both His hands are widely outstretched. He gives and spends (of His bounties) as He pleases..."*

"It is another form of the taunt to say, 'Then God's hands are tied up. He is close-fisted. He does not give!' This blasphemy is repudiated. On the contrary, boundless is God's bounty, and He gives, as it were, with both hands outstretched, a figure of speech for unbounded liberality." FN772.

2.3 Enmity to God's Angels

God says in 2:97-98, *"Say (Mohammed): 'Whoever is an enemy to Gabriel (should know that) he revealed this (Qur'an) to your heart by God's permission, it confirms the Scriptures revealed before it, and is a guidance and glad tidings for those who believe. Whoever is an enemy to God, His Angels and His Messengers and to Gabriel and Michael will surely find God an enemy to such unbelievers.'"*

"A party of the Jews in the time of Prophet Mohammed ridiculed the Muslim belief that Gabriel brought down revelations to Mohammed. Michael was called in their books 'the great prince which standeth for the children of thy people' (Daniel, xii 1). The vision of Gabriel inspired fear (Daniel, xiii 16-17). But this pretence-that Michael was their friend and Gabriel their enemy-was merely a manifestation of their unbelief in angels, Prophets and

God Himself; and such unbelief could not win the love of God. In any case it was disingenuous to say that they believed in one angel and not in another. Mohammed's inspiration was through visions of Gabriel. Mohammed had been helped to the highest spiritual light, and the message which he delivered and his spotless integrity and exemplary life were manifest Signs which everyone could understand except those who were obstinate and perverse. Besides, the verses of the Qur'an were in themselves reasonable and clear." FN101.

2.4 Enmity to God's Prophets and Messengers

The Qur'an tells us that all the Prophets and Messengers of God, from Noah to Mohammed, were persecuted by their own people and many of them were killed in defiance of the Truth. Their mission was held up to ridicule. However, mockery itself never discouraged them or deterred them of delivering God's Gospel of Unity.

God says in 6:10, "*And indeed before your time, (O Mohammed), many Messengers have been scoffed at; but those who mocked at them were overwhelmed by the Truth they had scoffed at.*"

And in 13:32, He says, "*Many Messengers before you (O Mohammed) were ridiculed. But I granted respite to the unbelievers, and finally I punished them. Then how (terrible) was my requital!*"

"*The punishment was in many cases deferred. But when it did come, how terrible and exemplary it was!*" FN1850.

God confirms again in 15:10-11, the mocking of His Messengers, "*(O Mohammed), We did send Messengers before you among the nations which have gone by. And whenever a Messenger came to them, they never failed to mock him.*"

And He says in 36:30, "*Sad is the state of the people! There never came to them a messenger, but they mocked him.*"

"*Ignorant men mock at God's Prophets, or anyone who takes Religion seriously. But they do not reflect that such levity reacts on themselves. Their own lives are ruined, and they cease to count. If they study history, they will see that countless generations were destroyed before them because they did not take Truth seriously and undermined the very basis of their individual and collective existence.*" FN3975.

The killing of the Prophets is mentioned in many verses in the Qur'an. For example, in 2:61 God refers to the conduct of those who rejected faith from the Children of Israel, "*...They were covered with humiliation and misery, they drew on themselves the wrath of God. This because they went on rejecting the Signs of God and slaying His Messengers without just cause. This because they rebelled and went on transgressing.*" And in 2:87, "*...But is it not true that every time a Messenger brought to you something that was not to your liking, you acted arrogantly; you called some Messengers liars and killed others?*"

In 3:21-22, God gives a stark warning to those who blasphemed and killed His Prophets, "*As to those who deny the Signs of God, and in defiance of right, slay the Prophets, and kill the people who command justice, announce to them a grievous chastisement. They are those whose works will bear no fruit in this world and in the Hereafter, nor will they have anyone to help.*"

And God says in 5:70, "*We took the Covenant of the Children of Israel and sent them Messengers. Every time there came to them a Messenger with what they themselves did not desire, some (of these) they called imposters, and some they slay.*"

"*Examples of the Prophets slain were: 'the righteous blood shed upon the earth, from the blood of righteous Abel unto the blood of Zacharias, son of Barachias, whom ye slew between the temple and the altar': Matt. xxiii. 35. Again John the Baptist, was bound, imprisoned, and beheaded, and his head presented to a dancing harlot: Matt. xiv. 1-11.*" FN 364.

But at the end, God and His Messengers must conquer, "*God has decreed: 'It is I and My Messengers Who must prevail', for God is Strong, Mighty.*" 21:58

A few examples from the Qur'an regarding the fierce resistance and the insults received by these men of God while delivering His Message:

A) Prophet Noah

In 7:59-64, the leaders of Noah's people refused to acknowledge him as a Messenger from God and accused him of being in manifest error. When he criticised the wickedness of his generation, he was laughed at and called a madman, for he mentioned the Great Day to come in the Hereafter. God's retribution came soon afterwards; the great Flood, in which his unbelieving people were drowned, but he and those who believed in him came into the Ark were saved. "*We sent Noah to his people. He said 'O my people! Worship God! You have no other God but Him. I fear for you the Punishment of a dreadful day!' The leaders of his people said: 'We can clearly see you are being misled.' He said, 'O my people! There is nothing wrong with me; on the contrary I am a Messenger from the Lord and Cherisher of the Worlds! I convey to you the Message of my Lord. I sincerely advise you, and I know from God something that you do not know. Do you wonder that there has come to you a reminder from your Lord, through a man of your own people, to warn you, so that you may fear God and receive His Mercy?' But they rejected him, and We delivered him, and those with him, in the Ark. But We drowned those who rejected Our Signs, they were indeed a blind people!*"

And in 11:27, the Chiefs of the Unbelievers among his people said, "*We see in you nothing but a man like ourselves and those who followed you are the meanest among us, nor do we see in you all any merit above us. In fact, we think you are liars!*"

These Chiefs also condemned him by saying, "*He is only a man possessed. Wait and have patience with him for a time.*" 23:25

In 71:5-9, we read about the response of his people to his Message, "*He said: 'O my Lord! I have called to my people night and day. But my call only increases their flight (from the right). And every time I have called to them, that You might forgive them, they would thrust their fingers into their ears, covered themselves up with their garments, grown obstinate, and given themselves up to arrogance. So, I have called to them aloud. Further I have spoken to them in public and secretly in private.*"

In 71:25 God tells us about His punishment to the unbelievers among Noah's people, "*Because of their sins they were drowned (in the flood), and they were made to enter the Fire (of punishment) and they had no helpers save God.*"

B) Prophet Hud

God sent Prophet Hud to the people of Ad. Their story belongs to Arabian tradition. They occupied a large tract of country in Southern Arabia. The people were tall in stature and were great builders. The leaders of the unbelievers among his people mocked him and said, "*We see you are in folly and we think you are a liar.*" 7:66

And in 11:53-54, they said, "*O Hud! You have not brought to us any clear evidence, and we are not going to forsake our gods merely because you say so. We are not going to believe you. All we can say is that some of our gods have afflicted you with evil...*"

In response to Hud's call to his people, they said, "*It is all the same for us whether you admonish us or not. This has been happening all along. We will not be subjected to any chastisement.*" 26:136-138. God says in 26:139, "*So they rejected him and We destroyed them...*"

C) Prophet Saleh

God sent Prophet Saleh to the Thamud people, who were the successors to the culture and civilisation of the Ad people. Their story also belongs to Arabian tradition. Their seat was in the north-west corner of Arabia, between Madinah and Syria.

In 7:75-79, we are told that the leaders of the arrogant party among his people mocked the believers who were from the lowly and the humble, because they believed that Saleh was God's Messenger. Saleh took the side of the unprivileged and was therefore himself attacked. When the arrogant party insolently defied the order of their Lord, they said to Saleh, "*O Saleh! Bring about your threats if you are a messenger of God!*" The retribution was not long delayed. A terrible earthquake came and buried the people and destroyed their boasted civilisation. And God saved Saleh and those who believed.

D) Prophet Abraham

In several verses in the Qur'an, we are told that Prophet Abraham faced fierce resistance when he invited his people to denounce their idols and believe in the One True God. In 19:46 his father threatened to stone him to death. In 29:24 his people suggested either to kill him or burn him alive. In 37:97 they suggested to build a furnace and throw him into the blazing fire. In 21:68 they said, "*Burn him and give victory and support to your gods...*" God in 21:69 commanded the fire to be cool and a means of safety for Abraham. In 21:70 God says, "*They planned against him, but We made them the greater losers.*". And in 37:98 He says, "*They plotted evil against him, but We made them the ones most humiliated.*"

E) Prophet Lut

Lut was a nephew of Abraham and was sent as a Prophet and Warner to the people of Sodom and Gomorrah, cities utterly destroyed for their unspeakable sins. He said to his people, "*Do you commit lewdness such as no people in creation ever committed before you? For you practice your lusts on men in preference to women. You are indeed a people transgressing beyond bounds.*" 7:80-81. So when Lut condemned their lust for unnatural crime, they said "*Drive them (Lut and his family) out of your city, they are people who want to be clean and pure.*" 7:82. So purity was Lut's crime in the sight of the wrong doers. And in 26:167 they said, "*If you don't stop preaching, O Lut! you will assuredly be cast out.*" Eventually God destroyed the cities and its people including Lut's wife, who was a sympathiser, and saved Lut and his daughters.

F) Prophet Shuaib

Prophet Shuaib was sent to the people of Madyan (North-East the Sinai Peninsula) with this message, "*O my people! Worship God, you have no other god but Him. Now has come to you a clear Sign from your Lord. Give just measure and weight, nor withhold from the people the things that are their due, and do not do mischief on the earth after it has been set in order. That will be best for you if you have Faith. And do not squat on every road, breathing threats, hindering from the path of God those who believe in Him and seek to make it crooked. But remember how you were little, and He gave you increase. And see what was the end of those who did mischief.*" 7:85-86.

The leaders of the arrogant party among his people said, "*O Shuaib! We shall certainly drive you out of our city and those who believe with you, or else you shall all return to our religion...*" 7:88. On another occasion they said, "*O Shuaib! We do not understand much of what you say. In fact, we see you weak in our midst. Were it not for your family, we should have certainly stoned you, for you have no great position among us.*" 11:91. They practically say, "*Don't you see that we have all the power and influence, and you, Shuaib, are only a poor Teacher? We could stone you or imprison you or do what we like with you! Thank us for our kindness that we spare you, for the sake of your family. It is more than you yourself deserve!*". In 11:94 God informs us of the fate of those who rejected Shuaib, "*And when our command came to pass, We saved Shuaib and those who believed with him, by special Mercy from Us. But the mighty blast seized the wrong-doers, and they lay lifeless in their homes by the morning.*"

G) Prophet Moses

Prophet Moses was not only ridiculed and insulted by the Pharaoh of his time, but also by many of his followers from the Children of Israel. When Moses brought manifest Signs from God, to Pharaoh and his Chiefs, they accused him in 7:109 and 10:76 that he is a well-versed sorcerer. And in 20:63 they said, referring to Moses and his brother Aaron, "*These two are magicians, who want to drive you out of your land with their magic and to destroy your excellent way of life.*"

In 17:101, Pharaoh said, "*O Moses! I think that you are bewitched.*" And in 26:27 he said to the audience, "*This messenger of yours who has been sent to you is mad.*" And in 28:38 he said to his Chiefs, "*No god I know for you but myself.*" Then he turned to his Chief of Staff and said to him in a very sarcastic way, "*O Haman! Bake bricks out of clay and build a lofty palace for me so that I may mount up to look for the god of Moses, even though I believe that he is a liar.*" In 40:26 Pharaoh threatened to kill Moses, saying, "*Let me kill Moses, then let him invoke his Lord. I fear that he will change your religion or cause mischief to spread in the land.*" Moses said in 44:20, "*And I have sought refuge in my Lord, lest you stone me to death.*"

In 43:51-53 Pharaoh gave a speech from his palace addressing his people and condemning Moses, "*O my people! Does not the kingdom of Egypt belong to me? And all these rivers flow beneath me! Can't you see? Am I not better than this Moses who is despicable and cannot speak clearly? Why he is not wearing gold bracelets? Or why angels are not accompanying him in procession?*" God responded in 43:54-55, "*He made fools of his people and they obeyed him. Truly they were a people rebellious against God. When at length they provoked Us, We exacted retribution from them, and We drowned them all.*"

In 7:129 Moses' people accused him of being the reason for their persecution, "*We have had nothing but trouble, both before and after you came to us...*"

In 61:5 Moses said to his people, "'*O my people! Why do you vex and insult me, though you know that I am the messenger of God sent to you?*' *Then when they went wrong, God let their hearts go wrong. For God doesn't guide those who are rebellious transgressors.*"

In 5:21-26 we are told about the argument between Moses and his people when he commanded them to enter the Holy Land. Their response in 5:22 was so repulsive, "*O Moses! In this land there are very ferocious and tyrant people and we will not enter it until they leave it. Once they leave it, we shall enter.*" Then in 5:24 they uttered blasphemy, "*O Moses! We shall never enter it as long as they are in it. Go you and your Lord and fight, while we sit here.*" God cursed them in 5:26, "*The (Holy) land will be out of their reach for forty years. They will wander through the earth (Sinai) in distraction. So don't grieve over these rebellious people.*"

H) Prophet Aaron

Before Prophet Moses went to the mount to receive the Torah, he appointed his brother Prophet Aaron to be in charge. After Moses left, his people turned their golden ornaments into a bull and worshipped it. God told Moses what his people did. We are told in 7:150, that when Moses came back, he was angry and grieved. He said, "*Evil is the course you have followed in my absence. Would you hasten the retribution of your Lord?*" He put down the Tablets, seized his brother by his beard and the hair of his head, and dragged him towards himself. Aaron said, "*Son of my mother! The people overpowered me and almost killed me. Don't make the enemies rejoice over my misfortune and don't consider me to be among the wrongdoers.*"

I) Mary and Prophet Jesus

In 4:156 God refers to the false charge against Mary by those who blasphemed from among the Children of Israel, that she was unchaste, "*That they rejected Faith that they uttered against Mary a grave false charge.*"

"*Such a charge is bad enough to make against any woman, but to make it against Mary, the mother of Jesus, was to bring into ridicule God's power itself. Islam is especially strong in guarding the reputation of women. Slanderers of women are bound to bring four witnesses in support of their accusations, and if they fail to produce four witnesses, they are to be flogged with eighty stripes and debarred from being competent witnesses.*" FN662

In 4:157-158 God refers to the evil planning and plotting by the same people to kill Jesus, and how did God foil their plot and saved him, "*That they said (in boast), 'We killed Christ Jesus the son of Mary, the Messenger of God.' But they neither killed him nor crucified him. Only a likeness of that was shown to them. And those who differ therein are full of doubts, with no certain knowledge. But only conjecture to follow, for of a surety they did not kill him. In fact, God raised him up unto Himself, and God is Exalted in Power, Wise.*"

J) Prophet Mohammed

Most of the challenges and insults faced by the previous Prophets and Messengers of God, were also experienced by Prophet Mohammed (pbuh) the last and final Messenger of God. In many places in the Qur'an we are told that his people called him liar, magician, mad, poet, possessed, soothsayer, bewitched, etc. And when they saw him, they scoffed at him saying, "*Is this he whom God sent as a messenger!*" 25:41. To comfort and support him God said to him in 6:10, "*Messengers before you were mocked, but their scoffers were hemmed in by the thing that they mocked.*" And in 13:32: He says, "*Messengers before you were indeed mocked, but I gave the unbelievers respite, then I seized them and how (terrible) was My retribution!*"

They also attacked the revelation he received. God says in 8:31, "*And when our Signs (the Qur'an) are rehearsed to them, they say: 'We have heard this (before). If we wished, we could say (words) like these. These are nothing but tales of the ancients.'*" And in 21:5 they said, "*These are but confused dreams or he has simply forged it or he is a poet. Let him bring us a Sign like the ones that were sent to (prophets) of old.*"

There is a Hadith (a Prophetic Tradition) in Al-Bukhari (3421) and Muslim (2781), that a Christian man embraced Islam and the Prophet (pbuh) used him to write the Revelation. The Prophet (pbuh), not being able to read or write, had to appoint people to write the Qur'an. Whenever he received a Revelation through Archangel Gabriel, he would call his scribers and dictate to them what he received, and they would read back to him what they wrote. This Christian man who became a Muslim wrote several verses from the Qur'an. Then he decided to denounce Islam and reverted back to Christianity. He claimed that what he wrote was his own words and Mohammed (pbuh) was not aware of what was written. This was a direct attack on the Prophet (pbuh) and the Qur'an. However, the Prophet (pbuh) did not respond to his false allegations and fully ignored him as if nothing happened. What a beautiful example to us all on patience and tolerance, even in times of false accusations and recriminations.

Later when this man died his people buried him, but the earth threw him out after they left. His people said, "*look what the followers of Mohammed did*". So they dug a deeper grave, but the same thing happened again and again. Then they realised that it has nothing to do with Mohammed's (pbuh) followers. What God commanded the earth to do was in response to his blasphemy.

In 8:30-31 we are told that the pagans made three plots against Mohammed (pbuh), "*Remember how the unbelievers plotted against you (Mohammed), to imprison you, or kill you, or exile you. They plot and plan (evil) and God too plans (to defeat evil), but the best of planners is God.*"
"*The plots against the Prophet in Makkah aimed at three things. They were not only foiled, but God's wonderful working turned the tables, and brought good out of evil in each case. (1) They tried to hold the Prophet in subjection in Makkah by putting pressure on his uncles, relatives, and friends. But the more they persecuted, the more the little Muslim community grew in faith and number. (2) They tried to injure or slay him. But the wonderful example of his humility, perseverance, and fearlessness furthered the cause of Islam. (3) They tried to get him and his followers out of their homes. But they found a new home in Madinah from which they eventually reconquered not only Makkah but Arabia and the world.*" FN1203.

In 111:1-5 we read the story of an uncle of the Prophet (pbuh), his nickname was Abu-Lahab, which means "Father of Flame", from his fiery hot temper and his ruddy complexion. He was one of the most inveterate enemies of Islam. He cursed the Prophet (pbuh) while preaching, saying "Perdition to you!". His wife was a woman of equally passionate spite and cruelty against the sacred person of the Prophet (pbuh). She used to tie bundles of thorns with ropes of twisted palm-leaf fibre and carry them and strew them about on dark nights in the paths which the Prophet was expected to take, in order to cause him bodily injury. The verses in 111:1-5 condemn them both and promised them an eternal punishment in a fire of blazing flame in the Hereafter.

The attacks on Prophet Mohammed (pbuh) were not only limited to physical attacks on him or his followers or casting doubts on the revelation he received, but went beyond that when the hypocrites in Madinah falsely accused his wife Aisha, the daughter of his best friend Abu-Bakr, of committing adultery. Chapter 24 of the Qur'an tells the story and how did God cleared her.

2.5 Is the Qur'an Anti-Semitic?

The Qur'an clearly states how God defended the Children of Israel at the time of Moses and how He delivered them to safety. He fully defeated and destroyed their enemy, Pharaoh and his host, who were also an enemy to God.

Unfortunately, some Jewish academics and politicians, claim that the Qur'an contains verses which incite hatred against them. They demand that these verses should be removed from the Qur'an to make it 'Jewish friendly'.

Muslims believe that the Qur'an is a Divine Revelation from God to Mohammed (pbuh) and no one has any authority to tamper with its contents. However, Muslim scholars must make an effort to explain to non-Muslims as well as Muslims, the meanings of these verses and the historic background for its revelation. Especially, that the Qur'an was revealed over a period of 23 years, which witnessed many encounters between Muslims and Jews. Also they must point out Islamic tolerance towards the followers of other religions.

On 19th February 2015, a Jewish academic sent a letter to the Editor of the Guardian accusing the Qur'an of being behind the increase of anti-Semitic sentiment in the West:

"Antisemitism is on the rise but above all it is an Islamic issue. While it is politically correct to be concerned about caricatures of Muhammad, the fact that the Qur'an calls Jews cursed, traitors, the greediest of men, liars, corrupters and apes (to name but a few of the more nasty epithets) is never mentioned. It is not just the Israel-Palestine issue that can turn Muslims to antisemitism. It comes straight out of the book held to be the direct word of God – even if it also contains calls to peace." - Professor Emanuel de Kadt Utrecht University and Brighton.

In response to his comments, I wrote to him. Sad to say, he wrote back saying he didn't want to be engaged in any dialogue. I felt so sorry for his students.

On 8th May 2018, The Telegraph newspaper reported: "On 22nd April 2018, an open letter was published in La Parisien newspaper and signed by nearly 300, argued verses of the Qur'an calling for the 'murder and punishment of Jews, Christians and disbelievers' should be removed because they are 'obsolete'.

"Signatories included former French President Nicolas Sarkozy and former Prime Minister Manual Valls as well as intellectuals and other public figures such as actor Gerard De Pardieu. The signatories in the letter said, 'Islamist radicalisation' was to blame for what it described as a 'quiet ethnic purging' in Paris region, with abuse forcing Jewish families to move out."

On Thursday, 31st October 2019, Lord Malcolm Pearson went on national television (Sky News) to make a number of unsubstantiated, derogatory, and Islamophobia claims including:

- "Muslim birth rate is going up 10 times faster than ours"

- "In 12 years-time, 11 local authorities, including Birmingham, will be Muslim majority"

- "The Qur'an instructs Muslims not to mix with Jews and Christians"

- And, "one of the World's leading Muslims said to a friend of mine the other day: "We really don't need to go on blowing you up, all we need is to wait because we will take over your culture through the power of the womb and ballot box"".

It is deeply concerning that he was able to propagate such baseless statements without confrontation and request by the presenter to provide any evidence. Lord Pearson is a known Islamophobe who has hailed far-right extremist Mr Stephen Yaxley-Lennon (pseudonym 'Tommy Robinson") as a 'friend' and has frequently invited him to Parliament.

My response to the above is as follows:

Firstly, I will respond to the claims made by Lord Pearson. Then I will provide a response to those who claim that the Qur'an is Anti-Semitic.

My response to Lord Pearson...

I will only respond to his third comment as the rest are based on statistical analysis and forecast. His 4th comment is so mean and mathematically wrong.

In response to him saying "The Qur'an instructs Muslims not to mix with Jews and Christians.", it is mentioned in verses 5:51 and 5:57 of the Qur'an. But unfortunately, there was no Muslim present to explain to him and the audience, the reason for the revelation or the meaning of these verses. Ironically, there are radical Muslims who promote Lord Pearson's allegations.

God says in 5:51, "*O you who believe! Don't take the Jews and the Christians for your friends and protectors. They are but friends and protectors to each other. And he amongst you that turns to them (for friendship) is of them. Verily God doesn't guide a people unjust.*"

The instruction in this verse is that a Muslim country should not use or rely on Jews or Christians to wage war against another Muslim country, the key focus here bring on the word "protectors" as in wartime.

And in verse 5:57, God says, "*O you who believe! Don't take for friends and protectors those who take your religion for a mockery or sport, whether among those who received the Scripture before you, or among those who reject Faith. But fear God if you have Faith (indeed).*"

A.Y.Aly says in FN768, "*It is not right that we should be in intimate association with those to whom religion is either a subject of mockery or at best is nothing but a plaything. They may be amused, or they may have other motives for encouraging you. But your association with them will sap the earnestness of your Faith, make you cynical and insincere.*"

In 5:5, God tells us that we are allowed to eat the food of the People of the Book and they are permitted to eat our food. We are also permitted to marry their chaste women and they will have equal rights like chaste Muslim women. So, a Muslim man can marry a chaste Jewish or Christian woman and she is permitted to continue to practice her religion.

"*This day (all) things good and pure are made lawful to you. The food of the People of the Book is lawful unto you and yours is lawful unto them. (Lawful unto you in marriage) are (not only) chaste women who are believers, but chaste women among the People of the Book, revealed before your time, when you give them their due dowers, and desire chastity, not lewdness or taking them as lovers. If anyone rejects faith, fruitless is his work, and in the Hereafter he will be in the ranks of those who have lost (all spiritual good)." 5:5*

In FN700, A.Y. Aly says, *"Islam is not exclusive. Social intercourse, including inter-marriage, is permitted with the People of the Book. A Muslim man may marry a woman from their ranks on the same terms as would marry a Muslim woman, i.e., he must give her an economic and moral status, and must not be actuated merely by motives of lust or physical desire."*

And in 60:8-9, God clearly states the only condition for not befriending non-Muslims, *"God does not forbid you, with regard to those who don't fight you for (Faith), nor drive you out of your homes, from dealing kindly and justly with them; for God loves those who are just. God only forbids you, with regard to those who fight you for (your) Faith, and drive you out of your homes, and support (others) in driving you out, from turning to them (for friendship and protection). Those who turn to them (in these circumstances), are wrong."*

A.Y.Aly says in FN5421, *"Even with Unbelievers, unless they are rampant and out to destroy us and our Faith, we should deal kindly and equitably, as is shown by our holy Prophet's own example."*

My response to allegations that the Qur'an is Anti-Semitic...

Does the Qur'an describe the Jews, who blasphemed and rejected faith, as apes and pigs?

The answer is yes, not only in the Qur'an, but also in their own Books and by the tongues of their own prophets as explained below.

The Qur'an shows that God is critical of those who reject faith, blaspheme, practice evil and violate His Commandments. Evildoers are condemned by God irrespective of their race or origin, unless they repent, believe and do righteous deeds. God will change the evil of such persons into good as God is Oft-Forgiving, Most Merciful. No one is favoured by God except on the score of righteousness.

The Qur'an, (7:163-166), tells the story of a Jewish fishing community in a seaside village, they transgressed in the matter of the Sabbath, for on the day of their Sabbath their fish did come to them, openly (holding up their heads). But on the day they had no Sabbath, they did not come. This was a great temptation to the law-breakers, which they could not resist.

Another group (presumably) the righteous ones, denied by their heart what the law-breakers did. But a third group, the righteous-reformers spoke out to the sinners and admonished them. So the righteous said to the righteous-reformers, "Why do you preach to a people whom God will destroy or visit with a terrible punishment?"

The preachers replied, "To discharge our duty to your Lord and perchance they may fear Him."

When the sinners disregarded the warnings that had been given to them, God rescued those who forbade evil; but He visited the wrong-doers with grievous punishment, because they were given to transgression. When in their insolence they transgressed (all prohibitions), God said to them, "*Be you apes, despised and rejected.*"

The punishment for breach of the Sabbath under the Mosaic Law was death. "*Everyone that defileth it (the Sabbath) shall surely be put to death: for whosoever doeth any work therein, that soul shall be cut off from among his people*": (Exod. xxxi.14).

Who were the people who incurred the curse of God? See Deut. xi. 28, and xxviii. 15-68, and numerous passages like Hosea viii. 14, and ix. 1.

Who provoked God's wrath? See numerous passages like Deut. i. 34: Matt. iii.7.

Who forsook God, and worshipped evil? See Jeremiah, xvi. 11-13.

For men possessed by devils, and the devils being sent into swine, see Matt. viii. 28-32.

The Qur'an, in 5:78-79, says, "*Curses were pronounced on those among the Children of Israel who rejected Faith, by the tongue of David and of Jesus the son of Mary: because they disobeyed and persisted in Excesses (transgressed all limits). Nor did they forbid one another the iniquities which they committed: evil indeed were the deeds which they did.*"

See Matt. xxviii, *33* ("*Ye serpents, ye generation of vipers, how can ye escape the damnation of Hell?*"); also Matt. xii. 34.

So, the law-breakers among the Children of Israel are condemned by God in their own Books and by the tongue of their own Prophets like David and Jesus.

They are also condemned by God in the Qur'an as a warning to any law-breakers among the Muslims. There are many verses in the Qur'an where God condemns the hypocrites among the Muslims and promises them a great punishment in this life and the Hereafter. Also those among the Muslims who wage war against God and His Messenger (Mohammed pbuh), are severely punished in this life (5:33-34) and a heavy punishment is theirs in the Hereafter, unless they repent and adjust their conduct.

The Slain of the Men of the Jewish Tribe of Banu Qurayzah by Prophet Mohammed (pbuh)

Did the Prophet Mohammed (pbuh) commit holocaust against the Jews?

The slaughter of the men of Banu Qurayzah was shocking to many people who are not familiar with their treason.

If it was not mentioned in 33:26-27 of the Holy Qur'an, we as Muslims would have rejected the story as it contradicts with the nature of the Prophet (pbuh) and his teachings.

"*And those of the people of the Book who aided the (enemies), God took them down from their strongholds and cast terror into their hearts, (so that) some you slew, and some you made captives. And He (God) made you heirs of their lands, their houses, and their goods, and of a land which you had not frequented (before). And God has power over all things.*" 33:26-27.

"The Jewish tribe of the Banu Quraizah were counted among the citizens of Madinah and were bound by solemn engagements to help in the defence of the City. But on the occasion of the Confederate siege by the Quraish and their allies they intrigued with the enemies and treacherously aided them.

"Immediately after the siege was raised and the Confederates had fled in hot haste, the Prophet turned his attention to these treacherous 'friends' who had betrayed his City in the hour of danger. They were filled with terror and dismay when Madinah was free from the Quraish danger. They shut themselves up in their castles and sustained a siege of 25 days, after which they surrendered, stipulating that they would abide by the decision of their fate at the hands of Sa'd Ibn Mu'az, chief of the Aus tribe, with which they had been in alliance." FN3701-3702

It is a known fact that the Jews, at the time of Prophet Mohammed (pbuh), only accepted their own Law. It was the Jews themselves who suggested the appointment of Sa'd Ibn Mu'az as an arbiter.

The Prophet accepted their choice. Sa'd applied the Jewish Law of the Old Testament when he judged in the matter.

FN3703 and 3704 read, *"Sa'd applied to them the Jewish Law of the Old Testament, not as strictly as the case warranted. In Deut. 20:10-18, the treatment of a city 'which is very far off from thee' is prescribed to be comparatively more lenient than the treatment of a city 'of the people, which the Lord thy God does give thee for an inheritance', i.e. which is near enough to corrupt the religion of the Jewish people. The punishment for these is total annihilation: 'thou shall save alive nothing that breatheth' (Deut. 20:16).*

"The more lenient treatment for far-off cities is described in the next note. According to the Jewish standard, then, the Banu Qurayzah deserved total extermination-of men, women and children. They were in the territory of Madinah itself, and further they had broken their engagements and helped the enemy.

"Sa'd adjudged them the mildest treatment of the 'far-off' cities which is thus described in the Jewish Law: 'Thou shalt smite every male thereof with the edge of the sword: but the women and the little ones, and the cattle, and all that is in the city, even all the spoil thereof, shalt thou take unto thyself, and thou shalt eat the spoil of thine enemies, which the Lord thy God hath given thee' (Deut. 20:13-14). The men of the Banu Qurayzah were slain: the women were sold as captives of war: and their lands and properties were divided among the Muhajireen."

So the Prophet Mohammed (pbuh) cannot be accused of committing "holocaust" against the Jews.

Does the Qur'an Commend the Righteous Jews?

The answer is yes. There are numerous verses where God praises the righteous Jews for their good conduct, for example:

"O Children of Israel, call to mind My special favour which I bestowed upon you, and that I preferred you to all others." 2:47

"Among the People of the Book are some who, if entrusted with hoard of gold, will (readily) pay it back; others, who, if entrusted with a single silver coin, will not repay it unless you constantly stood demanding..." 3:75

"Not all of them are alike: Of the People of the Book are a portion that stand (for the right); they rehearse the Revelation of God all night long, and they prostrate themselves in adoration. They believe in God and the Last Day; they enjoin what is right and forbid what is wrong; and they hasten in all good works. They are in the ranks of the righteous. Of the good that they do, nothing will be rejected of them, for God knows well those that they do right." 3:113-115

"And there are, certainly, among the People of the Book, those who believe in God, in the Revelation to you, and in the Revelation to them, bowing in humility to God. They will not sell the Revelation of God for a miserable gain. For them is a reward with their Lord, and God is swift in account." 3:199

"Of the people of Moses there is a section who guide and do justice in the light of truth." 7:159

"We broke them up into sections on this earth. There are among them some that are the righteous, and some that are the opposite. We have tried them with both prosperity and adversity, in order that they may turn to Us." 7:168

Please remember that Prophet Mohammed, peace be upon him, married a Jewish woman, Sapheia, who was given by God the title of "the mother of the believers".

His swords were made by a Jew in Madina. When the Prophet (pbuh) died, his shield was mortgaged with a Jew, to show us that among the Jews there are those who abide by God's Commandments and do not take usury.

As previously stated, a Muslim man is permitted to marry a chaste Jewish or Christian woman. She does not have to embrace Islam and will have the same rights as a Muslim wife, as stated in verse 5:5.

The food of the People of the Book is lawful to Muslims and the food of the Muslims is lawful to the people of the Book, again as mentioned in 5:5.

It was the Muslims who protected the Jews during their persecutions in Europe and provided a safe haven for them.

In 2:109 and 3:186, God commands the Muslims to tolerate and forgive, insults from the People of the Book.

"Many of the People of the Book (Jews and Christians), wish to turn you back into disbelievers after you have accepted the faith, out of their selfish envy, (even) after the truth has become manifest to them. Yet, pardon and overlook till God brings about His command. Surely, God is powerful over all things." 2:109

And He says in 3:186, "*You shall certainly be tried and tested in your possessions and in your own selves, and you will surely hear from those who have been given the Book before you (Jews and Christians) and from the idolaters, much that is offensive and hurtful. But if you are patient and fear God, that is the best course.*"

Islam is a religion of peace, tolerance and justice. It condemns the killing of innocent people anywhere in the world irrespective of their religion or race even if Islam is insulted or ridiculed. Do not blame the Qur'an, blame those who do not understand it among the Muslims and non-Muslims.

2.6 How Should Muslims Respond to Insults Against Prophet Mohammed, The Qur'an and Islam?

A) God Defends Mohammed (pbuh)

In many places in the Qur'an we are told that God will suffice Mohammed (pbuh) so it is not beholden upon us to defend him. It is God who is protecting and shielding him from those who mean mischief, as He did with all His previous Prophets and Messengers.

God says in 37:171-173, "*We have already given Our promise to Our Messengers, that they would certainly be victorious and that Our forces shall triumph.*"

And He says in 40:51, "*We will, without doubt, give victory to Our messengers and those who believe, (both) in this world's life and on the Day when the Witnesses will arise (Day of Judgement).*"

I give below a few examples from the Qur'an showing that God is enough and sufficient for Mohammed pbuh:

1) In 2:137 God says, "*So if they believe in that you believe in, then they are rightly guided. But if they turn away, they are in open opposition (to Divine Guidance) and God will suffice you against them. He is the All-Hearing, the All-Knowing.*"

2) In 15:94-95, "*So proclaim openly what you are commanded and turn away from the idolaters. We defend you against those who mock.*"

"*If the whole world is ranged against Mohammed the Prophet of God, and scoffs at all that is sacred, the sense of God's presence and protection outweighs all. And after all, the scoffers are creatures of a day. Soon will they find their level and be undeceived as to all their falsehoods. But the Truth of God endures for ever.*" FN2016

3) In 39:36, "*Is God not sufficient for His servant (Mohammed)? But they try to frighten you with other (gods) besides Him! For such as God leaves to stray, there can be no guide.*" God is reassuring the Prophet (pbuh) that He is enough for all the protection he needs, all the rest and peace he craves for, and all the happiness he can imagine.

4) In 5:67, "*O Messenger! Proclaim the (Message) which has been sent down to you from your Lord, for if you do not then you will not have delivered His Message. And God will defend and protect you from people (who mean mischief). For God doesn't guide those who reject Faith.*"

"*Mohammed had many difficulties to contend with, many enemies and dangers to avoid. His mission must be fulfilled. And he must, as he did, go forward and proclaim that Message and fulfil his mission, trusting to God for protection, and unconcerned if people who had lost all sense of right rejected it or threatened him.*" FN777

5) In 16:126-128, "*And if you punish, let your punishment be proportionate to the wrong that has been done to you. But if you show patience, that is indeed the best (course) for those who are patient. (O Prophet) be patient, for your patience is but with the help from God. Nor grieve over them, and do not distress yourself because of their evil plotting. For God is with those who fear Him and those who do good.*"

"*In the context this passage refers to controversies and discussions, but the words are wide enough to cover all human struggles, disputes, and fights. In strict equity you are not entitled to give a worse blow than is given to you. Lest you should think that such patience only gives an advantage to the adversary, you are told that the contrary is the case, the advantage is with the patient, the self-possessed, those who do not lose their temper or forget their own principles of conduct.*" FN2163

The Prophet (pbuh) is told here that he need not entertain any such fears. Patience (with constancy) in those circumstances was in accordance with God's own command. Nor was he to grieve if they rejected God's Message. The Prophet (pbuh) had done his duty when he boldly and openly proclaimed it. Nor was his heart to be troubled if they hatched secret plots against himself and his people, God would protect them. The righteous are told that they should not yield to human passion or anger or impatience and that they should go on with constancy doing good all round them. To attain the Presence of God in the sense of 'I am with you' is the culmination of the righteous man's aspiration.

6) God's curse is on those who malign and cause annoyance to God and His Messenger Mohammed (pbuh) as stated in 33:57, "*Those who annoy God and His Messenger are cursed by God in this life and the Hereafter, and has prepared for them a humiliating punishment.*"

7) God confirms again in 9:61, the punishment of those who insult the Prophet (pbuh), "*And among them (the hypocrites) are men who molest the Prophet, saying: 'He is all ears.' Tell them: 'He listens to what is best for you. He believes in God and trusts the believers and is mercy for those of you who believe.' But those who molest the Messenger of God will have a painful punishment.*"

B) How does God Expect Muslims to Respond?

Muslims' response to insults to the Prophet Mohammed (pbuh) or the Qur'an or Islam in general, must comply fully with God's Commands in the Qur'an and the Tradition of the Prophet (pbuh) himself. There is no doubt that whenever Muslims hear or see any type of insults to their religion, it hurts them so much.

These insults are not new as many of the Orientalists in the past spent many years living in the Middle East to study Arabic and Islam. Some of them were guided to the Light and embraced Islam, but others were bent on attacking Islam, and the Prophet (pbuh). For example, some of them claimed that the Prophet (pbuh) was a paedophile because when he married Aisha, she was nine years old and he was 53 years old. They accused him of forcing his adopted son Zaid to divorce his wife Zainab for him to marry her. They claimed that he was a womaniser who had nine wives and refused to divorce any when the number was limited to four. They declared that the Qur'an is not a Divine revelation, in fact it was taught to Mohammed (pbuh) by a Christian monk. Some Jews accused him of committing a holocaust against the Jews in Madina. All these allegations were due to lack of understanding of the Qur'an and lack of awareness of the customs and traditions of the communities at the time of the Prophet (pbuh).

There are many publications by imminent Muslim scholars who have responded to these allegations. But unfortunately, not many people read them. When the issue of immigration makes its way to the forefront of the news, commonly during the times of the European elections, radical right-wing political groups react with hate campaigns against Muslims and Islam. Previously, in their ignorance, they produced nasty images to depict the Prophet (pbuh), which angered many Muslims.

An organisation called Faith Freedom International specialises in regularly publishing hate material against Prophet Mohammed (pbuh) and Islam. They are a group of **"Confused Muslims"**. In one of their publications they said, "*Dear conscientious Muslims: Question yourselves- isn't this compulsive dogma of following a man who lived 1400 years ago, leading us to doom in this changing world? Who are we deceiving? See how our Ummah (people) have sunk into poverty and how we lag behind the rest of the world? Isn't it because we are following a religion that is outdated and impractical? In this crucial moment of history, when a great catastrophe has befallen us and a much bigger one is lying ahead, should not we wake up from our 1400 years of slumber and see where things have gone wrong?*"

And in their conclusion, they claimed, "*We know too well that it is not easy to denounce our faith as it means denouncing a part of ourselves. We are a group of freethinkers and humanists with Islamic roots. Discovering the truth and leaving the religion of our fathers and forefathers was a painful experience. But after learning what Islam stands for, we had no choice but to leave it. After becoming familiar with the Qur'an, the choice became clear: it is either Islam or it is humanity. If Islam is to thrive, humanity must die. We decided to side with humanity. We are still Muslims culturally, but we no more believe in Islam as the true religion of God. We are humanists. We love humanity. We endeavour for the unity of humankind. We work for equality between men and women. We strive for the secularisation* of Islamic countries, for democracy, and freedom of thoughts, beliefs, and expressions. We have decided not to live anymore in self-deception but to embrace humanity, enter the new millennium hand in hand with people or other cultures and beliefs in amity and in peace. We denounce the violence that is eulogised in Qur'an as holy war (Jihad). We condemn killing in the name of God. We believe in sacredness of human life, not in the inviolability of beliefs and religions. And we invite you to join us and the rest of the humanity and be part of the family of humankind with love, camaraderie and peace."

I give below a few examples from the Qur'an on how God expects Muslims to respond:

1) "*Quite a number of the People of the Book wish they could turn you (Muslims) back to infidelity after you have believed, from selfish envy, after the Truth has become manifest unto them. But forgive and overlook, till God brings about His command, for God has power over all things.*" 2:109

Response advised within Qur'an: Here we are commanded to turn away from the insults, to ignore, to treat the matter as if it didn't affect us and to forget and to obliterate from one's mind.

2) "*You shall certainly be tried and tested in your possessions and in yourselves, and you shall certainly hear much that will grieve you from those who received the Book before you (Jews and Christians) and from the idolaters. But if you persevere patiently, and fear God, then that indeed is a matter of great resolution.*" 3:186

Response advised within Qur'an: the trial or test is part of our faith, calling for patience and trust in God.

"*Not wealth and possessions only (or want of them), are the means of our trial. All our personal talents, knowledge, opportunities, and their opposites, in fact everything that happens to us and makes up our personality is a means of our testing. So is our Faith: we shall have to put up for it many insults from those who don't share it.*" FN493

So, if we fear God and guard against evil whilst persevering patiently, no insults can harm us.

3) In 29:46, God directs us on how to argue with the Jews and the Christians, "*And don't dispute with the People of the Book, except in the best way and fairest manner, unless it be with those of them who do wrong, but say 'We believe in the Revelation which has come down to us and in that which came down to you; our God and your God is One; and it is to Him we submit our will to His Will as Muslims.'*"

Response advised within Qur'an: "*Mere disputations are futile. In order to achieve our purpose as true standard-bearers for God, we shall have to find true common grounds of belief, as stated in the latter part of this verse, and also to show by our urbanity, kindness, sincerity, truth and genuine anxiety, for the good of others, that we are not cranks or merely seeking selfish or questionable aims. Of course those who deliberately trying to wrong or injure others will have to be treated firmly, as we are guardians of each other. With them there is little question of finding common ground or exercising patience, until the injury is prevented or stopped.*" FN3472 & 3473.

4) In 3:64, God encourages the followers of the Qur'an to have a dialogue of peace and understanding with the People of the Book, the Jews and the Christians, by saying, "*O People of the Book! Come to common terms as between us and you, that we worship none but the One True God, that we associate no partners with Him, that we don't erect from among ourselves, lords and patrons other than God. If they then turn back, say: 'Bear witness that we (at least) are the ones who have submitted ourselves exclusively to God (as Muslims).'"*

Response advised within Qur'an: Speak with peace and understanding seeking to build bridges rather than deepen any divides, look for commonality first.

5) "*Already He (God) has sent you in the Book, that when you hear the Message of God held in defiance and ridicule, you are not to sit with them unless they turn to a different theme, if you did you would be like them. For God will gather the hypocrites and those who defy Faith, all in Hell.*" 4:140

Response advised within Qur'an: "*Where we see or hear Truth held in light esteem, we ought to make our protest and withdraw from such company, not out of arrogance, as if we thought ourselves superior to other people, but out of real humility, lest our own nature be corrupted in such society. But it is possible that our protest or our sincere remonstrance may change the theme of discourse. In that case we have done good to those who were inclined to hold the Truth in light esteem, for we have saved them for ridiculing Truth.*" FN649

So by peacefully walking out we have demonstrated our objection to the insults. So no violent reaction and not even uttering a word of contempt.

6) "*When you (Mohammed) see those who engage in vain discourse about Our Signs, turn away from them unless they turn to a different theme. If Satan ever makes you forget, then after recollection, don't sit in the company of those who do wrong.*" 6:68

Response advised within Qur'an: "*If in any gathering truth is ridiculed, we must not sit in such company. If we find ourselves in it, as soon as we realise it, we must show our disapproval by leaving.*" FN891

So, it is repeated again in this verse that there be no violence in response to insults. Just walk out peacefully.

7) God commands the Prophet (pbuh) in 33:48 to disregard and ignore the insolence of his enemies, "*Don't yield to the unbelievers and the hypocrites and disregard the hurt that comes from them, and put your trust in God. God suffices as the Guardian to entrust one's affairs to.*"

Response advised within Qur'an: "*Men of little or no Faith will often lay down the law and tell better men than themselves what to do. In case of refusal they shower insults and injuries. No attention is to be paid to them. It is their way. All will be right under the government of God.*" FN3737

8) "*And the servants of (God) Most Gracious are those who walk on the earth in humility, and when the ignorant address them, they say, 'Peace'.*" 25:63

"*Ignorant: in a normal sense. Address: in the aggressive sense. Their humility is shown in two ways: (1) to those in real search of knowledge, they give such knowledge as they have and as the recipients can assimilate; (2) to those who merely dispute, they don't speak harshly, but say 'Peace', as much as to say, 'May it be well with you, may you repent and be better'; or 'May God give me peace from such wrangling'; or 'Peace, and Good-bye; let me leave you!'*" FN3123

Response advised within Qur'an: So, God expects us to respond peacefully to any aggressive confrontation.

9) "*(O Mohammed) Hold to forgiveness, command what is right, but turn away from the ignorant.*" 7:199

"*God comforts the Prophet and directs his mind to three precepts: (1) to forgive injuries, insults, and persecution; (2) to continue to declare the faith that was in him, and not only to declare it, but to act up to it in all his dealings with friends and foes; (3) to pay no attention to ignorant fools, who raised doubts or difficulties, hurled taunts or reproaches, or devised plots to defeat the truth: they were to be ignored and passed by, not to be engaged in fights and fruitless controversies, or conciliated by compromises.*" FN1170

Response advised within Qur'an: Response advised within Qur'an: Those who claim to be the followers of the teachings of the Prophet Mohammed (pbuh), must comply fully with God's three Commands in this verse. It is clearly stated again that there be no violence in response to any insults, injuries, or persecution. Just ignore the ignorant.

10) Another example of how the true believers should respond to vanity is given in 28:55, "*And when they hear vain talk, they turn away therefrom and say, 'To us our deeds, and to you yours. Peace be on you. We do not desire the ignorant.'*"

Response advised within Qur'an: "*The righteous don't encourage idle talk or foolish arguments about things sacred. If they find themselves in some company in which such things are fashionable, they leave politely. Their only rejoinder is: 'We are responsible for our deeds, and you for yours; we have no ill-will against you; we wish you well, and that is why we wish you to know of the knowledge we have received; after that knowledge you can't expect us to go back to the ignorance which have left.*" FN3387

11) God commands Muslims in 6:108 not even to insult the idols of the idol worshippers, lest they out of spite revile God in their ignorance.

Response advised within Qur'an: "*God in His infinite compassion bears with them, and asks those who have purer ideas of faith not to vilify the weaknesses of their neighbours, lest the neighbours in their turn vilify the real truth and make matters even worse than before. God will forgive and send His grace for helping ignorance and folly. In so far as there is active evil,*

He will deal with it in His own way. Of course, the righteous man must not hide his light under a bushel, or compromise with evil, or refuse to establish right living where he has power to do so." FN936

12) Repelling evil with good is ordained by God in several places in the Qur'an. For example, in 13:22 God commends those who ward off evil with good, for they are not revengeful, but anxious to overcome evil with good. Thus breaking the chain of evil which tends to perpetuate itself. *"Those who patiently persevere, seeking the countenance of their Lord, establish regular prayers; spend (in charity) out of the bounties We bestowed on them, secretly and openly; and turn off Evil with good. Theirs will be the (heavenly) Home, Gardens of Eden which they will enter..."* 13:22-23

And in 23:96 He commands the Prophet (pbuh), *"Repel evil with that which is better. We are well acquainted with which they allege (against you)."*

Response advised within Qur'an: *"Whether people speak evil of you, in your presence or behind your back, or they do evil to you in either of those ways, all is known to God. It is not for you to punish. Your best course is not to do evil in your turn, but to do what will best repel the evil. Two evils do not make a good."* FN2934

In 28:54 we are told again that one of the attributes of the true believers is that they avert evil with good.

I will conclude with verse 41:34 where God answers the question 'How can your enemy become your close friend?' - *"(O Prophet) Nor can Goodness and Evil be equal. Repel the evil deed with one which is better, and you will see that he, between whom and you there was enmity, shall become as if he was an intimate friend."* What beautiful Divine advice for making peace between people!

"You don't return good for evil, for there is no equality or comparison between the two. You repel or destroy evil with something which is far better, just as an antidote is better than poison. You foil hatred with love. You repel ignorance with knowledge, folly and wickedness with the friendly message of Revelation. The man who was in the bondage of sin, you not only liberate from sin, but make him your greatest friend and helper in the cause of God. Such is the alchemy of the Word of God." FN4504

2.7 Conclusion

We have discussed that insulting or ridiculing God or His Messengers, or His Angels, or His Revelations is not a new concept; it has been taking place throughout history and through the times and lives of many Prophets.

Muslims should never resort to violence to respond to the mockers. God will deal with them in His own way in this life and the Hereafter, as stated in many verses in the Qur'an. For example God says in 16:45-47, *"Are those who plan evil so sure that God will not make the earth swallow them up, that punishment will not come on them from some unimagined direction, that it will not catch them suddenly in the midst of their comings and goings, for they cannot frustrate God, or that it will not catch up with them gradually? Indeed your Lord is Kind and Merciful."*

"The wicked plot against Prophets of God in secret, forgetting that every hidden thought of theirs is known to God, and that for every thought and action of theirs they will have to account to God. And God's punishment can seize them in various ways. Four are enumerated here..." FN2071

God says in 58:5-6, *"Those who oppose God and His Messenger (Mohammed) will be brought low, like those before them. We have revealed clear messages, and humiliating torment awaits those who ignore them, on the Day when God will raise everyone and make them aware of what they have done. God has taken account of it all, though they may have forgotten. He witnesses everything."*

And in 58:20-21, He says, *"Those who oppose God and His Messenger (Mohammed) will be among the most humiliated. God has decreed, 'I shall certainly win and prevail, I and My messengers.' God is Powerful and Almighty."*

"There are various degrees of humiliation in the final state in the next world. But the worst is the humiliation of being numbered among those who ignominiously attempted to resist the Irresistible." FN5361

God confirms in the Qur'an that Muslims will endure many insults from those who do not share their faith, which will grieve them. However, God commands them to turn away from the insults, to ignore, to treat the matter as if it did not affect them and to forget and to obliterate from one's mind. Fear of God and persevering patiently would eventually make them prevail.

God instructs Muslims not to argue or dispute with the People of the Book, unless it be in a way that is better than mere disputation. That is with kind words and good manners, except with those of them who do wrong.

Muslims are also commanded not to insult idols, lest their worshippers would ridicule or insult the One True God, the Creator of Heavens and Earth, and everything seen or hidden. Indeed, a closing chapter within the Qur'an (Surah 109, Al Kafiroon – The Unbelievers) relays in the most beautiful words, *"Say: O unbelievers! I do not worship what you worship. Nor do you worship what I worship. Nor will I ever worship what you worship. Nor will you worship what I worship. You have your religion and I have mine"*. We can take from this that there is no compulsion in religion and we can live with our faiths side by side in mutual respect and tolerance.

God orders Muslims that if they find themselves in a situation where God's Revelations or His Messengers are being ridiculed, just to walk out peacefully in protest, and not to respond violently.

God in 15:9, reassures Muslims that the protection of the Qur'an from corruption is His own responsibility, *"It is We, without doubt, who have sent down the Reminder (the Qur'an) and We will certainly guard it."*

"The purity of the text of the Qur'an through 14 centuries is a foretaste of the eternal care with which God's truth is guarded through all ages. All corruptions, inventions, and accretions pass away, but God's pure and holy Truth will never suffer eclipse even though the whole world mocked at it and were bent on destroying it." FN1944.

So whether the enemies of Islam would burn copies of the Qur'an or shred them or step on them with their shoes, the text of the Qur'an is protected by God as it is deeply engraved in the hearts, minds and souls of every Muslim.
Believers must rejoice and feel secure to know that God is their defender as He says in 22:38, *"Surely God defends those who are true believers. Surely God doesn't love the treacherous ingrate."*

God in 61:7-9, gives comfort, and solace to Muslims that it is His responsibility to defend Islam and His Messenger, *"And who does greater wrong than he who invents a lie against God when he is invited to (accept) Islam. And God does not guide the wrongdoers. They seek to extinguish the Light of God with their mouths, but God will perfect His Light, irrespective of how much the unbelievers may hate this. It is He who has sent His Messenger (Mohammed) with the Guidance and the Religion of Truth, so that He may exalt it above all (other) religions, however much the idolaters may be averse."*

"God's Light is unquenchable. A foolish, ignorant person who thinks of extinguishing it is like a rustic who wants to blow out electric light as he might blow out a rush candle! 'With their mouths' also implies the babble and cackle of ignorance against God's Truth. The more the foolish ones try to quench God's Light, the clearer it shines to shame them!

"There is really only one true Religion, the Message of God submission to the Will of God: this is called Islam. It was the religion preached by Moses and Jesus; it was the religion of Abraham, Noah, and all the prophets, by whatever name it may be called. If people corrupt that pure light, and call their religions by different names, we must bear with them, and we may allow the names for convenience. But Truth must prevail overall." FN5441 & 5442.

Chapter Three- Islam Empowers Women

3.1 Introduction

The Prophet Mohammed (pbuh), the final and the last Messenger of God, was born into a community in which men's primary concern was their honour and women were associated with shame and seen as burdens. Women were generally dehumanised and treated as commodities to be inherited or given in marriage to whomsoever her male guardian chose. This suffering of women was not only confined to Arabia, but it was experienced in many parts of the world.

The Prophet Mohammed (pbuh), starting with his own community over 1400 years ago, and through Divine Revelation, brought revolution to the world, restoring dignity and humanity to its womenfolk, and radically changing the way in which believing men treated their women.

How was this revolution brought about? How can the Prophet's (pbuh) example help us correct the behaviours of some Muslim communities in the UK who have adopted the customs of the time of ignorance (i.e. pre Islamic time), as if the Prophet (pbuh) had never come to the people with his Message from God?

Taking action to end violence against women and girls, is an initiative, which the Prophet Mohammed (pbuh), actively supported throughout his life. In this Chapter, I will present the message that he preached in this regard and the example he set for all of us to follow.

On 14th July 2012, I organised a conference in cooperation with the Association of Muslim Lawyers and Redbridge Police to support the strategy of the Mayor of London and the Metropolitan Police to take action in ending violence against women and girls. The focus of the conference was to bring prevention to the heart of all initiatives to combat violence against women and girls and focus on rape, sexual assault, sexual exploitation, trafficking, forced marriage, female genital mutilation (FGM), domestic violence, economic deprivation, and violence committed in the name of honour.

The conference was addressed by several professional speakers and the Police Borough Commander CSI Sue Williams.

3.2 My Speech at the Conference

3.2.1 Women's Rights in Islam
In Islam, men and women have equal rights but different responsibilities. The Prophet (pbuh) said, *'Women are the sisters of men'*, (reported by Ahmad, Abu-Dawood & Al-Tarmidhi). Before God we are all equal. The most honoured in the sight of God is the righteous, not the men, not the women, not the black, not the white, not the rich, not the poor, but the God fearing and the best in conduct as stated in 49:13.

The liberation of women started over 1400 years ago following the revelation of the final and last Divine Revelation, the Holy Qur'an.

During the 23 years of the mission of Prophet Mohammed (pbuh), and the following years of the four Muslim rulers, women enjoyed their rights. Later when spiritual values were lost and people became dogmatic and manipulated the interpretation of the religion, they reverted to old traditions and women started to suffer again.

So, what are women's rights in Islam? Let me mention some of them now, and later I shall elaborate on the ones relevant to today's theme.

1) The right to live with dignity in a safe and non-hostile environment.
2) The right to seek knowledge and education.
3) The right to work, as long as it is lawful. Whatever she earns is her own property; it does not belong to her husband or her father or her guardian.
4) The right to ownership of assets in any form.
5) The right to inherit.
6) The right to choose her future husband, and the right to receive a dowry from him.
7) The right to keep her maiden name after marriage.
8) The right to include certain conditions in the Islamic Marriage Contract.
9) The right to divorce her husband under certain conditions. This divorce is known in Arabic as Al-Khola.
10) Women have equality with men regarding forms of worship, reward, and punishment. Both sexes have spiritual as well as human rights and duties in an equal degree and the future reward of the Hereafter, as pointed out in 33:35.
11) Women are given the accountability and responsibility for themselves, their families, and the society they live in.
12) Islam respects the opinion of women and highly recommends that they should be consulted and invited to participate in the decision making process whether at home, or at community level, or national, or international.

13) As mentioned in verse 31:14, God acknowledges the pain women endure during pregnancy and further acknowledges the pain they go through when giving birth in verses 46:15. Moreover, God grants those women who die when delivering their child, the rank of a martyrdom. These are facts which men should appreciate and be considerate of.

14) Islam protects the reputation and the honour of chaste women against slander, as stated in versus 24:4-5.

15) According to verse 4:34, it is the responsibility of men to support women even if the woman is working and earning: "*Men are the protectors and maintainers of women, because of the physical strength God gave them and because they spend of their property (for the support of women)*...So, no husband is doing his wife a favour by financially supporting her. It is her right to be economically supported as per the Islamic Marriage contract.

3.2.2 Addressing Violence Against Women

A) The Right to Live with Dignity in a Safe and Non-Hostile Environment:

Female infanticide was practiced before the advent of Islam by the pagan Arabs. It is a major crime condemned by God and totally prohibited in Islam.

In 16:58-59, God describes the mental status of some men who hated to have daughters, "*When news is brought to one of them of the birth of a female (child), his face darkens, and he's filled with inward grief. With shame he hides himself from his people, because of the bad news he has had. Shall he retain it on surface and contempt, or bury it in the dust? Ah! What an evil (choice) they decide on?*"

So a man like that would bury his newly born daughter alive. This is known in Arabic as 'Waad'. Verses 81:8-9 tell us that on the Day of Judgement the baby girl who is buried alive by her parents will be asked, "*What crime did you commit to justify your killing?*"

Unfortunately, to date there are some parents who hate to have daughters and, in some cultures, Muslims as well as non-Muslims, the woman would abort if she were told that she is carrying a female child. Some men would even threaten their wives that if they continue to deliver girls, they will divorce them.

The Prophet (pbuh) informed these ignorant men, over 1400 years ago, that it is the male sperm which determines the sex of the child. No man should blame his wife; instead, he should blame his lazy Y sperms! God tells us in 42:49-50, that it is He who determines who should have what, "*To God belongs the Dominion of the Heavens and the Earth. He creates what He wills; He grants females to whomever He pleases, and males to whomever He pleases, or grant them a mix of males and females, and causes whomever He pleases to be barren. He is All-Knowing, All-Powerful.*"

In 17:31, we are told that poverty can lead some people to kill their own children, especially the girls, *"Don't kill your children for fear of want, We shall provide sustenance for them as well as for you. Verily the killing of them is a great sin"*.

Muslim women in some countries suffer from "Civil Waad", i.e. they are fully deprived from their Civil Rights, e.g. home imprisonment, no education, no travelling, no passport, no employment, not even allowed to drive a car, or show her face, or consent to get married.

The Prophet (pbuh) said, *"Whoever has a daughter and did not kill her, and did not insult her, and did not favour his son over her, God will reward him with paradise."* (Abu-Dawood)

In another Hadith he said, *"If you have one or more daughters and you bring them up righteously, they will act like a shield to protect you from the Hellfire"*.

Prophet Mohammed (pbuh) before he became a Prophet at the age of 40 had four daughters whom he treated with great respect, kindness and affection, at a time when it was a disgrace to have daughters who were buried alive by their own idol worshipping parents. He instructed men to be kind, caring and generous to all female members of the family.

B) No to Forced Marriages:

I received the following question from a young woman who says, *"My father wants me to marry the son of his business partner, whom I do not like. My father threatens me that if I do not accept his decision, he would disown me and deprive me from any inheritance. In Islam, is it my choice or my parent's decision to choose a husband for me? I'm not worried about inheritance, but I love my family and also, I cannot spend the rest of my life with someone I don't like. Please advise."*

So before talking about forced marriages, let me mention something about arranged marriages.

Islam recommends that before getting married, a man and a woman have the right to see each other in an environment governed by Islamic etiquettes. It is unfair and unacceptable practice in Islam that the bride and the groom will see each other for the first time in their lives on the day of marriage.

Marriage in Islam consists of three stages, namely engagement, registration and wedding. Each stage has its own rules and regulations.

Islam permits introductory marriages, that is when a man and a woman are introduced to each other, and it is up to both of them to decide to proceed or not.

In Islam no one can force a woman to marry against her will, even her father. A woman complained to the Prophet (pbuh) that her father married her to his nephew against her will. The Prophet (pbuh) called the father and told him that the decision is in the hands of the daughter. The daughter replied: "I have accepted what my father has done, but I wanted to teach the women that their parents have no right to force them to marry against their will." reported by An-Nasaie. What a brave woman!

In another Hadith, a woman called Khansaa bent Khozam Al-Ansareia, who was either a divorcee or a widow, came to the Prophet (pbuh) and told him that her father forced her to marry against her will. The Prophet (pbuh) nullified her marriage, reported by the Group, except Muslim.

The UK government is considering making forced marriages a crime. Is this a good idea? A Family Lawyer suggested that if it becomes a crime, the daughter who married against her will might find it difficult to report her father, whilst now she can, as the father will not be punished.

Islam gave women a new status; it wanted to create a new woman as much as a new man. However, the old ethos soon robbed the woman of that status. Unfortunately, over time some societies and cultures have reverted back to pre-Islamic ways and effectively taken away the status, respect and protection afforded to women in Islam. A close study of the Qur'an would reveal that she was given full autonomy in matters of marriage. Her marriage depended on her approval being given under her own conditions. However, the Jahiliya (pre-Islamic time of ignorance), practice of contracting marriage by her Wali (marriage guardian) on her behalf re-established itself and her approval was reduced to a mere nod or silence. From playing an active role in her own marriage she came to be relegated to a passive position.

C) No to Domestic Violence:

There are battered husbands and battered wives. But today we are addressing domestic violence against women. Unfortunately, it is happening in many families in the UK, Muslims as well as non-Muslims. Examples of other forms of domestic violence than just physical, are acid violence, marital rape, emotional blackmail, economic deprivation and psychological torture.

No marriage is without issues
There is no marriage without problems. Resolving to violence against a wife or a daughter or a mother or a sister is un-Islamic. It does not solve the problem. God says in 21:127, "*And We have not sent you (Mohammed) but as mercy to all the worlds (to all creatures)*". So, any act which lacks mercy is un-Islamic.

Verse 2:228 reads, "*...and women shall have rights similar to the rights against them.*"

No such thing as perfection
Verse 4:19 Reads, "*And live with them (the women) honourably on a footing of kindness and equity, if you dislike them (the wives), it may be that you dislike a thing and God brings through it a great deal of good*".

Display kindness in all actions

Even in the case of divorce, and during the waiting period, God says in 65:2, "...*either take them back in kindness or part with them in kindness...*". Also, in 65:6, He says, "*Lodge them where you dwell, according to your wealth and means, and do not harass them (do not annoy them to make life hard and difficult for them) ...*"

Focus on the positive

The Prophet (pbuh) said, "*No believing man should hate his believing wife. If he dislikes a part of her conduct, he would surely like another*", reported by Muslim. In other words, do not look for faults in your wife. Look for any positive aspects or any good character and focus on these to compensate for any faults. Also look into your own faults and work on remedying these.

Be the best to your family

The Prophet (pbuh) also said, "*Be kind to women for you have taken them by God's covenant and earned the right to have intimate relations with them by God's Word.*", reported by Muslim. In another Hadith he said, "*The best among you is he who is the best to his family and I am the best one among you to my family*", reported by Ibn-Hebban and Tohfat Al-Ahwazy.

We are from each other

The Prophet (pbuh) also said, "*Be kind to women, a woman is created from a bent rib, and the most bent part of it is its top. If you try to straighten it, you will break it, and if you leave it, it remains bent. So be good to women*", reported by Muslim and Al-Bukhari.

Patience is a virtue

Exercising patience, not being rude or aggressive, being able to control anger, being able to forgive and forget and overlook are great Islamic virtues. Verse 3:134 reads,"...*and those who restrain (their) anger and pardon people, and God loves those who do good (to others).*"

Control your tongue

God says in 4:148, that He doesn't like rudeness and vulgarity, "*God does not love the public utterance of hurtful speech, unless (it be) by one to whom injustice has been done. For God is He Who hears and knows all things.*"

As to those women on whose part the husband fears rebellion, disloyalty and ill contact, four steps are mentioned in the Qur'an in verses 4:34-35, to be taken in that order, this is based on the assumption that the husband is God-fearing and that he has given his wife all her rights:

(1) Perhaps verbal advice or admonition may be sufficient.

(2) If not, sex relations may be suspended.

(3) If this is not sufficient, some slight physical correction may be administered, but Imam Al-Shafi considers this inadvisable, though permissible, and all authorities are unanimous in deprecating any sort of cruelty, even of the nagging kind. The maximum physical admonition

from a man towards his wife is akin to the act of smacking the back of her hand with a tooth brush (explained further in (4) below).

At the end of these three steps God says,"...*but if they return to obedience, don't seek against them means of (annoyance), (don't seek ways to harm them), for God is Most High, Great (above you all)."*

(4) If the above stages fail, a family council is recommended as stated in 4:35, "*If you fear a breach between the two, appoint an arbitrator from his people, and an arbitrator from her people. If they both want to set things right, God will bring about reconciliation between them as God is All-Knowing, All-Aware."*

It must be made clear that, the Prophet (pbuh) never in his entire life raised a hand on any of his wives. He regarded those who do that as the meanest in the society. The maximum physical correction a man can administer is by using a "Miswak", a toothbrush, gently smacking the back of the hand. It is not for causing pain but to show the disgust of the husband regarding the ill contact and disloyalty of the wife.

A Hadith in Muslim clearly defines the only time that this form of discipline may be used. The Prophet (pbuh) said in his farewell Hajj, "*...Fear God regarding women, for they are your helpers. You have the right on them that they do not allow any person you don't approve to enter your house. However, if they do that, you are allowed to discipline them lightly. They have the right on you that you provide them with their provision and clothes in a fitting manner."*

In another Hadith reported by Ibn-Maja and Al-Tarmidhi, the Prophet (pbuh) said in the farewell Hajj that the only time when physical discipline can be used **if the wife commits a form of open lewdness.**

So, a wise and God-fearing husband would simply follow the instructions given above and would allow enough time between each one of them to enable the wife to reflect on her behaviour and come back to her senses.

D) No to Honour Killing:

Honour killing is an ancient tradition, still sometimes observed in many parts of the world.

Killing is a major sin in Islam. There is no justification whatsoever for killing an innocent soul:

1) God says in 5:32, "*On that account We ordained for the Children of Israel that if anyone slew a person, unless it be for murder or for spreading mischief in the land, it would be as if he slew the whole people, and if anyone saved a life, it would be as if he saved the life of the whole people...".*

2) God commands us in 17:33, "*Do not take life which God made sacred, except for just cause. And if anyone is slain wrongfully, We have given his heir authority to demand*

a Qasas (Law of retaliation or to forgive), but let him not exceed bounds in the matter of taking life for he is helped (by the law)."

3) Verse 4:93 reads, "*If a person kills a believer intentionally, his recompense is Hell, to abide therein forever, and the wrath and the curse of God are upon him, and a dreadful punishment is prepared for him.*"

What is mentioned here is the punishment in the Hereafter. The legal consequences enforceable by human society, are mentioned in verse 2:178.

4) If a man or a woman are accused of committing fornication or adultery, then the punishment stated in verse 24:2 would be implemented by the ruling Islamic government, not by members of the families. This punishment will only be carried out if they either confess, or the woman becomes pregnant, or four eyewitnesses saw the act of penetration, as stated by God in 24:13. The punishment in verse 24:2 reads, "*The woman and the man guilty of committing adultery or fornication, flog each of them with a hundred stripes; Let not compassion move you in their case in a matter prescribed by God, if you believe in God and the Last Day; and let a party of the believers witness their punishment.*"

5) Suppose a husband accuses his wife of having an affair! Should he kill the wife and her lover, or apply verses 24:6-9? In these verses God says, "*And as for those who accuse their wives and have no witnesses except themselves, let him swear four times by God that he is telling the truth and the fifth one invoking the curse of God on him if he is telling a lie. And the punishment shall be averted from her if she testifies four times by God that he is a liar, and fifth one invoking the curse of God on her if he is telling the truth*".

So, if she does not take this step, the charge is held approved and the punishment follows. In either case the marriage is dissolved, as it is against human nature that the parties can live together happily after such an incident.

E) No to Female Genital Mutilation (FGM):

Another crime committed against young girls in the name of religion, is female genital mutilation (FGM). The least form of FGM is female circumcision. It is practiced in Egypt, Sudan, Somalia, along with some other African countries. Some immigrants from these countries continue to practice it in the UK or send their daughters on holiday to their countries of origin to get it done there.

Most Arab and Islamic countries view it as un-Islamic, but some people believe the Prophet (pbuh) approved it. The people who practice it rely on weak (unauthentic) Prophetic Tradition (Hadith). In one Hadith the Prophet (pbuh) said, "*Circumcision is a tradition for men and an honour for women*". According to Al-Albani (a Muslim Jurist who specialises in the science of Prophetic Tradition (Elm Al- Ahadith), this Hadith is weak as there is debate regarding its authenticity, (It is recorded under number 1935 in the book of weak Hadith by Al-Albani).

The other Hadith: A woman used to perform circumcision in Madina, the Prophet (pbuh) told her, "*Don't abuse (i.e. do not go to extremes in circumcising); that's better for the woman and more liked by her husband*". This Hadith is reported by Abu-Dawood, who said that it is weak (unauthentic).

Al-Azhar Supreme Council of Islamic Research, the highest religious authority in Egypt, has condemned the practice calling it harmful and saying it is not based on Islamic law. Dar Al-Ifta, the authority of issuing legal religious opinions, also condemned it. Egypt officially banned FGM in 2007. Why did it take so long to ban an evil practice, which goes back to the time of the pharaohs?!

Women in Islam have the right to have an enjoyable fulfilling sex life with their husbands. FGM denies women this right. It causes many marriages to collapse due to women's frigidity in addition to problems with periods and obstetric complications.

I give below opinions of contemporary scholars and jurists on female circumcision:

Sheikh Sayyid Sabiq quite frankly says that female circumcision is not compulsory and leaving it is not a sin. There is nothing in the Qur'an or the Tradition of the Prophet (pbuh) to prove that it is compulsory. All the reports that have been mentioned in this regard are weak and unauthentic and cannot be taken as evidence in this regard. The Sheikh supported his argument with the following saying of Ibn al-Mundhir who was one of the senior scholars in Fiqh and Hadith, "There is no reliable report or a Prophetic Tradition to be followed regarding female circumcision".

He also argues that nothing can be considered compulsory unless there is supportive evidence on that: whether it is a Qur'anic verse, a Hadith that is authentic in its source and chain of narration or a consensus of the prominent scholars. Regarding this (female circumcision), there is nothing to support it from the Qur'an, the authentic Hadith or consensus of scholars. In the Islamic Sharia, nothing can be approved except with evidence and evidence is lacking in this case. Therefore, if a girl was not circumcised this is not considered a violation of the Sharia or a breach to the religion. (Al-Tahrir magazine 28/10/1958).

Dr Sheikh Mohammed Sayyid Tantawi, Grand Imam of Al-Azhar expressed his view regarding female circumcision saying: "What I see after reviewing the views of some of old and contemporary scholars on circumcision that it is a compulsory Sunnah (Prophetic Tradition) for males. This is because of the existence of authentic texts that encourage doing it. However, there is no authentic Sharia text to be used as a proof on female circumcision. I see that this is a tradition that spread in Egypt from a generation to another and it is about to decline and become extinct among all classes especially among the learned people. The fact that many of the Muslim countries that are full of knowledgeable scholars have left the practice of female circumcision is one of the proofs that this act is a tradition and not supported by any authentic Sharia text. Therefore, I see that the final opinion on female circumcision must be that of physicians. If they say that it is harmful, it must be left because physicians are the people of knowledge in this regard.

"The Grand Imam Mahmoud Shaltut opined in his book (Al-Fatwa) that, "*there is nothing in Sharia, manners or medicine that calls for female circumcision or makes it compulsory*".

He also says in his book that "female circumcision is an old practice that was known to people from the beginning of humanity and they continued to practice it until Islam came and they (males and females) continued to practice circumcision under Islam. However, we don't know exactly if this was practised based on human thoughts and instructions of natural instincts that guide people to remove extra unwanted things that carry no benefit or cause some harm and dirt if left un-removed...Or that they practised this based on some religious instructions given by a prophet or a messenger in the past...
What is important to us is to know its relation to the religion and the ruling of Islam regarding it."

Egyptian Dar Al-Ifta: Female Circumcision is Prohibited Under the Sharia and has to be Confronted, Sunday 23rd June 2013:

The Egyptian Dar Al-Ifta stated on Sunday that female circumcision (FGM) is prohibited under the Islamic Sharia and requested the country's responsible administrations and bodies to exert more effort in order to confront and stop this phenomena. Dar Al-Ifta further said that this phenomena is a non-religious issue but it rather pertains to the medical heritage of people and their own traditions.

The Egyptian Dar Al-Ifta has participated in the events of the National Day for Confronting Female Circumcision. The event was attended by Dr Mohammed Wisam Khidr who is a senior researcher and head of the Administration of Written Fatwa and Jurisprudence of Minorities. He attended as a deputy to Dr Shaqwqy Allam, the Mufti of the State. The event was held in the headquarter of National Council of Population and was coordinated by the Ministry of Health, the Al-Azhar University's International Islamic Centre for Population Studies and Research, the Egyptian Coalition on Children's Rights, the UNICEF, other medical and human rights organisations and national and international mass media. The event's slogan was **"We are all responsible...No for female circumcision."**

Dr Wisam confirmed in his speech that since the middle of the last century, Al-Azhar scholars dealt with the issue of female circumcision through the juristic rules and principles of jurisprudence based on the objectives of the Islamic Sharia; and they stressed that any practice that is proven by scientific research to be harmful to the health must be prohibited under the Islamic Sharia for causing harm to oneself or to others, is prohibited in Islam.

Wisam added that Dar Al-Ifta interacted early with the medical and scientific research issued by recognised medical institutions and neutral international health organisations. As these researchers have proven the severe harm and negative consequences of female circumcision, Dar Al-Ifta has issued in 2006 a statement that confirms that this practice is a form of tradition and not an Islamic rite and that a person who studies the case carefully will opine only the prohibition of this practice.

He also referred to the fact that Dar Al-Ifta has contributed to the preparation of and participated in the International Conference of Muslim Scholars on the prohibition of violating women's bodies. The conference was held in Al-Azhar and Dar Al-Ifta in 2006. The conference recommended that female circumcision must be delegalised and called for issuing laws and rules to classify that practice as a crime and punish whoever conducts or participates in it.

Dr Wisam referred to the scientific facts and medical researches that prove with certainty the benefits of male circumcision and the harmfulness of female circumcision. **He explained that recent medical and scientific researchers have proven that there is no relationship between female circumcision and the decrease in the sexual desire. Chastity is achieved by proper upbringing, not by cutting the part.**

The Sharia rulings clearly state that when any doubt enters, the associated Corporal punishment whilst permissible must be waived. Female circumcision cannot be allowed, based on weak Hadith, due to its proven physical and psychological harm and its negative complications. Even if the Hadith were strong and considered authentic, the very fact that the act medically has been proven harmful would not support the case in question.

In his speech Wisam said: Female circumcision is not a religious or ritual issue in principle, but is an issue that relates to the medical heritage and traditions, explaining that after search and investigations, we found that **this custom is practised in a hurtful and harmful way that makes us say it is prohibited under the Sharia, contrary to male circumcision which is an Islamic ritual by consensus.**

The above was my speech at the Conference held at our Mosque at South Woodford, London, on 14th July 2012.

3.3 My Personal Involvement in Combatting FGM

The conference inspired me to continue my work to empower women to combat FGM in the UK.

On Saturday 29th March 2014, I spoke at the Conference organised by the "Sexual Offences, Exploitation and Child Abuse Command", The Metropolitan Police. The title of my talk was **"Dispelling Myths".**

Detective Chief Superintendent Keith Niven, wrote to me on 4th April 2014:

"Dear Mohammed

I am writing to thank you for your contribution to our Conference at the Holiday Inn, Gloucester Road on Saturday 29th March 2014. The concept was to reach out to members of the community affected by female genital mutilation and highlight the health risks, illegality of the act and the lack of any religious foundation to its existence. This could only be done by involving a wide range of speakers who could either explain the dangers from a professional standpoint such as yourself or who have been so brave to speak out as survivors from various communities. The hope was for the audience to resonate with those on stage.

The feedback has been simply overwhelming both from those who spoke and those who attended that day. We have been humbled by the impact this has had and wish to develop our community contact further in our continued efforts to empower people to turn their backs on the practice and come forward with information on those who carry out the abuse.

Thank you again.

Yours sincerely

Keith Niven
Detective Chief Superintendent
OCU Commander
Sexual Offensive, Exploitation and Child Abuse Command"

On 23rd June 2014, I was a speaker at "Tackling FGM in the UK Conference", which gave an update on progress towards meeting the recommendations in the Intercollegiate Report on FGM. The title of my speech was **"Is FGM a Religious Obligation?"**.

Susan Bookbinder, a journalist and broadcaster, chaired the update on that symposium at the Royal College of Obstetricians and Gynaecologists in London. Two government ministers, Norman Baker MP, Minister of State for Crime Prevention, and Jane Ellison MP, Parliamentary Under Secretary of State for Public Health, addressed the conference.

On Friday 27th June 2014, Ms Bookbinder wrote a very well informed and comprehensive article in the **Jewish Telegraph**, titled **"23,000 girls in the UK at risk of genital mutilation"**.

"...FGM is associated with what can only be described as misogynistic ideals of femininity and modesty, including the notion that girls are 'clean' and 'beautiful' after being cut.

"There are no religious scripts prescribing the practice, but the myth that FGM is a Muslim ritual is one which has acted as a very effective barrier to change.

"It is a barrier I have seen torn down very effectively by Dr Mohammed Fahim. He is the Metropolitan Police chaplain and head Imam of South Woodford Mosque and is emphatic on the issue.

"'FGM is a crime committed against young women and girls in the name of religion', he said.

"Dr Fahim has campaigned against FGM for 30 years and insists there is no scripture in the Koran which supports or prescribes FGM. To the contrary there is no authentic Sharia text to approve female circumcision, however it is compulsory in males.'

"It is a position supported by the British Medical Association and the Muslim Council for Britain.

"In a joint statement on Monday they declared: 'Some people who practice FGM believe it to be an Islamic practice. This is not true, FGM is not a Muslim requirement'.

"Dr Fahim is passionate about promoting harmony, cohesion and understanding and leads a Jewish, Muslim and Christian tour of Israel each year.

"Being at the forefront of the campaign to end FGM in the UK and being Jewish, people often ask me about what they call 'MGM' (male genital mutilation). 'Isn't male circumcision the same?' they ask. I put this question to Dr Fahim. 'No, it is not,' he replied. 'There are no benefits to the woman, only harm. Whereas male circumcision is entirely beneficial. It is cleaner, healthier, due to the non-retention of urine under the foreskin and it can ultimately prevent the risk of cancer. In the woman, it is exactly the opposite.'

"Smiling, Dr Fahim went on to elude the other benefits of male circumcision...which Jewish men and women alike can enjoy.'Therefore,' he continued, 'I prefer to call it male genital beautification.'"

On 19ᵗʰ June 2014, I attended the "Religious Declaration on FGM" at the Ministerial Conference Room at the Home Office, London. I signed, with other Religions Leaders, the following Declaration:
"We, the signatories recognise that:

"Female Genital Mutilation, in all its types, is a great violation of the rights of girls and women.

"Female Genital Mutilation is child abuse and a violation of the child's bodily integrity as well as their right to health.

"Female Genital Mutilation can have serious consequences for a woman's health and in some instances can lead to death.

"Female Genital Mutilation is not a religious requirement. Causing harm and distress is not condoned by our faith."

I took part in the making of several applications and films on social media. **"Let's Talk FGM"** is one of the iPad and website applications produced by NHS Oxford Health, designed to facilitate discussions about FGM between health professionals and the people they serve. A great amount of professional work went into it. I mentioned in this application that there is not a single Prophetic Tradition to confirm that Prophet Mohammed (pbuh) had carried out any form of circumcision on any of his daughters or granddaughters. So, let those who claim to be practicing Islam by hurting young women and girls, stop doing that and follow the example of the Prophet Mohammed (pbuh).

I also became the Religious Adviser to **"Desert Flower Foundation UK".** Waris Dirie is the President of the Foundation. She, being a sufferer herself, led a very vigorous campaign against FGM. Her books **"Desert Flower"** and **"Desert Children"** are great inspirations.

3.4 A Critical Analysis of the Debate Between Traditionalists and Feminist Muslims Regarding the (re-) Interpretation of Islamic Sources:

In my quest to empower women, I share below the essay I wrote when I was studying Islam, Judaism, and Muslim-Jewish Relations at The Woolf Institute, Cambridge University, in the academic year 2007/08:

A) Introduction

This essay provides a critical analysis of the debate between 'traditionalist' and 'feminist' Muslims regarding the [re-] interpretation of Islamic sources.

I shall first examine how a selection of classical traditionalists have interpreted some of the so called 'problematic' Qur'anic verses in reference to women and will thereafter analyse how feminists like Wadud and Barlas differ in their interpretations. The verses in question are: (4:34), (2:282), (4:11) and (4:3). For the purposes of this discussion, I have taken the exegetical works of Ibn-Kathir, Al-Nasafi, Al-Sha'rawi and Al-Jalalayn to be representatives of the 'traditionalist' thought.

In the following sections I shall explain how the traditionalists and feminist have defined the words – "qawwamun" (in charge of women), "faddala" (favoured above women) and "idribuhunna" (beat women), (4:34). I shall also discuss women's testimony (2:282), polygyny (4:3) and women's share of inheritance (4:11).

B) Is Man Superior Over Woman?

In reference to *qawwamun*, Ibn-Kathir states that 'the man is responsible for the woman, and he is her maintainer, caretaker and leader who disciplines her if she deviates'. As for *faddala* he states "men excel over women and are better than them for certain tasks. This is why prophethood was exclusive for men. The Prophet (pbuh) said people who appoint a woman to be their leader would never prosper". Al-Jalalayn regards *qawwamun* to be synonymous with 'musallatun' that is men have absolute power over women; they discipline them forcibly to correct them. According to Al-Jalalayn, the word *faddala* in this context refers to the man's superior intellectual capacity as God has favoured men with knowledge, wisdom (and therefore, the capacity) to be in charge.

Al-Nasafi on the other hand, whilst affirming the traditionalist stance that *qawwamun* refers to man's superiority over women, seems to dilute the absolutist facet of this superiority by stating that this power is to be used by men to command women to do good and forbid them from evil. In defining *faddala*, Al-Nasafi states: "men are dominating and have supremacy over women because Allah has given men more wisdom, determination, physical strength, ability to fight in battles, perfection in fasts, prayers, prophethood, leading prayers…". Again, Al-Nasafi seems to justify the reason for man's authority over women by furnishing a number of circumstances which exemplify man's greater capacity to lead and carry out tasks which under Islamic law, which women have not been required to undertake.

According to Ibn-Kathir, idribuhunna means: "if advice and ignoring her in bed do not produce the desired results – you are allowed to discipline the wife without severe beatings subject to what the prophet stipulates. In a hadith reported by Abu-Dawud, Al-Nasir, Ibn-Majah and Ahmad when he was asked about the rights of the wife, he said: 'To feed her when you eat, clothe her when you buy clothes for yourself, refrain from striking her face or cursing her…" Ibn-Kathir further refers to a hadith in Muslim (8:886) which was delivered by the Prophet (pbuh) in Arafat on the farewell Hajj wherein he clearly defines the only circumstance in which a husband is permitted to strike his wife – "fear Allah regarding women for they are confined to you, you have the right on them that they do not allow any person whom you dislike to sit on your bed; however if they do that, you are allowed to strike them lightly".

Both Al-Jalalayn and Al-Nasafi on the other hand simply refer to a literal definition of idribuhunna and both state it means "striking without (excruciating) pain/violence/intensity".

It is also worth referring to some modern interpretations in order to observe the transition that has taken place in the genre of Qur'an interpretation throughout Islam's history.

Abdullah Yusuf Ali translates Qur'an (4:34) as, *"(Husbands) are (qawwamun) the protectors and maintainers of their (wives) because Allah has given the one more (strength) than the other, and because they support them from their means… As to those women on whose part you fear disloyalty and ill-conduct, admonish them (first), (next), refuse to share their beds, (and last), (idribuhunna) beat them (lightly)"*.

He further states that *qawwamun* is "one who stands firm in another's business, protects his interests and looks after his affairs". He says that "if verbal advice or suspension of sex relations are not sufficient, then some slight physical correction may be administered; but Imam Al-Shafi'i, considers this inadvisable though permissible and all authorities are unanimous in deprecating any sort of cruelty even of the nagging kind".

Al-Sha'rawi says, regarding verse 4:34, *"some commentators limited the meaning to husband and wife in spite of the fact that it talks about men and women in general – therefore the verse is not limited to the man and his wife. The father is responsible for his daughters as the brothers for his sisters. Qawwam is the emphatic verbal participle and is therefore a person who is tirelessly stands up to look after the people he is responsible for; therefore the verse is not meant to oppress women – rather it means that men should struggle to support women, protect them and provide for them"*.

As for idribuhunna, Al-Shar'rawi states that "striking is conditional upon never causing bleeding or breaking a bone – only to display disgust – consequently scholars have since authorized the use of a toothbrush".

In sum, Muslim women have been offended by the interpretation of the traditionalists. One can therefore appreciate the comments made by Muslim feminist Fatima Mirnisi, "A hadith in Al-Bukhari which was narrated to me by my teachers when I was a little girl, hurt me – it quotes the Prophet (pbuh) states that 'dog, donkey and woman could annul man's prayer whenever they pass between him and kiblah.' I was shocked to hear that sort of hadith and never repeated it with the hope that silence would wipe it out of my mind. I asked, how the beloved Prophet (pbuh) could relate a hadith which hurt a little girl so much". This lead feminists such a Wadud and Barlas to regard the above verses as problematic for which reason they attempted to yield a new interpretation in order to eliminate the fear from the minds of women.

Kassam refers to Wadud's work entitled Qur'an and Women, who in her attempt to recover an egalitarian voice for women, took her lead from the University of Chicago scholar Fazlur-Rahman, who suggests that 'All Qur'anic passages, revealed as they were in a specific time in history and within certain general and particular circumstances, were given expression relative to those circumstances.' This is in contradiction with views shared by male Muslims Scholars of the classical era, who regard the Qur'an to be a sacred text and eternally valid for all time.

Wadud, who relies upon her linguistic analysis of the Arabic language, tried to assign new meanings to a number of Qur'anic verses which she regards as problematic – namely the verses which have traditionally been read to justify man's superiority over women. Kassam states that Wadud says that "some male interpreters of the Qur'an have claimed that men are preferred by God over women with respect to intelligence, physical constitution, determination and physical strengths without ever citing any place in the Qur'an text that says this (p. 35)". Moreover, Wadud isolates two terms that have been used by male commentators to signify the inherent superiority of male over females. The first is daraja (Q 2:228), meaning, 'to prefer', usually 'over something else'. She concludes that the context of the verse 2:228 is clearly the issue of divorce, whereby the use of *daraja* relates to the fact that men are indeed ranked above women only in their ability to divorce their wives without third party intervention, whilst women have to rely on a judge to divorce them. In the same vein, she also interprets *faddala* in Q 4:34 to mean that men have an economic responsibility for women, not that men are superior to women because of their physical strength or ability to reason, which is how classical traditionalists have understood this verse.

Turning our attention to another feminist – Barlas in her study, *Believing Women' in Islam*: Unreading Patriarchal Interpretations of the Qur'an; she analyses the Qur'an's outlook on the role and rights of mothers, fathers, wives and husbands. She claims that the Qur'an repudiates the concept of 'father-right/ruler' and makes similar criticism of a husband's privileges over his wife.

According to Kassam, Wadud interprets idribuhunna in verse 4:34 as scourge, which is from the verbal root *daraba*. Meaning 'to hit' or 'to strike'. Wadud suggests, however, that it includes in its lexical field the meaning – 'to give or set an example', and is further contrasted with its intensive form, *darraba*, which means 'to strike repeatedly or intensely'. Since the less intensive form is used, Wadud reads the use of the term *idribu* from *daraba* not as permission, but a severe restriction of existing practices.

Barlas also states that *daraba* means 'to set an example' and refers to other interpretations such as 'forsaking' or 'preventing women from going outside their homes'. Like Wadud, her interpretation clearly opposes the traditional interpretation, which permits men to strike their wives.

Both choose not to concede that 'idribuhunna' refers to one of the stages whereby a wife is disciplined. Instead they both remove *idribuhunna* out of its context to eliminate any connotations that this was indeed meant to be a sanctioned form of discipline. The Prophet (pbuh) during his farewell Hajj, clearly limited the option of striking to the circumstances of infidelity. Thereby implicitly disallowing this verse to justify disciplining one's wife at any time the husband sees fit. Then one could argue that this 'discipline' serves a purpose as this may in turn avoid a marriage termination.

C) Polygyny – Is It Man's Right?

Concerning polygyny, Barlas, in her interpretation of Q 4:3, points out that this verse has a very specific purpose; that of securing justice for female orphans – an option shared by Wadud. Both writers contradict traditionalists views that polygyny is one of women's rights as a woman may choose to marry a married man and be treated equally. Blame and repudiation seems to be assigned solely to men who engage in such marriages – not the woman who accepts to marry a married man.

D) Women's Testimony

Another controversial aspect in regarding women's testimony. Verse 2:282 states "...*And get two witnesses, out of your own men and if there are not two men, then a man and two women, such as you accept (competent), for witnesses, so that if one of them errs, the other can remind her...*"

In interpreting the above verse, Ibn-Kathir states, "...*this requirement is only for contracts, that directly or in-directly involve money. Allah requires that two women take the place of man as witness, because of the woman's shortcomings as the prophet describe*". He then goes on to quote a hadith from Muslim (1:87) confirming that the Prophet (pbuh) stated that women have shortcomings in mind and religion. Other traditionalists share this view.

Wadud on the other hand, in her analysis of the above verse, claims "this practice was based on a woman's relative unfamiliarity at the time with financial matters – a circumstance that has now changed. So, the verse should, by extension, never have been universally applied to make two women's legal testimony bear the weight of one man's".

Wadud, like most traditionalists, has understood the word *tadhel* in verse 2:282 to mean 'forget'. An alternative explanation of *tadhel* could mean to deny the transaction by giving false testimony, not to mentally forget it, due to social pressure or blackmail from male relations. A woman may be rendered an easier victim as opposed to a man, upon whom such pressures would be more difficult to exert. In such a circumstance, the second woman would therefore be called in to admonish (tozakker) the first woman, not to mend the shortcoming of the first woman's forgetfulness. Verse 2:283 confirms this, *"And conceal not the evidence, for he who hides it, surely, his heart is sinful"*.

E) Women's Share of Inheritance

In this section the following verses from the Qur'an and prophetic traditions regarding the law of inheritance in Islam, will be critically analysed.

"From what is left by parents and those nearest related there is a share for men and a share for women, whether the property be small or large, a determinate share. But if at the time of division other relatives, or orphans, or poor, are present, give them out of the (estate), and speak to them words of kindness and justice." 4:7-8

"…Here the general principles are laid down that females inherit as well as males, and that relatives who have no legal shares, orphans, and indigent people are not to be treated harshly, if present at the division." FN514. This is a recommendation from God to share the inheritance with those who have no legal right to inherit.

And in 4:11-14, God specifies the shares, *"God directs you as regards your children's (inheritance); to the male, a portion equal to that of two females; if only daughters, two or more, their share is two-thirds of the inheritance; if only one, her share is a half. For parents a sixth share of the inheritance to each if the deceased left children; if no children, and the parents are the (only) heirs, the mother has a third; if the deceased left brothers (or sisters), the mother has a sixth. (The distribution in all cases is) after the payment of legacies and debts. You do not know whether your parents or your children are nearest to you in benefit. These are settled portions ordained by God; and God is All-Knowing, All-Wise. In what your wives leave, your share is a half, if they leave no child; but if they leave a child, you get a fourth; after payment of legacies and debts. In what you leave; their share is a fourth, if you leave no child; but if you leave a child, they get an eighth; after payment of legacies and debts. If the man or woman whose inheritance is in question, has left neither ascendants nor descendants, but has left a brother or a sister, each one of the two, gets a sixth; but if more than two they share in a third; after payment of legacies and debts; so no loss is caused (to anyone). This is a commandment from God and God is All-Knowing, Most Forbearing. Those are limits set by God. Those who obey God and His Messenger will be admitted to Gardens with rivers flowing beneath, to abide therein eternally and that will be the Supreme achievement. But those who disobey God and His Messenger and transgress His limits will be admitted to a Fire to abide therein eternally; and they shall have a humiliating punishment."*

"The principles of inheritance law are laid down in broad outline in the Qur'an; the precise details have been worked out on the basis of the Prophet's (pbuh) practice and that of his Companions, and by interpretation and analogy. Muslim jurists have collected a vast amount of learning on this subject, and this body of law is enough by itself to form the subject of life-long study. Here we shall deal only with the broad principles to be gathered from the Text, as

interpreted by the jurists. (1) The power of testamentary disposition extends over only one-third of the Property; the remaining two-thirds are distributed among heirs as laid down. (2) All distribution takes place after the legacies and debts (including funeral expenses) have first been paid. (3) Legacies cannot be left to any of the heirs included in the scheme of distribution; or it will amount to upsetting the shares and undue preference of one heir to another. (4) Generally, but not always, the male takes a share double that of a female in his own category." FN516

All the traditionalists are in agreement with the above explanation in FN516.

In verse 1:180, God commands that parents and relatives are to be included in the will, *"It is prescribed for you, when death approaches any of you, if he leaves wealth, that he makes a bequest to parents and next of kin, according to reasonable manners. (This is) a duty upon those who fear God."* This verse contains the command to include parents and relatives in the will, which was obligatory, according to the most correct view, before verses 4:11-14 about the inheritance were revealed. Hence verse 1:180 was **abrogated**, so fixed shares of the inheritance for deserving recipients were legislated by God. Therefore, deserving inheritors take their fixed inheritance without the need to be included in the will or to be reminded of the favour of the inherited person.

God states in 4:34 that it is the responsibility of the man to financially support his family, *"Men are the protectors and maintainers of women, because God has given the one more (strength) than the other, and because they support them from their means..."* Thus, a son is entitled to get double the share of his sister because the burden of supporting his family falls on his shoulders. The sister may have a husband who is responsible to financially support her, hence she does not have to spend anything out of her share of the inheritance. It is highly recommended to leave a will as stated by the Prophet Mohammed (pbuh) in a Hadith in Al-Bukhari and Muslim, *"It is not permissible for any Muslim who has something to will to stay for two nights without having his last will and testament written and kept ready with him."*

As stated above, traditionalists agree regarding verses 4:11-14, that if the deceased does not leave a will then the estate will be distributed as mentioned in theses verses. But if he leaves a will, it should not include anyone who is already entitled to inherit. And also not to be more than one-third of the total legacy. This is based on a Hadith narrated in Sunnan Abu-Dawood and others that the Prophet (pbuh) said, *"God has given each heir his fixed share. **So there is no will for a deserving heir.**"* However, the will can include relatives that do not qualify as inheritors, or any other recipients, to bequeath up to a maximum of one third. The third to be bequeathed, is mentioned in a Hadith recorded in Al-Bukhari and Muslim that when one of the Prophet's companions Sa'd bin Abi-Waqqas told the Prophet (pbuh) that he is leaving his estate to others, the Prophet (pbuh) put an upper limit on that by saying,*"...Yes, one-third, yet even one-third is too much. It is better to leave your inheritors wealthy than to leave them poor, begging from others."* Al-Bukhari mentioned in his book that Ibn Abbas said, *"I recommend that people reduce the proportion of what they bequeath by will to a fourth (of the whole legacy) rather than a third, for God's Messenger said: 'One-third, yet even one-third is too much.'"*

In the following example I will explain some of the inheritance rules mentioned in verses 4:11-14 to make it clearer. A man has one wife, one son, two daughters, parents, one sister and one brother. The man did not leave a will. His estate will be distributed as follows, once all debts have been paid: His wife gets an eighth, each one of his parents gets a sixth (man's share here is equal to a woman's share), the rest will be divided among the three children, the boy gets double the share of a sister. The deceased's sister and brother do not inherit from him because he has a son.

If the man left a will and bequeathed that an amount goes to his sister and brother, equally, (here we have an equal share for the brother and the sister), then this amount must be paid firstly, and the balance to be distributed as explained above. Scholars insist that it should not be more than one third of the entire estate as confirmed in the Hadith mentioned earlier.

Contemporary scholars argue that in the same way as verses 4:11-14 **abrogated** verse 1:180, these verses have also abrogated the Hadith that says that there is no will for a deserving heir. They continue to say that the will is mentioned three times in these verses, which are regarded as final command from God concerning inheritance. So everyone has the choice either not to leave a will, although it is highly recommended in the Hadith mentioned above, and the estate will be distributed in accordance with the shares mentioned in 4:11-14, or to leave a will and change the allocations based on the personal circumstances. For example, if a man has a daughter who has special needs, he may bequeath more to her than to her healthy siblings. Or he may give his wife more than her designated share of one-eighth if he feels that none of his children will look after her once he has gone. One opinion claims that those who are entitled to inherit must agree to any extra allocations to those among them who are allocated more than what God has commanded. So the children must agree that their mother would inherit more than one-eighth. I remember when my wife and I were re-writing our wills, we asked our son if he is agreeable that he takes the same share like his sisters. He said yes. So each one of my three children (one son and two daughters) will get a third each of my estate.

Concerning inheritance, Wadud disagrees with the statement in verse 4:11, "... *to the male, a portion equal to that of two females...*" Here, her knowledge of inheritance law may be questioned because in her commentary she ignores the fact that a father and a mother can inherit equal shares, should their son pass away.

On the other hand, traditionalists unanimously agree among themselves that this is God's Law, and no one can change it. They refer to verse 4:13 wherein people are explicitly reminded not to transgress boundaries set by God. The Qur'an defines the general rules and sets clear boundaries within which every individual is required to examine his/her family circumstances and through mutual consultation, distributes wealth without violating the limits set by God. It could be argued that if men and women should have equal shares of inheritance, then women should discharge men from all their financial responsibilities towards them.

F) Conclusion

In conclusion, we can see from the above discussion that the hermeneutics of certain verses in the Qur'an by some male traditionalists have offended women. Thus, giving the impression that the Qur'an is a misogynistic text. This has led some feminists to strive to find new meanings to problematic gender verses causing them at times to take a radical view of Islam whilst ignoring some of its main teachings.

3.5 Confused Terminology: Is it Hejab or Khimar? Is God wrong? Should women veil their faces?

I give below my lengthy response to a Muslim woman who claimed that the Niqab (face cover - veil) is a religious obligation on all Muslim women as they must all emulate the wives of the Prophet Mohammed pbuh, she claims.

"My dear sister in Islam

May God's Peace, Mercy and Blessings be upon you.

Following the creation of Adam, Allah taught him the names of all things. Adam even excelled the angels by what God taught him. This shows us the importance of education and knowledge. (2:31-33).

The first revelation which came to the Prophet Mohammed pbuh, commanded him to read and write. (96:1-5).

According to UN statistics, unfortunately, over 65% of the Muslim world can neither read nor write. The majority of the Arabs cannot even read the Qur'an and if they read it they don't understand it. What a disaster!

One of the major weaknesses prevalent in the Muslims of today, is that they do not know how to discuss or debate or disagree with the other. It is either my way, or the highway!!!

To claim that women should cover their faces to emulate the wives of the Prophet pbuh, is absolute nonsense. In fact, the wives of the Prophet pbuh were not asked to cover their faces. They were asked to screen themselves completely from men whom they are not allowed to mix with, 33:53. And anyway by simply covering your face you will never be like the wives of the Prophet pbuh, neither in their knowledge, conduct, nor their righteousness.

The majority of the women who wear a Niqab don't cover their eyes. So having such a face cover you still can see men and gaze at them and they can see your eyes and communicate with you through them. So a face cover is not like a Hejab which fully obscures any vision.

God does not judge us by our looks or our wealth, He judges us by our conduct and what is in our hearts, as reported by Muslim. He forgave a prostitute who gave a drink to a thirsty dog! (Al-Bukhari)

We must all make an effort to understand the Qur'an in Arabic.

Do you understand the meanings of the following words in Arabic? Hejab, Khimar, Gilbab and Niqab?

Where are the first three words mentioned in the Qur'an? And what do they mean? Please go and find out, you will learn a lot.

In verse 33:53, the word Hejab حجاب was mentioned in relation to the wives of the prophet only, not to any other women, "....and when you ask (his wives) for anything you want, ask them from behind a screen (حجاب), that makes for greater purity for your hearts and for theirs ....."
Following this revelation a screen was placed between the wives of the Prophet pbuh and the public. Neither these strange men can see the Prophet's wives nor can the wives see them, for the purity of both hearts as stated in the verse.
This is the meaning of Hejab حجاب in this verse: I can't see you and you can't see me, but we can hear each other.

So the word Hejab never meant a face cover (Niqab) and never meant a head cover (Khimar) for a woman.

The word Hejab is mentioned in the Qur'an in eight chapters: 7:46, 17:45, 19:17, 33:53, 38:32, 41:5, 42:51 and 83:15. Every time it is referred to, it reflects the same meaning of a screen or a curtain or a partition.

The word Khimar (a head cover) is mentioned only in verse 24:31: "And tell the believing women to lower their gaze and preserve their chastity, and to display of their adornments only that is apparent, and to draw their head-coverings (Khimar) over their bosoms..."
The message here clearly states that women should cover their cleavage with the Khimar they have on their heads. It doesn't say cover your hair and your cleavage.
Unfortunately, there are women who use their cleavage to get ahead in life. So if a woman is not wearing a head scarf, or a short head cover, she must still cover her cleavage by wearing a top which would do that.

God never referred to the head cover of a woman in the Qur'an as Hejab, He called it Khimar. In fact, it is a form of blasphemy to change the word of God and call the head cover Hejab. Who should be blamed for this? Is God wrong and needed someone to correct Him?! It is the radical men who wanted to continue to imprison the women, after they have been liberated by the Prophet pbuh, by imposing on them the word Hijab which suggests isolation and segregation against women.

In 4:46, 5:13 and 5:41, God condemns those from among the Children of Israel who changed words in the Torah from their context and distorted their meaning. This is a deterrent to the Muslims, however some Muslims did the same.

The word Gilbab جلباب is mentioned in 33:59, "O Prophet! Tell your wives, your daughters, and the believing women, that they should cast their Gilbab (outer garments) over their persons (when out of door); that will be better so that they may be recognised (as chaste) and not molested. And God is Oft-Forgiving, Most Merciful."

"This is for all Muslim women, those of the Prophet's household, as well as the others. They were asked to cover themselves with outer garments when walking out of doors. Gilbab, plural Galabib: an outer garment; a long gown covering the whole body, or a cloak covering the neck and bosom. The object was not to restrict the liberty of women, but to protect them from harm and molestation. In the East and in the West a distinctive public dress of some sort or another has always been a badge of honour or distinction, both among men and women. This can be traced back on the earliest civilisations. Assyrian Law in its palmiest days (say, 7th century B.C.), enjoined the veiling of married women and forbade the veiling of slaves and women of ill fame: see Cambridge Ancient History, III.107." FN3764-3766

Going back to the wives of the Prophet pbuh, God confirms in 33:27-34, that they are not like any of the other women. Please read these verses and make an effort to understand them.

The Prophet's wives had a completely different code of conduct, their punishment was doubled 33:30, and their reward was doubled 33:31. They are commanded to stay at their homes: وقرن في بيوتكن
"And stay quietly at your homes, and make not a dazzling display, like that of the former times of ignorance ..." 33:33.

If you want to be like the Prophet's wives stay at home!!!
Don't go out at all.
Don't drive a car.
Don't use public transport.
Don't go to work.
And when you cover your face, you must make sure you can't see any man, this is the meaning of حجاب Hejab as described above.
Is this convenient? Does this make sense? Is this a practical religion?
God commands women to be modest in the way they dress, the way they walk, the way they talk and the way they conduct themselves.

In verse 33:34, the wives of the Prophet pbuh, were commanded to teach the public what was rehearsed to them in their homes by the Prophet pbuh, of the revelations of God and (words of wisdom). Can you emulate them in this and benefit humanity? It is hard work, is it not? Not as easy as covering the face!

The wives of the Prophet were not allowed to marry after his death (33:53). Why are you allowed to marry if your husband divorces you or dies? Because your husband is not the Prophet and you are not a wife of the Prophet.

There is an authentic Hadith in Al-Bukhary no. 1838, where the Prophet pbuh commands women not to cover their faces or wear gloves during the state of Ihram when they are performing Hajj or Umra. Millions of women go for Hajj and Umra every year and they mix with foreign men while performing their rituals, especially in the very crowded Tawaf (going round the Kaba). If the face of a woman is "Awra", something which should not be seen, how can the Prophet pbuh command women to show it in public?

Contemporary Scholars like Abu-Shuqqa, Al-Ghazaly, Shaltoot, Al-Sharawy, Al-Qaradawy, Ali Gomaa and Saqr, after they critically analysed and examined the evidences of those who support the Niqab, concluded that their evidence is not sound as it is based on weak Hadith and wrong interpretation and no ruling can be derived based on weak Hadith. They concluded that the Niqab is not a religious obligation. However, if there are others who believe it is, it is their choice.

That is why I'm suggesting if you could kindly read their work to answer your question. Please start with the link I sent you regarding Al-Qaradawy.

In his book Current & Modern Fatwas, 2nd Volume, page 312, the question he addressed was: Is the Niqab compulsory? He fully examined the claims of both parties, those who are against it and those who are for it. He stated that the claims of those who are for it (and they are a minority, as he says) are not sound and not founded and not reliable.

I also sent you an article by Justice Qazi Faez Isa, Judge at the Supreme Court of Pakistan, in response to a resolution requiring that wearing a veil should be made compulsory for every girl above 12 years of age. It might help you to understand the ruling of Niqab in Islam. He started his article by saying: "If God directs women to veil their faces, then Muslims have no option but to abide by this command. But if on the other hand our Benevolent Creator has not imposed any such injunction, no man can impose it. An attempt to add to the commands of God Everlasting is an abomination and completely unacceptable in Islam. No matter how well intentioned a man may be such desire can't be substituted for God's law and it is not permissible to diverge from the truth."
He ended his research by saying: "Those who want to blacken the faces of women and reduce them to mere objects must remember that God the Omnipotent directs believing men to lower their gaze (24:30). If women were veiled there would be no need for men to lower their gaze. The Commandment to lowering one's gaze is often brazenly flouted. Would it then not be more appropriate to legislate for affixing blinkers on men's eyes, like those on a mule or donkey, rather than having the effrontery to put rags on the faces of 12-year old-girls?."

The scholars I referred to above have listed many authentic Hadith and many sound interpretations of the Qur'an, proving that women were not covering their faces at the time of the Message whether before the revelation of chapter 24 (Al-Noor) and chapter 33 (Al-Ahzab) or after. Please study what Sheikh Mohammed Al-Albany wrote in his book Ar-Rad al-Mufhim

Verse 33:52 reads: "It is not lawful for you (Mohammed) to marry more women after this, nor to change them for (other) wives, even though their beauty attracts you..." How can their beauty attract him (pbuh) if the face is covered?

There is a Hadith in Muslim, Ahmad and Al-Tabarani, that the Prophet pbuh went out and saw a woman who sexually aroused him and came home and slept with one of his wives. He

said to his companions if this happens to any of you, then approach your wives. So if the women were veiled, how could this have affected the Prophet pbuh?
I personally refuse to accept this Hadith even if it is classified as Sound. Why? Because it contradicts with the sublime nature of the Prophet pbuh. He was Qur'an walking on earth. He was the leader of the righteous. How can he go out gazing at women to the extent that he would be sexually aroused?

The Niqab existed before Islam, it was the tradition or the custom of some women to wear it. Those who decided to wear it after Islam were not asked to remove it except in state of Ihram, this also includes while saying their five daily prayers. But it was never promoted nor forced upon other women during the time of the Prophet pbuh.

If I live in a country such as Saudi Arabia, where sexually frustrated men gaze at and devour each woman they see, I would ask my wife to cover her face even if she is so ugly. Not because it is a religious obligation, but because these awful men are invading my privacy and not lowering their gaze as commanded by God in 24:30.

Look at how many women are performing Hajj every year and in compliance with the command of the Prophet pbuh they don't cover their faces or wear gloves during Ihram. Are they committing a punishable sin by showing their faces in the most Holy site whilst performing their Hajj?

I hope it is clear from the above that the covering of the face of a Muslim woman is not a religious requirement.
The wives of the Prophet had completely different status and were subject to different rules and regulations and they have never been commanded to cover their faces but to screen themselves from strange men.

A Muslim woman must be modest in the way she is dressed, the way she conducts herself, the way she walks and the way she talks. She should never be in a closed place with strange man (non Mahram) on their own.
She must seek knowledge and be educated and seek lawful employment to help herself, her family, her community and the world she lives in.

If you are convinced that the Niqab is a religious obligation, it is entirely your choice and I'm not asking you to remove it. However, if you are living in the West you have to comply with the dress code of the country you live in as long as you are dressed modestly.

May God guide us all to His Straight Path, increase our knowledge, forgive our sins and admit us all to His Gardens of Bliss. Amen"

The following is the final response I received from her:

"Thank you for your time. I have understood and decided even more clearly now Alhamdulellah from all the correspondence from yourself about the issue of face veil. Thank you.

I'm spiritually and intellectually more confident that what you promote about the face veil is wrong. And that it is in actual fact promoted by Islam as either highly recommended or obligatory.

Now I part with my opinion and you with yours and you will never have the right to deny me and others our opinion even if you post it on your webpage.

I ask Allah to keep us steadfast upon His deen and to remove every misguided leader amongst us and to replace them with those upon the haqq Ameen.

Please do not send me any further information on this issue."

The attitude of this woman and her supporters is very similar to those confused young women who fled the UK and joined terrorist groups like ISIS in Syria and Iraq. They brought damnation on themselves and painted Islam as a religion of violence and terror.

3.6 Conclusion

The Prophet Mohammed (pbuh) brought a radical change to his community and in doing so he upturned the status quo at the time, upsetting many influential people.

He enforced the "Family Law" which God revealed to him. He introduced rights to women, which women in the West are still fighting to acquire. Women must fight for their rights, which were given to them by God, but denied by men.

Women should not feel shy or embarrassed to learn about their religion. Aisha, the wife of the Prophet (pbuh) said, "*I really admire the women of Madina for the way they sought knowledge. Their sense of reserve (Haiaa) did not prevent them from learning*". It was the wives of the Prophet (pbuh) who taught religion to men as commanded by God in 33:34, "*And recite what is rehearsed to you in your homes, of the Signs of God and His Words of Wisdom, for God understands the finest mysteries and is well acquainted (with them)*"

The concept of honour existed at the times of ignorance before Islam. The Prophet (pbuh) preached a radically different idea of honour in the sight of God. God does not look at our race or tribes or images or our wealth, but He looks at our hearts and our deeds. Consequently, the most honoured in the sight of God is the most righteous.

FGM is not a practice that is endorsed by God or his final Messenger Prophet Mohammed (pbuh)

Because procreation is necessary for human survival, marriage is encouraged in Islam, though it is not made compulsory. It is also through this institution that the rights of women, both as wives and mothers, can be safeguarded. Marriage in Islam guarantees social stability and a dignified existence for both a woman and a man. Marriage in Islam is not merely a sexual urge which brings a woman and a man together; it has a higher end, an exalted motive, and is a relationship of love and mutual respect.

The institution of marriage as developed from the traditions of the Prophet (pbuh) is one in which a woman freely chooses her husband, having the right to conduct her own marriage as stated by Imam Abu-Hanefa and add any lawful conditions to her Islamic marriage contract. The idea of forced marriages is alien to Islam.

The Prophet (pbuh) was never violent towards his wives and daughters. God commanded believing men to treat women with kindness even in potentially fraught circumstances like divorce. Unfortunately, there are Imams in the UK who endorse violence and argue that the Qur'an allows men to beat unfaithful wives. Any Imam who does this should be deported or jailed for supporting violence against women.

In Islam women have equal rights with men, under God's universal Moral Law.

God says in 4:124, "*Whoever does righteous deeds, male or female, and is a (true) believer, such will enter paradise, and not the least injustice will be done to them.*"

And He says in 16:97, "*Whoever does righteous deeds, whether male or female, whilst being a (true) believer, We will make them live a gracious life and grant them their reward (in the Hereafter) for the best of what they used to do.*"

So righteous men and women, are promised by God, to enjoy a good and pure life in this world and a great reward awaits them in the Hereafter.

God says in 33:35, "*For Muslim men and women, for believing men and women, for devout men and women, for true men and women, for men and women who are patient and constant, for men and women who humble themselves, for men and women who give in charity, for men and women who fast, for men and women who guard their chastity, and for men and women who engage much in God's remembrance, for them God has prepared forgiveness and a great reward.*"

"*A number of Muslim virtues are specified here, but the chief stress is laid on the fact that these virtues are as necessary to women, as to men. Both sexes have a spiritual as well as human rights and duties in an equal degree, and the future reward of the Hereafter.*" FN3719

God informs us in 4:1 that men and women have been created from a single being, and hence they enjoy equal status.

The Qur'an gives equal rights to both sexes, and it does not discriminate between them in respect to personal, democratic and human rights.

Therefore, women must fight for their rights which are clearly extolled and stipulated within the Qur'an and Hadith. Do not blame Islam, blame the men who highjacked women's rights.

136

PART II - DECLINE OF MUSLIM NATIONS

Chapter 1 -The Four Jewels of Nations' Prosperity

1.1 Introduction

The question that arises time and time again is that, if Islam is such a great religion, why are Muslim countries in a big mess? Indeed why do Muslims travel to non-Muslim countries to seek employment or medical advice or education? Why do they invest in these countries? Why are there always unending queues in front of the embassies of non-Muslim countries? Why do Muslims perilously sail the oceans in a rubber boat, braving the waves and risking their lives to reach the shores of a non-Muslim country? Finally, why do Muslims decide to emigrate to these countries (in more conventional and safe ways) and rejoice when they attain a foreign nationality?

Do you know what the answer is?

The answer to these and many more similar questions is quite simple and obvious. It is because all purported Muslim governments and the majority of Muslims worldwide are non-Qur'an compliant. They do not follow or adhere to the teachings of the Qur'an in their daily practices and dealings.

God informs us in 25:30 that His Messenger Mohammed (pbuh) will say, *"O my Lord, Truly my people treated this Qur'an with neglect."*

Whether *"my people"* refers to his tribe, or his followers, it is equal as they all took the Qur'an for just foolish nonsense.

In 47:24, God questions those who do not make an effort to study and implement the Qur'an, *"Do they not then earnestly seek to understand the Qur'an, or are there locks on the hearts?"*

In 19:59-69, we are told that the latter generations have ruined worship and have followed lusts and they will meet perdition, *"But after them there followed a posterity who missed prayers and followed after lusts. Soon, then, they will face destruction. Except those who repent and believe, and work righteousness. These will enter the Garden and they will not be wronged in the least."*

God says in 10:13-14, *"We destroyed generations before you when they did wrong. Their Messengers came to them with Clear Signs, but they would not believe. Thus We do requite those who sin. Then We made you heirs in the land after them, to see how would you behave."*

If we betray God's trust and guidance given to us through the Qur'an, then we are doomed to be lost and remain unguided and destroyed. This happened to the Abbasi Empire in the time of Harun-ar-Rashid and the Muslim Empire in Spain and the Turkish Empire in its palmiest days, and indeed, to the Muslims and non-Muslims of our own days.

Unfortunately, in Muslim countries there is often overt and accepted, corruption, nepotism, injustice and human rights violations, which have become the norm. These corrupt practices having seeped into organisational and power structures over generations and perpetuated over time.

God says in 30:41, *"Corruption, (evil and mischief) are spreading (becoming the norm) in the land and the sea because of the evil which the hands of people have earned, so that He (God) may make them taste some part of the evil they have done, in order that they may turn back (from evil)."*

A.Y.Aly says in FN3556, *"God's Creation is pure and good in itself. All the mischief or corruption was introduced by Evil, viz., arrogance, greed, selfishness, etc. As soon as the mischief has come in, God's Mercy and Goodness step in to stop it. The consequences of Evil must be evil, and this should be shown in such partial punishment as 'the hands of people have earned,' so that it may be a warning for the future and an invitation to enter the door of repentance."*

1.2 The Secular West

When Muslims, in the past, read the Qur'an, they understood it, sincerely applied it, and acted upon its Moral Law in all their dealings. Accordingly, they ruled their empires with knowledge and justice.

But what made the non-Muslim secular countries successful without having the Qur'an?

When the very famous Egyptian Scholar Imam Mohammed Abdu visited France in the late 19th Century, he said *"I found Muslims without Islam"* and when he returned to Egypt he said *"I found Islam without Muslims."*

The people in Europe impressed him with their discipline, manners, etiquettes, cleanliness, kindness and knowledge. They were not noisy. They did not litter the streets. They formed queues without supervision. They respected the traffic. They were extremely helpful and human in their dealings.

They were always on time. They loved everything green, they adored public parks and looked after them. They did not pluck flowers. They were so kind to the animals. They fulfilled their promises. They looked after the elderly and the young, and more and more good qualities which impressed him so much greatly.

In fact they followed God's Moral Law which they found in the Torah and the Gospel. Whilst the Muslims did not follow God's Moral Law in the Qur'an. As there is only One God, His Moral Teachings are the same.

The meaning of Islam is *"submission"*. That is to submit your will to the Will of God by obeying all his commands. Islam is the religion of unity and harmony. It is the religion of all God's Prophets and Messengers from Adam (pbuh) to Mohammed (pbuh) including but not limited to Noah, Abraham, Moses and Jesus (peace be upon them all).

1.3 Radical Muslim Teachers

A Turkish story...
What prompted Kamal Ataturk, the founder of modern Turkey, to create secularism in Turkey? The extremist Mullas (the religious teachers) who misinterpreted Islam, objected to any reforms he introduced, which they regarded as non-Islamic. They were crushed by him. He claimed that he did not need the Islam practiced and preached by these fanatics to modernise Turkey. He even changed the Turkish alphabet from Arabic to Roman and banned women from covering their heads. It was the misconception of Islam by these Mullas which made Kamal Ataturk denounce the religion and abandon the Qur'an.

A Saudi Story...
When the late King Faisal of Saudi Arabia introduced the education of women, he was fiercely opposed by radical religious teachers from the Wahhabi sect. But he just ignored them and went ahead with it.

An interesting article was published in the New York Times newspaper in December 1965, titled *"Faisal's Reform Effort Resisted by Some Saudis- Radio Is First Step in Moves Toward Modernisation."*

"A few months ago a delegation of religious leaders, teachers and judges appeared before Prince Faisal in Jeddah to protest the use of women's voices by the national radio network. In their views, this was shameful. After all had spoken, the Prince declared that he was as good

a student of the Islamic religion as anyone present and that he recalled that the Prophet Mohammed (pbuh) had delighted in recitals of a poetess named Al-Khamsa. 'So what is so shameful about women's voices now?' he asked. Then, to the consternation of the sheikhs, he announced that in a few months they would not only be hearing women's voices, but also would be seeing their faces on something called television."

These ignorant fanatics did not even understand the meaning of verse 33:34, which was addressed to the wives of the Prophet Mohammed (pbuh): *"And recite what is rehearsed to you in your homes, of the Signs of God (the verses of the Qur'an) and His Wisdom, for God is All-Subtle, All-Aware"*. In this verse God commands the wives of Prophet Mohammed (pbuh), to teach and make known and publish the Message which they learn at home from the holy Prophet Mohammed (pbuh), the fountain of spiritual knowledge.

A blind man's conviction...
The Grand Mufti, the Head of the Religious Opinions Committee of Saudi Arabia, who died in May 1999, was a blind man who insisted until his death, that the Earth, the planet we live on, is flat and does not move.

He misinterpreted several verses from the Qur'an to justify his ignorance. Even when he was told that the satellite images and the astronauts saw it as a sphere, he did not change his mind. In his response, he said, *"those who saw it are Kafer (non-believers) and we should not accept their testimony."* Unfortunately, many of his Fatwas (religious opinions) were so radical that it made the lives of many people so difficult.

In 1998, I was traveling from Madina in Saudi Arabia to Makkah by a private taxi. The driver was an officer with the National Guards. He entered into a conversation with me for four hours insisting that the earth is flat. He referred to the verses the Grand Mufti used. I explained the scientific meanings of these verses, and provided other verses which clearly state that the Earth is like a ball! But I totally failed in convincing him.

The misinterpretation of the teachings of Islam by these radicals, whether followers of Wahhabism in Saudi Arabia or Talibans in Afghanistan or Khomeini in Iran, has caused great injustice to women, and radicalised some young Muslims, men and women, causing some to turn to terrorism.

Islam, over 1400 years ago, has introduced rights to women, which women in the West are still struggling to reach. But these rights were denied to women in Muslim countries because of the militant and fanatic views of these ignorant Mullas.

We must understand that the Qur'an tells us how to live a pure and good life to prepare ourselves for the next life that is the 'Eternal Life' after death. This is not only mentioned in the Qur'an, but it was also mentioned in both the Old and the New Testaments. God says in 3:3-4, *"It is He (God) who sent down to you (Mohammed) in truth, the Book (Qur'an) confirming what went before it; and He sent down the Torah and the Gospel before this as a guide to mankind, and He sent down the Criterion (of judgement between right and wrong)*

(Qur'an). Certainly those who reject faith in the Signs of God will suffer the severest chastisement and God is Exalted in Might, Lord of Retribution."

And He says in 5:44, *"It was We who revealed the Torah (to Moses), therein was guidance and light..."*

In 5:46, God confirms, *"And in their footsteps We sent Jesus the son of Mary, confirming the Torah that has come before him, and We sent him the Gospel, therein was guidance and light..."*

But what about successful and prosperous Buddhist countries like China, Japan and South Korea? Whether Buddha was one of God's Prophets or not, they also had a Code of Conduct embedded in their culture and in their daily dealings.

1.4 My Japanese Encounter

I visited Japan in May 2016 for the first time. I was so impressed by everything I experienced during my stay. This ranged from the warmth of the welcome, the cleanliness and order of things and spaces and the respect that seemed afforded to all guests.

As I mentioned earlier, whether Buddha was one of God's Prophets or not, the Japanese had a Code of Conduct which was an integral part of their daily practices.

I will give below my feedback, from an Islamic perspective, regarding my visit.

A) No Tips Please, we are Japanese

The first evening we went out for a walk. We sat in a café and had a drink. We started to chat to a young Japanese man sitting next to us. He was extremely polite and knowledgeable. When we got the bill we left a tip. To our surprise he told us that giving tips in Japan is an insult as people are proud to serve. What!! Please tell the rest of the world especially Muslim countries and the Americans who pester you to tip them.

B) Welcome to Japan

The first Saturday in Tokyo we took the train to Tokyo station to visit the Imperial gardens and palace. When we got out of the station, we saw a tourist guide with a flag and few people with him. We asked him for directions to the palace. He said we can join him as he is going there and this is a free guided tour. What?!

Apparently he was a volunteer and he does this at the weekends. He is an IT professional. He was not the only one. There were so many other volunteers, men and women who do this job on regular basis. Their knowledge of the Japanese history and culture is amazing. One of the guide's first name was Isamu. I was very pleased to discover that I must have some Japanese blood in my genes as my middle name is Essam. Isamu in Japanese means brave. So, I'm only 80% brave!

We were so impressed by the magnificent landscape of the Japanese garden around the palace.
What an art! And what an effort to maintain it. The guide pointed out to us a huge area planted with tea shrubs.
I asked him if I can pluck a leaf. He said: *"Do it when I'm not looking!"*
I immediately felt embarrassed as my Japanese hosts, clearly were striving to tolerate people like me. I could not dare to pluck more than one tea leaf. It reminded me of our visit to the Holy site of Mount Sinai, in Egypt, where the Blessed burning bush is located. I felt so tempted to pluck several leaves.
I did not have any consideration that if everyone is plucking a leaf from this Holy tree it might soon run out of leaves. Whilst the Japanese guide was so concerned about one tea leaf from a huge plantation.

We were given 15 minutes break to use the facilities. The guide said: *"We are meeting here in 15 minutes. I mean 15 minutes."*
My wife said: *"German time!"*
He replied: *"Better than German time"*. I was so impressed to hear that. I realised they are people who know the value of time. A great Islamic virtue which is ignored by almost all Muslims worldwide. God in chapter 103 of the Qur'an, swears by the time and confirms that man is always in loss if not utilising it properly.

The comment made by the guide reminded me of a funny incident we had when we visited Bermuda Island several years ago. We were running to catch a boat. When we arrived at the port gasping and sweating, the guard said: *"Don't run. No one runs here. The boat will wait for you."* What a relief!
It also reminded me of how many hours I had to wait to conduct various Nikahs (an Islamic marriage) because either the groom or the bride or both are never on time. Unfortunately to be on time means nothing to many Muslims.

At the end of the tour we were offered the opportunity to wear a Japanese Kimono to have photos. The Japanese are people who dearly love their country and are so proud of their culture.

C) Cleanliness

Everything surrounding you in Japan is spotlessly clean. This is not solely due to their skills at cleaning but very much their culture, which prevents them from littering the environment. This is an Islamic virtue. The Prophet Mohammed (pbuh) said, *"Removing any form of harm from the road is a form of charity."*

I reflected back to when I arrived from Cairo, Egypt into London in July 1970. I was so impressed with the cleanliness of the streets. Upon expressing my admiration to my English professor at the London School of Economics (LSE). He said: *"We are dirty. But we are good in cleaning."*

A simple tip from my wife, Dr Sonia Kandil, has enabled me to keep my car relatively litter free. Previously, I used to keep rubbish under the seat next to me until I found a chance to dispose of it. She advised me to always have a plastic bag attached to the gearstick and when it is full, just bin it. Many thanks to her for keeping the environment and my car clean. A very simple tip to adopt and solution to those who keep throwing rubbish out of their cars.

D) Noiseless Nation

The Japanese are very quiet people. You cannot even hear them talking to each other or on their phones and they generally talk very little. They cover their mouths when they yawn and put their hands on their phone when they talk. Another great Islamic virtue. They communicate like ants. I hope they have an enjoyable sex life!

They reminded me of Luqman in Chapter 31 in the Qur'an. He was honoured by God and given Divine Wisdom. He commanded his son, among other things, to lower his voice otherwise he will sound like a donkey. I think he was the father of the great Japanese nation. Today unfortunately, there are many countries in the world dominated by donkeys.

During the week we spent in Japan, I did not hear any drivers hooting. It reminded me of a funny conversation I had several years ago with a Swiss group of tourists flying back from Cairo to Geneva.
I asked them how their visit was. They replied: *"It was lovely!"*. I asked them how they found the noise of the cars hooting all the time, often for no reason at all? They said: *"We loved it. It is the music of Cairo."* Well! This is their taste; I personally prefer to listen to Mozart!

D) A Rushing Nation

The Japanese we saw looked stressed, smiled little and sounded very serious. They do not smile that much. They have to work very hard and long hours to satisfy their demanding bosses and ensure the prosperity of their country for all future generations. You can see many of them falling asleep on the metro. They not only think of their own prosperity, but the prosperity of future generations. You can see the traces of the painful past engraved on their foreheads. But they are content, honest, hardworking, organised, and courageous.

You would see them rushing to work in the early morning like robots. The majority of the men are dressed in dark suits. Women are elegantly dressed as well but no colour coordination when it comes to matching the bags, shoes and outfits. Their style is very striking and individual.

As a nation which is always rushing, we had a very interesting experience with the taxi driver who took us from Tokyo airport to our hotel. Unfortunately, he took us to the wrong Marriott hotel and very quickly put our suitcases on the curb and rushed back into his cab. I had to knock on his window to inform him that this was not the right hotel. Then he kept apologising saying: *"I'm sorry. I'm really sorry. I did not read the address properly. I thought there was only one Marriott. Your hotel is a new one."* Then he took us to the correct hotel and refunded us US $30 which was half of the money we had already paid.

He has great Islamic values. What an honest man who also admitted making a mistake. If we were anywhere else in the world, I'm sure we would have been charged for the extra journey and no apology would have been received.

The second funny experience we had was when we were supposed to meet our tour operator at the hotel to join an organised tour to Mount Fuji. We gave her our booking vouchers with our names on them. She checked them against the list she had. Then she took us on a coach to another hotel to pick up more passengers. Then suddenly she panicked and said to us in a very painful tone that we were the wrong clients. She had to hurry us back in a taxi to our hotel to meet the right guide and kept apologising for this mistake and paid for the taxi. I think they make such mistakes because they are constantly rushing.

The taxi driver and the tour operator reminded me of myself being in haste all my life which still causes me a high level of stress and anxiety. But I can see that some elements of this have helped me to achieve many things in my life, simultaneously. Unfortunately, the anxiety I suffered from led to severe depression in the latter part of 1970. It was only the grace and mercy of God which saved me from this dreadful illness.

No wonder that Japanese employers are obliged to introduce de-stressing programmes for their employees whether in offices or factories. You will also see "Relaxation Rooms" for men and women where people try to spend some time away from their daily problems.

My parents used to call me *"Agool"* since my childhood which means *"in haste all the time"*. God says in 17:11, *"...Indeed man is hasty."* And He says in 21:37, *"Man is hasty by nature. I shall certainly show you My Signs. Don't ask Me to be hasty."*
I remember a time, many years ago, when I picked up my (or what I thought was mine) suitcase at Miami airport, USA, and realised once I arrived at my hotel that it was the wrong one. At that time, all Samsonite bags looked the same and even had the same key. Funnily enough, it belonged to a Japanese woman. When I called her, I was so angry and I accused her of picking up my suitcase. She said, *"no your suitcase is still at the airport"*, as she checked the label before picking it up. I apologised immediately for not checking the label. She came to the hotel, picked up her suitcase and I had to return to the airport to pick up mine. How many times did I put petrol in my diesel car or vice versa?! Again, I think I definitely have Japanese genes!

D) The Japanese Toilets

It is an invention worth writing a novel about! The design and cleanliness of public toilets is another story. The electronic control panel reflects the ingenuity of the Japanese engineers. The heated toilet seat, the different types of sprayers to wash and clean yourself, the automatic flushing and the hot air for drying were amazing. I was expecting a hand to come out to wash my butt! What about the music you can play while sitting to add more to your privacy if you suffer from wind!

Why did they have to go through all these complicated designs to clean themselves? In UK hospitals, you will always see a sign saying, *"Did you wash your hands?"* Or *"Use the pump".* MRSA became a major concern in British hospitals causing the death of many patients.

The Japanese realised the importance of cleanliness and hygiene. They must be aware of how much love God has for those who purify themselves. God says in the Qur'an, *"God loves those who repent and loves those who purify themselves."* 2:222

How many times I visited some Muslim countries and struggled to find a public toilet, let alone it being clean or not. Due to this I was compelled to either use the bush or not to drink for a whole day out.

E) The Organised Chaos

Scramble pedestrian crossings were an experience of its own! People were crossing diagonally and perpendicularly without any confusion. When the traffic light changes, a beautiful piece of music plays to alert people to cross.

To maintain a fast flow of pedestrians the curb is divided into two parts. One side for the going flow and the other one for the coming flow.

The trains and the metro services are another wonder. They are always on time. Guards on the trains and on the platforms can be seen all the time. Not like TFL in London who refuse to appoint guards on long trains, compromising passengers' safety.
Millions of passengers would use the services everyday. Music is played before every announcement. Despite trains being packed at rush time, people are still so organised, well-disciplined and patient. No pushing, no shouting, no queue jumping and most impressively, no body odour! This is something I always dread to endure when travelling on the London Underground in the hot days of the summer. The Japanese on the other hand, smell so nice!

You can see police officers everywhere. They are extremely helpful. They would even walk with you to guide you to your destination. Similar help you would get from normal people who would change their travel plan or drop their partner to walk with you all the way to get you to your address.

F) A Bowing Nation

We travelled on the bullet train from Tokyo to Osaka. Our tickets were booked for the 13:07 train with reserved seats and we ensured we arrived an hour and a half earlier to our station. Instead of waiting until 13:07, we decided to take the 12:07 train. We were concerned about our seat reservation, however, when we read the information on the display screen, we realised that the first three cars of every train have free seating. So we went on the earlier train. As the train is a very long train, the car number and the seat number are marked on the platform.

When the conductor entered the train carriage, he bowed to greet all the passengers. Then he started to check the tickets. You could not even hear him when he was talking or saying *"Ari Gatto"* which is *"thank you"* in Japanese. He had a big smile on his face. He looked very elegant and pleasant in his uniform. When I asked him for something, he squatted to make eye contact with me.

This gesture of being on the same level with people when engaging with them really struck me as such a powerful, yet simple way to connect so well with people. Something like this would very rarely happen in other parts of the world. Just before leaving the carriage he bowed again.

When those who were selling food and drinks appeared, he or she bowed to greet the passengers. They had a beautiful uniform but again you could not hear any voices when the people are ordering food or drinks. I remembered the trains in Egypt and India when those who are selling food on each platform would deafen your ears. Maybe this is the music they play in such countries.

A plastic bag was given to each passenger on the train to collect any rubbish and passengers were instructed to take their rubbish with them and dispose of it in the recycling bins on the platforms.

Passengers were constantly reminded to show consideration to others whilst moving their luggage.

So bowing is a form of greeting each other rather than shaking hands. It is like saying: *"Peace be on you"*. You can witness this anywhere you go. This is a form of spreading peace among the people as recommended by Prophet Mohammed (pbuh), *"...Spread peace among yourselves by greeting each other..."*, reported by At-Tarmidhi. I remembered how many times in Saudi Arabia I said *"Peace be upon you"* and was totally ignored.

A few years ago, I received a telephone call from my very dear friend Superintendent Carl Lindley from New Scotland Yard. In addition to being a police officer in the Metropolitan Police, Carl is also a professional karate trainer. He said he was having problems with Muslim children who were refusing to bow at the beginning and the end of each fighting session. He added, *"If they don't bow they will be disqualified."* He asked me if I can issue a memo to the parents of the Muslim children to explain that this was not a religious ceremony. I issued a statement explaining that bowing here was not a form of worship. It was rather a form of showing respect by greeting the person in front of you in a very peaceful manner.

G) Hiroshima

On Wednesday 25th May 2016 we travelled from Osaka to Hiroshima by the Bullet Train. As we travelled, we remembered being told in history about the devastation this city experienced during the Second World War. So, to finally be able to witness ourselves at the place of such a human tragedy, weighed heavily upon us. I came with so many mixed feelings and emotions. Surprisingly, we were made aware that two days later, President Obama would be visiting as well. He was the first ever USA President, who was still in Office at the time, to visit Hiroshima.

I was so impressed and surprised to see a very modern city with beautiful spacious avenues and parks, and very expensive department stores. It reminded me of Paris or Barcelona. Is it possible that this is the city which was fully destroyed on August 6th, 1945 by the first atomic bomb ever used in warfare? Where was the destruction? Was it in the buildings or the souls of the Japanese people?

What a great testament to a great nation that managed to recover so quickly from such a great tragedy and dealt so positively with its pain and suffering.

We visited the Peace Memorial Park area and were so amazed to see the Atomic Bomb Dome. "It is a symbol of Hiroshima, conveying to us the horror of nuclear weapons and appealing for world peace", stated the Hiroshima's Sightseeing Guide Map. The building was severely damaged and burnt. It is now a UNISCO World Heritage Site.

We saw a great number of school children in different school uniforms coming to visit the park. In spite of their young age they were well disciplined with serious and studious looks on their faces.

Each group had its own guide. They spent some time in front of the Children's Peace Monument. They came to the monument in waves. They prayed and bowed and offered so many colourful flags of peace.

The message was to forgive, forget and overlook and to work together to build peace in the world. I like the expression "to build", as peace is not an imaginary quantity in mathematics or a science fiction. It is a structure which we should all contribute towards its existence even by contributing one single brick of love or sacrifice, or both.

We also visited the Hiroshima Peace Memorial Museum. It was so painful to see images of the horrors and cruelty of man towards his fellow man. The extent of the destruction was beyond any imagination. My eyes were tearful. It reminded me of my five visits to the Holocaust memorial in Israel, *"A Hand & A Name"*. Again, you can see the atrocities committed by one group against the other, for no other reason but being of different religion or ethnicity. Unfortunately, people very often forget that we are all brothers and sisters in humanity and that there will be a Day of Judgement when we will all be called to account.

The school children were queuing for hours to read each and every displayed exhibit. In spite of their young age, they were so eager to live every moment of the past, irrespective of how painful it was to reflect on how great their leaders were who took them from the depths of hell into prosperity. Those honest, sincere and devoted leaders who managed to wipe the tears and dress the wounds of the entire population, with one hand and build a new confident generation with the other hand. Thus to achieve one of the best and strongest economies in the world.

H) Conclusion

During our stay we never witnessed nudity or vulgarity or any apparent tattoos or even boys and girls kissing in public. They have true Islamic virtues. They do not need religious police to monitor them as they do in Saudi Arabia and Iran, which created a generation of hypocrite Muslims. We did not see anyone sleeping rough on the road or begging as we see many of these in Muslim and European countries.

The Japanese who survived the war were not People of the Book, they were not Jews or Christians or Muslims, or even believers in the One True God. It was their great values which survived the nuclear attack and made them a super nation in less than two decades.

I wonder, why the Muslim nations of today are so behind? Is it their religion? Or their lack of understanding and applying Islamic values which excel any man made values?

The Japanese are a great nation without any doubt. We Muslims of today, are only Muslims by name. We are nothing compared to these people. We are *"...the scum and rubbish like that carried down by a torrent, useless froth on rain water",* as stated by the Prophet Mohammed (pbuh) over 1400 years ago in the Hadith recorded in Sunan Abi Dawud. These are powerful words of the Prophet (pbuh) which need to be reflected upon.

We misinterpreted our religion and made it an excuse for our failures and lack of achievements.
Islam became symbolised by a beard and a white robe for a man and a headscarf for a woman. Simple adornments that failed to penetrate deeper to achieve beautiful manners and etiquette. We did not seek knowledge as the Qur'an commands us. We lack sincerity and devotion. We do not perfect our work. Unfortunately, there are many Muslims (as there are many of other faiths and none) who are a bunch of lazy hypocrites and beggars seeking every type of help from non-Muslim countries.

If the Japanese would just believe in the One True God, they would be admitted to Gardens of Bliss. They would enter from any of its eight gates.

On the other hand, if the Muslims of today continue to ignore God's Moral Law in the Qur'an, if they will not refrain from killing each other, if they will not eradicate corruption, if they will not seek knowledge, if they will continue to ignore human rights and deny women their Divine rights, if they will not show kindness to orphans and widows and feed the poor and the needy, they will be queuing at the front of the seven gates of Hell, waiting for its 19 angels to open for them.

1.5 God's Moral Law and the Four Jewels of Nations' Prosperity

When the non-Muslim countries applied their religious beliefs in their daily practices, they acquired the 'Four Jewels' of building a prosperous nation, namely:

1) **Seeking and acquiring knowledge.** العلم

2) **Hard work with sincerity and dedication.** العمل

3) **Manners and etiquettes.** الاخلاق

4) **Justice and equality for all.** العدل

They decorated their Constitutions with these 'Four Jewels'. The general population of most of the non-Muslim countries have great love for their countries and think of the future generations. Their rulers are held accountable by the court and ultimately by the people who democratically elected them.

A corrupt individual is tried and prosecuted. People created a world where no one can get away with abuse of office or any crime, however minor or serious.

God's Moral Law is exhibited in all His Divine Revelations, namely, the Torah (the Old Testament) to Moses, the Psalms to David, the Bible (the New Testament) to Jesus and the Qur'an to Mohammed (pbuh).

Non-Muslim countries eventually separated their religious practices from their lives and became secular. However, they maintained the 'Four Jewels' of prosperity in their Constitutions.

Whilst the Muslim countries lost both, their religious practices and their existence and became fully dependent on non-Muslim countries to support and feed them. This is the reality which is facing the Muslim world today. What a sad and a very embarrassing situation!

So the main reason behind the backwardness of Muslim countries and the decline of Muslim nations is the distorted version of Islam that exists in their governments and minds. Please do not blame Islam. Blame the Muslims who distorted the Divine Message.

1.6 What does God say about these Four Jewels in the Qur'an?

In the next sections, I will examine some of the relevant verses in the Qur'an which refer to these great qualities.

1.6.1 First Jewel: Seeking and Acquiring Knowledge

The First Command

When God spoke to Moses for the first time, He said, *"I'm God, there is no other god but Me. So only serve Me and establish regular prayers for My remembrance"* 20:14

And when Jesus spoke to his people from the cradle, he said, *"I'm indeed a servant of God, He has given me revelation and made me a prophet. And He has made me blessed wheresoever I be, and has enjoined on me prayer and giving charity as long as I live"* 19:30-31

And when Arch Angel Gabriel brought down the first Divine revelation on Mohammed (pbuh), God said: *"Read in the name of your Lord and Cherisher, who created- created man, out of a leach-like clot. Read and your Lord is Most Bountiful, He who taught (the use of) the pen. Taught man that which he didn't know"* 96:1-5

So the first command in the Holy Qur'an was to eradicate illiteracy, to oblige people to learn how to read and write. Thus, seeking knowledge to serve God by serving humanity, is an obligation on every Muslim, male or female. Unfortunately, according to UNESCO's Institute for Statistics, over 65% of Muslims worldwide can neither read nor write. What a shame!

God Expects Every Practising Muslim to be a Scientist!

Every time I study the Qur'an, I come across many verses which command us to reflect and ponder on God's creation in the heavens and the earth. They are like an appeal to man's own intelligence and wisdom.

We are instructed to examine our own creation and look at the food we eat, the water we drink, the trees we burn for energy, and the air we breathe.

It is not my intention to list all the verses in the Qur'an where scientific evidence or a fact has been mentioned or referred to. The Qur'an is not a book of science. The Qur'an is a book of Signs from God for guidance. I'm only giving below a few examples to illustrate the point that it is a religious obligation on us all to search and research the world we live in, which was created by God and entrusted to us all. Our aim in doing that is to save our planet.

It is our responsibility, as God's Vicegerents, to endeavour to protect the earth and improve the quality of life for all the children of Adam and all other God's creatures who share this planet with us.

God says in 29:19-20: *"Have they not seen how does God originate creation, then repeats it, truly that is easy for God. Say 'Travel through the earth and see how did God originate creation; so will God produce a later creation, for God has power over all things'"*.

"If we actually go through this wide earth, we shall see the wonderful things in God's Creation-the Grand Canyon and the Niagara in America, beautiful harbours like that at Sydney in Australia, mountains like Fujiyama, the Himalayas, and Elburz in Asia, the Nile with its wonderful cataracts in Africa, the Fiords of Norway, the Geysers of Iceland, the city of

the midnight sun in Tromsoe, and innumerable wonders everywhere. But wonders upon wonders are disclosed in the constitution of matter itself, the atom, and the forces of energy, as also in the instincts of animals, and the minds and capacities of man. And there is no limit to these things. Worlds upon worlds are created and transformed every moment, within and presumably beyond man's vision. From what we know we can judge of the unknown."
FN3441

In 21:30-33, God informs us regarding the Big-Bang theory, the predominance of water on our Globe that all life began in the water, the role played by the mountains in stabilising the earth in its rotation, the floating or swimming of all celestial bodies in their orbits.

"Do not the unbelievers see that the heavens and the earth were joined together (as one unit of creation), before We split them asunder? And We made from water every living thing. Will they not then believe?

"And we have set on the earth mountains standing firm, lest it should shake with them, and we have made therein broad highways (between mountains) for them to pass through, that they may find their way.

"And We have made the heavens as a canopy well-guarded, yet they turn away from its Signs.

"It is He who created the Night and the Day, and the sun and the moon, each is floating in its orbit." 21:30-33

God says in 2:164, *"Behold! In the creation of the heavens and the earth; in the alternation of the Night and the Day; in the sailing of the ships through the Ocean for the benefit of mankind; in the rain which God sends down from the skies, and the life which He gives therewith to an earth that is dead; in the beasts of all kinds that He scatters through the earth; in the change of the winds, and the clouds which they trail like their slaves between the sky and the earth; (here) indeed are Signs for a people who have sense".*

Yes in the above there are Signs of God's Sovereignty for people who use their brains to think, reflect and contemplate on His creation.

And God says in 3:190-191, *"Behold! In the creation of the heavens and the earth, and the alternation of Night and Day, there are indeed Signs for people of understanding. People who remember God standing, sitting, and lying down on their sides, and contemplate the (wonders of) creation in the heavens and the earth, (with the saying): 'Our Lord you have not created (all) this in vain. Glory to You! Give us salvation from the punishment of the Hell Fire'".*

And He says in 13:2-4 *"It is God who raised the heavens without any pillars that you can see; then He established Himself on the Throne. And He has subjected the sun and the moon! Each one runs (its course) for a term appointed. He regulates all affairs, He explains the Signs in detail that you may believe with certainty in the meeting with your Lord. And it is He Who spread out the earth, and set thereon mountains standing firm, and (flowing) rivers; and of* every fruit He placed in it two in pairs (male and female). He draws the Night as a veil over the Day. Behold, verily in these things there are Signs for those who reflect! (Those who use their brains to think and consider).

"And in the earth are neighbouring plots (tracts), and gardens of vines and fields with vegetables, and date-palm trees growing out of single roots or otherwise; all watered with the same water, yet we prefer in taste some of them over the other. Behold, verily in these things there are Signs for those who understand".

In the following verses 16:10-16, God attracts our attention to the rain He sends down from the sky, from which humans and animals drink, and the various vegetables and fruits the earth produces upon receiving this rain.

Then He reminds us regarding the night and the day and the sun, the moon and the stars. Following that, He enumerates the benefits we get from the sea. Besides, He mentions the role played by the mountains to stabilise the earth in its daily rotation around its axis and in its orbit around the sun.

We are then told that He created on the earth, rivers and passages for our guidance. Also the use of stars to guide us in the darkness while travelling in the land or sailing in the sea. Shouldn't we be grateful to our Lord, the Most Bountiful?

"It is He Who sends down rain from the sky from it you drink, and out of it (grows) the vegetation on which you feed your cattle. With it He produces for you vegetables, olives, date-palms, grapes, and every kind of fruit. Verily in this is a Sign for those who reflect.

"He has made subject to you the Night and the Day; the sun and the moon; and the stars are in subjection by His Command. Verily in this are Signs for people who use their brains (those who have sense).

"And what He has created for you in the earth is of diverse colours. There is indeed a Sign in this for people who are mindful (people who take heed).

"It is He Who has subjected the sea to you, that you may eat from it flesh that is fresh and tender, and you may extract from it ornaments to wear; and you see the ships cleaving through it, that you may seek of God's bounties. And that you may be grateful.

"And He has set up on the earth mountains standing firm, lest it should shake with you; and rivers and ways, that you may guide yourselves, And marks and sign-posts; and by the stars (people) guide themselves."

Should we not all be grateful to God regarding the above mentioned favours and bounties? Do we really care about the environment we live in? Should we not all strive to introduce new scientific methods to slow down or curb the current pace of climate change, which is terrifying? Sometimes I feel the Day of Judgement is approaching extremely fast!

I recently came across a contemporary scientific explanation of verses 13:41 and 21:44, where God confirms that our planet is shrinking from both ends, i.e. the North and the South Poles which are melting because of Global Warming.

"Have they not seen that We gradually reduce the earth from its outlying borders?" 13:41 & 21:44

Contemplating on My Food is a Divine Command

Every time I am having something to eat or drink, I reflect on God's command in verses 80:24-32.

"Let man look at his food, (and how We provide it). For that We pour forth water in abundance, and We split the earth in fragments, and produce from within the earth, grains and grapes and fresh vegetation, and olives and dates, and enclosed Gardens, dense with lofty trees, and fruits and fodder, a provision for you and your cattle."

Prophet Ibrahim when he was defining God to his people, who were idol worshippers, said, *"It is He who feeds me and gives me a drink."* 26:79

My Breakfast Menu

In the following section I will examine a few verses from the Qur'an regarding what is on my breakfast menu. Normally, I have water, milk (as well as dairy products like cheese and butter), honey, dates, grapes, and bread.

1) Water
God says in 56:68-70: *"Have you seen the water which you drink? Is it you who bring it down (in rain) from the clouds or it is We? If We would have willed, We would have made it saltish (and unpalatable). Then why do you not give thanks?"*

The water of the seas and oceans is salty. But when it evaporates it is sweet. And the clouds which are formed from this evaporation process are carrying fresh and sweet water. But God has the power to turn it into salty water even whilst it is descending.
God explains to us in 30:48-49, the Water Cycle and His power in directing the clouds to drop their water on specifically chosen people who were in desperate need for rain: *"It is God Who sends the winds, and they raise the clouds. Then He spreads them in the sky as He wills, and breaks them into fragments, until you see rain-drops issue from the midst of them. Then when He has made them reach such of His servants as He wills, behold they do rejoice. Even though, before they received (the rain), just before this, they were in utter despair!"*

And in 24:43, He explains how He forms the clouds and the different types of rain which would come out of them including hail stones.

"Have you not seen that God makes the clouds move gently, then joins them together, then makes them into a heap? Then you will see rain issue forth from their midst. And He sends

down from the sky mountain masses (of clouds) wherein is hail. He strikes there with whom He chooses and He turns it away from whom He wills. The vivid flash of its lightning well almost blinds the sight."

"Artists, or lovers of nature, or observers of clouds will appreciate this description of cloud effects-thin clouds floating about in fantastic shapes, joining together and taking body and substance, then emerging as heavy clouds heaped up, which condense and pour forth their rain. Then the heavy dark clouds in the upper regions, that bring hail,-how distinct and yet how similar! They are truly like mountain masses! And when the hailstones fall, how local their area! It hits some localities and leaves free others almost interlaced! And the lightning-how blinding flashes come from thunderous clouds! In this Book of Nature can we not see the hand of the powerful and beneficent God?" FN3019

2) Milk
In 16:66 God attracts our attention to the source of the delicious pure and palatable milk we drink. Can you imagine it comes from excretions and blood in the stomachs of the cattle? The excretions refer to the faeces or the refuse in their bellies. It sounds disgusting. But it is the power of God which makes it possible.

"And verily in the cattle you will find an instructive Sign. From what is within their bodies, between excretions and blood, We produce, for your drink, milk, pure and agreeable to those who drink it."

"Milk is a secretion in the female body, like other secretions, but more specialised. Is it not wonderful that the same food, eaten by males and females, produces in the latter, when they have young, the wholesome and complete food, known as milk? Then, when cattle are tamed and specially bred for milk, the supply of milk is vastly greater than is necessary for their young and lasts for a longer time than during the period they give suck to their young. And it is a wholesome and agreeable diet for man. It is pure, as it is typified by its whiteness. Yet it is a secretion like other secretions, between the excretions which the body rejects as worthless and the precious blood-stream which circulates within the body and is the symbol of life itself to the animal which produces it." FN2095

3) Grapes and Dates
God warns us in 16:67 regarding the misuse of date-palm and grapes by turning them into intoxicants instead of enjoying them as wholesome food, "And from the fruit of the date-palm and the vine, you get out strong drink, and wholesome food. Verily in this is a Sign for those who are wise."

"There are wholesome drinks and food that can be got out of the date-palm and the vine: e.g. non-alcoholic drinks from the date and the grape, vinegar, date-sugar, grape-sugar, and dates and grapes themselves for eating." FN2096

4) Honey
God says in 16:68-69, "And your Lord inspired the bee saying: Chose your habitations in the hills and in the trees and in that which man builds (beehives); then eat of all flowers and

fruits, and follow the ways of your Lord, made smooth (for you). There comes forth from their bellies a drink of varying colours, wherein is healing for mankind. Verily in this is indeed a Sign (from God) for people who reflect."

"The bee assimilates the juice of various kinds of flowers and fruits, and forms within its body the honey which it stores in its cells of wax. The different kinds of food from which it makes its honey give different colours to the honey, e.g., it is dark-brown, light-brown, yellow, white, and so on. The taste and flavour also varies, as in the case of heather honey, the honey formed from scented flowers, and so on. As food it is sweet and wholesome, and it is used in medicine." FN2098

5) The Splitting of the Seed-Grain and the Date-Stone
My bread comes from wheat or maze grain. Is it not amazing how hard a seed-grain or a date-stone may be, and when it is planted it splits and sprouts? The seed divides, and one very tender part shoots up, against gravity, seeking the light, and forming leaves and the visible parts of the future tree, and the other soft part digs down into the dark, forming the roots and seeking just the sustenance from the soil, which is adapted for the particular plant.

God says in 6:95: "It is God Who causes the seed-grain and the date-stone to split and sprout. He causes the living to issue from the dead. And He is the one to cause the dead to issue from the living. That is God, then how are you deluded away from the truth?"

The Various Stages of Man's Physical Growth

In the following verses God talks about the science of embryology and human development as manifested in the different phases which man goes through starting in his mother's womb until his death.

God says in 42:49-50, "To God belongs the kingdom of the heavens and the earth. He creates what He wills. He gifts to whom He wills females and He gifts to whom He wills males. Or He gives both males and females (or twins), and He leaves barren whom He wills, for He is full of knowledge and power."

It is very interesting to further examine verse 42:49. When God is talking about gifting boys and girls to whom He wills, He referred to the females in Arabic as 'Enatha' and referred to the males as 'Al-Zukoor'. So, in the Arabic language, by having 'Al' before the word, it would make it definite in number. This means that God would make the number of girls more than the number of boys. This is a fact we are witnessing in many countries worldwide.

The idol worshippers, before the revelation of the Qur'an began, used to bury newly born girls alive. They regarded it shameful to have girls. God is telling them here that although you may think that the crime you are committing would diminish the number of girls, I will make the number of girls more, because I know what I'm doing and I have power over everything.

I remember I came across a Muslim man who had six daughters. Every time his wife delivered a baby girl, he screamed at her *'I want a son'*. The poor woman would say *'It is in the hands of God. Be grateful for having a child. There are many people who are struggling to get one."* And the ungrateful husband would say *'You are the one who is carrying and delivering the baby. It is your fault nothing to do with me'*. Then she became pregnant for the 7th time. The husband threatened her saying *'If you give me another girl, I will divorce you'*.

What an ungrateful, ignorant husband! Did he not know that it is the sperm of the man which determines the sex of the baby? Nothing to do with the woman. Please do not blame your wife, blame your lazy Y sperm which lost the race in getting to your wife's egg before the X one.

Unfortunately, some Muslim women abort if the scan shows they are carrying a girl. This is considered as a major crime in Islam as stated in 17:31: *"And don't kill your children for fear of want. We shall provide, sustenance for them as well as for you. Surely the killing of them is a great sin"*. In China, this evil practice was the norm for years when they had the one-child policy.

In 56:58-59, we are told that the Creator is God and not the one who emitted the human seed: *"Have you seen the sperms you ejaculate? Is it you who create them or are We the Creator?"*

In the following verses 22:5-7, God describes the phases man goes through in his mother's womb and in this life. *"O mankind! If you have doubt about the Resurrection, (consider) that We created you out of dust, then out of zygote (fertilised ovum - sperm and egg), then out of leech-like clot, then out of a morsel of flesh, partly formed and partly unformed, in order that We may manifest (Our power)to you. And We cause whom We will to rest in the wombs for an appointed term, then we bring you out as babies, then (foster you) that you may reach your age of full strength; and some of you are called to die, and some are sent back to the feeblest old age, so that they know nothing after having known (much). And (further), you see the earth barren and lifeless, but when We pour down rain on it, it is stirred (to life), it swells, and it puts forth every kind of beautiful growth (in pairs). This is so, because God is the Reality. It is He Who gives life to the dead, and it is He Who has power over all things. And verily the Hour of Judgement will come. There can be no doubt about it, or about (the fact) that God will raise up all who are in the graves."*

The information given above became available to man very recently with the advance of medical sciences, enabling greater detail, clarity and visual depictions through scan advancements to see embryonic stage by stage growth.

In our physical life we see how strength is evolved out of weakness and weakness out of strength. The helpless baby becomes a lusty man in the pride of his manhood, and then sinks to a feeble old age. Living for old feeble age would result in memory loss and the person becomes demented. This illness is known as 'Dementia' or 'Alzheimer's'. Again only discovered very recently. This is also confirmed in 16:70 *"It is God Who creates you and* takes your souls at death. And of you there are some who are sent back to a feeble age, so that they know nothing after having known (much); for God is All-Knowing, All-Powerful."

In some cases if man lives so long that he falls into a feeble old age like a second childhood; he forgets what he learnt and seems almost to regress. The back of the man who walked proudly straight and erect is now bent. He loses many faculties including his sharp sight and hearing and may become double incontinent. This is also confirmed in 36:68, "If We grant long life to any, We cause him to be reversed in nature. Will they not then understand?"

So how can medical sciences help man in his old age? This became a new topic in "Geriatric Medicine" to address the physical needs of old people and of course we are seeing in many countries the impact and cost associated with higher numbers of the ageing population.

In verses 23:12-16, God mentions again the stages of creation in the womb, but He adds a very amazing fact regarding the formation of bones and how does He clothes them with flesh. "We created man from a wet earth. Then We placed him as a zygote (fertilised ovum) in a place of rest, firmly fixed. Then We made the zygote into a leach-like clot. Then out of that clot We made a (foetus) lump; then We made out of this lump bones and clothed the bones with flesh; then We developed out of it another creature. So blessed be God, the Best to create. After that, at length you will die. Then on the Day of Resurrection, you will be raised up."

In verse 39:6, God mentions the three veils of darkness inside the womb, "...He creates you in the wombs of your mothers, in stages, one after another, in three veils of darkness..."

The three veils of darkness which cover the unborn child are: the caul or membrane, the womb, and the hollow in which the womb is enclosed. This knowledge was not known to us until recently with the advance of medical sciences.

Finally, God reiterates in 40:67 the various stages of man's physical life; "It is He Who has created you from dust, then from a fertilised ovum, then from a leach-like clot, then He gets you out (into the light) as a child, then lets you (grow and) reach your age of full strength, then lets you become old, though of you there are some who die before, and lets you reach a term appointed, in order that you may understand."

"So the various stages of man's physical life are: (1) first, simple matter (dust); (2) the sperm-drop in the father; (3) the fertilised ovum in the mother's womb; (4) put into the light, as a human child; (5) youth and full maturity; (6) decay; and (7) death. In some cases the latter stages are curtailed or cut off; but in any case, a Term appointed is reached, so that the higher purpose of God's Will and Plan may be fulfilled in each given case, that man 'may understand.'" FN4444

Divine Knowledge

In the following section I give examples of the Divine knowledge which God taught some of His Prophets and Messengers, as well as some ordinary men whom He chose to honour with very special knowledge. God's Grace was not only limited to man but also included creatures from the animal kingdom.

A) Adam and the Angels

Verse 2:30, tells us that before the creation of Adam, God informed the angels that He is going to create a vicegerent on earth. The angels were not that happy. They said, *"Would You place therein one who will make mischief therein and shed blood, whilst we do celebrate Your praises and glorify Your Holy (Name)?"* God responded by saying: *"I know what you don't know."*

Immediately following the creation of Adam, God started by educating him: *"And He taught Adam the names of all things; then He placed them before the angels, and said: 'Tell Me the names of these if you are right.'*

They said: 'Glory to You. We only know what You have taught us. It is You who is perfect in knowledge and wisdom.' God said: 'O Adam! tell them their names.' When (Adam) told them their names, God said: 'Did I not tell you that I know the secrets of the heavens and the earth, and I know what you reveal and what you conceal?'" 2:31-33

"It would seem that the angels, though holy and pure, and endued with power from God, yet represented only one side of Creation. We may imagine them without passion or emotion, of which the highest flower is love. If man was to be endued with emotions, those emotions could lead him to the highest and drag him to the lowest. The power of will or choosing would have to go with them, in order that man might steer his own bark. This power of will (when used aright) gave him to some extent a mastery over his own fortunes and over nature, thus bringing him nearer to the God-like nature, which has supreme mastery and will. We may suppose the angels had no independent wills of their own; their perfection in other ways reflected God's perfection but could not raise them to the dignity of vicegerency. The perfect vicegerent is he who has the power of initiative himself, but whose independent action always reflects perfectly the will of his Principal. The angels in their one-sidedness saw only the mischief consequent on the misuse of the emotional nature by man; perhaps they also, being without emotions, did not understand the whole of God's nature, which gives and asks for love. In humility and true devotion to God, they remonstrate: we must not imagine the least tinge of jealousy, as they are without emotion. This mystery of love being above them, they are told that they don't know, and they acknowledge not their fault (for there is no question of fault) but their imperfection of knowledge. At the same time, the matter is brought home to them when the actual capacities of man shown to them." FN47

B) Noah and the Ark

God sent Noah as a Messenger and Prophet to his people. He remained among them for 950 years as stated in 29:14. He faced fierce rejection and ridicule from his own people.

God informed Noah in 11:36 that, *"None of your people will believe except those who have already believed. So don't grieve any longer over their (evil) deeds."*

And He commanded him in 11:37 *"And construct an Ark under Our eyes and Our inspiration...."*

So Noah who was a preacher, a Messenger and Prophet of God, had now been given, in his old age, the knowledge of how to become a marine-engineer.

He was instructed in 54:13 on how to build an Ark on a dry dock, using broad planks of wood with male and female endings to fit into each other, as a form of fixation. This is similar to the male and female endings on the pieces of a puzzle. The Ark was to be used to save all the believers and members of the animal kingdom as stated in 11:40and 23:27, from an imminent flood.

How did Noah communicate with the different species to bring them on board and how did he tame them? This was another knowledge which God taught him.

Then he became a sailor, steering the ship through waves towering like mountains, as stated in 11:42. Then God commanded the earth to swallow up the water and the sky to withhold the rain. And the water abated and the Ark rested on Mount Judi, and all the believers and the animals were saved, as stated in 11:44.

C) Joseph and the Interpretation of Dreams

In 12:22, we are told that when Prophet Joseph attained his full manhood, God gave him power and knowledge. So through the vicissitudes of his fortune in Egypt, he grew in knowledge, judgement, and power.

Following the interpretation of the Egyptian King's dream by Joseph and how impressed the King was with him, he offered Joseph a choice of any role he wished to play in the Egyptian government. God tells us in 12:55, that Joseph said, *"Set me over the store-houses of the land. I'm a good keeper and knowledgeable."* In other words, he said, *"I'm honest and have sufficient knowledge to deal with the Egyptian economy to utilise the seven years of plenty and to face the seven years of famine."*

He deliberately asked to be put in charge of the granaries and store-houses, and the drudgery of establishing them and guarding them, for the simple reason that he understood that need better than anyone else. He was prepared to take this role upon himself, rather than throw on to another, the obloquy of restricting supplies in times of plenty.

God mentions in 12:101, the prayer said by Prophet Joseph, at the end of his welcoming speech to his parents and his eleven brothers and their families when he welcomed them all in his house in Egypt. He said: *"O my Lord! You have indeed bestowed on me some power (or authority) and taught me something of the interpretation of dreams. You are the Creator of the heavens and the earth! You are my Protector in this world and in the Hereafter. Take my soul (at death) as one submitting to Your Will (as a Muslim), and unite me with the righteous (in the next life)."*

His reading of events and dreams had saved millions of lives in the great Egyptian famine. He admitted that this knowledge was bestowed on him by God. He took no credit to himself for the attribution and blessings of God.

D) Moses and the Wise Teacher

After God spoke directly to Moses and gave him the Torah, Moses thought that he knew everything. But God wanted to teach him a lesson. He told him that there was a wise man who knew more than him on certain topics.

God advised Moses to meet this man to learn from him. In 18:60-82, we are told about a fascinating encounter where Moses became the student of this wise man. Moses asked him if he can keep his company to learn from what God had taught him. The man agreed subject to Moses not asking any questions before he was, in time, told the interpretation of each event. Moses promised to be patient, as every student should be whilst acquiring knowledge.

They marched very quickly and when they went on a boat the first thing this man did was to make a hole in it. Moses became so angry and said: *"did you make a hole to drown it's people?"* The Teacher responded by saying: *"Didn't I tell you that you will not be patient."* Moses said *"Sorry!"*

Then they rushed again and they saw a young boy standing in front of his house. The Teacher took a knife out and cut the throat of the little boy. Moses went mad... "How dare you kill an innocent soul?" he shouted! The Teacher said, *"Did I not say you will not be able to persevere patiently with me?"* Moses said, *"Sorry! If I do it again, we will separate."*

Then they proceeded very quickly. They arrived into a village, very exhausted and hungry. The people of the village were so mean and unwelcoming. They refused to provide any hospitality to them. The Teacher, followed by Moses, walked through the uneven and narrow lanes of the village until they reached an old house. There was a big crack in one of it's walls, and the wall was about to collapse. The Teacher took out of his bag some material and filled the crack in a brilliant way to prevent the wall from falling down.

Moses was so angry with his Teacher. *"These people were so nasty to us. You could have charged them for your service!"* said Moses.

The Teacher looked at him and said, *"That is it. Now we have to part from each other. But before you go let me give you the interpretation of which you could not be patient about."*

Moses' face was full of regrets. He looked at his teacher with tearful eyes. He was now listening very carefully to what his Teacher was going to say.

"O Moses. The boat belonged to very poor people operating in the sea. There was a tyrant king who was capturing every ship by force. So I wanted to make a defect in the boat so when the king's men come to take it they will see the hole and will leave it.

"As far as the young boy I killed is concerned, his parents were very righteous and if he would have grown up he would have chosen to be very evil towards his parents. So God wanted to give them another child who will choose to be righteous, and this one would go to heaven because he died as a martyr.

"As far as the wall is concerned, it belongs to two orphan boys living in the city. Their parents were very righteous. Underneath it there is a hidden treasure which belongs to them. So God wanted them to reach their age of consent and come to retrieve their treasure. If the wall would have collapsed the treasure would have been exposed and the evil people of this village would have devoured it.

"I did all that based on knowledge and orders I received from God."

Moses regretted being impatient. Seeking knowledge requires a lot of patience and hard work. Moses was saying to himself if I was patient, surely I would have learnt more from this Teacher who received Divine knowledge from God.

E) Zul-qarnain (the King with the Two Horns) and the Iron-Lead Barrier

In 18:83-98 God tells us the extent of the power and knowledge He bestowed on the "King with the Two Horns" (Zul-qarnain). God gave him power and provided him with the ways and means for his great work, which he used for justice and righteousness.

Three of his expeditions are described in the Qur'an.

In the third expedition, we are told that in his travel, he arrived among a people who were skilled in the working of metals. Apparently they were a peaceful and industrious race, much subject to incursions from wild tribes who were called Gog and Magog. Against these tribes they were willing to purchase immunity by paying the Conqueror tribute in return for protection. The permanent protection they wanted was the closing of a mountain gap through which the intrusions were made.

The Conqueror refused to accept any remuneration from them as they were his subjects. He asked them to help with labour and materials.
He applied his knowledge of engineering and metallurgy to build an impregnable mass of metal made out of an alloy of blocks of iron and molten lead. The iron-lead wall was sufficiently high to prevent it being scaled and sufficiently strong to resist any attempt to dig through it.

The Conqueror said, "This is a mercy from my Lord. But when the promise of my Lord comes to pass (on the Day of Judgement), He will make it into dust, and the promise of my Lord is true."

F) Saul and David Fighting Goliath

God tells us in 2:246-247, that when the Children of Israel asked their Prophet Samuel to appoint a King to lead them in their fight against the tyrant Goliath, he informed them that God had chosen Saul to be the new King. However, they objected to his appointment saying: *"How can he exercise authority over us when we are better fitted than he to exercise authority, and he is not even gifted with wealth in abundance?"*

The people's fickleness appeared immediately after he was named. They raised all sorts of petty objections to him.

Samuel said: *"God has chosen him above you and has gifted him abundantly with knowledge and bodily prowess. God grants His authority to whom He pleases. God is All-embracing and He knows all things."*

So the main qualities of Saul were knowledge and physical strength, two major attributes required to lead an army to face the tyrant Goliath.

God tells us in 2:251 that in the battlefield, David slew Goliath and God gave David power and wisdom and taught him whatever (else) He willed.

David was not only a shepherd, a warrior, a king, a wise man, and a prophet, but was also endowed with the gifts of poetry and music.

God informs us in 21:79-80 that He made the hills and the birds celebrate His praises in unison with David. He made the iron soft for him and taught him the making of coats of mail to guard the warriors from each other's violence.

Thus *"the making of coats of mails is attributed to David. It is defensive armour, and therefore its discovery and supply is associated with deeds of righteousness in 34:10-11, in contrast with the deadly weapons which man invents for offensive purposes. Indeed, all fighting, unless in defence of righteousness, is mere 'violence'."* FN2734

G) Solomon the Young Judge

When Solomon was young, his father David would invite him to sit with him while judging between people.

In 21:78-79, we are told about a dispute between a farmer and a shepherd. *"The sheep got into a cultivated field by night and ate up the young plants, causing damage, to the extent of perhaps a whole year's crop. David was king, and in his seat of Judgement he considered the matter so serious that he awarded the owner of the field the sheep themselves in compensation for his damage.*

"His son Solomon, a mere boy of eleven, thought of a better decision, where the penalty would better fit the offence. The loss was the loss of the fruits or produce of the field of vineyard; the corpus of the property was not lost. Solomon's suggestion was that the owner of the field or vineyard should not take the sheep altogether but only detain them long

enough to recoup his actual damage, from the milk, wool and possibly young of the sheep, and then return the sheep to the shepherd.

"David's merit was that he accepted the suggestion, even though it came from a little boy. Solomon's merit was that he distinguished between corpus and income, and though a boy, was not ashamed to put his case before his father. But in either case it was God Who inspired the true realisation of justice. He was present and witnessed the affair, as He is present all the time." FN2732

H) Solomon and the Ant

Following the death of King David, Solomon became the new king. In 27:19, we are told of what he said at his coronation ceremony, *"O you people! We have been taught the speech of birds, and we have been given of everything. This is indeed Grace Manifest (from God)."*

"The spoken word in human speech is different from the means of communication which birds and animals have between each other. But no man can doubt that they have means of communication with each other, if he only observes the orderly flight of migratory birds or the regulated behaviour of ants, bees, and other creatures who live in communities. The wisdom of Solomon consisted in understanding these things in the animal world and in the lower fringes of human intelligence." FN3255

In 27:18-19, we are told about a very caring and responsible ant who carried out a risk assessment and sent SOS message to its community commanding them to get into their habitations as quickly as possible before Solomon and his army crush them (under foot) without knowing it.

Solomon, while marching with his army in the Valley of the Ants, heard the ant's message of distress and immediately stopped marching to save the ants. He smiled when he heard the voice of the distressed ant and gave thanks to God for giving him such knowledge to enable him to look after every subject in his kingdom.

I) Solomon and the Hoopoe

In another occasion, as mentioned in 27:20-28, Solomon was challenged by a Hoopoe, a member of his air force, who just returned from a reconnaissance journey to Sheba.

The beautiful graceful bird told Solomon that he has information which Solomon does not have. He told him that he visited Sheba and found its Queen and its people worship the sun instead of worshiping the One True God. This believing Hoopoe was commanded to fly back all the way from Jerusalem to Sheba to deliver a letter from Solomon to its Queen inviting them to believe in the One True God.

The Queen of Sheba, upon receiving Solomon's letter, decided in her wisdom, to travel to Jerusalem, a distance of almost 3,000 km, to confer with Solomon to avoid an imminent attack on her country.

We are told in 27:38-44, that while she was travelling, Solomon decided to surprise her on her arrival. He sought the help of knowledgeable members of his cabinet to bring her throne to Jerusalem before she arrived. So he asked them, *"who can bring her throne to me before they believe"*.

A brute Jinni said: *"I can bring it here before this meeting is over."*

But a man, a human being like Solomon, who had Divine knowledge from a certain Book, which Solomon did not have, said: *"I can bring it here before you blink!"*

And he did it! He moved the throne at the speed of light from Sheba to Jerusalem. Solomon did not have this knowledge, but a member of his cabinet had it. Solomon was so grateful to God for bestowing such a great favour on him.

Solomon commanded that her throne should be disguised to put her to a test. When she arrived, she was asked: *"Is this your throne?"* She replied: *"It seems the same!"*
She must have thought to herself, how could this be her throne? It was in her palace when she started her journey many days ago!

Then she was asked to enter the Grand Palace. Its floor was made of slabs with smooth polished glass that glistened like water. She thought it was water, and tucked up her clothes to pass through it, showing her bare feet and ankles. This was a very undignified position for a woman, especially for one in the position of a Queen. She felt so humiliated that she could not tell the difference between water and glass and by showing her legs she added more embarrassment to herself. Solomon immediately told her the real facts, upon which she felt grateful and joined herself with Solomon in praising God.

Eventually, the Queen of Sheba and her people followed Solomon and believed in the One True God and became Muslims. Thanks to the Hoopoe who saved Sheba and its Queen.

1.6.2 Second Jewel: Hard Work with Sincerity and Dedication

There are many verses in the Qur'an which command people to believe and do good righteous deeds. In the sight of God, these two activities are inseparable.

Good righteous deeds, referred to in the Qur'an, do not only include performing religious rites. Acquiring knowledge and developing professional skills to enable you to find a job to support yourself and your dependents and to serve humanity, is a great deed.

Whatever job you may do, if you are doing it to the best of your ability, seeking the pleasure of God, it is regarded as a form of worship. Being mindful of every act we take and words we utter, enables us to be more measured and aware of our actions and intentions. This further enables us to combine this form of mindfulness with our worship to our God. Mindfulness has of course been proven to diminish anxiety and help us in our overall general health and wellbeing.

God says in 16:97, *"Whoever does good righteous deeds, man or woman, and has Faith, We will make him live a life which is good and pure. And We will reward them (in the Hereafter) according to the best of their actions (in this life)."*

"Faith, if sincere, means right conduct in everything we do, in every job we perform, in every task we carry out.

"When these two, faith and conduct, confirm each other, God's grace transforms our life. Instead of being troubled and worried, we have peace and contentment; instead of being assailed at every turn by false alarms and the assaults of evil, we enjoy calm and attain purity.

"The transformation is visible in this life itself, but the reward in terms of the Hereafter will be far beyond our expectations." FN2137

And in 9:105, He commands us to work as our deeds will be witnessed by Him, His Messenger (Mohammed) and all the believers.

Prophet Mohammed (pbuh) said in a sound Hadith, in Abu-Yala: "God loves that if anyone of you would do a job, to perfect it."

God commands us in 103:1-3 to value time and not to waste it. Unfortunately, many Muslims are not conscious regarding the importance of time. Man is not only made out of body and soul. Each one of us is here for a limited time, predetermined by the Creator before we came to this planet. So from the moment we are born our clock is ticking away.

So if you don't want to be a loser, you must invest your time slot in this life properly. Do not waste time, because you are in fact wasting your life. You must have faith, work righteous deeds and enjoin the truth and perseverance, so you will prosper in this life and attain salvation in the Hereafter.

1.6.2.1 All God's Messengers are Commanded to Work

In 23:51, God commands His Messengers to eat from what is good and pure and work righteously as He is well acquainted with what they do. I give below examples of jobs practiced by some of God's Messengers.

A) Noah

As stated earlier, Noah was a Prophet and Messenger of God, but after 950 years of his mission as a preacher, he was commanded to build an ark to save the believers and members of the animal kingdom. So in his old age, he became a carpenter to build the first ever ship on a dry dock in the middle of the desert, under God's supervision.

Then his next job was to go out in the wild and gather a pair from each animal species. He became a very experienced zoologist who ensured the welfare of all the animals he brought on the ark.

Finally, he became a sailor who steered his ship in a very rough sea with waves as high as mountains.

Today there is no such thing as a *"job for life"*. So there is no harm in changing your career to survive recessions and labour market changes and demands. Being adaptable and open to change is the pre requisite to surviving hard recessions and tough economic climates and times.

B) Hajar the wife of Abraham

God tells us in 14:37 that Prophet Abraham left his beautiful young wife Hajar and their little baby Ishmael in a barren valley in Makkah, next to the ruins of the House of God. He left them with this prayer: *"O our Lord! I have made some of my family to dwell in a valley without cultivation, by Your Sacred House; in order, O our Lord! That they may establish regular prayer. So fill the hearts of some among people with love towards them, and provide them with sustenance that they may give thanks."*

When Hajar ran out of provisions, she immediately had to look for help to save her baby. Although she was a true believer, she did not expect Heaven to send down sustenance on them. She looked around, but the valley they were in, had no water or vegetation or even people.

She saw two hills opposite each other, Al-Safa and Al-Marwa. She climbed Al-Safa and looked around but could not see anything, so she came racing down in the scorching heat. She was so concerned about her little boy who was screaming from hunger. She walked through the valley until she got to the other hill, Al-Marwa. She went all the way up. Again she could not see anyone. She did this journey seven times, and suddenly she heard a voice. She saw an angel next to her son who struck the ground and water started gushing. That was the source of the well of ZamZam in Makkah.

In the honour of this great woman who exerted such a tremendous effort to save her child, God made the walking between these two hills one of the religious rites of pilgrimage. It is important that we reflect on this being one of the rites of pilgrimage and all who complete these rites are also honouring the actions of a woman, Hajar. I mention this in response to those who say women are not valued or important in Islam. We must strive to earn our daily bread. It is shameful in Islam to beg.

C) Abraham and Ismael

Abraham and Ishmael were both Prophets and Messengers of God. But they became the bricklayers appointed by God to rebuild His House in Makkah, the Kaba (the Cube). Abraham was in his late nineties, but his old age had never been an excuse not to perform his duties to the best of his ability.

It was not below his dignity to act as a bricklayer. He never complained about the huge size of the rocks he and his son had to carry to build the four walls of the Kaba, the House of God.

They both had to go around the structure several times to erect the four walls. And in the memory of the great services and sacrifices offered by these two men, it became a religious obligation on Muslims to go around the Kaba seven times as part of the rites of pilgrimage.

D) David and Solomon

The Qur'an tells us in 21:79-80 and 34:10-11 that Prophet David was taught by God how to make coats of mail from iron to be used as a defensive armour.

And Prophet Suleiman had great managerial and engineering skills to control the Jin and Satans to participate in the construction of the Temple in Jerusalem as stated by God in 34:12-13.

E) The King of the Two Horns

Also, as stated earlier, we are told in 18:93-98 about Zul-qarnain (the King of the Two Horns), who was a great metallurgist, who applied his scientific knowledge to save a nation from a fierce aggressive neighbour by building a wall made out of an alloy of iron and lead.

F) Moses

Prophet Moses, was brought up as a prince in the palace of Pharaoh, with all the riches and comforts that this afforded. However, after he fled Egypt, he readily accepted a job offered to him by his future father-in-law. This job was to look after the cattle and the land, for minimum of eight years or maximum of 10 years, in return for marrying one of his two daughters as stated in 28:27.

G) Mary the Mother of Jesus

In 19:24-26, we are told that immediately after Mary delivered her baby Jesus, he spoke to her and asked her to shake the date-palm so fresh ripe dates would fall on her for her to eat.

This task is impossible even for a young healthy man to do. So we can imagine the demands this would have placed upon Mary, immediately after child birth. Why did God do this to help a weak woman who just delivered a baby? Because we must all work for our daily bread. Maybe she just hugged the trunk of the date-palm and God made the dates drop upon her.

1.6.2.2 A Lesson from the Birds

There is a great lesson for us all in the birds. They leave their nests with empty tummies, in the early morning, after they have praised the Lord, and return in the evening with full tummies. Then they say their prayers and go to sleep. But they must go out in search for their daily sustenance. God will not send food to them while they are resting in their nests.

"Can you not see that Allah it is whom all who are in the heavens and the earth praise including the birds on the wing? Each one knows his prayer and the (method of) His glorification, and Allah knows that which you do" - Surah 24:41

1.6.2.3 Rewarding of Deeds

God tells us in 99:7-8, that man will be rewarded for every good deed he does in this life, irrespective of how big or small it may be. Similarly, he will be called to account regarding any evil he does in this life, irrespective of how big or small it may be.

If he believes in the Hereafter, then his reward will not only be in this life, but also in the next life, the Eternal Life after death. But if he does not believe in the life after death, then his reward will only be limited to this life, as stated by God in 2:200, 25:23 and 11:15-16.

1.6.3 Third Jewel: Manners and Etiquettes as per God's Moral Law

The Qur'an has many verses instructing us on how to conduct ourselves to live a pure and good life in preparation for the next Eternal Life. Our duty is to hold fast by faith and lead a good life.

Muslim and Al-Bukhari reported that when Ayesha, the wife of Prophet Mohammed (pbuh) was asked how was his character? She answered, *"He was Qur'an walking on earth."* In another Hadith, in Muslim, she said *"His character was the Qur'an"*. God says in 68:4: *"And you (Mohammed) are certainly on the most exalted standard of moral excellence"*. So Prophet Mohammed (pbuh) understood God's Moral Law in the Qur'an and implemented it fully. Consequently, he was a perfect example for anyone whose hope is in God and the Last Day, and who engages much in the praise of God, as stated in 33:21.

The basis of the Moral Law is man's own good, and not any benefit to God, for God is above all needs and worthy of all praise; i.e. even in praising Him, we don't advance His Glory. When we obey His Will, we bring our position into conformity with our own nature as made by Him.

It is sad to say that the majority of the Muslims worldwide lack these etiquettes and manners. They may be educated or rich or enjoy high status in society, but they lack kindness, mercy, sincerity, generosity, discipline, humbleness, honesty, and many more. We are commanded by God to be kind to our parents, our children, our relatives, our neighbours, the orphans, the poor and the needy, the stranger wayfarer, and even the environment we live in.

We have in the Qur'an and in the Tradition of Prophet Mohammed (pbuh), a full description of God's Moral Law, which is for our own good to follow.

I have studied most of the verses in the Qur'an which refer to God's Moral Law. A list of these verses has been provided in the Appendix. I will only give below a few examples from this list regarding how our moral conduct should be.

A) Surat Al-Imran (the Family of Imran)- Chapter 3

Verses 3:133-136

133. "Be quick in the race for forgiveness from your Lord and for a Garden whose width is that (of the whole) of the heavens and of the earth, prepared for the righteous."

134. "Those who spend (freely) whether in prosperity or in adversity; who restrain anger, and pardon (all) people, for God loves those who do good."

135. "And those who, having done an act of indecency or wronged their own souls, earnestly bring God to mind and ask for forgiveness for their sins. And who can forgive sins except God? And are never obstinate in persisting knowingly in (wrong) they have done."

136. "For such the reward is forgiveness from their Lord, and Gardens with rivers flowing underneath, an eternal dwelling. How excellent a recompense for those who strive (to do good)."

In the above verses (3:133-135), God commands the following Moral Qualities (Moral Law) (Moral Etiquettes) (Moral Conduct):

1) Take part in the "Spiritual Marathon"
We should strive as in a race with each other towards all that is good whilst seeking the pleasure of our Lord and His forgiveness and hoping for an eternal abode in His Gardens of Bliss.

2) Be generous whether in prosperity or in adversity
Another definition of the righteous. So far from grasping material wealth, they give freely, of themselves and their substance, not only when they are well off and it is easy for them to do so, but also when they are in difficulties, for other people may be in difficulties at the same time.

3) Restrain anger

The righteous person will not get angry when other people behave badly towards him. He will not respond foolishly as he is in full control of all his faculties. He will not utter a word of contempt or use physical violence.

4) Forgive people
If you have the upper hand in any situation you must, as a righteous person, not only control your anger, but also forgive and cover other people's faults.

5) Be quick in repenting if you have done something wrong
The righteous man is not necessarily perfect. When he finds he has fallen into sin or error, does not whine or despair, but admits his sin and asks for God's forgiveness. And his faith gives him hope. If he is sincere, that means that he abandons his wrong conduct and makes amends. Sin is a sort of oppression of ourselves by ourselves. This follows from the doctrine of personal responsibility, as opposed to that of blind fate or of an angry God or gods lying in wait for revenge or injury on mankind.

B) Surat Al-Anaam (The Cattle) - Chapter 6

Verses 6:151-153

151. Say: "Come, I will rehearse what God has (really) prohibited you from": Don't join anything with Him; be good to your parents; don't kill your children for fear of poverty, We provide sustenance for you and for them; don't come near indecent deeds, whether open or secret; don't take life, which God has made sacred, except by way of justice and law. Thus He commands you, that you may learn wisdom."

152. "Don't come near the orphan's property except to improve it, until he attains the age of full strength; give measure and weight with (full) justice. No burden do We place on any soul, but that which it can bear. Whenever you speak, speak justly, even if a near relative is concerned. And fulfil the Covenant of God. Thus He commands you that you may remember."

153. "Verily, this is My Way leading straight, then follow it and don't follow other paths, they will scatter you about from His Path. Thus He commands you that you may be righteous."

In the above verses (6:151-153), God commands the following Moral Qualities (Moral Law) (Moral Etiquettes) (Moral Conduct):

1) Don't give partners to God
We should recognise that God is the One and Only Lord and Cherisher of all the Worlds. Those who give partners to God will say: "If God had wished, we should have not given partners to Him, nor would our fathers, nor should we have had any forbidden thing." The pagans' argument is false, for it implies (a) that men have no personal responsibility, (b) that they are the victims of a Determinism against which they are helpless, and (c) that they might therefore go on doing just what they liked. It is also inconsistent, for if (b) is true, (c) can't be true. Nor is it meant to be taken seriously.

2) Be good to your parents

The mention of goodness to parents immediately afterwards suggests: (1) that God's love of us and care for us may -on an infinitely higher plane- be understood by our ideal of parental love, which is purely unselfish; (2) that our first duty among our fellow creatures is to our father and mother, whose love leads us to the conception of divine love.

3) Don't kill your children on a plea of want
Arising from that divine love is the conception of our converse duties to our children. God provides sustenance (material and spiritual) not only for us, but for them. Hence any custom like the Pagan custom of sacrificing children to Moloch stands condemned.

4) Don't come near indecent deeds
God commands moral prohibitions against lewdness and all unseemly acts, relating to sex or otherwise, open or secret.

5) Don't take a life which God has made sacred
Killing an innocent soul is prohibited by God. It is not only that human life is sacred, but all life is sacred even in killing animals for food.

6) Don't come near orphan's property except to improve it
Orphans to be treated with tender affection and respect. Helpless creatures ought to be treated as sacred trusts.

7) Give measure and weight with justice, do not cheat
We have to deal justly and rightly with others. We are apt to thinking too much of ourselves and forgetting others.

8) Speak justly even if a near relative is concerned
The truth must always prevail, irrespective of the closeness of ties and relationships.

9) Fulfil the Covenant of God
Fulfil all contractual obligations or promises you made or contracts you signed. God was the Witness and you will be questioned about them on the Day of Judgement.

10) Stay on God's Straight Path
Our attention is called to the Straight Way, the Way of God, the only Way that leads to righteousness.

C) Surat Al-Isra (Journey by Night) or Bani Israel (The Children Of Israel)- Chapter 17

A) Verses 17:22-39

22. "Don't take with God another god; or you (O man!) will sit in disgrace and destitution."

23. "Your Lord has decreed that you worship none but Him, and that you be kind to parents. Whether one or both of them attain old age in your life, don't say to them a word of contempt, nor repel them, but address them in terms of honour."

24. *"And, out of kindness and mercy, lower to them the wing of humility, and say: "My Lord! Have mercy on them both as they did care for me when I was little."*

25. *Your Lord knows best what is in your hearts. If you do deeds of righteousness, verily He is Most Forgiving to those who turn to Him again and again (in true penitence)."*

26. *"And give to the kindred their due rights, as (also) to those in want, and to the wayfarer. But don't squander (your wealth) in the manner of a spendthrift, (an extravagant irresponsible way)."*

27. *"Verily spendthrifts are brothers of the Satans. And the Satan is to his Lord (Himself) ungrateful."*

28. *"But if you turn away from them, seeking from your Lord the mercy which you hope for, then speak to them a kind word."*

29. *"Don't make your hand tied (like a niggard's) to your neck, nor stretch it forth to its utmost reach, so that you become blameworthy and destitute."*

30. *"Verily your Lord provides sustenance in abundance for whom He will, and restricts (it for whom He will), for He is aware of His servants and can see them."*

31. *"And don't kill your children for fear of want. We shall provide sustenance for them as well as for you. Verily the killing of them is a great sin."*

32. *"And don't come near adultery, for it is an indecent (deed) and an evil way."*

33. *"And don't kill the life which Allah Has made sacred except for just cause. And if anyone is slain wrongfully, we have given his heir authority (to demand Qisas or to forgive), but let him not exceed bounds in the matter of taking life, for he is helped (by the law)."*

34. *"And don't come near the orphan's property except to improve it, until he attains the age of full strength. And you should fulfil (every) engagement, for (every) engagement will be enquired into (on the Day of Reckoning)."*

35. *"And give full measure when you measure, and weigh with a balance that is straight. That is better and fairer (for you) and best in the end."*

36. *"And don't concern yourself with anything of which you have no knowledge, for surly the hearing, the sight, and the heart all of them will be called to account for it (on Judgement Day)."*

37. *"And don't walk on the earth with insolence, for you can't penetrate the earth, nor reach the mountains in height."*

38. *"The evil of all this is hateful in the sight of your Lord."*

39. *"These are among the (precepts of) wisdom which your Lord has revealed to you. And don't take with God another object of worship, lest you should be thrown into Hell, blamed (by yourself) and rejected (by Him)."*

In the above verses (17:22-39), God commands the following Moral Qualities (Moral Law) (Moral Etiquettes) (Moral Conduct):

1) Don't take with God another object of worship
God has decreed that you worship none but Him. For there is none worthy of worship except God. If foolish men turn to false objects of worship, they will not only be disappointed, but they will lose the respect of their own fellow-men, and spiritually they will be reduced to destitution. All their talents and their works will be of no avail.

2) Be kind to your parents
"And out of kindness and mercy lower to them the wing of humility"
The metaphor is that of a high-flying bird which lowers her wing out of tenderness to her offspring. There is a double aptness. (1) When the parent was strong and the child was helpless, parental affection was showered on the child. When the child grows up and is strong, and the parent is helpless, can he do less than bestow similar tender care on the parent? (2) But more: he must approach the matter with gentle humility, for does not parental love, remind him of the great love with which God cherishes His creatures? There is something here more than simple human gratitude; it goes up into the highest spiritual realm.

We are asked to honour our father and mother, not "that thy days may be long upon the land which the Lord thy God giveth thee" (Exod. xx. 12), but upon much higher and more universal grounds, such as befit a perfected revelation. Firstly, not merely respect, but cherishing kindness, and humility to parents, are commanded. Secondly, this command is bracketed with the command to worship the One True God. Parental love should be to us a type of divine love. Nothing that we can do can ever really compensate for that which we have received. Thirdly, our spiritual advancement is tested by this. We can't expect God's forgiveness if we are rude or unkind to those who unselfishly brought us up.

3) Do not forget the rights of your poor relatives, as also those in want and the wayfarer
The worship of God is connected to kindness to parents, kindred, those in want, those who are far from their homes though they may be total strangers to us. It is not mere verbal kindness. They have certain rights which must be fulfilled.

However, you may have to "turn away" from people for two reasons. (1) You may not have the wherewithal with which to entertain them and give them their rights; or (2) you may have to give them a wide berth because their thoughts conflict with yours. In either case there is no need to speak harshly to them. Your words should be those of "easy kindness", i.e., the sort of kindness (not merely frosty politeness) which flows from empathy and understanding and smooths over unnecessary difficulties in human intercourse.

4) Do not be wasteful. Those who are wasteful are Satan's brothers

All charity, kindness, and help are conditioned by our own resources. There is no merit if we merely spend out of bravado or for idle show. How many families are ruined by extravagant expenses at weddings, funerals, etc. or (as they may call it) to "oblige friends or relatives", or to give to able-bodied beggars? To no one was this command more necessary than it is to Muslims of today.

Spendthrifts, those who spend their wealth in an extravagant irresponsible way, are not merely fools. They are of the same family as the Satans. And the Satan himself fell by his ingratitude to God. So those who misuse or squander God's gifts are also ungrateful to God.

5) Don't be stingy (miser) (tight fist) and do not over spend

We are not to be so lavish as to make ourselves destitute and incur the just censure of wise men, nor is it becoming to keep back our resources from the just needs of those who have a right to our help. Even strangers have such a right. But we must keep a just measure between our capacity and other people's needs.

If a foolish spendthrift pretends that his generosity, even if it ruins himself, is good for other people, he is reminded that God will take care of all. He knows everyone's true needs and cares for them. He gives in abundance to some, but in all cases He gives in just measure. Who are we to pretend to greater generosity?

6) Don't kill your children for fear of want

The Arabs were addicted to female infanticide. In a society perpetually at war a son was a source of strength whereas a daughter was a source of weakness. Even now infanticide is not unknown in other countries for economic reasons. This crime against children's lives is here characterised as one of the greatest of sins.

7) Do not come near adultery (fornication - sex outside marriage)

Adultery is not only shameful in itself and inconsistent with any self-respect or respect for others, but it opens the road to many evils. It destroys the basis of the family: it works against the interests of children born or to be born; it may cause murders and feuds and loss of reputation and property, and also loosen permanently the bonds of society. Sexually transmitted diseases are on the increase because of sex outside marriage. Not only should it be avoided as a sin, but any approach or temptation to it should be avoided.

8) Do not take life which God has made sacred

Under the strict limitations there laid down, a life may be taken for a life. The heir is given the right to demand the life; but he must not exceed due bounds, because he is helped by the Law.

9) Do not come near orphan's property except to improve it

If an orphan's property is touched at all, it should be to improve it, or to give him something better than he had before, never to take a personal advantage for the benefit of the guardian. A bargain that may be quite fair as between two independent persons would be, under this verse, unfair as between a guardian and his orphan ward until the latter reaches his full maturity of strength and understanding.

10) Fulfil any promise or engagement you make
We are commanded to honour every engagement or agreement or promise we make or a contract we sign as these will be questioned about on the Day of Judgement as we made God our Witness.

11) Do not cheat when you measure or weigh
Giving just measure and weight is not only right in itself but is ultimately to the best advantage of the person who gives it.

12) Do not spy on people
Idle curiosity may lead us towards evil, through our ignorance that it is evil. We must guard against every such danger. We must only hear the things that are known to us to be of good report, and see things that are good and instructive and entertain in our hearts feelings or in our minds ideas that we have reason to expect will be spiritually profitable to us. We shall be called to account for the exercise of every faculty that has been given to us. This goes a little farther than a famous sculpture on a Japanese temple in which three monkeys are shown as putting their hands to their ears, eyes and mouths, respectively, to show that they were not prepared to hear any evil, or see any evil, or speak any evil. Here idle curiosity is condemned. Futility is to be avoided even if it does not reach the degree of positive evil.

13) Do not walk on the earth with insolence
Insolence, or arrogance, or undue elation at our powers or capacities, is the first step to many evils. Besides, it is unjustified. All our gifts are from God.

The Moral Law, as expounded in 17:22-39 is far in advance of the bare Decalogue (the Ten Commandments) in that it searches out motives, and draws pointed attention to the weak and helpless if we are to reach any real understanding of God. It begins with a mention of the worship of God, the One True God and ends with a similar mention to close the argument, thus emphasising the fact that the love of God embraces the love of man and practical help of our fellow-creatures.

B) Verse 17:53

53. Say to My servants that they should (only) say those things that are best; for Satan does sow dissensions among them. Satan is indeed a manifest enemy to man.

The above verse commands the following Moral Quality:

1) Be considerate in your speech
This command refers to two situations. (1) Even to your enemies and the enemies of God you should speak fair: who are you to judge others? Judgement belongs to God alone, for He knows you (i.e., all mankind) best, and your personal knowledge is at best imperfect. And Satan is always trying to divide mankind. (2) Amongst yourselves, also you should not entertain suspicion, but speak politely according to the best standards of human speech. A

false or unkind word may destroy all your efforts at building up unity, because the forces of disruption are more numerous than the forces of unity.

C) Verse 17:78

78. Establish regular prayers from the declining of the sun (from it's zenith) till the darkness of the night, and the recital of the Qur'an in morning prayer. Indeed the recital of the Qur'an at dawn is witnessed.

The above verse commands the following Moral (Religious) Obligation:

1) Keep up the five daily prayers
This command refers to the five daily canonical prayers, viz,: the four from the declination of the sun from the zenith to the fullest darkness of the night, and the early morning prayer, Dawn prayer, (Fajr prayer), which is usually accompanied by a long reading of the holy Qur'an. The four afternoon prayers are: Zuhr, immediately after the sun begins to decline in the afternoon; Asr, in the late afternoon; Maghreb, immediately after sunset; and Isha, after the glow of sunset has disappeared and the full darkness of the night has set in. The morning prayer, which starts at least one and half hours before sunrise, is specially singled out for separate mention, because the morning is a "peaceful hour" and special influences act on the soul awaking from the night's rest. Special testimony is borne to the prayers of this hour by the angelic host.

D) Verse 17:110

110. Say: "Call upon God, or call upon Al-Rahman (The Lord of Mercy), be whatever name you call upon Him, (it is well), for to Him belong the Most Beautiful Names. And do not recite very loudly in your prayer, nor very quietly, but seek a middle course between them."

In the above verse God commands the following Moral Qualities:

1) Invoke God by any of His Beautiful Names
God can be invoked, either by His Gracious Name Allah, which includes all attributes, or by one of the names implying the attributes by which we try to explain His nature to our limited understanding. The attribute of Mercy in Al-Rahman was particularly repugnant to the Pagan Arabs; that is why special stress is laid on it in the Qur'an.

2) Do not disturb others with your noise while reciting in your prayers
All prayers should be pronounced with earnestness and humility, whether it is congregational prayer or the private outpouring of one's own soul. Such an attitude is not consistent with an over-loud pronunciation of the words, though in public prayers the standard of permissible loudness is naturally higher than in the case of private prayer. In public prayers, of course, the call to prayers (the Azan) will be in a loud voice to be heard near and far, unless you live in a country which does not permit this. But the recitation from the Qur'an should be neither so loud to disturb others or to attract the hostile notice of those who do not believe nor so low in tone as not to be heard by the whole congregation.

This Moral Quality should be observed when Muslims are using a multi-faith room, which is dedicated to all religions whether it is at an airport or at the work place.

D) Surat Al- Muminun (The Believers) - Chapter 23

A) Verses 23:1-11

"1. Successful indeed are the Believers.
2. Those who humble themselves in their prayers.
3. Those who avoid vain talk.
4. Those who are active in giving Zakat.
5. Those who guard their modesty.
6. Except with those joined to them in the marriage bond, or (the captives) whom their right hands possess, (for in their case) they are free from blame.
7. But those whose desires exceed those limits are transgressors.
8. Those who faithfully observe their trusts and their covenants.
9. And those who (strictly) guard their prayers.
10. Those will be the heirs.
11. Who will inherit Paradise. They will dwell there eternally."

In the above verses (23:1-11) God commands the following Moral Qualities (Moral Law) (Moral Etiquettes) (Moral Conduct):

1) Humble yourself in your prayers:
Humility in prayer as regards (1) their estimate of their own worth in Allah's presence, (2) as regards their estimate of their own powers or strength unless they are helped by Allah, and (3) as regards the petitions they offer to Allah.

2) Avoid vain talk
By being mindful and aware of what we say, we can strive to only speak well and avoid and type of vain talk

3) Be active in giving Zakat
The giving of Zakat enables us to participate in charity and this in itself reminds us of the needy and those who may not have all that we have.

4) Be modest
A believer must guard himself against every kind of sex abuse or sex perversion. The new psychology associated with the name of Freud, traces many of our hidden motives to sex, and it is a common knowledge that our refinement or degradation may be measured by the hidden workings of our sex instincts. But even the natural and lawful exercise of sex is restricted to the marriage bond, under which the rights of both parties are duly regulated and maintained.

5) Be trustworthy
Trusts may be express or implied. Express trusts are those where property is entrusted or duties are assigned by someone to some other whom he trusts, to carry out either

immediately or in specified contingencies, such as death. Implied trusts arise out of power, or position, or opportunity; e.g., a king holds his kingdom on trust from God for his subjects. Covenants create obligations, and express and implied trusts and covenants taken together cover the whole field of obligations.

6) Guard your prayers

In verse 2 we were directed to the spirit of humility and earnestness in our prayers. Here we are told how necessary the habit of regular prayer is to our spiritual well-being and development, as it brings us closer to God, and thus sums up the light of the Seven Jewels of our Faith, viz:
(1) Humility
(2) Avoidance of vanity
(3) Charity
(4) Sex purity
(5) Fidelity to trusts
(6) To covenants
(7) An earnest desire to get closer to God

So believers who practice these moral qualities explained above in 23:1-11, will succeed. They will prosper, thrive and achieve their aims to obtain salvation from sorrow and all evil. In the life to come, there is no doubt that every person will see the fruit of his life on earth and the righteous will inherit heaven, in the sense that they will attain it after their death here.

B) Verses 23:57-61

"57. Verily those who are so conscious about the fear they have for their Lord.
58. Those who believe in the Signs of their Lord.
59. Those who do not associate any partners (in worship) with their Lord.
60. And those who dispense their charity with their hearts full of fear, because they will return to their Lord.
61. It is these who race to do good things and they will be the first to get them."

In the above verses (23:57-61) God commands the following Moral Qualities (Moral Law) (Moral Etiquettes) (Moral Conduct):

1) Fear the Lord

We should live in awe for fear of our Lord. The fear which is akin to love. A feeling of a great respect sometimes mixed with fear. We do not fear the Lord because we are so concerned about His wrath. But because of the love we have for Him, we do not want to do anything wrong which would upset Him.

2) Believe in your Lord's Signs

Have faith in all the Lord's Messages and Messengers.

3) Don't associate any partners with your Lord

The oneness of God is paramount.

4) Give to charity with a heart conscious of your return to your Lord
Their hearts are full of reverence for God and fear lest their charity or their hearts be not good enough for acceptance before their Lord; for they have the certainty of a future life, in which they will stand before the Judgement Seat. They fear for their own worthiness, but they hope in Faith.

5) Race to do good deeds
If you have the above qualities it will make you hasten to do good deeds and you will outstrip others therein.

E) Surat Luqman - Chapter 31

Verses 31:12-19
- *"We bestowed wisdom on Luqman: 'Show your gratitude to God.' Any who is grateful does so to the profit of his own soul. But if any is ungrateful, verily God is free of all wants, worthy of all praise.*
- *Luqman said to his son by way of instruction: 'O my son! Don't join in worship (others) with God, for false worship is indeed the highest wrong doing.'*
- *And We have enjoined on man (to be good) to his parents. In travail upon travail did his mother bear him, and in two years was his weaning. (Here the command), 'Show gratitude to Me and to your parents, to Me is your final goal.*
- *'But if they strive to make you join in worship with Me things of which you have no knowledge, don't obey them. However, keep their company in this life with justice and consideration, and follow the way of those who turn to Me (in love). In the end the return of you all is to Me, and I will tell you all that you did.'*
- *'O my son!' (Said Luqman), 'if there be but the weight of a mustard seed and it was hidden in a rock, or anywhere in the heavens or the earth, God will bring it out, for God understands the finest mysteries, and is well acquainted with them.'*
- *'O my son! Establish regular prayers, enjoin what is just, and forbid what is wrong. And persevere patiently whatever (tests) may befall you, for this is firmness of purpose in the conduct of affairs.*
- *'And do not swell your cheek (for pride) at people, nor walk in insolence through the earth, for God does not love any arrogant boaster.*
- *'And be moderate in your pace, and lower your voice, for the harshest of all sounds without doubt is the braying of asses.'"*

In the above verses (31:12-19), God commands the following Moral Qualities (Moral Law) (Moral Etiquettes) (Moral Conduct)

1) Give thanks to God
We must always be grateful to God and acknowledge His favours and bounties upon us. He has given us of everything we have asked Him for. If we try to count God's favours, we could never reckon them. He has lavished us with His blessings seen, and unseen. God promised that if we are grateful, He will give us more. God never changes the Grace He has bestowed upon any people until they first start to abuse His favours. Then He will remove it from

them.

2) Never to associate any partners with God in any form
Always remember God is One and has no partners.

3) Be kind to your parents even if they are of a different religion
Respect for parents transcends all religions and is a right that all parents have over their children; for them to show respect and kindness.

4) Show gratitude to your parents
Displaying your gratitude and vocalising your thanks to your parents is important.

5) Establish regular prayers
The 5 daily prayers help create the order and routine of worship and helps keep us away from sin.

6) Enjoin and practice what is right, fair and just
Adopt fairness and do justice in all you say or do.

7) Forbid what is wrong without being aggressive or violent
Speak up when you see or hear of a wrong, but with measured tone and behaviour and no violence.

8) Persevere patiently in facing trials and tribulations in life
The testing of good men by calamities, and evil men by leaving them in the enjoyment of good things is part of the trials of God, in which some freedom of choice is left to man.

9) Do not show off
Be humble. Do not be arrogant. Do not hurt the feelings of other people. Show respect and kindness to those who are less fortunate than you. Be kind and helpful to those less endowed in any respect than ourselves.

10) Be moderate in everything you do in life. No to extremism!
Take the middle way and strive to be measured in your speech and behaviour so that others want to come towards you and consult and connect with you.

11) Do not be a nuisance to others
Lower your voice and your music! Do not be rude or aggressive. Live in peace with yourself and everyone around you.

F) Surat Al-Hujurat (The Inner Chambers)- Chapter 49

Verses 49:11-13

11. "O you who believe! Let not some men among you laugh at others. It may be that the (latter) are better than the (former). Nor let some women laugh at others. It may be that the (latter) are better than the (former); nor defame, nor be sarcastic to each other, nor call each other by (offensive) nicknames. Ill-seeming is a name connoting wickedness, (to be used of one) after he has believed. And those who don't desist are (indeed) doing wrong.

12. O you who believe! Avoid suspicion as much (as possible); for suspicion in some cases is a sin. And don't spy on each other, nor backbite each other. Would any of you like to eat the flesh of his dead brother? No, you would abhor it. But fear God, for God is Oft-Returning, Most Merciful.

13. O mankind! We created you from a single (pair) of a male and female, and made you into nations and tribes, to get to know each other (not to despise each other). Verily the most honoured of you in the sight of God is (he who is) the most righteous of you. And God has full knowledge and is well acquainted (with all things)."

In the above verses (49:11-13), God commands the following Moral Qualities (Moral Law) (Moral Etiquettes) (Moral Conduct)

1) No to mutual ridicule
Mutual ridicule ceases to be fun when there is arrogance or selfishness or malice behind it. We may laugh with people, to share in the happiness of life; we must never laugh at people in contempt or ridicule. In many things they may be better than ourselves.

2) No to defamation
Defamation may consist in speaking ill of others by the spoken or written word, or in acting in such a way as to suggest a charge against some person whom we are not in a position to judge.

3) Do not be sarcastic to each other
A cutting, biting remark or taunt of sarcasm is an evil act, and must be avoided.

4) Do not call each other by offensive nicknames
An offensive nickname may amount to defamation. But in any case there is no point in using offensive nicknames, or names that suggest real or fancied defect. For example, even if a man is lame, it is wrong to address him as "O lame one!" It causes him pain, and it is bad manners. So too when referring to a man in a derogatory way, in the case of the rude remark, "the black man".

5) Avoid suspicion
Most kinds of suspicion are baseless and to be avoided, and some are crimes in themselves, for they do cruel injustice to innocent men and women.

6) Do not spy on each other
Spying, or enquiring too curiously into other people's affairs, means either idle curiosity, and therefore futile, or suspicion carried a stage further, which almost amounts to sin.

7) No to backbiting
Backbiting also is a brood of the same genus. It may be either futile but all the same mischievous, or it may be poisoned with malice, in which case it is a sin added to sin.

8) No to Superiority Complex

We are all brothers and sisters in humanity. We are all the children of Adam and Eve. Before God we are all one, and he gets most honour who is most righteous.

9) Get to know each other

God created us all equal. He gave us a free will and endowed us with the same faculties. We are commanded here to make an effort to get to know each other, not to despise or abuse or exploit each other. Same family members must make more effort to understand each other. This will lead to peace at home which will lead to peace in the world.

A summary of God's Moral Law mentioned above, as stated in Chapters 3, 6,17,23,31 and 49 of the Qur'an, is given below:

A) Faith and Religious Practices

- Believe in the One True God. Do not take with Him another object of worship. Never to associate any partners with Him in any form.
- Believe in your Lord's Signs.
- Fear the Lord.
- Stay on God's Straight Path.
- Give thanks to God.
- Invoke God by any of His Beautiful Names.
- Keep up the five daily prayers.
- Humble yourself in your prayers.
- Do not disturb others with your noise while reciting in your prayers.
- Guard your prayers.
- Be active in giving Zakat.
- Give to charity with a heart conscious of your return to your Lord.
- Be quick in repenting if you have done something wrong.
- Take part in the Spiritual Marathon. Race to do good deeds.

B) Dealing with Others

- Be good and kind to your parents even if they are of a different religion.
- Show gratitude to your parents.
- Do not kill your children for fear of want.
- Do not forget the rights of your poor relatives and also those in need and the wayfarer.
- Restrain anger.
- Forgive people.
- Speak justly even if a near relative is concerned.
- Do not walk on earth with insolence.
- Be considerate in your speech.
- Avoid vain talk.
- Be modest.
- Be trustworthy.
- Enjoin and practice what is right, fair and just.
- Forbid what is wrong without being aggressive or violent.
- Persevere patiently in facing trials and tribulations in life.

- Do not show off.
- Be moderate in everything you do in life.
- Do not be a nuisance to others.
- No to mutual ridicule.
- No to defamation.
- Do not be sarcastic to each other.
- Do not call each other by offensive nicknames.
- Avoid suspicion.
- Do not spy on eachother.
- No to backbiting.
- No to superiority complex.
- Get to know each other.

1.6.4 Forth Jewel: Justice and Equality for All

In the following section, I will refer to a few verses from the Qur'an regarding God's Justice and what does He expect from us?

In 16:90, God commands the doing of three good deeds and forbids three evil deeds: *"God commands justice, the perfection of doing good, and giving (charity) to relatives. And He forbids all indecent deeds, injustice and transgression.*
And He says in 4:58, *"God commands you to return things entrusted to you to their rightful owners, and when you judge between people you judge with justice. Surely how excellent is the teaching which He gives you, for God hears and sees all things."*

And in 4:135, He says, *"O you who believe! Stand out firmly for Justice, as witnesses to God, even as against yourselves, or your parents, or your relatives, and whether it be (against) rich or poor, for God can best protect both. Don't follow the lusts (of your hearts), lest you swerve, and if you distort (justice) or decline to do justice, surely God is well-acquainted with all that you do."*

"Justice is one of God's attributes. One of His Most Beautiful Names is 'Al-Adl', the 'Source of Justice'. To stand firm for justice is to be a witness to God, even if it is detrimental to our own interests as we conceive them or the interests of those who are near and dear to us. Some people may be inclined to favour the rich, because they expect something from them. Some people may be inclined to favour the poor because they are generally helpless. Partiality in either case is wrong. Be just, without fear or favour. Both the rich and the poor are under God's protection as far as their legitimate interests are concerned, but they cannot expect to be favoured at the expense of others. And He can protect their interests far better than any man." FN644-645

To do justice and act righteously in a favourable or neutral atmosphere is meritorious enough, but the real test comes when you have to do justice to people who hate you or to whom you have an aversion. But no less is required of you by the higher moral law, as God states in verse 5:8:
"O you who believe! Stand out firmly for God, as witnesses to fair dealing, and let not the hatred of others to you make you swerve to wrong and depart from justice. Be Just; that is next to piety, and fear God for God is well-acquainted with all that you do."

God warns us in 2:188 not to use our own property for corrupting and bribing others-judges or those in authority- so as to obtain some material gain even under the cover and protection of the law:

"And don't eat up your property among yourselves for vanities, nor use it as a bait for the judges, with intent that you may eat up wrongfully and knowingly a little of (other) people's property."

We must understand that supporting oppressors and those who are unfair and unjust, is strongly condemned by God as mentioned in 11:213: *"And don't incline to those who practice injustice, or the Fire will burn you; and you will have no protectors from God and you will be defeated."* God also says in 2:258 that He does not guide the unjust and in 3:57 He states that He does not love unfair people, and they will never prosper (6:21).

Unfortunately, injustice in all its different forms, whether between members of the same family who are violating Personal Family Law, or between individuals who are defrauding and cheating each other, or between a tyrant ruler who enslaves his subjects, or any person who abuses his position and betrays the trust, will continue to be the norm practised by those who have no fear of God and those who don't believe in accountability on the Day of Judgement. On that day there will be no injustice as stated by God in 40:17: *"This Day will each soul be requited for that which it has earned. No wrong (will be done to anyone) this Day, God is indeed swift at reckoning."* The judgement will be carried out by the One and Only Judge who knows all the secrets of our hearts and minds and our motives and intentions (40:19). All the facts of what we did in this life will be presented to us as said in 58:6: *"On the Day when God will raise them all together. He will inform them of what they did. God has kept account of it, though they have forgotten it. God is Witness over all things."*

It is so reassuring that God does not involve any person whatsoever in His Judgement (18:26). And He is never unfair as stated in 4:40: *"God is never unjust in the least degree. If there is any good (done) He doubles it, and gives (the doer) from Himself a mighty reward."* And in 10:44 He confirms His justice: *"God doesn't wrong people in anything, but people wrong themselves."*

1.7 Conclusion

In this Chapter, I detailed what Muslim Nations should embrace and embed to begin to reverse the state of humiliation they currently live in and become prosperous again. They must become Qur'an compliant. God says in 47:24: *"Do they not then earnestly seek to understand the Qur'an, or are there locks on their hearts?"* Or are we going to be of those who will say to God on the Day of Judgement: *"We were constantly busy looking after our businesses and our families."* 48:11

Muslims must make a real effort to study God's Moral Law in the Qur'an and sincerely apply it in their daily practices. They must implement the true moderate message of Islam as preached and practiced by Prophet Mohammed (pbuh) and to reject fanaticism and radicalism. Verse 2:143 commands this: *"Thus we have made you a moderate (a middle) nation, so that you may act as witnesses over mankind and that the Messenger (Mohammed) may be a witness over you"*.

In an authentic Hadith (in Sunan Abi Dawud) the Prophet Mohammed (pbuh) informed us that many nations would collectively gang up against Muslims, in spite of their great numbers, like the beasts gathering around their prey, or hungry people on their food. Why? Because the love of this life, and hate of leaving this world, has fully saturated our hearts. Sadly we have lived to witness this day.

The state of humiliation and disgrace Muslim countries suffer from, will not be reversed until and unless they hold fast, all together, to the Rope of God and not to be divided, as ordered in 3:103.

They must eradicate corruption from their systems as commanded in 11:116-117: *"If only there had been, among the generations before your time, people with a remnant of good sense, to forbid corruption on the earth! We saved only a few of them, while the unjust pursued the enjoyment of plenty, and persisted in sin. Your Lord would not destroy any town without cause if its people were acting righteously."* God here is referring to leaders who have a balanced good sense that stands firm to virtue and withstands the lusts and pleasures of this world. They are not deterred by fear from boldly condemning wrong, despite it being fashionable or customary. It is leaders possessed of such character that can save a nation from disaster or perdition. The scarcity of such leaders-and the rejection of the few who stood out- brought ruin among the nations whose example has already been set out to us, in the Qur'an, as a warning.

Education, hard work, good manners and justice for all, are the ingredients for happy and prosperous nations.

We all must seek the love of God and His Messenger as commanded in 3:31-32, *"Say (Mohammed): 'If you do love God, follow me; God will love you and forgive you your sins; for God is Oft-Forgiving, Most Merciful.' Say (Mohammed): 'Obey God and the Messenger.' But if you turn back, God doesn't love those who reject faith."* The Lord and Sustainer of all the Worlds, states in 24:52 that those who obey Him and His Messenger and fear Him and observe their duty to Him, will prosper and be triumphant.

Chapter 2 -White Supremacy and Satanic Diplomacy

2.1 Introduction

Following the election of President DT in 2016, a white American said: *"One of the greatest qualities of President DT is that he 'Speaks his mind!' America never had such a great president like him. He is our hero. He is so brave. He is out to defend the rights of the white Christians against the invasion of non-white, non-Christians. It is us, the whites, who created this country. He will not stop me from buying a gun to shoot the invaders."*

Are we really hearing these sentiments, expressed so openly in current times?! What a sad statement to hear! I wonder, did everyone who voted for DT share this radical and racist view? If this equates to what his supporters feel and is the way they **'speak their minds',** **then may God save the righteous from an imminent Divine Wrath.** Is Covid-19 in response to the conduct of those who did upset God?

2.2 The White Satan and the Creation Ceremony

The story of the creation of Adam is mentioned in the Qur'an in chapters 2, 4, 7, 15, 17, 18, 20 and 38.

Before Adam's creation, God sent an invitation to all the angels and to the King of the Jinn to attend Adam's Creation Ceremony. The invitation had the following message written on it: *"I will create a vicegerent on Earth, a man called Adam, created from sounding clay from mud moulded into shape. When I have fashioned him in due proportion and breathed into him of My Spirit, fall down prostrating yourselves unto him."*

The King of the Jinn was so swift to be there on time. He raced with the angels to occupy a prominent seat near the stage. He didn't want to miss such a great opportunity to watch the creation of a man from clay. *'"A man from clay to rule the Earth"* he thought to himself. *"What about me? Why God didn't chose me as His vicegerent. Surely I'm better than the angels who are only created to obey, but can't even make a decision. God created me with a free will so I can make decisions to save the Earth. I think God is making a big mistake here and surely He will regret it later. Definitely I'm going to tell him that. I will **speak my mind** to Him in front of all the angels."*

Fireworks started and a Big Bang could be heard so loudly and Adam the first human being appeared on the stage.

All the angels fell down in prostration to him as commanded by God. The King of the Jinn stood up looking at Adam, the newest creation by God. He gazed at the angels who had their foreheads on the floor, in prostration. He murmured to himself, "wh*at stupid angels these are who humiliated themselves to such an ugly creature! O my God! He is black! Did God forget him in the oven? Surely he is over cooked! God created the angels from light and created me from smokeless fire, so we both glow. But this man looks like as if the light was turned off".* The King of the Jinn continued to murmur to himself.

Then God asked him: "*What is your reason for not being among those who prostrated themselves? What prevented you from prostrating when I commanded you?".* The King of the Jinn responded in a very arrogant manner: "*I used my free will which You created me with. I decided not to prostrate myself to a man, whom You created from sounding clay, from mud moulded into shape. Surely I'm better than him, You created me from fire and created him from clay. **I'm speaking my mind, my Lord.**"*

That was the first ever racist remark passed by a creature of God towards another one. He felt he was more superior to Adam because of his origin. The King of the Jinn exhibited his rebelliousness born of arrogance. Notice his subtle wiles, his egotism in putting himself above man, and his falsehood and delusion in ignoring the fact that God had not merely made man's body from clay, but had given him spiritual form. In other words, had taught him the nature of things and raised him above the angels. So when man uses his free will correctly and submits his will to the Will of God he is better than the angels in God's sight.

That is why the angels were commanded to prostrate themselves to Adam and not the other way round.

God said in 7:13 to the King of the Jinn: *"Get down from here. It is not for you to be arrogant here. Get out, for you are of the meanest (of creatures)."*

Then God gave him several titles. He called him '**Shaitan**' (this is an Arabic word which is equivalent to Satan in English). It means he went out of God's Way, God's Straight Path. And He named him '**Iblis**' which means he despaired of the Mercy of God. He did not believe that God would have forgiven him if he would have said sorry. His arrogance also prevented him from saying sorry as he felt it was below his perceived superiority to Adam and dignity to apologise. When Adam and Eve succumbed to temptation and ate from the forbidden tree they said sorry to God because they had faith in His Mercy and Forgiveness. Another name given to the King of the Jinn was '**Rajeem**' which means 'the rejected and accursed one'. Also God called him **Al-Gharoor**, the Chief Deceiver.

So he is now fully decorated and adorned with the most awful attributes. The King of the Jinn became the King of Evil, the original father of all the Devils.

Satan turned towards God, without showing any remorse, and said: *"Give me respite till the day they are raised up."* So God granted him respite till the Day of Resurrection.
Satan said: *"Because You have thrown me out of the Way and You have preferred this despised and despicable creature over me, I will surely bring his descendants under my sway. I will lie in wait for them on Your Straight Way. Then I will assault them from before them and behind them, from their right and their left, nor You will find, in most of them, gratitude for Your mercies and favours. I will make evil fair-seeming to them on the Earth. I will lead them all astray except Your servants amongst them who are sincere and purified by Your Grace."*

"...Surely, I will take of your servants an appointed portion. And surely, I will lead them astray, and I will arouse (deceiving) desires in them, and surely, I will command them and they will slit the ears of the cattle, and surely, I will command them and they will alter the creation of God..." 4:118-119

God said, *"Get out from here, despised and expelled. The Curse shall be on you till the Day of Judgement. If any of them follow you, I will fill Hell with you all."*

"Another instance of Iblis's subtlety and falsehood. He waits till he gets the respite. Then he breaks out into a lie and impertinent defiance. The lie is in suggesting that God had thrown him out of the Way, in other words misled him, **he spoke his mind** again, whereas his own conduct was responsible for his degradation. By his own arrogance and rebellion he fell. The defiance is in his setting snares on the Straight Way to which God directs Adam and his children.

"The assault of evil is from all sides. It takes advantage of every weak point, and sometimes even our good and generous sympathies are used to decoy us into the snares of evil.

"Man has every reason to be grateful to God for His loving care and yet man in his folly forgets his gratitude and does the very opposite of what he should do." FN1001 & 1002.

2.3 Adam's Wedding and Satanic Diplomacy

Adam's and Eve's wedding was a commemorative occasion, celebrated by Heavens and Earth. God introduced all the guests to Adam one by one, and amazingly Adam memorised all the names. There was only one creature who was not invited to the wedding due to his enmity to Adam. That was Satan, the king of the Devils.

Adam and Eve were created to live on earth, not in Heaven. Their honeymoon was planned in the most beautiful garden on earth or maybe temporarily, somewhere in Heaven.

God, the Most Merciful, warned both the bride and the groom, about Satan and told them that Satan is their true enemy, so they must take him as enemy and never to befriend him, otherwise they will lose God's Bounties.
God said: *"O Adam! Dwell you and your wife in the Garden, and eat from wherever you wish, but don't come near this tree, lest you become of the unjust."* Verse 7:19.

God added: *"O Adam! Verily, this is an enemy to you and your wife, so let him not get you both out of the Garden, as you will land in misery. There is therein (enough provision) for you not to go hungry, nor to go naked, nor to suffer from thirst, nor from the sun's heat."* Verses 20:117-119.

So God, in His wisdom, introduced to Adam and Eve their manifest enemy and alluded them to the test of temptation. He warned them not to come near a specific tree in the Garden. He didn't say *"Don't eat from it"*. He said *"Don't come near it"*. Because if they come near it they may be tempted to taste it's fruits. Then they will lose everything.

Satan now felt he can use diplomacy to tempt both of them. He whispered evil to Adam saying, *"O Adam! Shall I lead you to the tree of Eternity and to a Kingdom that never decays?"* 20:120.

The suggestion of Satan is clever, as it always is. It is false, and at the same time plausible.

Then Satan began to whisper suggestions to both of them saying: *"Your Lord only forbade both of you this tree, lest you should become angels or you live forever. He swore to them that he was their sincere adviser."* 7:20-21.

Unfortunately, they believed Satan and fell into temptation and ate from the forbidden tree. The honeymoon was over. The Garden became a desert, the water evaporated, and the sun blazed on their heads. If they would have just listened to the advice of their Lord and not to the evil whispers of Satan they would have had an eternal honeymoon.

In spite of the fact that they had lost everything they had, they did not blame each other or insult each other or fight with each other. They did not leave each other. If they would have walked away on that day none of us would have been here today. Instead they remained supportive to each other. They did not lose the love they had for each other and their faith in God's Mercy and Forgiveness. They felt very sorry and ashamed of what they have done. So they both turned to their Lord in repentance saying: *"Our Lord we have wronged our own souls and if you don't forgive us and bestow Your Mercy on us, we shall certainly be lost."* 7:23.

They both said sorry and asked for God's forgiveness. Something Satan refused to do when he refused to prostrate himself to Adam.

So God graciously forgave them as stated in verse 2:37, and they began their new lives and struggle on planet earth.

On the Day of Judgement, when all the matters have been finally decided, Satan will be permitted by God to address the children of Adam and broadcast his final sermon, as stated at verse 14:22 *"It was God Who gave you a promise of Truth. I too promised, but failed in my promise to you. I had no authority over you except to call you, and you listened to me. Then don't reproach me, but reproach your own souls. I can't listen to your cries, nor can you listen to mine. I reject your former act in associating me with God. For wrong-doers there must be a grievous Chastisement."*

"After the Judgement, Evil declares itself in its true colours. Frankly it says: 'I deceived you. The promise of God was true, but you believed me rather than God. I had no power to force you. I had but to call you, and you came running after me. You must blame yourselves. Did you think I was equal with God? I know too well that I was not and never could be. If you did wrong, you must suffer the Penalty.'" FN1897.

Satan has a large army of wicked seducers, including many willing men and women who will follow his evil suggestions and whisperings and carry these out for him. God says in 6:112 that there are Satans among humans and Jinn, inspiring each other with flowery discourses by way of deception and delusion. But eventually they will all be defeated and thrown into the Hell Fire.

2.4 Dementia & Speaking Your Mind

I was the manager and proprietor of Greenmantle Care Home for 30 years, in Woodford Green, London where I cared for old people with dementia.

The majority of the carers were from the ethnic minorities. One day, a carer reported to me that Mrs AB told her *"I don't want a black carer to touch me."*

"And what did you say to her?" I asked.

She replied *"I told her sorry we have no white staff to clean your poo. So I'm afraid it is only me who will wash you."* I said to her: *"Please don't be upset you know she has dementia. She doesn't mean it."*

She replied, *"Yes Dr Fahim I know that. But what she said has always been in her mind. When she had mental capacity she controlled her tongue. But the moment she lost control she is now saying the hate she used to conceal."*

I said to myself *"Yes. She is right."*

Then, I telephoned the daughter of Mrs AB, and asked her to come to see me.

When she came, I told her what happened. I said: *"I'm aware that your mother has dementia and she did not mean what she said as **she speaks her mind** and she has no control over what she says. Even God would forgive her for what she says as she has no mental capacity. But please can you just talk to the carer as she felt what your mother said was a very hurtful racist remark."* The daughter immediately apologised and said *"It is sad what my mother said especially that we are Jews."*

I remember I had a visitor from Saudi Arabia who was admitted to a private hospital in Harley Street, London. A black nurse came to attend to him. He said to me in Arabic: *"I didn't come all the way from Saudi to be nursed by a black woman. I want a white nurse with blue eyes and golden hair"*. I was so disgusted to hear that from someone who claims to be a Muslim and he himself is a man of colour. I said: *"If I translate what you said to me we will both go to jail. This is not Saudi where you have no respect for Human Rights. If you are not happy you can leave now."* Of course, he stayed. That was a non-demented racist Muslim Arab who **spoke his mind.**

Once a black Racial Equality Officer visited the hospital in London, where my wife used to work, to train medical staff regarding new legislation. The English Head of my wife's department said in a very arrogant manner: *"When I treat my patients, I treat them equally, but what is in my heart and mind is my own choice."* **He spoke his mind!**

One of my wife's colleagues, a black Christian nurse, was very badly discriminated against by white staff. She said: *"I believe in life after death. I'm praying to God to bring me back as a white person."*

When my wife was examining a white patient before anaesthetising him for surgery. He said to her: *"I don't want an Indian doctor to examine me!"* **He spoke his mind!**

My wife replied: *"Hard luck I'm not Indian."* She could have easily cancelled his operation due to him being abusive, and he would have definitely had to re-join the waiting list. But, being a professional doctor and caring person, she decided to ignore his derogatory remark and go ahead with his surgery.

I think the first ever racist comment I heard was from a neighbour in Egypt when I was at the age of seven or eight. We had a porter serving our block of flats. It is very sad to say that in many Muslim countries the rich would always look down on the poor.

The porter's wife delivered a boy and called him 'Jameel', which means in Arabic, beautiful. Her husband went to the registration office and obtained a birth certificate for his newly born son. One of the neighbours had a five year old son also called 'Jameel'. So when she was told that the porter's son had been named the same like her own son, you could hear the rudest and the harshest comments like, *"How dare you name your son like my son. You are a porter and we are your masters. If you don't go and change his name we will kick you out from here"*. The poor porter had to go back to the registration office to change the name of his son and obtained a new birth certificate to satisfy the ego of one of the tenants. Thank God, there will be a Day of Judgement and Life After Death where there will be no injustice on that day.

These are a few examples of people from one ethnicity looking down on people from another ethnicity or people from the indigenous population discriminating against people from the exogenous population or people from the same country discriminating against each other.

This is happening all the time among all races because of 'Superiority Complex'. It is prevalent among the Arabs, the Asians, the Africans and the Europeans, and among the adherents of all religions. Even in telling jokes we will target a specific group of people within a country to make fun of. In Egypt we tell jokes about the people from Upper Egypt that is the south of Egypt. In Britain we would tell jokes about the Irish. I don't think this is appropriate as we should show respect and love to each other rather than making fun of them even if we are just joking to make someone laugh.

So if you are a ruler **who speaks his mind** and you have full mental capacity you will be held accountable, in this life and the Hereafter, for inciting hatred among any of your subjects. You may be excused if you are 'demented' and I will offer you free accommodation in my Care Home to save humanity from your evil thoughts.

2.5 My First Job

In 1972 and after I completed my Master in Computer Science from the University of London, I applied for a job with a Consulting Engineering firm in London. I was to join their Research & Development (R&D) department as a computer scientist to develop computer applications in Civil & Structural engineering.

In the interview, I made it clear that I have a Bachelor in Aeronautical Engineering and a Master in Computer Science and that I worked in the aircraft industry and the computer industry for four years.

The owner of the company, who was a white English gentleman, said to me at the end of the interview: *"We already have a Chinese working for us, there is no harm in trying an Egyptian."*

I was hurt so much to hear that from an educated man, but I needed the job so I had to accept his racist comment and eat humble pie.

His remark brought back a lot of memories. He had obviously forgotten the British colonisation of Egypt and the demoralisation of its people and the looting of its wealth and the repeated barbaric massacres.

Lord Cromer, in 1919, sentenced my grandfather Sheikh Ahmad Hatata, a lawyer from Al-Azhar University, to death following the revolution against the British occupation to Egypt. The sentence was later reduced to 25 years imprisonment, but he was released after five years due to his ill health. Unfortunately, one of his legs was amputated in the prison due to lack of medical treatment for his diabetes.

How did my grandmother and her children manage to survive whilst my grandfather was in prison? Did Lord Cromer think of that? Or was it the 'White Supremacy' which justified these acts of terror against innocent people living in their own country?

My mother was very patriotic. She used to say: *"I love Egypt. I don't like anyone to say anything bad about it. My father was a hero. He fought against the British occupation. He declared the independence of Al-Menia Province, in southern Egypt. He became the ruler and was given the title 'Emperor'. He organised his army and police force. If you don't believe me go and see his statue in the Town Hall of Al-Menia."*

I was not that sure of what she was saying regarding the title of her father and the independent state he created. So recently I checked her story on social media. And to my surprise, everything she said was true. Maybe I should take part in the BBC programme 'Meet your Ancestors'.

My father was an agriculture engineer, graduated from King Fouad University in Cairo in 1941. He was responsible for the protection of Egyptian crops from insects' attacks. A role similar to what Prophet Joseph did in Egypt many years ago before him. During my school holidays, and as a child, I used to accompany him on his tours of the cotton fields to check the performance of the teams responsible for fighting the 'cotton worms'. The cotton was the most important agricultural crop in Egypt. He explained to me that the butterfly would lay eggs on the leaves of the cotton plant. When the eggs hatch the little worms would feed on the leaves and the cotton plant would die. The fighting team comprised mainly young women supervised by a man. If my father was not happy with their performance, he would tell them off in Arabic and end his message with 'F...king Egyptians', in English. I was only six years old and I didn't understand the meaning of his words in English.

When I went to London in July 1970, I asked a colleague at work to teach me all the rude words in English, so if anyone would say a rude comment to me, I would understand what they said. Then and only then, I understood the meaning of the 'F' swearing word. O my God! How could my father, such a devout Muslim, and a very cultured and educated man swear at these poor people?

After four years I went back to Egypt on holiday. I asked my father regarding what he used to say to these poor peasants over 20 years ago. To my surprise, he said he didn't know what it meant! He added, *"We had a white English teacher at secondary school, who used to shout at us and say 'F...king Egyptians'"*. I said, *"father, this is a very rude swear word in English, so please don't ever say it again."*
It was so sad to hear about the Superiority Complex of a white English teacher who looked down on his students, simply because he was the occupier, **who spoke his mind**.

I remember very well the Suez Aggression in 1956 when Britain, France and Israel attacked Egypt following the nationalisation of Suez Canal by President Naser. We had to paint all the windows in blue and study with the light of a candle. In the event of an air raid, the sirens would sound and we would switch all the candles off. Unfortunately, we didn't have shelters to seek protection in.

I was ten years old. I walked into an army camp and volunteered to join the Army to defend Egypt against the aggressors. I think my mother's genes of being so patriotic had engulfed me. The army officer said: *"You are a very brave boy. Ask your father to come."*
I said: *"My father is a full time Civil Servant."* The Officer said: *"Then he is exempt."* Can you imagine the destruction and the killing of so many innocent people simply because Egypt restored what belonged to her from the hands of the aggressors?

Let me return to the interview for my first full time job in London. I forgot about the racist remark of my employer and tried to erase it from my mind. I persevered patiently and worked so hard. Some of my colleagues were so jealous of me because I used to work during my lunch break and I used to take the work home to increase my output. Something I found my fellow English colleagues were not used to. I also used to say my daily prayers next to my desk in front of everyone. Nobody ever said anything. On the contrary they showed great respect. I remained in this job for nine years.

Due to my qualifications and experience, the Firm was awarded a huge job from the PSA (The Property Service Agency) of the DOE (Department of the Environment) to produce a computer application to design buildings with special engineering features. I became the project manager for the duration of the project which lasted for three years.

I also managed, whilst working full time, to complete in 1978 my PhD in 'Airports Planning using Computer Simulation Models'. The Firm was involved in designing a number of airports in the UK and overseas including Belfast, Shetland, Gatwick, Amman and Kuwait airports, and my research work was key to this design stage.

The Financial Times wrote on 19th August 1975, under **Computing** a long article titled 'Evaluating airport parameters'. The article referred to my work. In summary it said: '...Dr Fahim is working with the Airport Design Group of Sir Frederick Snow and Partners, consulting engineers, to use a model which simulates the flow of people through the different areas of the terminal building as well as different airport activities including car parking facilities, check-in, security, immigration, etc. The model takes account of incoming luggage and gate allocation for arriving and departing aircraft...'

The Computer Weekly wrote on 4th September 1975: '**Airport planning model designed by student**- An Egyptian PhD student has provided the initial inspiration and most of the design effort in the development of a second suite of simulation software for airport planning, on behalf of consulting engineers Sir Frederick Snow and Partners. The simulation will place particular emphasis on efficient flow of passengers and baggage within the terminal building...'

I also produced a computer application for designing "Storm Sewer Networks using RRL Method."

In 1975, the Firm was awarded the design of a major water supply scheme in Saudi Arabia for one million pounds fee, and I was delighted to have played a major role in this bid acquisition too.

I share this to underline that we must not allow the hate of the others, due to ethnicity or faith or gender, to stop us from doing what is right and achieving and excelling in life. I always applied verse 41:34 in dealing with people who hated me or felt jealous of me: *"Good and evil can't be equal. Repel evil with what is better and your enemy will become as close as an old and valued friend."*

FN4504 reads: *"You don't return good for evil, for there is no equality or comparison between the two. You repel or destroy evil with something which is far better, just as an antidote is better than poison. You foil hatred with love. You repel ignorance with knowledge, folly and wickedness with the friendly message of God's Revelation. The man who was in the bondage of sin, you not only liberate from sin, but make him your greatest friend and helper in the cause of God."*

My two role models who fought hatred with love and passion were Prophet Jacob and his son Prophet Joseph. They both embarked upon two different rehabilitation plans to save the ten sons of Jacob who hated Joseph to such an extent, that they wanted to kill him but eventually decided to throw him into a well to get rid of him. I always emulate their style in dealing with hatred.

My employer and I became very close and good friends. It is always ignorance which is the chief contributory factor that leads to fearing each other. But once we start to get to know each other, we share curiosity and ask when we do not know rather than assume, there will be no fear and no hatred. My employer was so appreciative of what I did in my nine years while working in his firm, that upon my resignation, he offered a 50% increase in my wages as an inducement to stay. But unfortunately, I had to go to start my own Project Management Consultancy in Regent Street, London, where I was managing major construction projects and water supply schemes in the Middle East.

2.6 The Irish Conflict

I was not aware of the cause of the conflict in Northern Ireland between the Catholics and the Protestants.

My boss, the Head of R&D was Irish Protestant from Belfast, with PhD from Queens University. He used to tell me awful things about the Catholics in his City.

Academically he was highly qualified, but spiritually he was empty. He had a lot of hatred towards the Irish Catholics and supported the presence of the British troops in Northern Ireland.

It took a while for me to understand the main cause of the conflict, but I will never condone any terrorist attacks by any conflicting parties (or indeed anyone), towards innocent people anywhere in the world.

2.7 Our British Citizenship

When I applied for Naturalisation in 1978 to become a British Citizen we had to advertise in the local newspaper in Woodford Green, London, to allow anyone with any objections to come forward and voice these.

Subsequently we were visited by a police officer from New Scotland Yard who inspected our house and looked at our bank statements and even at my wife's jewellery. She said before leaving: "I don't think you will have any problem in getting your naturalisation. You are not dirty like the Pakistanis I visit." Was it really necessary to say that?

I didn't feel comfortable with her comment, but **she spoke her mind.** From a professional point of view this should not have been vocalised. Unfortunately, I believe the police force at that time was suffering from 'Institutional Racism' and many may say this is still the case in some sectors and levels.

When my wife was getting her British naturalisation application form countersigned by her white boss at the hospital he said: *"You will be British. But you will never be English!"* Was this a necessary comment from a medical professional to a colleague? But **he spoke his mind!** I am so proud to be a British Muslim from an Egyptian origin.

2.8 Neighbours from Hell

In 1981 my house in Woodford Green, London, and my cars used to be attacked on regular basis by our criminal neighbours, who hated to have 'Wogs' living next to them. Even I didn't understand the meaning of the 'Wogs' stickers which they stuck on my car and my house. These criminal neighbours used to slash the tyres of our cars, put black bags full of rubbish on the top of our cars, spit on the mirrors of our cars. Some nights you would have a flying ball-bearing smashing the window of the front room. We had two little children. We lived in constant fear. We spent so many sleepless nights.

We lived there for four years without any problems at all, and we could not comprehend why this was suddenly happening to us? We later discovered that our neighbours two sons had been in prison and they had been released. They continuously used to fight with their parents and we often saw them running after each other in the garden and shouting verbal abuse. I felt sorry for the parents who were in their early fifties.

When the police came for the first time, he said to me, *"You look English. But the moment you open your mouth you are a foreigner."* Thank you, officer, for being so helpful and reassuring! Great! **He spoke his mind!**

The sleepless nights and the fear and the anxiety we experienced could not be explained. We were advised that we must move away from these nasty neighbours. We were also advised to immediately have a 'For Sale' sign in front of our house so these terrorising neighbours would get the message.

Fortunately, by the Grace of God the Almighty we managed to move out of the area. But imagine if one day the whole country would become hostile to the ethnic minorities because of the hatred incited by the politicians, **who speak their minds,** where would we move to?

2.9 Racism and the European Disintegration

In May 2006 I was invited by the Home Office to attend a five day residential course called '20:20' run by a company called 'Common-Purpose'.

The course included different topics regarding "Governance - who's pulling the strings? The Idea of Europe? Wealth creation and global influences, and international trends & looking ahead". The course was attended by several very senior Civil Servants from almost every ministry. I was attending in my capacity as a Muslim Chaplain/Imam. The Home Office funded my placement which was about £7,000. I was the first ever Muslim Chaplain/Imam to be funded by the Home Office to attend this course as it was part of the Government agenda to combat radical Islam and extremism.

I was not surprised to discover that the majority of the participants as well as the organisers knew nothing about Islam apart from what the media espouses. I had the opportunity of introducing Islam to a large number of them. I offered my services free of charge to visit and talk to their employees about Islam.

This encounter inspired me to design my Islamic Christmas cards. So instead of sending a copy of the Qur'an to members of the Royal Family, or every MP at Westminster or a minister or a senior civil servant, I would utilise the occasion of Christmas and send the story of Mary and Jesus as mentioned in the Qur'an, whilst wishing everyone a Merry Christmas and a Happy New Year.

As part of the course, we visited No.10 Downing Street and whilst waiting for the PM Tony Blair, we had a meeting with his private secretary. He was a small Irish man who looked like me. He shared that he wrote all the speeches of the PM and the PM would just add or delete whatever he wished.

Is it possible that the PM's secretary left a note to Cherie recommending 'Weapons of Mass Distraction by Wonder Bra' to her. It seems Tony picked it up by mistake and as he was not sure of the spelling of his Irish secretary, he read it as 'Weapons of Mass Destruction'. Hence, he had to start his war against Iraq? The fault was Cherie's - she had asked the secretary to recommend a bra to her. As she is a barrister, I think she meant the 'bar'. But the Irish guy, under the influence of a pint of Guinness from the 'bar' thought it was 'bra'.

On a more serious note, we could not wait anymore for the PM to come as we had to travel to Brussels by Eurostar. We travelled to the European Parliament to meet our EMPs (European Members of Parliament). When we arrived at the reception the security prevented a woman member of our team from entering because she had a dog and she is not blind. "We can only allow dogs for the blind and you are not blind" said the security guy. She could not hear what he said because she was deaf. We told the security that this dog is to support the deaf. They said, in a very arrogant way, that they never heard of dogs guiding the deaf. She felt she was discriminated against because of her disability, therefore we all refused to enter if she was not going to join us. To our surprise when we met her on our first day, we asked her why had she got a dog? She said because she was deaf. Honestly, none of us ever heard of this before. But you live and learn. The first night at the course, the fire alarm went off and the dog pulled her out of bed.

Dogs are amazing animals! They are trained to sniff drugs or food or money or explosives. There are now dogs who are trained to diagnose cancer. So do you think a Dr Dog, especially if he is a white one, would think he is more superior to a dog who is sniffing drugs? No, because Dr Dog knows well that they are all dogs, irrespective of their colour or profession, and they are extremely careful in **speaking their minds when they bark.** Very often when dogs meet they greet each other. Something we lack as human beings.

We called our EMP to come downstairs to see us. It took a while for him to persuade the security guy to allow her to enter with her dog. Again it is ignorance which can lead to discrimination against innocent people. In spite of the Disability Discrimination Act which was introduced in 1995, many disabled people are still being discriminated against.

We were escorted during our tour to the European Parliament by several EMPs. I asked the question: *"Why did we have to create a European Union when we already had a very successful Common Market?"*

The answer was amazing! Something we never thought of... "Because we wanted to make sure that there will never be wars again between European countries." said the EMP. No doubt it is a very good reason, but will it last?

We were told about the importance of 'lobbying' to get EU funds and the discrimination which the poor EU countries can face when it comes to grants.

Following Brexit a group of white leavers were asked why did you vote to leave? They replied *"We hate Romanians, Bulgarians and Polish. They are taking our jobs and our children's school places. They are occupying hospital beds and making the NHS waiting lists much longer."* So the war between European countries has already started.

During Brexit, unfortunately innocent EU citizens living in the UK started to be attacked, even killed, and their businesses destroyed. Can we say that those who voted to leave because of fear of immigration are racist? Have they ever thought of the economic contributions made by these EU immigrants? Or how are we going to replace such a huge work force, who are content to do some so-called menial jobs, whilst the indigenous population find it to be below their dignity?

Catalonia in Spain wants its independence. The Basque region wants its independence. The Flemish in Belgium desire their independence. The Corsicans want their independence. Scotland wants its independence. And more and more European countries will move towards disintegration.

So Europe very soon will be dismantled and wars due to economic recessions will be fought and the real victims will be the people from the ethnic minorities who will suffer the most.

On a funny note, I had an Italian friend from the north of Italy who used to tell me how much hate they have in the north towards those in the south of Italy. *"They are lazy. They are blood suckers. They are parasites. They live on us. We work so hard and pay a lot of tax, whilst they are sitting in the sun doing nothing. We should declare the independence of the north of Italy and keep our money for ourselves."*

So here it sounds like hate derived by economic discrimination.

Our mosque in South Woodford, London was burnt down by members of the NF (National Front) or maybe the BNP (British National Party) just before 9/11. BBC Panorama included this in one of their programs. What wrong had we done to them, for them to burn down our place of worship? Did the police fully investigate the arson attack? Not really.

We should not forget history. The same attitude was practiced by the Spanish Inquisition at the time of Queen Isabella when she sanctioned the killing and expulsion of innocent Jews and Muslims from Spain.

Then Hitler came with his ethnic cleansing policy which was followed by many countries in the world including the USA, China, Burma and modern Europe. What happened during the Bosnian war is something to be ashamed of. Unfortunately, we can see it happening again and again in our neighbourhood today. Will it ever stop? No, because Evil will always be present until the Day of Judgement.

A funny anecdote to share, I was flying first class from Jeddah, Saudi Arabia to Madina. The stewardess, a young white English girl asked me, *"What is your nationality?"* I replied *"British"*. She said *"No you can't be!"* I said "Excuse me! Why not". She said *"Because you have an accent"*. So I said in a very loud but polite voice, to ensure other passengers on the plane could hear me, *"Don't you know that there are five nationalities in Britain? You can be either English or Irish or Welsh or a Scottish or a bloody foreigner. I'm the bloody foreigner!"*

The entire plane burst into laughter! An English stewardess working in first class does not know the meaning of being *"British"*. I am so proud to be a British Muslim from Egyptian origin.

2.10 God's Moral Law - What does God Say Regarding White Supremacy?

2.10.1 A Colourful Creation

God says in 30:20, *"Among His Signs is this, that He created you from dust; and then behold, you are human beings scattered (far and wide)!"*

"In spite of the lowly origin of man's body, God has given him a mind and soul by which he can almost compass the farthest reaches of Time and Space. Is this not enough for a miracle

or Sign? From a physical point of view, see how man, a creature of dust, scatters himself over the farthest corners of the earth!" FN3524

And He says in 30:22, "And among His Signs is the creation of the heavens and the earth, and the variations in your languages and your colours; verily in that are Signs for those who are knowledgeable."

"The variations in languages and colours may be viewed from the geographical aspect or from the aspect of periods of time. All mankind was created from a single pair of parents; yet they have spread to different countries and climates and developed different languages and different shades of complexions. And yet their basic unity remains unaltered. They feel in the same way, and are all equally under God's care. Then there are the variations in time. Old languages die out and new ones are evolved. New conditions of life and thought are constantly evolving new words and expressions, new syntactical structures, and new modes of pronunciation. Even old races die, and new races are born." FN3527

God says in 35:27-28: "Have you not seen that God sends down rain from the sky? With it We then bring out produce of various colours. And in the mountains are tracts white and red, of various shades of colours, and black intense in hue. And so among people and animals and cattle, are they of various colours. Those who truly fear God, among His servants, are those who are endowed with knowledge. For God is Exalted in Might, Oft-Forgiving."

"Everyone can see how God's artistry produces from rain the wonderful variety of crops and fruits - golden, green, red, yellow and showing all the most beautiful tints we can think of. And each undergoes in nature the gradual shading off in its transformation from the raw stage to the stage of maturity.

"These wonderful colours and shades of colours are to be found not only in vegetation but in rocks and minimal products. There are the white veins of marble and quartz or of chalk, the red laterite, the blue basaltic rocks, the ink-black flints, and all the variety, shade, and gradation of colours. Speaking of mountains, we think of their 'azure hue' from distance, due to atmospheric effects, and these atmospheric effects lead our thoughts to the glories of clouds, sunsets, the zodiacal lights, the aurora borealis, and all kinds of Nature's gorgeous pageantry.

"In the physical shapes of human and animal life, also, we see variations in shades and gradations of colours of all kinds. But these variations and gradations, marvellous though they be, are as nothing compared with variations and differences in the inner or spiritual world.

"In outer nature we can, through colours, understand and appreciate the finest shades and gradations. But in the spiritual world that variation or gradation is even more subtle and more comprehensive. Who can truly understand it? Only God's servants, who know, i.e., who have the inner knowledge which comes through their acquaintance with the spiritual world - it is such people who truly appreciate the inner world, and it is they who know that the fear of God is the beginning of wisdom. For such fear is akin to appreciation and love - appreciation of all the marvellous beauties of God's outer and inner world (God is Exalted in Might) and love because of His Grace and Kindness (Oft-Forgiving). But God's forgiveness extends to many who do not truly understand Him." FN3910-3913.

2.10.2 Race Relations

In 49:11-13, God lays down golden rules governing our interrelationships with each other irrespective of our colour, or ethnicity or faith as we are all brothers and sisters in humanity and we are all the children of Adam and Eve.

"O you who believe, let not some men among you laugh at others (e.g. make fun of them - mock them - belittle them - ridicule them - discriminate against them). It may be that the (latter) are better than the (former).
Nor let some women among you laugh at others, it may be that the (latter) are better than the (former). Nor defame, nor be sarcastic to each other, nor call each other by (offensive) nicknames; Ill-seeming is a name connoting wickedness, (to be used of one) after he has believed. And those who don't desist are (indeed) doing wrong." 49:11

"Mutual ridicule ceases to be fun when there is arrogance or selfishness or malice behind it. We may laugh with people, to share in the happiness of life: we must never laugh at people in contempt or ridicule. In many things they may be better than ourselves!

"Defamation may consist in speaking ill of others by the spoken or written word, or in acting in such a way as to suggest a charge against some person whom we are not in a position to

judge. A cutting, biting remark or taunt of sarcasm is included in the word lamaza. An offensive nickname may amount to defamation, but in any case there is no point in using offensive nicknames, or names that suggest some real or fancied defect. They ill accord with the serious purpose which Muslims should have in life. For example, even if a man is lame, it is wrong to address him as 'O lame one!' It causes him pain, and it is bad manners. So in the case of the rude remark, 'the black man" FN4929 & 4930

And God says in 49:12: *"O you who believe, avoid suspicion as much (as possible) for suspicion in some cases is a sin. And don't spy on each other, nor speak ill of each other behind their backs. Would any of you like to eat the flesh of his dead brother? No never, you would abhor it. But fear God, for God is Oft-Returning, Most Merciful."*

"Most kinds of suspicion are baseless and to be avoided, and some are crimes in themselves, for they do cruel injustice to innocent men and women. Spying, or enquiring too curiously into other people's affairs, means either idle curiosity, and is therefore futile, or suspicion carried a stage further, which almost amounts to sin.

"Back-biting also is a brood of the same genus. It may be either futile but all the same mischievous, or it may be poisoned with malice, in which case it is a sin added to sin. No one would like even to think of such an abomination as eating the flesh of his brother. But when the brother is dead, and the flesh is carrion, abomination is added to abomination. In the same way we are asked to refrain from hurting people's feelings when they are present; how much worse is it when we say things, true or false, when they are absent." FN3931 & 4932

2.10.3 Getting to Know Each Other

In verse 49:13, God addresses all mankind: *"O mankind, We created you from a single (pair) of a male and a female, and made you into nations and tribes, that you may know each other (not that you may despise each other). Verily the most honoured of you in the sight of God is (he who is) the most righteous of you. And God has full knowledge and is well-acquainted (with all things)."*

"The above verse is addressed to all mankind and not only to the believers, though it is understood that in a perfect world the two would be synonymous. As it is, mankind is descended from one pair of parents. Their tribes, races, and nations are convenient labels by

which we may know certain differing characteristics. Before God they are all one, and he gets most honour who is most righteous." FN4933

It is reported by Ahmed in his Musnad (Book of Hadith), that the Prophet Mohammed (pbuh) said: *"O people, your Lord is one and your father (Adam) is one. There is no superiority of an Arab over a non-Arab, nor a non-Arab over an Arab, and neither white skin over black skin, nor black skin over white skin, except by righteousness. Have I not delivered the message?" They said, "The Messenger of Allah has delivered the message."*

So it is the righteous from Adam's family who will prosper, not the white, not the black, not the rich, not the poor. No one has the right to justify himself as God says in 53:32, *"...Therefore, don't claim purity for yourselves, He knows best who is the righteous, (who is conscious of Him)."*

"As God knows our inmost being, it is absurd for us to justify ourselves either by pretending that we are better than we are or by finding excuses for our conduct. We must offer ourselves unreservedly such as we are; it is His Mercy and Grace that will cleanse us. If we try, out of love for Him, to guard against evil, our striving is all that He asks for." FN5107

The Prophet Mohammed (pbuh) said, *"I swear by the One who has my soul in His hand, you will not enter Paradise until you believe, and you will not believe until you love one another. Shall I inform you of something which, if you do, you will love one another? Promote greetings amongst yourselves."* Reported by Muslim.

A man asked the Prophet (pbuh) *"Which act in Islam is the best? He replied, "To give food, and to greet everyone, whether you know or you don't."* Reported by Al-Bukhari and Muslim.

God says in 4:86, *"When you are offered a greeting, respond with a better one, or at least return it. God takes careful account of all things."*

The Prophet (pbuh) said, *"O people, exchange greetings of peace (i.e. say Peace on you to one another), feed people, strengthen the ties of kinship, and be in prayer when others are asleep, you will enter Paradise in peace."* Reported by Al-Tarmidhi.

Greeting each other and sharing food with each other would help us to get to know each other. Let us all strive to forge greater and more authentic connections with each other, be they with colleagues, neighbours or strangers. For at some point, are we not all strangers until we share our names and start to understand each other better?

When we all get to know each other, our initial apprehensions and fears dissipate, allowing greater understanding, increased tolerance and more allowances made for the differences. It is ignorance of each other and misconceptions in the world which create Islamophobia. We are all the children of Adam and Eve. We are all brothers and sisters in humanity.

The main reason which causes major family problems is because we do not know each other that well. This leads to strained relationships between members of the same family. I have been married for over 50 years and I do not think I know my wife that well. Do I know her likes and dislikes? Am I making an effort to address any of the issues she has with me or conversely, is she making similar efforts with me?

If members of the same family do not know each other that well, what about ethnic minorities and the host nations? What should we do to alleviate any fear or hate from the hearts of the indigenous population? How can we implement integration without losing our faith or watering down our religion?

2.10.4 Abolition of Slavery

Slavery was common in pre-Islamic times before the commencement of the revelation of the Qur'an. It was accepted by many ancient legal systems and it continued under Islam.

A conqueror in a battlefield would take prisoners of war as slaves to be sold in the slave market. Bandits would raid a village and burn it down and snatch people and sell them as slaves, maybe to the village next door. Joseph (pbuh) the son of Jacob (pbuh) was taken as a slave and sold in the slaves' market in Egypt. Pharaoh at the time of Moses, enslaved the Children of Israel in Egypt and persecuted them.

*"The **abolition of slavery** occurred at different times in different countries. It frequently occurred sequentially in more than one stage – for example, as abolition of the trade in slaves in a specific country, and then as abolition of slavery throughout empires. Each step*

was usually the result of a separate law or action. This timeline shows abolition laws or actions listed chronologically. It also covers the abolition of <u>serfdom.</u> *Although slavery is still abolished* <u>de jure</u> *in all countries, some* <u>practices akin to it</u> *continue today in many places throughout the world."* **WIKIPEDIA**

"Although Islam is much credited for moderating the age-old institution of slavery, which was also accepted and endorsed by the other monotheistic religions, Christianity and Judaism, and was a well-established custom of the pre-Islamic world, it has never preached the abolition of slavery as a doctrine." **Forough Jahanbaksh, Islam, Democracy and Religious Modernism in Iran, 1953-2000, 2001**

"The condition of slaves, like that of women, may well have improved with the coming of Islam, but the institution was not abolished, any more than it was under Christianity at this period." **Malise Ruthven, Islam in the World, 2000**

How did Islam Moderate Slavery?

I give below examples from the Qur'an on how Islam encouraged people to free slaves and to treat them kindly as brothers and sisters in humanity.

1) New Rules for Prisoners of War
These rules are meant to diminish the main source of acquiring slaves.
God says in 47:4: *"When you meet the unbelievers (in a battle), smite at their necks; at length, when you have thoroughly subdued them, bind a bond firmly (on them). Thereafter (is the time for) either generosity or ransom, until the war lays down its burdens. Thus you are commanded. But if it had been God's Will he could certainly have exacted retribution from them (Himself). But (He lets you fight) in order to test you, some with others. But those who are slain in the cause of God, He will never let their deeds be lost."*

"When once the fight is entered upon, carry it out with the utmost vigour, and strike home your blows at the most vital points (smite at their necks), both literally and figuratively. You can't wage war with kid gloves.
In the first onset there must necessarily be great loss of life; but when the enemy is fairly beaten, which means, in a Holy War, that he is not likely to seek again the persecution of Truth, firm arrangements should be made to bring him under control. I thus construe the

words 'bind a bond firmly (on them)', but others have construed the words to mean, 'after the enemy's numbers are fairly thinned down, prisoners may be taken'.

When once the enemy is brought under control, generosity (i.e. the release of prisoners without ransom) or ransom is recommended." FN4821 & 4822.

In the above verse, we have the following options regarding dealing with prisoners of war. Either to free them without ransom or exchange them with our own prisoners or ask for a ransom.

2) Kindness to Slaves

God commands in verse 4:36 kindness to slaves and others: *"Serve God, and don't join any partners with Him. And be good and kind to parents, relatives, orphans, those in need, neighbour who is related to you, neighbour who is stranger (not of kin), the companion by your side (wife and friends), the wayfarer (you meet), and (the slaves) whom your right hands possess; for God does not love the arrogant, the boastful."*

3) Encouraging the Believers to Free Slaves to Expiate a Sin Committed

A) God says in 4:92-93: *"Never should a believer kill a believer. But (if it so happens) by mistake, (compensation is due); if one (so) kills a believer, it is ordained that he should free a believing slave, and pay compensation to the deceased's family, unless they remit it freely. If the deceased belonged to a people at war with you, and he was a believer, the freeing of a believing slave (is enough). If he belonged to a people with whom you have a treaty of mutual alliance, compensation should be paid to his family, and a believing slave be freed. For those who find this beyond their means, (is prescribed) a fast for two months running, by way of repentance to God, for God has all knowledge and all wisdom. Whoever kills a believer intentionally, his recompense is Hell, to abide therein eternally, and the wrath and the curse of God are upon him, and a dreadful penalty is prepared for him."*

B) God says in 5:89 to those who violate their *oaths: "God will not call you to account for what is futile in your oaths, but He will call you to account for your deliberate oaths. For expiation, feed ten poor persons, on a scale of the average for the food of your families; or clothe them; or give a slave his freedom. If that is beyond your means, fast for three days. That is the expiation for the oaths you have sworn. But keep to your oaths. Thus does God make clear to you His Signs, that you may be grateful."*

"Vows of penance or abstention may sometimes be futile, or even stand in the way of really good or virtuous act. The general principles established are: (1) take no futile oath; (2) don't use God's name, literally or in intention, to fetter yourself against doing a lawful or good act; (3) keep to your solemn oaths to the utmost of your ability; (4) where you are unable to do so, expiate your failure by feeding or clothing the poor, or obtaining someone's freedom, or if you have not the means, by fasting. This is from a spiritual aspect. If any party suffers damage from your failure, compensation will be due to him, but that would be a question of law or equity." FN792

C) God says in 58:2-4 to those who abuse their wives by adopting an illegal form of divorce: *"If any men among you divorce their wives by Zihar (calling them mothers), they can't be their mothers. None can be their mothers except those who gave them birth. And in fact, they use words (both) iniquitous and false. But truly God is One that blots out (sins) and forgives (again and again). But those who divorce their wives by Zihar, then wish to go back on the words they uttered (it is ordained that such a one) should free a slave before they touch each other. This you are admonished to perform. And God is acquainted with (all) that you do. If any has not the means, he should fast for two months consecutively before they touch each other. But if any is unable to do so, he should feed sixty poor persons. This, that you may show your faith in God and His Messenger. And those are limits (set by) God. For those who reject (Him) there is a grievous Penalty."*

4) Freeing Slaves from Zakat Money

In verse 9:60, God defines the eight channels to which we can direct our Zakat (compulsory charity) money. One of them is to free slaves: *"Zakat is for the poor and the needy, and those employed to administer the (funds); for those whose hearts have been (recently) reconciled (to the Truth); for those in bondage; for those in debit; in the cause of God; and for the wayfarer. This is ordained by God, and God is full of knowledge and wisdom."*

5) Freeing Slaves is a Virtuous Deed

God states in 2:177 and 90:13 that freeing slaves is a good deed which brings us closer to Him. *"It is not righteousness that you turn your faces towards East or West; but it is righteousness to believe in God and the Last Day, and the Angels, and the Book, and the Prophets, and to spend of your wealth, out of love for Him, for your kin, for orphans, for the needy, for the wayfarer, for those who ask, and for the ransom of slaves; to be steadfast in prayer, and practice regular charity, to fulfil the contracts you have made; and to be firm and patient, in pain (or suffering) and adversity, and throughout all periods of panic. Such are the people of truth, the God-fearing." 2:177

And in 90:4-18, God says, "Verily We have created man into toil and struggle. Does he think that none has power over him? He may say (boastfully): I have squandered wealth in abundance. Does he think none can see him? Have We not made for him a pair of eyes? And a tongue and a pair of lips? And shown him the two highways? But he has made no haste on the path that is steep. And what will explain to you the path that is steep? (It is :) freeing the bondman; or the giving of food in a day of privation to a related orphan or to a very poor person (down) in the dust. Then he will be of those who believe, and enjoin patience, (constancy, and self-restraint), and enjoin deeds of kindness and compassion. Such are the companions of the Right Hand."

"The difficult path of virtue is defined as the path of charity or unselfish love, and three specific instances are given for our understanding: (1) freeing the bondman, (2) feeding the orphan, (3) feeding the indigent down in the dust. As regards the bondman, we are to understand not only a reference to legal slavery, but many other kinds of slavery which flourish especially in advanced societies. There is political slavery, industrial slavery, and social slavery. There is the slavery of conventions, of ignorance, and of superstition. There is slavery to wealth or passion or power. The good man tries to liberate men and women from all kinds of slavery, often at great danger to himself. But he begins by first liberating himself." FN6140

By reflecting on the FN above, it is so sad to say that there are rich Muslim countries in Arabia who employ very poor workers from poor Muslim countries and they continue to treat them like slaves. By doing that they are ignoring the teachings of the Qur'an and the tradition of the Prophet Mohammed (pbuh). No doubt White Satan has possessed them! There are many authentic Prophetic Traditions instructing us all to treat slaves with dignity and respect and show them kindness and mercy. They should only be given jobs which they can easily perform. We are even recommended to help them in implementing their duties. Abdul-Rahman Ibn Auf, one of the rich companions of the Prophet Mohammed (pbuh), would often walk with his slaves, and no one could differentiate between master and slave as they were both well dressed, well-nourished and treated with great mutual respect.

In conclusion, what the slaves, especially from the black communities, suffered in the hands of their white owners or any other owners was disgraceful, inhumane, and abhorrent by all human standards. This led to the abolition of slavery in the 19th Century. Whilst God introduced in the Qur'an, rules to free slaves and to moderate slavery were in existence since the 7th Century. Unfortunately we are still experiencing so many different types of slavery as mentioned earlier in FN6140.

2.11 The White Pharaoh and Anti-Semitism

Some politicians who **'speak their minds'** are inciting hatred against innocent ethnic minorities. This is similar to what the Pharaoh at the time of Moses (pbuh) did against the Children of Israel who lived and served in Egypt for centuries and saved the Egyptians from catastrophic economic disasters.

God says in 28:4-6: *"Truly Pharaoh exalted himself in the land and divided its people into sections, depressing a group among them, their sons he slew, but he kept alive their females. For he was indeed an evil-doer. And We wished to be Gracious to those who were being depressed in the land, to make them leaders (in faith) and make them heirs, to establish a firm place for them in the land, and to show Pharaoh, Haman (Chief Of Staff) and their hosts, what they were dreading from them."*
And in 28:8 He says, *"...for Pharaoh and Haman and (all) their hosts were men of sin."*

And in 26:52-56 He says, *"By inspiration We told Moses to travel by night with My servants; for surely you shall be pursued. Then Pharaoh sent heralds to (all) the Cities, (saying): 'These (Israelites) are but a despised minority and they have surely enraged us. And we are a multitude amply fore-warned.'"*

Can you imagine a ruler would describe the people from an ethnic minority as *"a despised minority who are raging furiously against us and we are taking every precaution to protect ourselves from them"*?

"For a king or ruler to make invidious distinctions between his subjects, and especially to depress or oppress any particular class of his subjects, is a dereliction of his kingly duties, for which he is responsible to God. Pharaoh and his clique were intoxicated with pride and race and pride of material civilisation, and grievously oppressed the Israelites. Pharaoh decreed

that all male sons born to his Israelite subjects should be killed, and the females kept alive for the pleasure of the Egyptians." FN3329.

"Pharaoh was trying to kill the Israelites. Instead, the Plagues of Egypt, invoked by Moses, killed thousands of the Egyptians, because 'they were steeped in arrogance, a people given to sin, 7:133'. In pursuing the Israelites in their flight, Pharaoh and his army were themselves overwhelmed in the sea." FN3332.

God says in 43:51-56 "And Pharaoh proclaimed among his people, saying: 'O my people! Does not the Kingdom of Egypt belong to me, and all these rivers flowing underneath (my palace)? What! Do you not then see?
Am I not better than this (Moses), who is despicable and can scarcely express himself clearly? Then why there are not gold bracelets bestowed on him, or why he does not have angels accompanying him in procession?' Thus he made fools of his people, and they obeyed him. Truly they were rebellious people (who rebelled against God). When at length they provoked Us, We exacted retribution from them, and We drowned them all. And we made them (a people) of the past and an Example to later ages."

"God is patient, and gives many and many opportunities to the most hardened sinners for repentance. But at length comes a time when His Justice is provoked, and the inevitable punishment follows. Pharaoh and his hosts were blotted out, and became as a tale of the past. Their story is an instructive warning and example to future generations." FN4656 & 4658

God says in 28:39-40 *"And he (Pharaoh) was arrogant and insolent in the land, beyond reason, he and his hosts. They thought that they would not have to return to Us!*
So We seized him and his hosts, and We flung them into the sea. Now behold what was the End of those who did wrong!"

The persecution of the Children of Israel in Ancient Egypt was an **unprecedented holocaust.** The good news is that ultimately God saved the Children of Israel and destroyed Pharaoh and his hosts. And that will be the end of every government which treads on the same path of these racist rulers.

2.12 Conclusion

A "Racist" is defined in the Cambridge dictionary as *"someone who believes that their race makes them better, more intelligent, more moral, etc. than people of other races and who does or says unfair or harmful things as a result"*

BBC reported on 20th June 2020, that the American dictionary Merriam-Webster agreed to change the definition of the word racism in 2020 after receiving an email from a young black woman, who suggested that the definition should include a reference to systemic oppression. This was following international anti-racism protests after the death of George Floyd in Minneapolis. Floyd died after a white police officer held his knee on Floyd's neck for nearly nine minutes, refusing to release his hold or pressure despite pleas from both George and horrified onlookers.

Merriam-Webster's current definition of racism:

1. A belief that race is the primary determinant of human traits and capacities and that racial differences produce an inherent superiority of a particular race

2. a) A doctrine or political program based on the assumption of racism and designed to execute its principles, b) a political or social system founded on racism

3) Racial prejudice or discrimination
In this Chapter, I explained how racism originated. I mentioned that the King of the Jinn who was invited to Adam's creation ceremony disobeyed God and refused to prostrate himself to Adam, on grounds of race. He was haughty and arrogant, and was of those who rejected faith. He claimed to be better than Adam, because God created him from fire and created Adam from clay. God cursed him for being a racist and kicked him out of His Mercy. He became the King of the Devils, the originator of all Satans.

He asked God to give him respite till the Day of Judgement and God granted it to him. He accused God of misleading him. He vowed to destroy Adam and his descendants, except God's chosen devotees. He used "Satanic Diplomacy" to seduce Adam and Eve. He persuaded them to disobey God and eat from the forbidden tree. So by deceit he brought about their fall. His wish was to make Adam and Eve suffer the same fate as him. However, Adam and his wife, foiled Satan's plan and repented and asked for God's forgiveness and they were forgiven. But sadly, their honeymoon was over. When they fell, they realised the evil. They were (and we are) still given the chance, in this life on a lower plane, to make good and recover the lost status of innocence and bliss.

Following the expulsion of our parents from the Garden, God promised to send Guidance through His Divine Revelations to His Messengers. He said: *"...and if, as is sure, there comes to you guidance from Me, whosoever follow my guidance, on them shall be no fear, nor shall they grieve"* 2:38

"In spite of man's fall, and in consequence of it, assurance of guidance is given. In case man follows the guidance he is free from any fear for the present or the future, and any grieve or sorrow for the past. The soul thus freed grows nearer to God." FN56

I also mentioned that the King of the Devils has his own army of Satans from the Jinn and the humans. They inspire each other with flowery discourses by way of deception as stated in 6:112.

"...The spirit of evil is ever active and uses men to practice deception by means of highly embellished words and plausible excuses and objections. God permits these things in His Plan. It is not for us to complain. Our faith is tested, and we must stand the test steadfastly." FN941

Racism leads to injustice, and injustice would lead to destruction of communities if not entire nations. What happened to the Children of Israel in Egypt at the hands of a tyrant Pharaoh, or to the Muslims and the Jews in Spain by a vicious Queen, or the Holocaust in Germany by a cruel and oppressive ruler, enslavement of Black Africans in the USA, or to the Muslims in Bosnia at the hands of criminal Serbs. These are only a few examples of racism practiced by many of us against each other on a daily basis. History, unfortunately, continually shows us the human cost and perpetuated trauma of racially motivated injustices.

People, whether they be leaders or followers, who engage in these racist attacks and onslaughts, ignore the fact that we are all brothers and sisters in humanity irrespective of our colour or ethnicity or religion. We are all equal in the sight of our Creator to whom we all belong and to whom is our return. He does not look at our images or our wealth, but He looks at our deeds and the intentions of our hearts. Surely the most honoured in the sight of God is the righteous. So let us all jointly and individually fight Satan, the promoter of evil in all its forms. *"Surely Satan is an enemy to you. Therefore, do take him as an enemy. He only invites his adherents to his way, that they may become companions of the Blazing Fire."* 35:6

Chapter Three- Inviting All to God With Insight

3.1 Introduction

Friday 3rd July 1970 is a date imprinted upon my mind as it marked my entry to the UK from Egypt, at the age of 24. A young graduate, just having completed my first university degree in Aeronautical Engineering and working in the aircraft industry for three years, I was ready for new experiences and new horizons.

Whilst living in Egypt, I only met Egyptian Muslims of the Sunni sect and Egyptian Christians of the Orthodox sect, who were a minority. We attended the same schools and universities and we lived in the same block of flats in peace and harmony. We congratulated each other whenever we had religious festivities. Our religious differences were never questioned when it came to forging strong friendships. We had no radical Islam in Egypt. We had a saying, "Religion belongs to God and Egypt belongs to all". By God's Grace, I have been a practising Muslim since my childhood. My parents were both secularly and religiously educated. They taught me God's Moral Law from a very young age, to avoid falling into temptation. I was brought up to fear doing anything wrong which could upset God, who loves me so much and this fear and love continue to remain strong foundations for me.

Before coming to the UK, I had never met a Jew in my life, although we had a considerable number of Jews in Egypt until 1956. My mother's dress maker was a Jew and my mother liked her tremendously. I had also never met Hindus, Buddhists, Sikhs, atheists or any other sect of Christianity or Islam. Suddenly I found myself in a London neighbourhood with all the colours and faiths of the most beautiful rainbow of humanity. How was I going to deal with all these people who did not share my religion or culture without losing my faith or watering down my religion? I asked myself this question many times!

So, in order to find the answer to this question, I embarked on a self-education programme to learn from the Qur'an and the tradition of Prophet Mohammed (pbuh) on how to achieve that. I always reflected on verse 49:13 of the Qur'an, "*O mankind! We have created all of you from a single pair of a male and female, and made you into nations and tribes that you may get to know each other (not that you may despise each other). Verily the most honoured of you in the sight of God is (he who is) the most righteous of you. And God has full knowledge and is well acquainted (with all things).*"

My religious education journey led me to join organisations like Rotary International, Multi-Faiths and Three Faiths Forums where I was so honoured and privileged to meet men and women from every corner of the world with faith or no faith. I even joined two universities in the UK, as a mature student, to learn about Chaplaincy and Muslim-Jewish relations.

As mentioned in 1.1.3.I, Chapter One, calling people to God is a form of "Jihad". My job is to pass on God's Message as detailed in the Qur'an and practiced by His Messenger, Prophet

Mohammed (pbuh). In doing that, I have literally followed the principles of religious preaching as detailed in I.1, Chapter One.

I give below examples of the work I have done in passing on God's Message. It was not an easy task. I have had to deal with some extremely aggressive and radical people who did not share my vision or quest. But I had to persevere patiently as commanded by God in 46:35: "*So bear with patience (O Mohammed) as the messengers endowed with firmness of resolve (before you) bore with patience...*". And in 27:79, He says, "*Put your trust (O Mohammed) in God, for you are on (the path of) manifest Truth.*"

God commands Mohammed (pbuh) in 12:108 to say,
"This is my way: based on clear evidence, I, and all who follow me, call (people) to God – glory be to God! I do not join others with Him"

3.2 My Involvement in Delivering God's Message

3.2.1 Three Faiths Forum - East London

Since 2001, I have been a member of the Executive Committee (EC) of the Three Faiths Forum in East London. Jews, Christians and Muslims would regularly meet in a mosque or a synagogue or a church to discuss a topic from the point of view of each religion. Once a year the Executive Committee would meet to recommend and chose the topics to be discussed for the entire year. The EC would choose speakers from each faith. There is no doubt that these meetings have dealt with many issues and cleared numerous misunderstandings. It created a platform to ask questions which would have caused a lot of embarrassment if they were asked outside the Forum. Very often you would hear comments which are not pleasant, but the Chair who is a member of the EC is knowledgeable enough to defuse any tension.

Unfortunately, there was one occasion when a Christian member of the EC decided to break away after almost ten years. He attacked Islam and Muslims openly. We were having our meeting in December 2015, at the offices of Members of Parliament, opposite Westminster Palace, and he as one of the three speakers started to attack Islam and Muslims and said, "Islam is Dangerous". I was the Chair in that meeting. The Muslim speaker was Mrs Khola Hasan, a brilliant speaker who beautifully responded to him and by the Grace of God, I successfully managed to control the Muslim crowd.

On 20th December 2015, I sent him the following message:

Subject: "Islam is Dangerous" Says Rev RH!

I think every religion is dangerous if it is in the wrong hands.

Islam is very dangerous if it is in the hands of radical and fanatics like Taliban or Al-Qaeda or ISIS or any other extremist groups anywhere in the world.

Christianity was extremely dangerous in the hands of someone like Hitler who killed several million Jews, exterminated people from other ethnicities and destroyed the civilised world.
The Spanish Inquisition which killed many Muslims and Jews was Christian.
The Crusaders who invaded the Holy Land and killed again many Muslims and Jews were Christians.
The countries which occupied many parts of the world robbing, demoralising and enslaving its people were Christians.
The Irish terrorists are Christians.
The Spanish Basque terrorists are Christians. The Corsican Terrorists are Christians.
Bush and Blair, the evil pair, who lied to invade and destroy Iraq are Christians.

Judaism is dangerous if it is in the hands of, for example, the radical Jewish settlers in Hebron.
So what really matters is how to differentiate between the true teachings of a religion and the conduct of its followers.

If God is the Most Merciful and the Most Compassionate and the Source of Peace and Justice, how can Muslims or Christians or Jews explain or justify the acts of violence committed by some of them in the name of God?

May God save us all from His Wrath."

Following the end of the year celebration of the Three Faiths Form, Rev RH sent the following message dated 21st December 2013:

"Dear all,

I came away from the last Thursday's meeting very uneasy. All my long involvement has been motivated by my deep respect for people of faith in an increasingly secular anti-religious world. As you know I entirely through my contacts through 3FF came to see Islam as at least potentially prone to strong disrespect of other religions and in some cases likely to lead religious young men into violence. This of course does not apply to the majority and certainly not my dear friend and brother Mohammed (Dr Fahim).

There were two things that deeply disturbed me on Thursday. First two Muslim girls gave the Islamic view of The birth of Jesus. In doing so they were obviously using material they are taught at Mosques. Among many other things I did not like they said that Christians had altered their Scriptures and that Jesus was not God's son. If in many Islamic countries such as Pakistan from where most of British Muslims come, if I had said comparable things about the Qur'an and Mohammed I would now be on death row. I felt like calling out that saying these things are offensive to Christians and incompatible with dialogue and respectful coexistence. I didn't want to upset the children who were merely doing what they had been told to do. So I said nothing. Christians normally don't. We are passive and allow all sorts of abuse to come our way. Muslims don't react so passively and when Mohammed or the Qur'an are deemed to be abused, they kill people, or certainly a percentage do.

The other thing that disturbed me was that all the Muslim girl children from as young as 4/5 *were wearing hijabs. I find this incredible. This fad has only really arisen in our country since 9/11 and with that is a sign of Islamic revival that draws much of its inspiration from Mawdudis and Sa'id Qutbs. Now with children of four wearing the hijab, does this mean they are sexual objects and therefore must cover themselves up? I have visited many Arab countries and have never seen Children covered up in this way. I can only assume that the Islamic parents there are making strong statements about their anger and even hate of British society, and if this is over-said, certainly their refusal to assimilate into our society. I know Mohammed (Dr Fahim) will agree with much of what I say here.*

I really think the 3FF should try and address these issues. As a minimum people ought to be warned not to say directly that the beliefs of the other two faiths are false. They ought to be warned and also they ought to apologize as this goes against the principles we worked out (largely written by me and corrected by David) in the charter.
If nobody else does not consider these issues important and that I am making an undue fuss, I am very sorry for you. The fact is that Islam in Britain is getting more, not less extreme. Talking to my sister afterwards and expressing my unhappiness I picked up Volume 4 of my 9 volume edition of Al Bakhari's Hadith. The first page I turned to there was a reference to Mohammed asking for a certain person to be assassinated and a Muslim agreeing to do so. We all just assume that religions ought to be peaceful, and their leaders are men of peace not violence. If you are brave you would, once my book on Islam is ready (sadly it is not at the printers yet), to have an intelligent Muslim answer me and explain why I am wrong (if indeed I am). I do not think any of you are brave enough unfortunately. These issues are just avoided. We all prefer the ostrich approach, but time is running out for this way of dealing with unwanted issues.

As the reproduction rate of a British Pakistani woman is approximately 3, while a good estimate of an equivalent British indigenous woman is 1.25 or less, we have little more than a generation to get used to a significantly larger Muslim community in Britain. I think these issues must be grappled with. I came to grapple with them through the East London 3FF but now I am outside partly because my unwanted (I never believed this until about 3 years ago, and even came round to Mohammed's house to discuss these issues when I was disturbed about having such terrible thoughts) conclusions. I could certainly never attend another meeting like last Thursday. I was highly offended at what was said about my Lord and Saviour and also my Holy Scriptures. I am also horrified to see dress politicized for children as young as four.

Your honestly and respectfully,

R H "

By distancing himself and removing himself from the Three Faiths Forum, we were unable to engage in a measured and respectful debate and constructive discussion on some of the key points he had raised. Yes, the Qur'an clearly states that Jesus is not God or son of God and God is not one of three. Muslims cannot change these facts and they will not compromise their religion or water down their faith because they live in a Christian country which believes in the opposite. Sad to say that the majority of those who claim to be Christians are in fact secular.

The Jews categorically deny Jesus and are still waiting for the Messiah to arrive. There are Jews who accused Mary of being unchaste, and the child she bore was illegitimate. There are Christians who accused the Jews of crucifying Jesus. I wonder why he was **NOT** highly offended at what the Jews said about His Lord and Saviour? Why did he not attack the Jews as he had attacked the Muslims? The answer may be that he would have been accused of being anti-Semitic.

He would have been aware that over 1.5 billion Muslims worldwide believe in Jesus Christ, the son of Mary. They believe in his mother's purity, his virgin birth, his Message, the Divine Revelation he received, all his Miracles, his ascension to Heaven, his second coming to earth and his ruling with peace and justice to establish absolute submission to the One True God.

In addition to these attacks on Islam and Muslims, he used to publish very hostile material in his newsletter 'Holy Trinity Quarterly' inciting hatred against Muslims. As his church was always almost empty, the newsletter used to be delivered by hand to many people in the neighbourhood, including Muslims. I will quote a few paragraphs from his article 'A Short History of Islam', Summer 2014 issue:

"In a recent radio news summary, the first five news items were about Islamic militancy in Iraq, in Pakistan, in Nigeria, in Kenya and in Birmingham. Why does Islam have this problem? Nobody seems to know. In 2001 I was a founding member of the East London Three Faiths Forum where Jews, Christians and Muslims came to share their faith with each other. It was my hope that as we learnt Mutual respect our society would become safer and better. Yet whilst chairing a meeting in 2010, I sadly realised that the Conservative Muslim man speaking could never assimilate into British society.

"He would not let his children partake of music lessons at school. Much of what it was to be Western -Beethoven and Beatles - would always be denied him. There was something essential to British culture that was being rejected, not only its music. He did not want to be part of its general feeling of togetherness, neither did he dress in a Western way. And yet he was born in England. He was not a radical but what if his children took seriously his sense of alienation further still?

"These questions where disturbing for me. I did not want to be anti-Muslims. So, I contacted a local Imam whom I greatly respect and asked to talk to him about my concerns. This gracious man agreed. I went round to his house and met people who were ready to help me with my search for understanding.

"My hosts believed that Islam was safe and peaceful. However right at the end a young Muslim woman suddenly stopped and said: 'it's strange! When our parents came to Britain they accepted and loved it. Now so many of the younger generation do not love it. Why has this changed?' Good question..."

Very often in the Three Faiths Forum meetings he would never refer to 'Israel' as 'Israel', he would call it 'Palestine'. Once, a Rabbi was so annoyed with him for saying that and in order to diffuse the situation, I responded by saying, "As this is a religious meeting, he is referring to its name in the Gospel and the Old Testament!"

And he never referred to 'Istanbul' by its name, he always called it 'Constantinople', as if the Muslims had never been there.

Once I invited him for a meal at a restaurant, my German son-in-law, who was previously a Catholic, sat next to him. When he discovered that my son-in-law embraced Islam to marry my daughter, he became quite agitated and quite angry at my son-in-law.

He used to organise trips to Germany to attend the "Passion Play" in Oberammergau. My wife and I joined him on one of the visits. I found the play to be anti-Semitic. If I would have known this in advance, I would not have gone.

In spite of the above, I kept a very good working relationship with him as I have been commanded by God in verses 2:109 and 3:186:

"Out of sheer envy, many of the People of the Book would be glad to turn you back into unbelievers after you have become believers even though the Truth has become clear to them. Nevertheless, forgive and overlook, until God brings forth His decision. Surely God has power over all things" 2:109

"You shall certainly be tried and tested in your positions and in your personal selves, and you shall certainly hear much that will grieve you, from those who received the Book before you and from the idol worshippers. But if you persevere patiently, and fear God, then that will be a determining factor in all affairs." 3:186

When he was diagnosed with cancer, my wife and I did not stop visiting him and praying for him. I used to take him, his wife and parents out for meals. I would also bring Asian food to him and his family, as it was one of his favourite cuisines. On many occasions he invited my wife and I to eat at his house; he was so generous. When I was bed-ridden for three months due to my back problems, he visited me several times. In spite of his illness, he cycled a long distance to get to me and to this day I am grateful to him for his care and friendship towards me. When he died, I was with him. My wife and I attended his funeral and hugged his parents and his wife.

His death reminded me of what Jesus would say on the Day of Judgement when God would ask him the following question in the presence of all mankind, as stated in 5:116-119, *"And God would say: O Jesus, son of Mary! Did you say to people: 'take me and my mother for two gods beside the One True God'? Jesus will answer: 'Glory to You! It was not for me to say what I have no right to say. If I had said it then You would have known it, You know what is in my mind and I do not know what is in Yours. You alone are the Knower of the unseen. I said to them only what You commanded me (saying) 'Worship God my Lord and your Lord.' I was a witness over them while I remained among them, and when You took me up, You were the Watcher over them, and You are the Witness over all things. If You punish them, they are Your servants and if You forgive them, You are the Exalted in Might, the Wise.' God will say: 'this is a day in which the truthful will profit from their truth. For them are gardens, with rivers flowing beneath, where they will abide forever. God will be pleased with them and they will be pleased with Him. This is the Mighty Triumph (the Great Salvation).*

3.2.2 Visits to the Holy Land

Through the Three Faiths Forum in East London, we organised several trips to the Holy Land, Israel and Palestine. So, for the first time in history Jews, Christians and Muslims in East London, joined hands on a journey of promoting peace, tolerance and understanding. The experience was so amazing, to the extent that I have done it so many times and I will continue, God Willing to do it again and again.

In response to our first visit to the Holy Land, the "Jerusalem Post" published a very powerful and enthusiastic report on 4th December 2008:

"Unexpected guests!

Israel's tourist Industry is on the up again following the downturn from the second intifada, with Jews across the world packing bathing suits or Shabbat clothes, depending on their destination in the country. Far fewer people have been boarding planes with a copy of the Koran in their hand luggage, hoping to fulfil the dream of praying at Jerusalem's al-Aksa Mosque.

But among those few were the 20-plus Muslims who recently travelled to the Holy Land for a busy one-week pilgrimage, organised by the East London chapter of the Three Faiths Forum - a UK-based initiative that encourages friendship and dialogue between Muslims, Jews and Christians..."

The "Ilford Recorder", a London newspaper, published a very interesting article on 13th November 2008, under "Muslims make history with a visit to Israel":

"Muslims, Jews and Christians joined together for a ground-breaking multi-faith pilgrimage to Jerusalem's Holy Land. The group of 26 formed the first ever visit to Israel and Palestine organised by predominantly Muslim group from Britain. A total of 23 Muslims took part in the pilgrimage and were joined by fellow members of the East London Three Faiths Forum. The trip was led by Imam Dr Mohammed Fahim of the South Woodford Community Centre, Mulberry Way, South Woodford, Rabbi David Hulbert of Bet Tikvah Synagogue, Perrymans Farm Road, Newbury Park, and Father Francis Coveney of St Anne's Line Roman Catholic Church, Grove Crescent, South Woodford.......

"Dr Fahim said he was proud to be the first British Imam to visit Israel and was delighted to have joined with other faith groups for the emotional adventure.

"Rabbi Hulbert said: 'A pilgrimage to the Holy Land by a predominantly Muslim group is truly a ground-breaking event and we felt truly proud that we came from Redbridge, reflecting the high level of tolerance and trust between all faiths represented in the Borough.'

The Jewish Chronicle wrote on 14th November 2008, under **"Muslim tour"**:

"A predominantly Muslim group has returned enthused from a visit to Israel under the direction of the East London Three Faiths Forum. The itinerary included the Church of the

Holy Sepulchre, the Western Wall, and Yad Vashem in Jerusalem; the Church of the Nativity in Bethlehem and the Dead Sea. The group also visited Nazareth and a Tiberias hospital serving Jews and Arabs. Co-organiser Imam Mohammed Fahim of South Woodford Mosque said: 'I was so impressed with the way the tour went. It is a very peaceful land and we were welcomed everywhere in a very friendly atmosphere.' He said the visit to Yad Vashem, Holocaust memorial, was of particular interest."

Unfortunately, the writer of the above article, had left out the visit the Muslims made to Al-Aqsa and Dome of the Rock mosques, and the fact that they prayed the Friday prayer there for the first time in their lives. Those were the main highlights of the journey to the Muslims in the group, including myself.
Since the first trip in 2008, Rabbi David Hulbert and I organised annual trips to the Holy Land. Each trip had its own experience and flavour, but they were amazing and challenging. The majority of the groups were Muslims.

The "Ilford Recorder" newspaper wrote a lengthy article on September 29th 2011:

"They stood united, visiting holy sites important to members of the Muslim, Jewish, and Christian communities in a week which helped to strengthen the ties between faiths. Thirty-six people made the visit to Israel and Palestine. Among them were three Jews, three Christians and 30 Muslims. The trip was the third, and largest, organised by Redbridge Three Faiths Forum, following successful visits in 2008 and 2010..."

3.2.3 Speaking at Holocaust Memorial Day

For many years I have been invited to speak at Holocaust Memorial Day in the London Borough of Redbridge. On 27th January 2009, and while delivering my speech, I experienced a very unpleasant situation. At the time I was writing my speech, there was a war going on in Gaza. I strongly felt I had to refer to it in my speech, if I'm addressing injustice in the world. I forwarded the draft of my speech to a Jewish friend of mine, who was a College Director, to check if I have said any inappropriate comments which would not be suitable for the occasion. He was so happy with what I wrote.

I give below the speech I delivered on the day. The theme was *"Stand up to Hatred"*:

"Dear brothers and sisters. May God's Peace, Mercy and Blessings be upon all of you.

I am honoured to participate in Holocaust Memorial Day.

According to the Oxford Dictionary hatred means active dislike, enmity or ill-will. Hatred might be due to jealousy, injustice, ignorance, arrogance or greed.

"Let me give you a few examples. Before the creation of Adam, God commanded the Angels and the Spirit to prostrate themselves to Adam once he was created. They all obeyed, except Satan. When God asked him, 'why did you not prostrate yourself to Adam when I commanded you?' Satan replied: 'I'm better than him. You created me from fire and him from Clay.' That was the first ever racist remark. He arrogantly despised the angels who

prostrated as well as the man to whom they prostrated to and he was in rebellion against God for not obeying His order. Arrogance, jealousy and rebellion were his triple crime. Thus, racism in any form is a crime against God.

"We are all brothers and sisters in humanity. God says in 49:13:
"Oh mankind! We created you from a single (pair) of a male and a female, and made you into nations and tribes, that you may know each (not that you may despise each other). Verily the most honoured of you in the sight of God is (he who is) the most righteous of you. And God has full knowledge and is well acquainted (with all things)"

"Unfortunately, animosity can lead to hate crimes. The first hate crime committed was by Cain, the son of Adam, who was puffed up with arrogance and jealousy, which led him to murder his righteous and innocent brother Abel.

"Another hate crime was committed when the children of Jacob decided out of jealousy to throw their brother Joseph in the well to get rid of him. Jacob stood up to hatred and embarked on a rehabilitation programme to save his children from the wrath of God. Eventually their repugnance to Joseph turned into true love. The prophet Mohammed said: 'Hate your enemy mildly, he may become your friend one day.' (Al-Termeze)

"I'm a preacher, not a politician. It is against my faith to incite hatred or sow enmity between people. I have a code of conduct to follow. God says in 16:125:
"Invite (all) to the way of your Lord with wisdom and beautiful preaching; and argue with them in ways that are best and most gracious: for your Lord knows best who have strayed from His Path, and who receive guidance."

"Unfortunately, there are politicians who would incite hatred to win an election and the political system does not check them. For example, my ward councillor comes from a party which invents lies against the ethnic minorities to win elections. Almost 30 years ago my house in Woodford and my cars were attacked on daily basis forcing me to move out of the area. Ten years ago, our mosque at South Woodford was burnt down. Hate crimes continue against the Muslim community and their buildings in the UK.

"Last October I visited the Holy Land with 22 Muslims, two Christians and Rabbi David Hulbert all from the Three Faiths Forum in East London on a mission of peace and reconciliation. While there we visited the Holocaust Memorial Yad Vashem in Jerusalem. It was a moving experience to see the level of atrocities committed against innocent civilians. I said to our Israeli guide: 'shame on those who deny the Holocaust. It is not the number; it is the principle. God says in 5:32:
'On that account: We ordained for the Children of Israel that if anyone slew a person -unless it be for murder or for spreading mischief in the land -it would be as if he slew the whole people. And if anyone saved a life, it would be as if he saved the life of the whole people'

"A similar verse is also in the Talmud. The Israeli guide hugged me while crying saying: 'God bless you Mohammed.'

"Unfortunately, in the last few weeks the world witnessed atrocities committed against innocent civilians in Gaza while the Israeli army was launching a disproportionate war against Hamas to silence their rockets of terror.

"Many Jews worldwide and in the UK condemned the killing of civilians. The article written by Avi Shlaim, Professor of International Relations at Oxford University, published in the Guardian on Wednesday 7*th* January 2009, and the one written by Uri Avenry 'How many Divisions?' published by Gush Shalom demonstrate that there are many intellectual Jews who support and stand firm for peace and justice.
"God confirms the great qualities of such people in verse 7:159: 'Of people of Moses there is a section who guide and do justice in the light of truth.'

"The Holocaust of the 2nd World War has not been the last of its kind. So, the question is, why couldn't we learn from history? Why can't we see the parallels in history? Why do we continue to hate and translate this hate into harm for other people?
At each stage, positions become more entrenched and communities around the world begin to take on a role not much different from football supporters who support their team right or wrong.

"God says in verse 4:135:
'Oh you who believe! Stand out firmly for justice as witnesses to God, even as against yourselves, or your parents, or your kin, and whether it be (against) rich or poor. For God can best protect both. Don't follow the lusts (of your hearts), lest you swerve, and if you distort (justice) or decline to do justice, verily God is well acquainted with all that you do.'

"And He says in verse 5:8:
'Oh you who believe! Stand firmly for God, as witnesses to fair dealing, and don't let the hatred of others to you make you swerve to wrong and depart from justice. Be just, that is next to Piety, and fear God. For God is well-acquainted with all that you do.'

"Disagreeing with a government's policy does not mean you become anti the people of that country. So let not the Middle East crisis affect the relationship between Muslims and Jews in Britain. Let us continue to respect and love each other and work together to achieve peace and harmony for our communities here and lasting peace in the Middle East. We must recognise the danger. If one group will fall, the other will follow."

Did I say anything wrong in the above speech? Did I incite hatred against anyone?

Surprisingly, the moment I mentioned Gaza, while delivering my speech, I could hear extremely aggressive comments thrown at me. Just after finishing, I was physically and verbally abused by some members of the Jewish community. One of them pulled the collar of my coat and shouted at me: **"How dare you mention Gaza? You have no sensitivity"**. My throat became so dry, but I had to fully control myself as I didn't want to create a scene.

While walking out, I met two Councillors from Redbridge, a husband and wife who were my neighbours. They both greeted me nicely and said: *"Well done for mentioning Gaza!"* I was so disappointed that they did not have the courage to publicly denounce the killing of innocent people in Gaza. They were concerned about losing their seats in the next election.

On Friday 30th January, and after delivering the Friday sermon at my mosque, I told the congregation what happened on the day. Two young men came to me and said: *"We are from Afghanistan. Shall we sort them out?"* I was shocked to hear that. I said: *"I know you love me so much. But as good practicing British Muslims we should never resort to violence. It is against God's Moral Law."* They thanked me and left peacefully.

Chris Grant, the Editor of the Ilford Recorder, wrote a very fair and supporting article on 29th January 2009, with the title **"Stifling debate not way forward in this crisis"**.

Under a photo of mine with a rabbi, Mr Grant wrote: ***"BRAVE STATEMENT: Imam Mohammed Fahim speaking at the Holocaust Memorial Day service on Tuesday, in Valentines Park, Ilford."***

Mr Grant said: *"...The Gaza crisis featured heavily during the Holocaust Memorial Day service on Tuesday. Redbridge Council leader Cllr Alan Weinberg's stark message was that 'the world has learned nothing. We are killing each other for no reason.' In his speech representing the Muslim community, Imam Mohammed Fahim, spoke out against racism and hatred towards all people, but also told of 'atrocities committed against innocent civilians in Gaza' and accused the Israeli army of launching a 'disproportionate war against Hamas to silence their rockets of terror'. That statement was brave in the circumstances and was not well received by some of those gathered. But Redbridge must be strong enough to allow debate about such issue. Surely, many of the conflicts in this world are caused by people not having a voice or being unable to have any say in their future. That's why measured debate must continue to be encouraged between the communities, in order that everyone's voice is heard."*

Mr H Harris, from Cranbrook Road, Gants Hill, wrote to the Editor of the Recorder, on 12th February 2009, attacking me:

"The Holocaust Memorial event at Valentines Park last week was well represented by all faiths and school children. Sadly, the Muslim cleric tarnished it by denouncing Israeli's bombing of Gaza. No one is proud that innocent people of Gaza were killed, but Hamas has, over the past two years, fired rockets into Israel. Why is it acceptable to give a preacher a platform to incite racial hatred?"

The Guardian newspaper wrote in their issue dated 29th January 2009: *"...During a ceremony at the Holocaust memorial garden in Valentines Park, Ilford, speakers including Dr Mohammed Fahim, Imam of South Woodford Mosque, Rabbi Aryeh Sufrin from the Chabad Lubavitch Centre, and Council Leader Alan Weinberg, spoke about the importance of the day and of the need to fight prejudice and hate in today..."*

Redbridge official newspaper "Redbridge Life", wrote in February 2009, under 'Council and faith leaders unite to oppose religious hatred':

"Council leaders from the three main parties have united with Jewish and Muslim leaders to collectively oppose any form of violence or hatred carried out in the name of their religions. The political and faith leaders decided to issue a joint statement to make it clear they believe religious tensions around the world must not be allowed to affect good community relations in Redbridge." I was so happy to be one of the signatories to the joint statement.

The Mayor of Redbridge, Cllr Mrs Loraine Sladden, wrote to me on 30th January 2009:

"Dear Dr Fahim

Holocaust Memorial Day

I wanted to write to thank you very much for the contribution that you made to Holocaust Memorial Day on 27th January.

I believe that it is very important to the community in Redbridge that we continue to commemorate those who suffered and died in the Holocaust and I thank you for your support. The presence of yourself as a representative of the Muslim community helps send a very positive message about community cohesion in Redbridge and I appreciate it.

Yours sincerely

Councillor Mrs Loraine Sladden
Mayor of Redbridge"

3.2.4 Speaking at Synagogues

I have been invited several times to many synagogues in the London area to speak about Muslim-Jewish encounter. I give below the highlights of two very interesting visits.

1) Visit to Finchley Synagogue, Kinloss Learning Centre on 24th May 2006:

"Dear Dr Fahim

On behalf of the Kinloss Learning Centre I would like to thank you for your words and sentiments at the interview I had with you last night.

You certainly succeeded in enlightening our audience on aspects of Islamic faith and outlook, and for the vast majority of us this was a unique experience. The feedback we have received has been very encouraging with many people telling us that it was a very memorable occasion through which they learnt a great deal. You endeared yourself to us all through your lovely personality and the sincerity and passion you have for your faith and traditions. We admire you for your earnest desire to increase outstanding between different faiths and to promote tolerance and harmony through effective education.

We are overwhelmed by your kindness in giving a generous cheque to our learning centre. Your gesture is greatly appreciated and will be put to good use.

We are very pleased that your wife and son-in-law came along for the evening and it was our pleasure to meet and welcome them. In my concluding remarks I said, 'may there be more like you', I certainly mean this and wish you every success in all your future endeavours.

With warm regards and grateful thanks.

Yours sincerely

RABBI EPHRAIM MIRVIS"

The Jewish Chronicle reported the visit in their issue dated 26th May 2006:

Imam donates funds to Finchley shul
"A London Imam surprised his Finchley Synagogue audience on Tuesday night when he ended his visit by handing over a £200 donation to its education centre. Dr Imam Mohammed Essam El-Din Fahim, the Egyptian-born imam of South Woodford Mosque, had been interviewed by Finchley's Rabbi Ephraim Mirvis for the Kinloss Learning Centre, the shul's educational programme. It was the first time an imam has visited the synagogue. 'Over the past two terms, we've run a course on Islam and the Jews with 200 people every week,' said Rabbi Mirvis. 'We wanted to hear a representative of Islam, whom I know as a person who wishes to promote understanding and tolerance.' Dr Fahim condemned suicide bombing, discussed passages in the Koran which link Jews to the land of Israel and praised assassinated Egyptian President Anwar Sadat for his peace work. At the end of the session, the two men embraced. 'You are an inspiration,' Rabbi Mirvis said. 'We are very touched by your wonderful gesture.' Rabbi Mirvis's interviews - last week with Michael Portillo and next week with chairman of the Commission for Racial Equality, Trevor Phillips - is one of 14 KLC courses on offer each week."

The following is the report in the Jewish News dated 25th May 2006:

"A LEADING London Imam this week denounced suicide bombings and called for greater understanding between faiths during an event at Finchley United Synagogue.

Dr Mohammed Fahim, of the South Woodford Islamic Community Centre was speaking with Rabbi Ephraim Mirvis during a session of the Kinloss learning Centre on Tuesday

Rabbi Mirvis said his guest explicitly told the 250-strong audience that suicide bombers were not representative of True Islam. The Rabbi added: 'He was very friendly and spoke about Jews as my brothers and sisters. He was very keen to promote better understanding between faiths. He added: 'there was a general sense of if only we would hear more from people like him.' The event was part of a five-part course where Rabbi Mirvis interviews a distinguished figure each week.

Last week, Michael Portillo took the hot seat while future guests include Commission for Racial Equality chief Trevor Phillips, Dennis MacShane MP, chairman of the All-Party

Parliamentary Inquiry Into Anti-Semitism and Marsha Gladstone, mother of Yoni Jesner who was killed in a suicide bombing in Israel"

The following is the response of Dr Ian Addleson, dated 29th May 2006, who introduced me to Rabbi Mirvis:

"Dear Mohammed

Your interview with Rabbi Mirvis last Tuesday was a resounding success in as much as you attracted a large audience and was listened to in silence.

You both were a wonderful blend of two faiths with leaders who display tolerance and understanding, and this was quite manifestly transferred to those who came to hear and learn. You answered all questions clearly and honestly, and in no small measure reassured us that true Islam was in friendship and tolerance with the true believers.

The whole hour was one of revelation and explanation that left us in no doubt that we can live together in peace and harmony when the spirit is willing. Sadly, there are elements in this world that are intent on railroading these good relationships, and we can only join with you in prayers for good sense to prevail and that we should live our lives in safety and security. And I am pleased to see how well you and the Rabbi got on - he had told me that at your initial meeting it did not take him long to warm to you, and felt the feeling was mutual.

Thank you for an interesting and informative hour among us, and I saw that you, Sonia and your son (or is he son-in-law?) appeared very much in demand and comfortable during the break. Even the Jewish Chronicle were told about you, and had a report in last week's edition, a cutting of which is attached. I might add that this is the first report about events at our learning Centre so obviously again you made an impact.

Your sincerely

Ian"

2) Visit to Cockfosters and N. Southgate Synagogue on 6th November 2006:

"Dear Dr Fahim

I wanted to reiterate my words of thanks to you on the evening of your visit and to express to you the feelings of my congregation.

The evening was a great success. It was informative, entertaining and above all else enormously enlightening to so many people to hear the true message of Islam so eloquently expressed. Unfortunately that is not the message that we all hear at all times and if only that message was expressed and heard more often, our own society here in Britain, and indeed societies throughout the world, would become safe and secure as extremism would increasingly be rooted out.

I sincerely hope that we will keep up our connection and that we will have more opportunities to collaborate together.

We are enormously touched and indeed overwhelmed by your most generous donation to our programme and I enclose a formal receipt.

With renewed thanks and warmest good wishes.

Yours sincerely

(Rabbi) Yisroel Fine"

Immediately following my visits to the above-mentioned synagogues, I received chocolate, fruits and flowers with beautiful thank you messages from both Rabbis. Many thanks for their generosity and their extremely kind gesture.

3.2.5 Speaking at Churches

As part of my involvement with the Three Faiths Forum, I was invited on many occasions to speak at churches of different denominations. I met so many amazing priests and pastors.

Rev Martin Hull, from Grove Hill Evangelical Church, in South Woodford, used to come regularly to attend the Friday prayer at our mosque. We used to meet very often at his office at his church to discuss different topics of interest to Islam and Christianity. I remember one day I said to him: "I have no intention of converting you to Islam." He immediately responded by saying: "But it is my intention to convert you to Christianity, because if you do your congregation will follow."

On 20th December 2013 he wrote:

"Dear Mohammad

Thank you for your friendship over the past year. I have continued to appreciate the rapport that we have developed and your willingness to engage in different conversations about Islam and Christianity. I am especially grateful to you for attending the evening with Rob Scott as I know you were feeling very weary at the time.

Rob suggested the enclosed book as he has found that it has helped his Muslim friends to understand the way in which Biblical Christianity approaches the whole matter of 'how we should now live'. I hope you also find it helpful - and perhaps there are things in it that we might be able to touch on when we next get together.

Thank you also for your concern for Father Robert. I understand that his recent treatment has been quite effective.

My wife, Corrie, and I have not forgotten our plan to have you and Sonia over for afternoon tea sometime.

With my very best wishes to you, your wife and family for 2014.
Martin"

And on 11th May 2018 he wrote:

"Dear Dr Fahim,

I do hope you and your wife and family are well.

I heard about the sad news of the death of Robert and wanted to make sure that you had heard, as I know that you counted him as a friend.

The notice below is from the web site at Holy Trinity.

I am sorry that I have not been able to join you at the South Woodford Mosque for quite some time. This has been due to a change in my schedule on Fridays when I now have a group Bible Study quite often at that time.

However, I have not forgotten you - and the warm welcome you always give me!

I do hope that the time of fasting for Ramadan proves to be useful to you.

With my best wishes,

Martin Hull

(Pastor - Grove Hill Evangelical Church)"

I responded to him on the same day:

"Dear Martin
I'm so glad to hear from you and to know that you are safe and sound.
I thought you have moved out of the UK in your missionary services.

Sonia and I went and saw Robert just before he passed away. God Willing, we will be attending his funeral.

Hope to see you soon.

Kindest regards to all family.

Mohammed"

3.2.6 Speaking at Education Institutions

I have been regularly invited to deliver talks at schools, colleges, universities and Local Authorities Education Services. My talks are not standard, in fact they are tailor-made to suit the age of the students and the audience mix. I found some of the pupils or students very eager to know about Islam from an outsider rather than relying on the Institution's RE (Religious Education) Programme or even Muslim classmates or colleagues.

Very often I would reflect on verse 12:108 in the way I structure my talks. God says to Prophet Mohammed to declare: *"This is my Way; I do invite to God, with a sure knowledge, both I and whoever follows me. Glory to God! And never I will join gods with Him."*
So, I try to emulate the style of Prophet Mohammed in the way he called the people to the Way of God.

I give below two responses, the first one is from London Borough of Harrow Education Services, dated 29th October 2002 and the second one is from Dr Challoner's Grammar School, in Amersham, Buckinghamshire, dated 13th May 1997

"Dear Dr Fahim

This is to thank you, most sincerely and warmly, for giving the Harrow SACRE Lecture 2002 on 17th October.

The audience was delighted by the talk, which was forthright, interesting, and highly informative. You had the audience on the edge of their seats and everyone went away much the wiser for your words. The question-time was equally absorbing and we were able to enjoy a high level of discussion on important topics, relevant to everyday life.

In short, your visit was highly successful and we are very grateful that you spared us your valuable time.

I passed on the invoice that you signed to our finance department. You will receive a cheque made out to you, explaining that this is to cover your expenses. The amount is our donation to your work and we would be grateful if you would pass it on.

With renewed thanks for giving us an inspiring evening.

Kind regards,

Yours sincerely

Pat Stevens
School Development Services"

I remember on that day I had a major problem with my stomach which prevented me from talking normally. Unfortunately, no medical treatment was available as no doctor was able to identify the cause of the problem. I was so concerned that I would not be able to deliver my speech. I had to rely entirely on the prayer said by Prophet Moses in 20:25-28, when God spoke to him for the first time and asked him to go back to Egypt to deliver the Message to Pharaoh and his Chiefs. Moses prayed: "O my Lord! Open my breast for me (relieve my mind), and ease my task for me, and loosen the knot from my tongue (the impediment from my speech) that they may understand what I say." I kept saying this prayer all the time while driving to get there. Thank God my prayer was accepted, and I spoke fluently.

The title of my talk was **"Happy Family in Islam"**. After I finished my speech, I was approached by a police officer who attended the lecture. He said, "*I thoroughly enjoyed your talk. I was not planning to stay, but after the first five minutes I realised that you are an honest speaker. I thought you were coming here to praise the Muslims and defend their violence. But you were so brave to condemn their ill practices. You clearly differentiated between Islamic teachings and cultural practices. Many thanks for coming.*" Comments like that make me feel so happy to continue my quest in trying to project the true message of Islam.

The following is the letter from Dr Challoner's Grammar School:

"Dear Dr Fahim,

May I, very belatedly, offer you my sincerest thanks for your inspiring lecture of last Tuesday here at Dr. Challoner's Grammar School.

I have had many of our students talking to me about Islam in response to last week, not least the Muslim youngsters who were in the room and who felt that your 'coverage' of their religious standpoint was excellently and sensitively put.

So often it is the case that young people need to be led towards cultural differences and to have them introduced to them in a knowledgeable and understanding way. I certainly felt that you were superbly successful in achieving that aim, to the great benefit of all.

May I thank you once again and express the wish that you may agree to come back to us again next year, if we can find a convenient time, and speak to the next 'layer' of Sixth Form students in their lectures.

I wish you a very happy and pleasant summer and look forward to our meeting again.

Chris Grant
Head of Sixth"

I was so delighted to become a regular speaker at the above school. I thoroughly enjoyed my interaction with the pupils, especially those who misjudged Islam by the conduct of its followers.

3.2.7 Speaking at Muslim Organisations

Most Muslim Organisations would annually celebrate certain Islamic events in the Islamic calendar. For example, they may celebrate the birth of Prophet Mohammed (pbuh), or the end of the fast of the month of Ramadhan, known as 'Eid-ul-Fitr', or the Feast of Pilgrimage, the Hajj, or the day of the journey by night taken by the Prophet (pbuh). With each talk, I had to ensure I covered the area to be addressed and structured the talk to enlighten people regarding the topic. I would carry out significant research work to ensure the authenticity of any references I would make to the Qur'an or Prophet Mohammed (pbuh). I also prepared myself to answer questions.

I give below two responses. The first one (1) is from **The United Muslims Association (UK)**, **in Morden, Surrey, dated 4th October 1998** and the second one (2) is from **Councillor Chris Noyce, Liberal Democrats, London Borough of Harrow, dated 16th January 2002.**

1) First Response

"Dear brother Dr. Faheem

As salaam-u-alaikum

'Seerat-un-Nabi'

The U.M.A. Committee on behalf of the entire membership wishes to thank you for your most valued participation in the above event held at Wentworth Hall Carshalton on Saturday 3rd October. We are further grateful for your kind 'hadiya' of £100. May Allah SWT shower you with His blessings and 'jazz-il-khair'.

Al'hamdo'lillah - your 'dars' on the topic of 'salaat' was very informative and greatly appreciated by all ages at the congregation. And we all eagerly await the next opportunity of meeting you in the not too distant a future - Insha'Allah.

Please also convey our thanks and best wishes to Mrs. (Dr.) Faheem and Miss Faheem.

Wasalaam

Yours sincerely

Syed Najmuddin Qadri
General Secretary"

2) Second Response

"Dear Dr Fahim

I am just dropping you a line to thank you very much indeed for the privilege of listening to your talk at the Harrow Islamic Society Eid function. It was extremely thought-provoking and I would appreciate the text of your speech or the notes as previously requested for further study.

May I say on behalf of myself and my partner Geraldine O'Neill that we very much enjoyed the evening and found your talk, as mentioned above, not only thought-provoking but very profound.

Best regards

Yours sincerely

Councillor C. D. Noyce"

3.2.8 Speaking on BBC World Service and Radio 4

I have successfully broadcast several radio programmes on BBC World Service and Radio 4. It has always been a great and enjoyable challenge as I had to address audiences worldwide. Hence, I had to make the material appealing to the varying worldwide nationalities that constituted the BBC listening audience.

The first encounter I had was with Kristine Pommert, a great Producer of Religious Programmes. She wrote to me on 4th April 1996:

"Dear Dr Fahim,

*Further to our telephone conversation yesterday, I now enclose our guidelines for **Words of Faith**. Please don't be dismayed by what at first sight might seem a rather weighty tome - most of it consists of sample scripts!*

As we discussed, the broadcast dates for your contributions on the Hajj are 29th and 30th April and 1st May. The format in each case is a straight talk, which should be about four minutes long. We agreed to do the recording on 17th April at 11 am. As I said, it would be helpful to have the scripts as far in advance as possible during that week.

As I need to prepare some programme trails before you actually come in, I should be grateful if you could give me a ring soon to let me know how you would like to be described in terms of your professional background etc.

Many thanks again for your interest in contributing to our programme. I very much look forward to receiving your scripts and meeting you in Bush House on the 17th.

Your sincerely

Kristine Pommert
Producer / Religious programmes"

On 29th April 1996, she wrote to me again:

*"Very many thanks for your letter of 25th April with your ideas for future editions of **Words of Faith**. I am delighted that you are interested in contributing more to the strand! I greatly enjoyed working with you and very much look forward to repeating the experience.*

As for future editions, all of the subjects you mentioned are interesting and worthwhile. If you agree, I would be happy to tackle the subject groups one at a time over a longer period. To make a start, I would be very interested to read what you have written about the biblical prophets mentioned in the Qur'an - I think this could be a fascinating subject for Muslim, Jewish and Christian listeners alike.

I don't think there's any need to worry about your accent, and unless our listeners say otherwise, I am very happy to put you on the air again! In any case, it's good to know that your daughters would be willing to read for us perhaps we could consider asking them to do something at a later stage to add a bit of variety to our range of speakers.

Thank you again for your interest in the programme and in the World Service. I very much look forward to hearing from you again.

Very best wishes

Kristine Pommert

Producer / Religious Programmes"

Kristine Pommert sent me a beautiful Christmas message:

"Dear Essam

Wishing you and your family every blessing for the New Year. Meeting you was one of the things that made 1996 special - I hope there will be further opportunities to work together in 1997! Very best wishes, Kristine."

To my surprise I was given a handwritten letter dated 2nd August 1996, addressed to BBC World Service, Bush House, London, written by a woman in Lanzarote, Canary Islands, Spain, commenting on my programme:

"Dear Dr Fahid

Excuse me if I did not catch your name correctly on Words of Faith this morning.

I was most impressed by what you had to say and felt it dealt very accurately with the cause of so many of the troubles in the world today.

I would be most grateful if you could let me know where I can obtain any other of your teachings.

Yours sincerely

Katherine Dickson - Wright"

I give below three responses from three other producers I worked with. The first one is dated 19th January 1999, from Sue Waldram, the second one is from Rosemary Hartill, dated 7th March 2001 and the third one is from Karen Maurice dated 17th April 2001:

1) *"Dear Dr Fahim,*

Fred, Ravinder and I send our heartfelt thanks to you for the lovely evening yesterday. I hope you heard the broadcast, but I'm enclosing a cassette in case. We really enjoyed meeting you and your family and friends, and felt very privileged to be included in such an occasion.

I really appreciate all the trouble you went to for our sakes, and it was the most interesting and enjoyable assignment we've had for ages! I certainly learned a lot, and we don't have many interviews where delicious cakes are offered (not to mention the wonderful dates - the tough dry ones I'm used to will never taste the same again!).

With best wishes and thanks from us all,

Sue Waldram"

The following is the response from Rosemary Hartill & Associates, dated 7th March 2001:

2) *"Dear Dr Sonya and Dr Mohammed*

I'm writing to thank you for all your really lovely kindness, hospitality and the very enjoyable time I had with you a few weeks back recording material for the BBC World Service radio series, 'Moslem Memories'. For me it was a truly memorable and happy day - one of those days when I realise what a pleasure and privilege it is to be able to come and meet and talk and make such programmes. I particularly appreciate the time you took because I can guess how busy you both are.

The lift over to East London was such a help - I gave my talk to the church group, and of course told them a little about how I had spent my day so enjoyably with you.

I was absolutely delighted with the results, and people at the BBC who have heard the series are pleased too. I shall send you cassettes soon, so I hope you will like them too.

Please find attached more information about the series, and times of transmission which began this week. You appear in all three programmes. Basmah appears in programme 2.

I found our conversation not only enjoyable, but illuminating, and I would so like to meet again sometime. I think I shall have to dream up another series! All the material on prayer and fasting was so good that I decided to focus on the fasting, and keep the prayer material back for possible transmission in another programme.

Please all three of you sign, date and return the contract, and you will receive some money soon - only a very small token of my real gratitude. In whose name shall I make out the collective cheque?

Kindest regards and thanks once again

Rosemary Hartill"

I received the following response dated 17th April 2001, from Karen Maurice, Producer, Radio 4:

3)"*Dear Dr Fahim*

Re: The Sunday Programme on Easter Day

Thank you for taking part in our Easter Day special Sunday Programme. Your contribution was invaluable and we are really appreciative of your time. The program has been received very well both by listeners (judging by the number of emails we have received) and senior management at Radio 4.

I have enclosed a copy of the programme and paperwork regarding guest payment/expenses will follow shortly.

Thank you once again.

Karen Maurice

Producer
Sunday Programme
BBC Radio 4"

What lovely responses from these amazing and grateful people who appreciated my time and effort. This reminds me of the ungrateful attitude of the Asian Muslim producers at TV Channel S. In the year 2006, they invited me to record, free of charge, 30 episodes, 20 minutes each, titled **"Light Upon Light"** to be broadcast during the blessed month of Ramadhan, one episode everyday before the sunset. Since then, the series has been repeated every year during the month of Ramadhan. As it was on at prime time and people enjoyed my talks, many companies were advertising during the programme. You can imagine the revenues the Channel was making. A friend of mine said: *'You must be receiving a lot of royalties every year!'* I responded by saying: *'They never even sent me a thank you card or a box of chocolate or just a bunch of flowers.'* I wonder! Are these Islamic manners? Of course not! But they are greedy, ungrateful souls.

3.2.9 Speaking at Rotary Clubs

I joined Redbridge Rotary Club in 1989. The first time I visited the Club, I wrote down my name as 'Dr Mohammed Essam El-Din Fahim'. During the first visit, members of the Club, to show a form of friendship, called me by my first name, Mohammed, which no one else has ever called me by. All my life, my family and friends called me by my middle name 'Essam'. So, from that moment in time I decided to introduce myself to any new friends or even strangers, as Dr Mohammed Fahim. Using 'Mohammed' would also give a clear message that I'm a Muslim. Unfortunately, some of my Muslim friends criticised me for joining Rotary as they considered it to be part of the secret Masonic Organisation, which is not true.

Our Club had 42 members from different ethnic backgrounds. However, the majority were Jews. It was now the first time in my life to have a very close and active encounter with Jewish people. We became so close. We ate together, we travelled together, we attended weddings and funerals together and we sang and danced together. My tailor was a Jew, my lawyer was a Jew, my plumber was a Jew, my accountant was a Jew, my estate agent was a Jew and my physiotherapist was a Jew.

My Jewish and Christian brothers and sisters elected me to be the Club President in 1997/98. I grab every opportunity to deliver the true message of Islam, without intimidating or alienating anyone. I compiled a speech to be delivered on the Change-Over night on Tuesday 1st July 1997. I give below some of the highlights of my speech:

"When God spoke to Moses after leaving Madianite, He ordered him to return to Egypt. Moses asked God to relieve his mind, to ease his task and to make him an eloquent speaker so people would understand what he says, and God said: 'Granted is thy prayer, O Moses!' 20:36.

"Today I pray that God will grant me the same as Moses and help and strengthen me with the Holy Spirit like Jesus to serve you and Rotary worldwide all my days. This is in return for the trust and honour you bestowed upon me by electing me as your President for 1997/98.

"The Lord whom we always praise in our Rotary Grace says: 'O! mankind We created you from a single pair of a male and a female and made you into nations and tribes to get to know each other (not to despise each other). Really the most honoured of you in the sight of God is he who is the most righteous of you.' 49:13.

"These are exactly the main objectives of Rotary:
1. To know each other, through the development of acquaintance and the development of international understanding.
2. To perfect our profession by applying the ideal of service to satisfy our customers in order to please our Creator.
3. To do good charitable deeds without expecting a reward from anyone.

"Rotary confirms the fact that we are all brothers and sisters in humanity as we are all the children of Adam and Eve. Rotary also firmly establishes the fact that we are all equal irrespective of our race, colour, religion, gender or creed. Look around you, you can see the best example in our Club."

"... The message I have tonight for all countries which do not allow Rotary to exist, especially some Muslim countries, is that by being a practising Muslim myself, if Rotary had

contradicted with my own beliefs, I would not be standing here today. On the contrary Rotary has helped me to understand the spirit of Islam and to implement its teachings.

"For example, when I heard Rotarian Terry Russell of District International Committee talking to us about 'send a cow project', my eyes were filled with tears. Do you know why? Because recently I came across a prophetic tradition by the Prophet Mohammed recommending 40 good deeds. The highest one on the list was sending a goat, not even a cow! That shows you how generous we are at Rotary. As I always wanted to send a goat, but I did not know how, it was Terry's talk which showed me the way.

"What makes me more proud to be a Rotarian is that among the 40 good deeds mentioned in this prophetic tradition were:

- *Helping the deaf, blind and partially sighted*
- *Helping those with a speech impediment and the mentally ill*
- *Helping the oppressed and the weak*
- *Helping man with his means of transport*
- *Comforting the bereaved, providing counselling and visiting the sick.*
- *Removing hazards from the road*
- *Providing water for people, animals and irrigation*
- *Spreading peace worldwide*

"As Rotarians, are we not doing this all the time? Are we not all making a difference by showing that Rotary does care?"

The above was part of my speech as the Incoming President for the Rotary year 1997/98.

We raised funds together for many humanitarian projects worldwide. In the Rotary year 1999/2000, I was the Chairman of the Foundation Committee. I utilised matching grants offered by Rotary Foundation to raise US $40,000 to assist an orphanage in Egypt to equip a small factory to produce carpets to support the orphanage. I was awarded 'Paul Harris Fellowship' which is the highest award in Rotary.

In the Rotary year 2000/2001, I was also the Chairman of the Foundation Committee. I raised US $50,000 to equip a hospital in Egypt with five kidney dialysis machines to provide free treatment to poor people. As a result of my fund raising campaigns, I brought to the Club over 50 Paul Harris Awards. We used to award them to members of our Club and the community at large, who would excel in their community work.

I introduced Islam to everyone in a very sensible and courteous manner. They were so pleased to hear about the true message of Islam. Some of my fellow Rotarians used to say: 'Mohammed! You sound like a Rabbi!' I remember once I invited a Rabbi as a speaker. One of my fellow Rotarians made a very funny comment, 'Mohammed! Why did you invite the Rabbi? I can't eat my ham!'

I became a very well-known speaker among Rotary Clubs in the London District 1130. I used to get invited by many clubs in our District to talk about Islam.

As an example of appreciation of my work, I give below the response of Rotarian Clive Amos, the Immediate Past President of Club of Tottenham & Wood Green, dated 26th October 1998:

"Dear Mohammed

Thank you for speaking to our club this evening.

I was telephoned by our secretary to say how good your talk was, how well it was received and that it had prompted many questions. He also said that I had arranged some very good speakers during the past two years, but that you were one of the best.

I am, therefore, very grateful to you for having given of your time to speak at the club and even more disappointed that I had to miss it. Although I was not present, I hope that your talk showed those present that there is more in this world that unites us as brothers and sisters than that which divides us.

With best wishes and many thanks.

Yours in Rotary Fellowship

Clive Amos"

3.2.10 Breaking Fast in Ramadhan with Different Communities

A) Breaking Fast in Ramadhan With Members of the Jewish Community

During the Holy month of Ramadhan, I was honoured to be invited with other Muslims in London to have our Iftar at the house of His Excellency Mark Regev, the Israeli Ambassador in London in June 2016 and 2017, and at the house of the Chief-Rabbi Ephraim Mirvis, in June 2017.

I received the following invitation, dated 17th May 2017, from His Excellency Ambassador Mark Regev:

"Dear Dr Fahim,

Asalaamu Aleikum,

At the time when the Middle East is facing significant challenges, it is more important than ever that we seek to build bridges and dialogue between religious communities. To this endeavour, I will be hosting an Iftar dinner on Monday 19th of June at 20:15 at a central London venue.

For this year's Iftar, we will explore a specially curated selection of Cambridge University Library's Genizah fragments, part of the world's largest collection of medieval Jewish manuscripts. Dating from the 9th to the 19th centuries, some 300,000 texts were deposited by the Jewish community of Old (Fustat) and preserved at the Ben Ezra, Egypt, synagogue.

Today, these manuscripts provide a rich insight into a millennium of Jewish and Islamic life in the region. Dr Ben Outhwaite, Head of the Genizah Research Unit at Cambridge University, will tell us the story of these unique texts and explain the lives of Jews during an era in which the vast majority lived in Islamic societies. I hope you will be able to join me on 19th June for what looks to be an incredibly enlightening evening.

Mark Regev
Ambassador of the State of Israel to the Court of St James's"

I received the following email, dated 14th June 2017, from Sophia Miller, Public Affairs Officer:

"Dear Dr Mohammed Fahim

I hope this finds you well. I would like to take the opportunity to introduce myself. My name is Sofia and I work in the public diplomacy department at the Embassy of Israel.

We are delighted that you will be attending the Iftar event Ambassador Mark Regev will be hosting on Monday 19th of June.

We were just wondering if you would be willing to say a few words just before we break the fast.

If you have questions, please do not hesitate to contact me. I look forward to hearing from you.

Many thanks,

Sofia"

No doubt I thoroughly enjoyed the event, as well as the rest of the guests. The Ambassador provided a room in his house for Muslim guests to offer the sunset prayer. What a great gesture from him.

The following is the response of His Excellency Ambassador Mark Regev dated 21st June 2017, after the event:

"Dear Dr Fahim

Please accept my sincerest thanks for joining me again this year at my Iftar dinner, for sharing your thoughts, and for kindly agreeing to open the proceedings.

I trust that you enjoyed the evening, and that like myself, you found the discussion enriching and full of hope.

As you know, conversations such as these are essential for Jews and Muslims to come together, and to build bridges for the betterment of a region that both our faith hold dear. I hope that our evening will serve as an example for others to do the same.

Once again, many thanks. I look forward to meeting with you again in the near future.

Mark Regev
Ambassador of Israel to the Court of St James's"

Unfortunately, not every member of my mosque was so supportive when I mentioned the above invitations. I clearly stated that we as Muslims should never decline any invitation which could lead to peace and understanding. God clearly states that we must make an effort to get to know each other. Building bridges is better than erecting walls. Our aim is to build more bridges and fill the gaps.

The first time I met Chief Rabbi Ephraim Mirvis, was when he invited me to speak at his synagogue in May 2006. The following is the invitation I received from him dated 24th May 2017 to break my fast at his house:

"Dear Dr and Mrs Fahim
To mark the first anniversary of the tragic murder of Jo Cox MP numerous events celebrating unity will be held throughout Britain. As part of this 'Great Get Together' initiative Valerie and I would be delighted if you could join us for an Iftar at our home on Sunday 18th of June from 20:45.

I have pleasure in attaching a formal invitation.

We very much look forward to welcoming you,

Chief Rabbi Ephraim Mirvis"

B) Breaking Fast in Ramadhan with Members of the Metropolitan Police Service

Muslims who are members of the London Muslim Community Forum were invited several times, by the Commissioner of the Metropolitan Police Service to break their fast during Ramadhan at New Scotland Yard. What an amazing experience to reinforce our Inter-Faith Dialogue. We should be grateful to God and Her Majesty, the Queen, for the Great Country we live in.

One of the greatest qualities of the British society is that we are all welcome to live together in peace and harmony whilst enjoying freedom of worship and showing mutual respect to each other. Again, what we used to say in Egypt we repeated it here: "We are proud to be British citizens of different ethnicities and beliefs. However, we are all brothers and sisters in humanity", as stated above in verse 49:13.

3.2.11 Police Chaplaincy - Do British Muslims Value the Police?

In the year 2002, I was approached by a fellow Rotarian at our Redbridge Rotary Club, who was a police officer working with the Metropolitan Police Service (the Met), to join a newly formed group by the Met, called **"Independent Advisors Group"** (IAG). The police were trying to encourage community leaders from all ethnicities to join the IAG, to create a dialogue with the diverse communities. I was so happy to join "Redbridge Independent Advisors Group" (RIAG). We would meet monthly to review the work of the police in our local Borough and to report any community issues or concerns. We received training on how the police conduct their daily duties, like stop and search or carrying out certain operations to target drug dealers or car theft or prostitution or knife crimes. We shadowed police officers to witness the way they handled people in their operations, and we would provide feedback regarding the way in which police officers dealt with the community.

There is no doubt that there are British Muslims who don't like the police as they feel they have been discriminated against because of their ethnicity or religion, especially when it comes to arresting innocent people in dawn-raids under the Terrorism Act, and then releasing them as they were the wrong people. There are Muslims who will never choose to join the police as they feel they will not have equal opportunity.

As the Chairman and Head Imam of South Woodford Mosque, the RIAG inspired me to create a major channel of communication with the local police force in Redbridge. I invited them regularly to our mosque on Fridays to address the congregation. We organised several conferences to deal with community cohesion, where the police were a major contributor. We strived to create an ethos of cooperation with the police whilst helping to instil in the community that they should really trust the police in what they are doing. We jointly tried to alleviate the fears of the community regarding any discrimination or racism because of their ethnicity or religion. All the Borough Commanders in Redbridge and the police officers were so helpful and cooperative. I personally felt so confident in the work carried out by the Met. Consequently, members of my community became so confident to approach me with their concerns to report them to the police and to ensure they were dealt with promptly. This exemplifies how trust and co-operation can be fostered more readily when local authorities and community support and protection services work in an open and collaborative way with faith and community leaders.

In November 2008, the Met went one step further and decided to recruit a Muslim Chaplain as a volunteer, as they did not have funds for this job. I volunteered and I became the first Muslim Chaplain to the Met in Redbridge. A job which I enjoyed so much. The spectrum of work I did was so amazing from providing pastoral support to educational sharing and building of tolerance. This comes from true understanding of religious and cultural differences and practices.

After joining the London Muslim Community Forum, I offered my services as a Muslim Chaplain to anyone in the London area.

I give below, an example of two conferences which were organised by the community and police.

1) Commander Mak Chishty, Sergeant Javaria Said and I spearheaded and successfully organised the first ever London Muslim Community Conference, sponsored by the Metropolitan Police on Saturday 16th November 2013 at the Waterlily, 69-89 Mile End Road, London E1 4TT. The **'Muslim Communities in London, The Law and Policing Conference'** addressed the following topics:

Session 1 - Muslims and the Wider Society

- Muslims and the mainstream media - Simon Israel
- Shariah (family) Law in Britain- Misapprehensions and misrepresentations - Khola Hasan
- Schedule 7 and the Muslim Communities - David Anderson QC and Ibrahim El-Nour
- The "Post-Woolwich" Environment - Nizar Boga
- Muslim Police Officers & Staff in the Metropolitan Police Service – Dal Babu
- Q&A Panel - Chaired by Commander Mak Chishty

Session 2 - Issues Within the Communities

- Opening - Commander Mak Chishty
- Take Action to End Violence Against Women and Girls - Dr Mohammed Fahim PhD
- Radicalisation and its Impact on Muslim Families – Sheikh Shams Adduha Muhammad
- Recruitment of Imams and Mosques' Madrasas - Mahmoud Attiya

- Muslim Communities and the Problem of Underachievement by Young Muslims - Dr Qadir Bakhsh PhD
- Anti-Muslims Hate Crimes & Tell MAMA - Fiyaz Mughal
- Q&A Panel - Chaired by Commander Mak Chishty
- Close - Nadia Ali

Prince Charles was invited to attend the conference, but unfortunately, he could not make it. The following is the response from Prince Charles' Programme Co-Ordinator, Trisha Windsor, dated 14th November 2013

"Dear Dr Fahim,

Thank you for your letter of 4th November, in which you very kindly invite The Prince of Wales to attend the Met and the London Muslim Community Conference on Saturday 16th November.

His Royal Highness's diary for November was confirmed several months ago and, very sadly, other long-standing commitments that day mean he is unable to join you. He is so sorry.

However, His Royal Highness was grateful to you for thinking of him and has asked that I pass on his best wishes for the success of the event.

Yours sincerely,

Trisha Windsor"

The conference was a great success. We all realised the importance of having such events to engage the community and the police in very positive and serious forums to address concerns and alleviate fears and distrust. Further conferences were organised and the Met was so helpful to fully support them. I spoke at all of them.

The following is the response of Commander Mak Chishty, West Area Commander, dated 25th November 2013.

"Dear Mohammed,

Asalaamu alaikum,

I wanted to personally acknowledge and thank you for making the conference a resounding success. Your time, efforts and presentation were very well received by the attendees and in particular the feedback from IPCC and other forces. You will be pleased to know that the conference was a huge success and we have already had numerous requests to replicate it around the country.

The most empowering aspect of the conference was that it was a community led conference for the community and not necessarily professional bodies and practitioners. This has provided local people with a platform to have their voices heard and an opportunity to reclaim issues affecting them. This is where we begin to mobilise communities against harmful effects of radicalisation.

Your qualified words and professional manner were essential in ensuring that the issues affecting the diverse communities of London were heard and provided a stage for dialogue between them and professional bodies. Through your brave actions of addressing difficult subjects affecting the Muslim communities of London, new relationships were built, while others were strengthened.

Thank you for your efforts, energy and time. I am committed to ensuring that this is not a one off event and look forward to your support in the future.

Yours sincerely,

Mak Chishty
West Area Commander"

2) On Monday 20th June 2019, the Trustees of South Woodford Mosque organised a conference to exhibit our community work and our cooperation with the police in London. Assistant Commissioner Ms Helen Ball and a number of police officers from the Met attended the conference.

The conference was a great achievement. It was another jewel in the crown of South Woodford Mosque. The following message was received from Assistant Commissioner Ms Helen Ball:

"Dear Friends

I wanted to sincerely thank you for your generosity and kind invitation to myself and colleagues to visit South Woodford Mosque. We were all so inspired by your commitment to the local community and impressed by the real improvements you have made through your tireless work.

The close relationship which has been forged between the Mosque, police and local community through such a positive and inclusive attitude is of great credit to all involved and I very much look forward to our future continued partnership.

Yours sincerely

Helen Ball QPM
Assistant Commissioner"

I'm helping to recruit more people from the Muslim ethnic minorities to join the Met. I hope I will succeed in my endeavour to persuade more Muslims to value our wonderful police services. I personally feel I became a part of this wonderful and highly professional organisation through my links. I also feel the pain when harm is caused to members of the police force, while they are out doing their job.

Following the murder of PC Andrew Harper, I sent the following message to Assistant Commissioner Ms Helen Ball, at New Scotland Yard:

"Dear AC Ms Helen Ball

I pray you are keeping well.

The Muslim community in South Woodford, London is shocked and saddened to hear about the brutal and mindless killing of the young Police Officer Andrew Harper.

Police officers are risking their lives on daily basis to protect us all. They are at more risk than army officers as they have to be physically engaged while fighting unknown criminals. They have no tanks or armed vehicles to combat the wrongdoers. They are on their feet and outside their police cars. Our prayers and our thoughts are with Andrew's family and friends.

As an old man, I'm writing this message with tearful eyes. I feel the pain of his family, his wife and his parents. I'm a father and a grandfather and I understand how painful it is to lose a son or a grandson.

May God Almighty shower His Mercy on Andrew and his family and admit him to His Gardens of Bliss. May God Almighty give his family and friends patience and perseverance and reward them for their calamity.

In honour and memory of Andrew who was killed in the line of duty protecting us all, and in recognition of his bravery and the greatest sacrifice he made I would like to send £1,000 (one thousand pounds) as a personal gift to his widow. It is just a token to show my personal love to Andrew and his family. Please advise how can I send it to her?

We are so grateful to our Police Force for all the work they are doing all over the Country whilst risking their lives to protect us all and to ensure our safety and well-being at all times.

May God Almighty bless you all and protect you from every evil and make you victorious in your fight against crime.

Hope to see you soon.

Please share my email with the Commissioner.

Kindest regards
Dr. Mohammed Fahim"

I received the following response from PC Suzanne Stanbrook, Romford Police Station on 19th August 2019:

"Dear Dr Fahim,

As always I am humbled by your beautiful words. You are an amazing man, leader and friend.

Your support for the police is second to none.

I am honoured to work with you.

May god be with you always.

Kindest regards

Suzanne"

I also received the following message from Assistant Commissioner, Ms Helen Ball, on 19th August 2019:

"Dear Dr Fahim,

As always, you are incredibly kind and caring. Thank you so much for contacting me over this. Your words always give strength and resilience. I will certainly let the Commissioner know.

You may already have seen that there is a JustGiving page for PC Harper's family. Would this be suitable for you to use? If not, please do say and I shall work out an alternative route for your extremely generous donation.

With kindest regards, as ever, Helen"

When I made my donation of £1,000, I posted the following message:

"May God shower Andrew with His Mercy and Blessings and admit him to His Gardens of Bliss and give his family patience and perseverance and reward them for their calamity. From the Muslim Chaplain to MPS."

As a Muslim Chaplain, I was approached by a Borough Commander who was so concerned about the welfare of her Muslim police officers who would be fasting during the long hours of the month of Ramadhan in the summer. As the fast could be for 19 hours without food or drink, she asked me if the supervisor can determine if a police officer should be asked not to fast, especially when they have to be racing on the roads?

I give below my response:

**"*Fasting during the long days of the summer:*

Fasting during the month of Ramadan is a religious obligation which must be observed by every healthy Muslim adult male or female who is not on a journey (i.e. not travelling) as detailed in verses 2:183-187, in the Holy Qur'an.

Fasting means to completely abstain from food, drink and the fulfilment of any sexual desire from dawn, (not sunrise) to sunset. Dawn is at least 1½ hours before sunrise, depending upon wherever you might be on planet earth. However, from sunset to dawn people go back to their normal life.

While fasting, the person must be in full control of all his faculties, no shouting, no rudeness and no swearing. If someone reviles or insults him, he must not respond, but simply reminds himself that he is fasting by saying to himself, "I am fasting" twice.

Times of dawn and sunset vary from one place on earth to the other. These times also change every day. For example, in the London area, dawn on 1st January is at 6:25am, sunrise is at 8:06am and sunset at 4:05pm, (about 10 hours of fast), whilst on 1st July dawn is at 2:52am, sunrise at 4:48am and sunset at 9:24pm, (about 18 hours of fast). These times in Scandinavian countries will be approximately 22 hours of fast in the summer and 4 hours in the winter.

Ramadan is the 9th month in the Muslim calendar. Since it is a lunar month, it comes 11 days earlier every year. So, it can be in the summer when the days are very long or in the winter when the days are short.
If someone is chronically ill or terminally ill, they have the right not to fast, but must pay a ransom by feeding a number of poor people equal to the days they could not fast. However, if they have no means to pay, then they are exempted.

Pregnant women and breast feeding women, if they fear that their child could be harmed, have the option not to fast but they must pay a ransom if they can afford it. Another religious opinion is that they must make up the days they missed later in the year when the reason for not fasting no longer exists.

Temporary sick people have the right not to fast but must make up the days later in the year before next Ramadan.

Anyone who is healthy, but by fasting anytime in the year could cause himself a health problem, as advised by his doctor, would be exempted from fasting. And again will have to pay the ransom if he can afford it.

Women during their monthly periods are not permitted to fast. They must break the fast and make up the days later.

Also, those who find it extremely difficult to fast any time in the year, have the right not to fast, but they must pay a ransom if they can afford it.

A person who is travelling also has the option not to fast, but must make up the days later.

The question we are trying to address here is:
If I am a healthy person, but due to the long days of the summer and the nature of my job I will find it extremely difficult to fast and I may cause harm to myself or others, but I can make up the days I missed later in the year when the days are shorter, can I do that?
The answer is:
In accordance with verse 17:13, every person is responsible for his own actions.
So it is important to carry out a risk assessment to see how your fast might affect your performance at the work place.
- *Maybe you should consider taking your annual leave during Ramadan.*
- *Maybe you try to fast a few days and see how your performance would be affected.*
- *May be if you stop having tea and coffee and stop smoking a few weeks before the start of the month, you might be able to fast.*
- *May be if you take a good predawn meal, it would help you fast.*
- *May be by staying away from food which makes you feel thirsty, it would help you fast.*

- *Why not fast the days when you are off duty?*

If you come to the conclusion that it is extremely difficult to fast as it would affect your performance at the workplace and may compromise your safety and the safety of others, then do not fast. But you must make up the days later in the year, as paying a ransom does not apply to a healthy person.

By Dr Mohammed Fahim"

3.2.12 School Chaplaincy

In the academic year 2013-2014, I was appointed as an Honorary Muslim Chaplain for Forest School, Leytonstone, London. The school has more than 1,500 boys and girls in equal proportion, from ages 4 to 18 years old. My eldest daughter and my son went there. The school follows the Church of England but accepts children from all faith groups.

The school was in the process of recruiting honorary chaplains from Judaism and Islam. Some of the Muslim children who worship at our mosque in South Woodford, London, recommended me to the Christian Chaplain. He invited me to come to the school to meet him. It was a great opportunity to confer with him. I found him to be very learned, tolerant and extremely kind and helpful. We discussed the role of the school chaplain and what the school expects me to do. I was told in the meeting that a few months ago he invited an Imam from East London Mosque, but unfortunately, he arrived very late after the assembly was over. I was asked to address the girls on Friday morning and the boys on Monday morning, during the assembly at the school chapel.

I arrived on time, thank God, for the first session on Friday morning. I went to the Chaplain's office to leave together to follow the procession to the chapel. The title of my talk was "the importance of persevering patiently whilst seeking knowledge". I told the story of Prophet Moses who was commanded by God to accompany a learned man to learn from him, as stated in the Qur'an 18:60-82. I had to squeeze the story in seven minutes. I do not read solely from any script, I prefer to talk and connect, so this time constraint was a challenge for me. When I finished, the girls gave me standing ovation. The Head Mistress started her vote of thanks by saying: "What a dynamic speaker!" I was so pleased that they liked my inaugural speech at the school assembly.

On Monday morning I arrived on time to address the boys. My talk was about "A father admonishing his son", as in 31:13-19. I went to the Chaplain's office to leave together. I greeted him but he sounded very unhappy. He said: "*I have received complaints from parents and teachers regarding your speech on Friday.*" I was so surprised to hear this, my throat became very dry, and I was also fasting on that day. I asked him what I had said that was wrong and what they didn't like? He replied: "*You used the word Martyr!!*" I tried to recall when I used this word and what the context was. I remembered when Moses was following the learned man, they came across a young boy, and the learned man killed him. Moses went mad and said, '*how can you kill an innocent soul?*'. The learned man told Moses that if this boy would have lived, he would have chosen to be a tyrant and he would have caused his righteous parents a lot of suffering and grief. The learned man continued, '*God in*

His Plan wanted him to die like that and have the reward of a 'Martyr' and God will give the parents in exchange another son who will be more caring and kind to them.' So, what was wrong in saying 'Martyr'? I did offer to respond to the mails received, to fully explain the context and interpretation but this was not taken up.

As I was not given any explanation regarding the nature of the complaint about the word 'Martyr', I conducted my own research. I discovered that an ex-pupil of Pakistani origin was allegedly accused of a terrorist attack in Pakistan which led to the killing of a foreign journalist. Terrorist groups regard those of them who are killed while carrying out an attack as 'martyrs'. The school was trying to detach itself fully from the history of this ex-pupil as if trying to say we have nothing to do with him. This led the entire school to become so paranoid!

I personally knew the parents of the boy. They were regular worshippers at our mosque and extremely helpful and righteous. But I never knew that they were his parents. I felt so sorry for them as they grieved a lot and lived in real pain. It was very sad that their only son became the source of grief for them. He reminded me of the boy who was killed by the learned man as explained in the story above.

New Chaplain
I subsequently worked with a new incoming school Chaplain (Fr Trathern) and we quickly formed a mutually respectful and understanding working relationship. We were both involved in organising the Friday prayer for the Muslim students. Even the girls were invited to join the prayers which was a great achievement.

I give below a few examples of the communications I had with my very dear brother Fr Trathen, regarding my involvement with the school:

1) On 27 March 2014, Fr Trathen wrote:

"Dear brother Mohammed,

Here at Forest School, the Chapel Talks Theme for Trinity (Summer) Term 2014 will be "My passion, my faith…"

I would very much like to invite you to speak about something you care about passionately, relating it in some way to your faith. The expectation is for up to seven minutes' talk duration and will, most likely, be framed with hymn and prayer/meditation, in our usual way (unless you want to suggest something exceptional!?!). You would be speaking to around 300 pre-teen and teenage students.
We would be, ideally, looking to have you speak on both a Monday and a Friday, on proximate dates (that way, you get to speak to Girls & Boys at their different Chapel times). If you can only offer for one date, I fully understand and will still be very delighted to hear from you!

Might you have a preferred date, or dates? Term starts back on 22 April and runs through until early July 2014.

I look forward to hearing from some of you, soon.

Go well,

Paul"

- On 13 Feb 2015, Fr Paul Trathen wrote:

"Dear brother Mohammed,

We live in difficult times, when our respective faiths are regularly misrepresented or misunderstood and where a few, act in the name of our faiths, but wreak horrors utterly at odds with their precepts and teachings.

I know that our students - Muslim and otherwise – value your visits to Forest School. As we reach the end of this half-term, I'm just writing, therefore, to remind you that we would be delighted to receive you if you can find any space in your diary in the months ahead.

Do please let me know what might be possible. Go well,

Paul"

- On 3 Jan 2016, Fr Paul Trathen wrote:

"Dearest brother Mohammed, Brother Jack & Sister Vanessa,

I am immensely grateful to you all for your intimations in recent times to offer to come to us at Forest School, to speak to students in Chapel.

I attach an Excel worksheet laying out the programme I have put together for this coming Lent Term, on the basis of offers made and agreed from a number of other contributors.

Can I ask that you please read it and let me know whether you might be willing and able to 'fill' any of the four slots as yet unallocated? You would be blessing the students simply by saving them from yet another talk from their Chaplain!!

Many thanks.
Go well,

Paul

Fr Paul Trathen

Vicar, St Peter-in-the-Forest, Walthamstow
Chaplain, Forest School"

- On 13 Jan 2017, Fr Paul Trathen wrote,

"Dearest brother Mohammed,

Happy new year to you and yours.

I am picking up on kind offers from folk to speak in Chapel at Forest School, this term, and am delighted that you are so willing, once again.

Could I ask if you might be able to come and speak on either or both of Monday 23 and Tuesday 24 January (i.e. the week after next)? It would be for the 8.40am slot, for a speaking-duration of just 7 or 8 minutes, as you have experienced here, on previous occasions. Alternatively, I would be keen to consider Monday 20 and Tuesday 21 February.

I would be able to meet your travelling expenses and a small honorarium payment.

I look forward to hearing back from you.

Many thanks. Go well,

Paul

Fr Paul Trathen

Vicar, St Peter-in-the-Forest, Walthamstow
Chaplain, Forest School
Priest-in-Charge, St Andrew, Leytonstone"

- On 16 Jan 2017, Fr Paul Trathen wrote,

"Dear brother Mohammed,

Many thanks for this kind offer. I will be delighted to have you speak with Lower School (11-13-year olds) on Monday 20 February and Middle School (14-16-year olds) on Tuesday 21 February.
Your offer of dinner is very kind, and I shall ask my wife about it and get back to you, soonest. Would your own wife be dining with us, too?

Many thanks. Go well,

Paul

Fr Paul Trathen

Vicar, St Peter-in-the-Forest, Walthamstow
Chaplain, Forest School

6) On 10 Feb 2017, Fr Paul Trathen wrote:

"Dear brother Mohammed,

It was such a blessing spending an evening with yourself, your wife, and friends, on the evening of Friday 27 January! And so very generous of you! Thank you!

I now write to just seek confirmation that you will be able to be with us as preacher at Forest School Chapel on Monday 20 and Tuesday 21 February, as per your earlier, kind offer? I know that, as ever, our students will benefit from your wisdom and kindness.

I do hope I shall hear from you that all stands in order for this to happen. Many thanks.

Go well,

Paul

Fr Paul Trathen

Vicar, St Peter-in-the-Forest, Walthamstow
Chaplain, Forest School
Priest-in-Charge, St Andrew, Leytonstone"

The reason I have listed the above communications between myself and Fr Paul, is to show the variety of work the Christian Chaplain brought to the school and how he strove to involve outside speakers to cater for the diverse religious backgrounds of the students, as well as to reassure the parents that the school is not promoting Christianity. This is something the school must pride itself for.

When my eldest daughter Dr Donia joined the school in 1982 as a pupil, I was not happy at all regarding the message the Chapel was delivering to the pupils. I honestly felt the school was trying to convert my daughter to Christianity, as missionary schools did in Egypt.

Consequently, I wrote to the school to raise my concerns. In response to my query I received the following letter dated 6th February 1984 from the Headmistress, Mrs M Taylor:

"Dear Dr Fahim

Thank you for your letter. I should like to point out that Religious Studies at Forest is treated as other academic subjects. It is accorded the same number of periods, homework and examinations as, say, History or Geography. The aim is to come to an understanding of religions and the religious view of life. Teaching is not confined to Christianity though, as we are in a Western culture, it looms large in the syllabus. The third year is devoted to the study of non-Christian religions and Hinduism, Buddhism, Islam and Judaism are studied. We do not believe the classroom is the place for evangelisation.

"Although Forest is a Church of England foundation, we do accept pupils from several different religious faiths. We stipulate that all girls must attend the short daily service or assembly for worship in the Chapel.

"I do hope that this information has clarified the situation regarding the teaching of Religious Studies at Forest. We pride ourselves on the absence of any kind of religious or other discrimination.

Yours sincerely

Mrs M J Taylor

"PS: I should be very pleased to discuss the matter with you if you would like to make an appointment. I am very anxious that you should feel completely satisfied. MT"

The above response was received when I was in my late thirties and almost 15 years before my involvement with South Woodford mosque. No doubt I was so anxious and concerned regarding my daughter's faith. Consequently, I had to spend more time with her to teach her the true message of Islam in a "Western culture".

Five years later my son Mohammed, joined the same school, so I was better prepared to deal with the same issue.

Having a Muslim Chaplain encourages many Muslim parents to get their children into the school. I used to have very pleasant encounter with the Muslim pupils. Some of them knew me previously from the mosque, or maybe they saw me for the first time when I addressed them. I always noticed that they were so jubilant to see me marching through the chapel. Some of them would wave to me or look at me with a big smile on their faces. Some parents would approach me after Friday prayer at our mosque to tell me that their children were so happy to listen to my talk at the Chapel. It made me feel so happy. I would also provide Islamic counselling, free of charge, to Muslim parents and children.

I remember one of the children said to me: "All the teachers and the Christian Chaplain when they march through the Chapel and reach the end, they would bow in front of the large cross placed there. But Muslim pupils noticed you don't do that. Please can you explain why?"

I responded by saying: "Muslims are not allowed to bow or prostrate to any religious symbols or images. In worship we only bow or prostrate to the One True God."

A New Concern!
I received a message from Fr Paul Trathen that the Headmaster of the boys' school would like to meet with me at his office. When I went to see him, he said: "I have a problem with some of the Muslim boys. They went to a local mosque and obtained a written 'Fatwa' that they are obliged to grow uncontrolled beards if they are really good Muslims. This is against

school regulations and they will be dismissed. I'm willing to turn a blind eye if it is just a very short one."

I told him that I will do my research and respond to him in writing. I fully appreciated his concerns because when young Muslims grow uncontrolled beards, they are 'profiled' as radicals or extremists which of course can take another step closer to the profile of a terrorist. I avoided asking him regarding Sikh pupils who are allowed to grow uncontrolled beards. I had to be very neutral and professional in my response.

I give below my response, which is a little lengthy, but I had to inspire and direct these pupils to what is more important than growing a beard:

"Subject: HAVING A BEARD: A REQUIREMENT OR A RECOMMENDATION?

INTRODUCTION

"Fatwa" is an Arabic word which means: a religious opinion or explanation to address a question or a concern regarding religious matters.

"The person who gives a Fatwa is known as Mufti. A Mufti must have special qualifications to assist him in giving such Fatwa.

"In Islam there are more than one School of Fiqh (jurisprudence) to interpret the Laws/ Codes of practicing the religion. So, the Mufti should present the views of all Schools of Fiqh.

"A Mufti must have full knowledge of the Sciences of the Qur'an in Arabic, as well as the Science of Hadith (Prophetic Traditions) and the Arabic language.
The local customs and traditions of the people in the environment or the country where the Fatwa will be used must be taken into consideration.

"It is a well-known fact that when Imam AL-Shafee (a leading Jurist of his time) left Iraq and came to live in Egypt, he realised that the Egyptians have different customs from the Iraqis. So, he altered his Fatwas as long as they did not contradict with the basic teachings of the religion.

"So a Fatwa given to people in Saudi Arabia or Egypt might not be suitable for me to use in the UK. For example, the Saudi scholars insist that the charity made at the end of the fasting month of Ramadhan must be from the food which people eat. So they insist on giving grains of rice or wheat or dates to the poor and the needy, while other scholars allow cash to be given instead.

"Prophet Mohammed, peace be upon him (PBUH), warned those who rush to give Fatwa without knowledge are rushing to take their seats in the blazing hell fire on the Day of Judgement.

"In every Muslim country a Mufti is either appointed by the Government or elected by the local Muslim Scholars Council. The Mufti is supposed to be the highest religious authority in

these countries, as he will address from a religious point of view, major issues in the fields of, for example, wars, the economy, politics and social events. Is the peace treaty between Egypt and Israel Islamically sound? Should I have a beard to be a good Muslim? Can I take a bank interest on my deposits? Should someone be executed? These topics for the Mufti to consider.

"In spite of this, we are now facing a barrage of Muftis on the Internet who read few Hadith or a couple of books and appoint themselves as Muftis. They can cause more harm to the people because of their ignorance and limited knowledge. Referring to a Hadith, without understanding or explaining the spirit of the Hadith will have negative repercussions.

"Sheikh Mohammed Naser Al-Albany, examined 14,654 Hadith in all books of Hadith, and concluded that 6,452 Hadith are weak or very weak or fabricated (i.e. false), and 8,202 Hadith are Good (Hasan) or Saheeh (Sound).
Al-Maktab Al-Islami, Beirut, P.O. BOX 11/3771 and Damascus P.O. Box 800 published the Third Edition of his work, in 1988.

"Egypt is well known to have a great reputation regarding the qualities of the Egyptian Muftis, many of whom have published various Fatwas. Their books are regarded as a great source of inspiration. I shall refer to some of them when I address the question of the beard.

HAVING A BEARD!
"Question Number 575: "Some groups insist that beards must be grown without control and accuse those who differ with them of straying away from religion and will not pray behind them as Imam in congregational prayers, what is the opinion of the religion regarding this?"

"The following is a summary of the reply to the above question by his Eminence Sheikh Ateya Saqr, Egyptian Mufti, in his book Al-Fatawy, page 243, volume 2, published by Al-Maktaba Al-Tawfeqia, Cairo, Egypt.

"There is a Sound Hadith in the book of 'Saheeh Al-Bukhari' and the book of 'Saheeh Muslim' which says: The Prophet (PBUH) said: **"Be different from the idol worshippers (Al-Mushrekeen), trim your moustaches and grow your beards."**
There is also another Sound Hadith in the book of 'Saheeh Muslim', which reads:
"Ten from the good nature (Al-fitra): trimming moustache, growing beard, using toothbrush (miswak), cleaning nostrils with water, clipping nails, cleaning between fingers and toes, removing under arm hair, shaving pubic hair, washing using water after defecation." The narrator of the Hadith said" I forgot number ten. It might be rinsing mouth with water."

"One group referred to the first Hadith and regarded having a beard as a requirement (Wajib). This means if you do it you will be rewarded for it and if you do not do it you will be punished for it.

"A second group looked at the other Hadith and claimed that it is a recommendation, (Mandoub) not a requirement. If you do it, you will be rewarded for it and if you do not do it you will not be punished.

So, it is up to each individual to choose whatever suits him and his environment.

"Sheikh Saqr also referred to Fatwa by his Eminence Sheikh Mahmoud Shaltoot, another Egyptian Mufti, page 210 of his book of Fatwas:
"...To copy the idol worshippers is prohibited in trying to imitate their religious conduct, but to imitate what is regarded as custom or general traditions there is no harm in this and it is not disliked or prohibited. Then he said: Surely matters of dress code and personal appearances, including shaving beards, is a custom which the individual should follow if this is desirable in his environment."

"The scholars are not in agreement that shaving beard is unlawful, and it is not the same as the prohibitions of robbery, usury or bribery. The above was a summary of the reply of his Eminence Sheikh Ateya Saqr.

CONCLUSION

"If the first Hadith requires Muslims to be different to the idol worshippers (this was when the Muslims were a minority), so if the orthodox Jews or the Sikhs or the orthodox Christians today grow beards, should not the Muslim then differ with them and shave their beards, if this is the meaning of being different?
If the non-believers wear trainers or shoes, should not the Muslims then walk bare feet to be different?
If the non-believers are driving cars, should the Muslims then ride camels?
"If the non-believers wear watches and use mobiles, should the Muslims then throw away their mobiles/watches and use the position of the sun to work out the time?
"Did Prophet Mohammed (PBUH) change his dress code after he became a prophet at the age of 40 or did he continue to wear the same like his own people who were idol worshippers?

"The idol worshippers at the time of Prophet Mohammed (PBUH), used to bury their newly born daughters alive, used to kill their own children for fear of want, used to commit lewdness openly and secretly, used to offer sacrifices to the idols, used to eat dead animals, used to drink and gamble, used to kill each other, used to go in worship around the House of God naked, etc. The Prophet Mohammed (PBUH), through divine revelation, forbade these acts but continued certain customs like celebrating Aqiqa (to announce the birth of a new-born at a gathering of family and friends with a meal). The custom of keeping a beard was prevalent among the pagans of Arabia before Islam but the Prophet (PBUH) did not banish it but asked the Muslims to trim their moustache to distinguish them as members of the new religious group, also for hygiene; the length of the beard is an individual choice but some follow the prophet in this act who did not let his beard grow out of proportion and used to regularly trim it. This is the meaning of the Hadith.

"The beard of the King of Saudi Arabia, the Custodian of the two holy shrines, who has to implement the fatwas of Saudi Muftis, is an example.

"Unfortunately, due to the negative media coverage about Islam in general and a group of Muslims in particular, the beard is now associated with "terrorists". This is a negative approach and regrettably those in the position of authority have not remained unaffected by this propaganda and the probability is that the police in the UK would stop and search those who have beards, more than those without.

"There is a Sound Hadith in Al-Baihaqi, Al-Hakim and Abu-Dawoud, which says:
The Prophet said, **"Be different from the Jews as they do not pray in their shoes or slippers"** (Al-Albany no. 3210). So that was what was happening at the time of the Prophet. Today Jews pray in their synagogues with their shoes and Muslims take off their shoes in their mosques. This is not because Muslims wanted to be different to the Jews, it is mainly because mosques now have carpets and at the time of the Prophet (PBUH), they had gravel.

"Muslims today ignore the main teachings of Islam and concentrate on trivial issues, which do not progress the cause of Muslims.

"I give below a checklist from the Qur'an and Prophetic Tradition, which should be completed by every Muslim pupil at the school.

"If the answer to all these questions is "YES", then have a beard.

1. Do you believe in the One True God, His Angels, His divine revelations, His Prophets and Messengers without making any distinction between them, The Day of Judgement and the life after death?
2. Do you fully submit your will to the Will of God and say, "I hear and I obey"?
3. Do you know how to purify yourself for prayers, perform your five daily prayers on time, humble yourself in prayer and perform Friday prayer in congregation?
4. Do you fast the month of Ramadan and pay your compulsory annual charity (Zakat)?
5. Do you intend to perform Hajj when you have the means?
6. Do you read the Qur'an in Arabic, understand what you read and apply what you understand to your daily life?
7. Do you teach the Qur'an to others? The prophet (PBUH) said: "deliver on my behalf even one verse from the Qur'an". He did not say deliver on my behalf one Hadith.
8. Are you kind to the orphans, the poor and the needy?
9. Do you walk on earth with humility and without showing off?
10. Do you lower your voice when you talk and control your temper?
11. Do you honour your contractual obligations?
12. Are you wasteful?
13. Do your actions conform to your talks?
14. Do you inspire and encourage people to do well?
15. Are you forgiving?
16. Do you invite all to the way of your Lord with wisdom and good preaching?
17. Do you abide by Gods Moral Law e.g. say no to lying, slandering, drinking alcohol, smoking, gambling, taking drugs, watching pornographic materials, having sex outside marriage, cheating, stealing, breaking your promises, acquiring wealth from illegal sources, taking usury, giving false witness testimonies, killing or come near lewdness openly or secretly?
18. Are you kind to your parents, neighbours and all God's creatures?

19. Are you polite and respectful of your teachers and colleagues and do your best to achieve good results at school?
20. Are you a law-abiding citizen who respects the host community amongst which you live?"

To my surprise I received on 9th April 2015, a similar query from a Police Borough Commander who asked me how to deal with Muslim police officers who grow uncontrolled beards? I shared with her the same response I sent to Forest school.

Girl's Uniform and Islamic Code of Dress
I also recall that the Head of the girls' school sought my advice regarding a new Muslim girl who was admitted to the school and wanted to wear a cloak on top of her school uniform. I suggested that the school should allow her to wear long sleeve shirts and a long loose skirt; this modest clothing thereby negating the need to wear a cloak.

No Girls to Pray Behind Boys
As a school Chaplain, I came across an interesting contentious issue between the Muslim pupils and the Headmaster in another school in East London. Muslim pupils, boys and girls, sought the permission of the school to perform Friday prayers during their lunch time. The Headmaster visited the hall where the prayer was to be held. He saw the girls were praying behind the boys. He immediately disapproved this practice. He said this is discrimination against the girls. The boy who organised the prayers explained to the Headmaster that this is an Islamic requirement as girls are not allowed to pray in front of the boys as this will be a source of distraction to the boys. The Headmaster completely refused to accept this explanation. Was the boy correct in what he said? Unfortunately, this is what the majority of Muslims believe in.

I said to the Headmaster, "The explanation which was given by the boy was incorrect. But he should not be blamed for this, as this is the opinion of the majority of the Muslims, due to ignorance. In the same way as men gaze at women, also women gaze at men as stated in the Qur'an 24:30-31. At the time of Prophet Mohammed (pbuh) women prayed behind the men in his mosque, because he allowed them to come to join the congregational prayers as late as they wanted and leave immediately after the prayer is finished as they had home responsibilities. Although congregational prayers are not an obligation on women, the Prophet (pbuh) in his wisdom, encouraged them to come. He even designated a door for them to use, so they don't disturb the men who are praying. So, it was not due to men gazing at them, it was mainly for the convenience of women." I also mentioned that when people are performing Tawaf (going round the Kaba) to perform Hajj or Umra, men and women can be seen very close to each other. I suggested to the Headmaster that the hall can be divided into two parts with a passage in the middle. The girls can pray in the right side and the boys in the left side, very similar to beautiful mosques in Malaysia. He was so pleased to hear that and he allowed the prayers to continue.

3.2.13 Community Chaplaincy

I'm honoured and blessed to be one of the ten trustees who started South Woodford Mosque, in London. I have been the Head Imam and the Chairman of Qur'ani Murkuz Trust (QMT), who owns the mosque, since its formation in 1999. Our mosque welcomes all Muslims from any sect. We empower women and children to attend congressional prayers. We have special circles for women. QMT has women trustees on its board. We also welcome non-Muslims from the local community, the police, school children and their teachers and parents to visit the mosque to find out more about the true message of Islam.

As an Imam and Chaplain, I visit the sick in hospitals, I attend funerals and I provide counselling to families in distress, all free of charge to please my Creator. I emulate what God's Messengers said to their people: "I have not asked you for any remuneration, for my reward lies only with God." 10:72, and many more similar verses in the Qur'an.

I give below a few examples of my engagement with the Muslim community:

1) Conference on "British Muslims and the Challenges of Drugs, Alcohol, Gambling and Unlawful Sex"

In serving the Muslim community, QMT trustees were pioneers in recognising and identifying the main problems facing young Muslims in Britain. We had to define the problems and find solutions relying on the help of professionals. We can't live in self-denial anymore. For example, you may hear very often some Muslim parents say: 'No way my son or daughter are having drugs or even drinking!' Unfortunately, such parents are displaying their naivety, seemingly blind to what their children may or may not be engaged in. The percentage of Muslim prisoners in the UK is more than the percentage of people from the indigenous population, and the Muslims are not more than 5% of the total UK population. When I was doing my Chaplaincy training at Pentonville prison in London, the majority of the Muslim prisoners were guilty of drug dealings and sexually abusing children.

QMT trustees were so proud to organise the first conference in London Borough of Redbridge, to address some of the major challenges facing Muslims in Britain. The conference took place on Sunday 10th October 2004. We had a panel of very highly professional speakers who addressed the following topics in a very courageous and open-minded approach:

- Medical implications of drugs
- Medical implications of alcohol, smoking and gambling
- Psychological implications of drugs, alcohol, smoking and gambling
- Legal implications of drugs, alcohol, smoking and gambling
- Drug misuse amongst Muslims
- Islamic views and solutions
- Medical implications of unlawful sex
- Physiological implications of unlawful sex
- Legal implications of unlawful sex

- Islamic views and solutions

During the question and answer session, the barrister who was addressing the legal implications (of points 4 and 9 above) asked me the following question, "Do you discriminate against people who are homosexual and what are the Islamic views regarding homosexuality?"

In response to his question I said, "Before I delve straight into Islamic views, let me mention what the teachings are for the Jews and Christians. Jews and Christians both believe in the entirety of the Old Testament. They cannot deny what is in their books, unless they do not believe.

When God, the Author and Publisher of all Divine Revelations, mentioned in the Qur'an the fate of the people of Lot, it was like 'copy' from His First Book and 'paste' into His Final Book, The Qur'an. Therefore, it was and is not something new which belongs to only Muslims. God prohibits the practising of homosexuality in the Qur'an and the Old Testament and regards it as a sin.

Whatever Gods Command on this topic may be, as practising People of The Books, we must fully adhere to His Commands. Having said so, we should not discriminate against anyone because of his/her sexuality as this is a personal choice and God endued us with many faculties and gave us free will. God has created us all equal and everyone is therefore responsible for his/her own actions and choices. We have no right to judge one another as The Only Judge is God, The One True God, who knows all what we conceal and reveal. No one has the right to claim purity for himself. God knows who is the righteous."

The conference was a great success, as demonstrated by the interaction and participation of the audience during the Q&A sessions. QMT trustees were adamant to organise more conferences to address topics like, for example, family issues, counter terrorism, women's rights, ending violence against women and young girls and integration.

It is worth mentioning, before the conference we invited young Muslims to respond to the following questionnaire:

"As a young British Muslim how did I resist the temptations of drugs, alcohol, gambling and unlawful sex? Was I weak? Did I fall into temptation? And if I fell, did I seek the help of my parent's or my friend's? Or was I too afraid or ashamed to tell them? What helped me to get back on the right path? Did my parents warn me during my childhood and adolescence to face these challenges? What more could they have done?"

We received so many interesting responses. The following is the response of my eldest daughter, Dr Donia Fahim Ph.D. She was 32 years old when she wrote it. It is one of the best responses we received. It is rather lengthy, but I felt I must share it with you:

"I was asked to write a personal account as to how I as a young British Muslim faced and dealt with the challenges of modern day life; in particular those related to the use of alcohol, illegal substances, premarital sex and gambling.

"Challenges that we have encountered here in Britain are also encountered in other countries around the world, including those with the predominant Muslim majority. It is

human nature to find a scapegoat for the trials and difficulties that we encounter throughout our lives. I often hear Muslims blaming and accusing the inappropriate behaviours exhibited by other Muslims on the permissive society, media advertising, and TV. But the truth of the matter is that we as Muslims around the world must face and fight back our own demons, which exist within each of us and between us.

"It is the responsibility of every Muslim to appropriately acquire knowledge about Islam. Islam is not a history or culture. It is a timeless religion based on faith and integrated practices. Islam is neither a secular nor an exclusionary religion and with our strength of faith we must be able to integrate appropriately within our societies. It is only by example that we will be able to teach and support one another. But how many of us truly understand the five pillars of our religion and our articles of faith? How many of us have sufficient and well-informed knowledge to be able to respond to Muslims and non-Muslims when they speak of Islam in a derogatory manner? Sadly, the current portrayal of Islam in the media is not the pleasant one, and I am sure that many of us read the inauthentic or dubious articles published on Islam with outrage. We need to respond to these articles and by speaking out we will be able to protect our faith and alter the stereotypes.

"Practicing Islam in a moderate manner is the protection for ourselves and of future generation. Attempting to understand and-implement the Qur'an, the prophetic traditions and Moral Laws of Islam is the only way that will make us feel strong enough to face and fight our desires and temptations.

"Parents have the primary responsibility to educate their children, but teaching is by example and not by rhetoric. A toddler who becomes used to seeing their parents praying will be more likely to emulate this behaviour later on in life than a child who only sees his parents praying occasionally. Children's early years are what shape their later life. It is important that parents adhere to the prophetic child rearing traditions with understanding as to how to bring up and deal with children. Parents need to pay attention to and understand the children's needs.

"When I look back on my childhood and formative years, I can recall many fond memories as well as struggles. But the great effort exerted by both of my parents to teach my siblings and I about Islam cannot be denied and this has been and is our protective shield. Like any family of course there are differences and conflicts, but I do believe it is the boundaries of Islam that have kept us together within healthy limits.

"My parents nurtured the seed of Islam that was in our hearts and with the grace of God this religion has undoubtedly been my supportive system. My parents were hard on me when I was growing up and extremely strict, far more than they were with my siblings. This is because I am the eldest and they were in an unfamiliar country where the system of living and culture was different to the one they came from. At times my parents were over protective and they were selective as to whom I could play and socialise with. When I was growing up, the notion of Islam was not as common as it is now. However, my school friends were generally respectful when I carried out any practices. On occasional visits to our home, they would witness us praying. During Ramadan, a lot of questions would be asked and some students would joke but again the majority would be respectful and would ask many questions to understand why we fast. They noticed that in every other way I was the same as them. We went out together, wore the same uniform, spoke the same language, and I attended chapel with them. Sadly, the tolerance shown by my school friends was far more than my Middle Eastern peers. I was never made fun of or mocked and now on reflection I can see that it was the security gained from my faith that helped me. It was when I was to go to university that my struggles began.

"My parents were afraid of university lifestyle hence were adamant that I should continue to live at home than staying at University's campus. I am the eldest and my parents were not familiar with the university system, although they gained all their post graduate qualifications in the UK. I was resentful that I couldn't live in Halls and be with my university friends. My parents would travel and leave me to oversee the family business and to look after my siblings and yet they were not allowing me to move into Halls. This provided a very mixed message but now as an adult I can understand their reasoning. However, I built up the resentment and anger.

"Whilst at university I was fortunate to have Muslim and non-Muslim friends which was a great form of support and again they respected my faith and practices. Ironically, I would use my friends' room to pray and they respected my faith. I desperately wanted to be a part of the university community. My friends would study together, socialise together and live together. I on the other hand would return home. Unfortunately, I was not able to share this with my parents and in order to stay with my friends at campus, I would lie to my parents. My only mistake was that I lied but I didn't drink, I didn't do drugs and I didn't have a boyfriend. When my parents found out that I had lied they did not take it well. But I only wish they had trusted me to be in halls for the first years of my degree. They had instilled in me the sense of morality and I knew what was right and what was unlawful, but I needed to experience being on my own; budgeting and being responsible for myself.

"University is a vital experience of life. You meet different people from different cultures, social backgrounds and religious beliefs. My faith and religion never had an adverse effect on me. On the contrary, the difficulties coping with adulthood and my family differences is what motivated me to read more about Islam; and I always took comfort in God's mercy and love.

"In my final year of university, my parents allowed me to move into the Halls. This was by far one of the most memorable times of my life. My closest friends were Muslims from different backgrounds as well as other non-Muslims who were conservative. When we did go out with friends who drank, it didn't bother us because we didn't and were not even tempted to. My protection was choosing friends who understood, respected and supported my bi-cultural and religious needs.

"The difficulty I did see amongst my friends and an ongoing difficulty that we face is that of relationships and marriage. It is the seed of faith that was nurtured by my mother that protected me. It is true that your friends can affect who you become, but I do thank God that I was and am shielded and protected by my faith.

"The prophetic tradition is clear regarding the rights of children and how they should be nurtured. If parents adhere to these recommendations, our future generations will grow up to be Muslims in the real sense. Not with fanaticism or extremism but in a moderate integrated manner. Teaching children about Islam begins immediately after birth and based on my experience and observations, I have listed some recommendations:

- Play and pray with your children.
- Reinforce positive behaviours by celebrating and praising your children's achievements.
- Always be involved in their school years, for example, make an effort to attend their concerts and speech days.
- Join the PTA so you can meet the parents of the children your child is at school with.
- Be a good example – practice what you preach.
- Listen to what your children are really saying.

- *Be prepared to answer difficult questions.*
- *Read, read, read ... knowledge is the most effective and powerful tool to understand the intricacies of Islamic law and jurisprudence and ethics, in order to be able to teach our children.*
- *If your children make mistakes, be compassionate and help them to understand the implications of their errors. The behaviour may be disliked but the child is still loved. God is most forgiving and His mercy is far greater than His wrath.*
- *Trust in God if you have done your duty as a parent and taught them well. God then will protect them and look after them."*

2) Solemnisation of Marriages

Our mosque is registered with the Local Authority for the solemnisation of marriages. So, we are allowed to conduct, both the Religious, (known in Arabic as Nikah), and Civil marriages at the same time in the presence of a Registrar. The mosque will issue an Islamic Marriage Certificate and the Registrar will issue the Civil Marriage Certificate. We don't allow segregation as the bride and groom must be present in the same room while the marriage is being conducted. Some couples may choose to do their Civil marriage outside the mosque and get their Islamic marriage in the mosque or their own homes or in a venue of their choice.

My voluntary job as Imam and Chaplain involves me in the fulfilment of many love stories when it comes to joining in holy matrimony the hearts of young people of different faiths or even of different Islamic sects. Islam allows a Muslim man to marry a Christian or a Jew. She has the right either to embrace Islam or to keep her religion. In either case she will enjoy the same rights of a Muslim wife. My job would be to introduce Islam to them in a very detailed and civilised manner, in a very relaxed and tranquil environment, and answer whatever questions are fired at me. Then I would ask the woman if she would like to embrace Islam or not? If she accepts Islam, I will give her a document to read which confirms her acceptance of the Religion and I will issue her with a certificate confirming this. However, it must be made clear that a Muslim man cannot marry an idol-worshipper. She must embrace Islam before I proceed to conduct their marriage. I don't claim any fees for the conversion process as it is fully dedicated to God.

On the other hand, a Muslim woman is only permitted to marry a Muslim man. So, in this case a non-Muslim man must embrace Islam before I would tie their knot. I make it very clear to the person who accepted Islam to continue to honour their non-Muslim parents as stated by God in 31:14-15.

When conducting the Religious marriage, (Nikah), and before accepting the marriage vows, I would give a humorous and constructive talk regarding the importance of marriage in Islam and the rights and obligations of each party. I design the talk to suit the guests' mix. I deliver it in English and Arabic. Very often I would receive positive responses from the bride, the groom and the guests. Some non-Muslim guests would approach me on the day saying: *"Many thanks for telling us about the true message of Islam. We were not aware of that!"* I donate any fee to my mosque and various other charities. I make it clear to the bride and the groom and the guests that religious marriages are **NOT** recognised in the English courts, hence they must have a Civil marriage to protect their rights and the rights of any future children.

3) Religious & Civil Marriages and the Role of a Sharia Council

As stated above, religious marriages are not recognised in the English courts, whether they took place in the UK or overseas. Muslims use the word Nikah to refer to an Islamic marriage, which is a religious marriage. However, State approved marriages which take place in Muslim Countries like Egypt or Pakistan are recognised in the English courts.

Under Islamic Law, a man has the right to divorce his wife without going through the courts. However, a Muslim woman can only divorce her husband through a judge. This form of divorce is known in Arabic as "Khol" خلع. The wife must give back to the husband the dowry he paid her when they got married.

To understand the problems which a Muslim woman may face if she wants to divorce her husband in England, let us examine the following scenarios:

1) In the case of a woman who had **ONLY** religious marriage i.e. Nikah, she will ask her husband to divorce her. If he fears God, he will give her a divorce by saying to her, face to face, or in writing that he divorces her. She must not move out of the house; she must continue to live there until she completes her "Waiting Period", known in Arabic as "Eddah". The "Eddah" is either three monthly periods or three months, if the woman does not have a monthly period, or after delivering the baby, if she was pregnant. After that, the divorce becomes absolute. This means she can now marry another man.

Unfortunately, not all Muslim husbands are God fearing. Now comes the problem! The man may refuse to divorce her unless she meets certain demands. He may blackmail her, requesting a huge sum of money. Some husbands take revenge from the wife and her family by psychologically torturing her and refuse to divorce her. The woman may have already left the matrimonial house and is fully supporting herself, but unfortunately will not be able to marry another man unless the husband divorces her.

The woman cannot take her case to an English court because her Nikah is not recognised. And the dilemma is that the divorce is only in the hands of the Judge of the land we live in, even if he is a non-Muslim.

What can she do now? She goes to a self-appointed Sharia Council to divorce her. But from an Islamic point of view they have neither religious nor legal power to grant the woman a divorce. They may conduct a Nikah or provide counselling but have no right to dissolve it. Many husbands are aware of this fact and they refuse to accept the ruling of a Sharia Council.

2) The second example is of a Muslim woman who had both religious (Nikah) and civil marriages in the UK. She can divorce her husband through an English court, and if the husband refuses to give her an Islamic divorce, the judgement by the non-Muslim judge will

be acceptable, although some Muslims do not want to accept the ruling of a non-Muslim judge.

Following the ruling of the judge, she will have to wait for three periods or three months or until the baby is delivered if she was pregnant, before she can remarry. This is an Islamic requirement.

My advice to women who want to get married in the UK, please do not only accept to have a religious marriage, Nikah, but you must also have a civil marriage, either before the Nikah or at the same time. Also, British Muslims must strive to establish Sharia courts in the UK to deal with family issues by qualified Muslim Judges.

4) Muslim Families in Crisis and My First Book

In addition to conducting marriages, I provide counselling, free of charge, to Muslim families in crisis who are experiencing family issues. Unfortunately, I became overwhelmed with so many problems which made my heart bleed. Family Law in Islam provides clear guidance on how to live a good, happy and pure life. Marriage in Islam is a solemn and very binding contract, and all its parties will be held accountable on the Day of Judgement. It clearly defines the rights and obligations of all members of the family. It strongly recommends reconciliation in any case of dispute. There is no marriage without problems. So, if families would follow God's Moral Law, they would prosper. I asked myself the question: "What is preventing people from following Islamic Family Law? The answer is very simple! They are not practicing God's Moral Law; they are only Muslims by name. I'm not claiming purity for myself, but this is the reality.

Consequently, I decided to publish a book based on stories of Prophets in the Old Testament, who are also mentioned in the Qur'an, to educate people on how to have a peaceful and happy home, free of domestic violence and hatred. The book is called **"A Father's Journey and a Son's Dream - The Story of Joseph, the Son of Jacob"**.

The book is about my dream of how to keep a family together. It might be a good read for parents who are struggling to keep peace and tranquillity at home. It might also be a great help for members of the same family who have stopped talking to each other and have forgotten how to sing "We are family". I dedicated all the proceeds to my mosque.

I shared my book with many dignitaries worldwide including Her Majesty the Queen, the Mayor of London and His Holiness the Pope. I give below a few responses I received about my book.

A) In my letter dated 13ᵗʰ March 2017, to Her Majesty I wrote:

"Your Majesty

I pray to God that Your Majesty is keeping well.

For the last ten years I have been sending Your Majesty a very special Christmas card which I have designed. The card is unique as it quotes verses from the Holy Qur'an. It is a card which aims to unite Christians and Muslims and bridge the gap.

And every year I would receive a response from either Your Majesty's Lady-in-Waiting, or the Senior Correspondence Officer, or the Director of the Private Secretary's Office. This is a great honour and I'm so grateful for that.

I have recently published a book called "A Father's Journey and a Son's Dream - The Story of Joseph the Son of Jacob". The book is about how to keep a family together.

May God reward your Majesty abundantly in this life and the Hereafter for your relentless efforts to keep the Royal Family together. The love, the devotion, the tolerance, the understanding, and the patience Your Majesty has exercised, are the key factors in achieving joyful, happy and peaceful outcomes.

It gives me great honour to send Your Majesty a copy of my book. I hope Your Majesty would enjoy reading it.

May God bless Your Majesty and the Royal Family.

May God Almighty save our Glorious Queen.

Dr Mohammed Fahim, Ph.D., M.Sc., B.Eng.

Chairman & Head Imam"

The following is the response from Her Majesty from Windsor Castle dated 10th April 2017:

"Dear Dr Fahim

The Queen wishes me to thank you for your letter with which you enclosed a copy of your book, A Father's Journey and a Son's Dream - The Story of Joseph the Son of Jacob.

Her Majesty was touched you have sent this publication for her to see and I am to thank you, very much, for your thought for the Queen in writing as you did.

Yours Sincerely
Lady-in-Waiting"

B) To His Holiness Pope Francis, I wrote on 1st April 2017:

"Your Holiness

I pray to God that Your Holiness is keeping well.

For the last ten years I have been sending His Holiness the Pope, a very special Christmas card which I have designed. The card is unique as it quotes verses from the Holy Qur'an. It is a card which aims to unite Christians and Muslims and bridge the gap.

And every year I would receive a response from the Pope's Assessors. The first response was from Monsignor Gabriele Caccia in January 2007, then from Monsignor Peter Wells from 2008 till 2016, and Monsignor Paolo Borgia in January 2017. This is a great honour and I'm so grateful for that.

I have recently published a book called "A Father's Journey and a Son's Dream", "The Story of Joseph the Son of Jacob". The book is about how to keep a family together.
May God reward your Holiness abundantly in this life and the Hereafter for your relentless efforts in promoting the importance of families in our societies today and how to keep a family together. The love, the devotion, the tolerance, the understanding, and the patience your Holiness has shown were the key factors in making people listen to your Holiness and achieving joyful, happy and peaceful outcomes.

It gives me great honour to send your Holiness a copy of my book. I hope your Holiness would enjoy reading it.

May God Almighty Bless your Holiness and support you with His Holy Spirit.

Kindest Regards

Dr Mohammed Fahim, Ph.D., M.Sc., B.Eng.

Chairman and Head Imam"

I received the following response from His Holiness dated 8th May 2017:

"Dear Dr Fahim

His Holiness Pope Francis has received your letter and the gift of your book, and he has asked me to thank you in his name. He appreciates the sentiments which prompted you to share your work with him.

Pope Francis wishes me to assure you of a remembrance in his prayers, and he invokes upon you the Almighty's blessings of joy and peace.

Yours sincerely

Monsignor Paolo Borgia
Assessor"

C) The following is the response I received from the Rt Hon Sadiq Khan, Mayor of London, dated 25th June 2018:

"Dr Fahim,

I wanted to write to you to thank you for gifting me a copy of your book 'A Father's Journey and a Son's Dream'.

Let me take this opportunity to wish you and your family Eid Mubarak!

Yours sincerely

Sadiq Khan
Mayor of London"

D) The following is the response from the Chief Rabbi Ephraim Mirvis, in London, dated 15th May 2017:
"Dear Dr Fahim

I'm writing to thank you for the signed copy of your book 'A Father's Journey and a Son's Dream' that you sent the Chief Rabbi.

It was very thoughtful of you to send the Chief Rabbi a copy.

Kind regards,

Louise Gould
Executive Assistant to the Chief Rabbi and CEO"

E) I received the following response from Dr Ed Kessler, the Director of the Woolf Institute, Cambridge, dated 9th April 2017:

"Dear Mohammed,

Thank you so much for the book.

I apologise for not replying sooner but you will be pleased to know that the book has been put into our library.

Thank you also for the Passover greetings.

I hope you are well and that your work is successful.

Best wishes and thank you again.

Ed"

F) The following is the response from the Embassy of Israel in London, dated 10th April 2017:

"Dear Dr Fahim

Thank you so much for the books and your kind message.

I look forward to reading your book and have forwarded the book to Mrs Regev (the mother of the Ambassador), as well, and she sends her gratitude as well.

Wishing you all the best,
Sigal

Sigal Mamistvalov
Chief of Staff to the Ambassador
Embassy of Israel
London"

5) The Muslim Imposter!

The word 'Imposter' means *'a person who pretends to be someone else in order to deceive others, especially for fraudulent gain'.* And the word 'Muslim' means *'submission of your will to God's Will by obeying all His Commandments and saying we hear and we obey'.* So how can the two words exist together?

The story goes back to summer 2009. A young Muslim man, Mr NR, decided to hire Murray Hall, in Loughton, Essex, for two hours, for Friday prayers for the Muslims living in Loughton. He communicated with a few Muslims in the area and set up 'Loughton Islamic Group'. He contacted Epping Forest Council, who agreed to do that at a cost of £50 per hour. This was a very good initiative and he should be thanked for doing this.

He called me out of the blue on 10th July 2009. I had never met him before. He informed me that he was organising Friday prayers at Murray Hall in Loughton. He also told me that the front door of his flat had been firebombed and he believed that this was done by the local BNP (British National Party), who already threatened him. BNP are a radical extremist right wing group who was already inciting a lot of hatred against the Muslims.

As I have developed a close working relationship with senior police officers at Ilford Police Station, I immediately called them to seek their advice. Mr NR invited me to lead the Friday prayer at Murray Hall. When I arrived at the Hall, I met local Councillors and a Police Inspector. The support Mr NR had from the Councillors and the Police Inspector was phenomenal.

The BNP attacked what the Councillors and I did to support him by launching a hate campaign full of lies, against the Muslims. They said in their Summer 2009 leaflet titled, **'Epping Forest Patriot BNP - The Voice of Loughton: NO MOSQUES IN LOUGHTON'**
*"Epping Forest Council, as you may already be aware, are allowing our new community centre, **Murray Hall,** in Borders Lane to be used as a **Mosque**. Neither local residents nor your local BNP councillors were informed or consulted over this, and many Loughton folk are **horrified** as one Borders Lane resident asked us:*

"Is this a stealth campaign to turn Murray Hall into Murray Mosque?" More worrying, is news that the Muslim group concerned are linked to the notorious **Mulberry Way Mosque,** South Woodford.

Planning permission for this establishment was 'granted' in 2000 after trembling local councillors in Redbridge surrendered to a **400-strong** mob who **rioted** at the planning meeting! Following this existing new addition to Woodford, life for local residents is certainty never dull..."

I met Mr NR for the first time on that Friday. My first impression of him was that he was a genuine man who was well composed, polite and respectful.

He told me that he was having problems with his wife and asked for help with this matter. I invited them to my house. He came with his wife and his stepson where I offered them marriage counselling. One of the issues that he raised was financial problems. I offered his wife training in my Care Home as a carer so she could contribute to the household income. I asked Mr NR how he was funding the hiring of Murray Hall? He said, he was paying for it out of his own pocket! I was surprised when he said that, as it is normal practice in the Muslim faith that worshippers would contribute towards any expenses.

On 12th August 2009, I received an email from Mr NR stating that he could no longer afford to pay for the hiring of Murray Hall. Consequently, he was planning on stopping the Friday prayer. As an Imam, I was disappointed to hear this. I then invited him to attend a trustees meeting at South Woodford mosque. It was agreed at this meeting that the mosque would financially support his efforts to retain Murray Hall. Subsequently, on 15th August I wrote him a cheque for £600. This sum was a loan and not a gift. Later in the week, he confirmed to me that money was paid for the hire of Murray Hall.

On Tuesday 18th August together with Mr NR, we were due to attend a multi faiths meeting at Epping Council to discuss his situation. En route I was to collect him from his home. When I pulled up outside in my car, I saw a police car parked there. I also saw his young stepson who was visibly upset. When I spoke to him, he told me that the shed where his bike was kept had been burgled and his bike had been stolen. I felt so sorry for him. I comforted him and told him that I would buy him a new one.

I picked up Mr NR and drove to Epping Council. At the meeting we were informed by the police that they were aware of the leaflets being distributed by BNP and were monitoring the situation.

On Sunday 23rd August 2009, I met Mr NR and his stepson. We went to the Halfords store in the High Street in Loughton. I bought a replacement bike for the boy. As we were walking back to my car, I was surprised when talking to Mr NR about his 'situation' when he suddenly said: "*I don't think there will be any more problems with the BNP now. It has gone so quiet, so don't worry.*" I said to him: "*I don't think so*".

A few days later I was in my office holding a meeting with a police sergeant when I received a telephone call from Mr NR. He told me that he had been kidnapped and taken to Epping

Forest by men purporting to be from the BNP, who then threatened him about the prayer meetings telling him to stop them.

When I asked how did they get in his house? He said that he was expecting a visit from Epping Council employees and thought that the callers were them, so he just let them in. As a result of this, I again spoke to the police which resulted in a major police operation being created to investigate the allegation. I also spoke to the national and local press and media, so the matter received the maximum coverage.

Mr NR and I were interviewed on several TV stations and the entire country was aware of the alleged 'kidnap'.

Vikram Dodd, from the National Guardian wrote on 27th August a long but brilliant article on page 4, analysing the whole situation:

"Muslim man claims he was abducted and threatened at knifepoint over prayer sessions"

"Racist attackers abducted a Muslim community leader at knifepoint, bundled him into a car and threatened his life unless he stopped running prayer sessions in a community hall that has been the target of the British National Party campaign. Police have confirmed they are treating the incident as a hate crime and are investigating links with an earlier firebomb attack on the same man's home."

At the end of the article, he wrote:

"Mohammed Fahim runs the nearest mosque to Loughton, four miles away in South Woodford, which was firebombed in 2000. He said racists have used the fears of new mosques in the area to stoke racial and anti-Muslim tensions. The BNP describes Fahim's Mosque as 'notorious' and claims it has incited violence. In fact, FAHIM works as a chaplain for the metropolitan police."

"VICTIM CLAIMS BNP FUELLED KIDNAP - Islamic group leader held at knifepoint", wrote The London Paper on 27th August 2009.

"Kidnapped Muslim dumped in forest", wrote Recorder, on 27th August 2009.

On Friday 28th August I went to Ilford Police Station to attend a meeting facilitated by the Borough Commander CSI PT. The meeting was attended by East Area Commander GC and Superintendent SG. I took with me a copy of the National Guardian newspaper. He introduced Commander GC as his boss. I remember very well me saying to him: "How can a kidnap happen in London? This is not Iraq!" I told him I had to install CCTV cameras around my house. He was so reassuring. I informed him that I'm traveling to Makkah, Saudi Arabia, on 1st September for three weeks.

While in Saudi, I received a call from Redbridge Police Borough Commander CSI PT, informing me that Mr NR had been arrested for faking his own kidnap. I was completely shocked to hear that. I asked him if he can address the congregation at South Woodford Mosque, in the interests of community harmony. Which he agreed to do. What an excellent police officer! Very fair and firm. I have known him since he came to Redbridge. He was also a guest speaker at my Redbridge Rotary Club. I have a lot of admiration and respect for him.

On my return I was told by a very senior police officer who knew me very well, that some of his colleagues thought I might have been a part of the 'faked kidnap'. I was so disappointed and very hurt.

I had a meeting with members of Loughton Islamic Group. They confirmed that Mr NR had stolen all the donations which he was given to pay for the renting the hall. I was so disgusted to hear that.

I had a conversation with his wife who told me that she thought he was involved in passport and visa fraud plus he had used all her credit cards to the maximum. She also thought that he had set the fire in his house himself when he had said that he had been firebombed and she doubted his kidnap claim. I was very disappointed to learn that she was aware of all this and never warned me, especially when I stretched a helping hand to her and her son.

A fellow Rotarian from Redbridge Rotary Club told me that Mr NR was renting his brother's house next door to him and he left without paying the rent. When the owner went in, he discovered that Mr NR was running a prostitution ring.

BNP in their leaflet dated autumn 2009, wrote: *"Attempt to smear BNP backfires - spectacularly!*
Ilford Muslim agitator Mr NR and his friends are campaigning to turn a Loughton Community Centre into a Mosque. All that stands in the way, are Loughton's residents and their local BNP Councillors, who want no such thing in their town. Mr NR has been all over TV and national newspapers, making allegations about 'death threats', 'arson attacks', on his home, and being kidnapped at knifepoint and frogmarched through Epping Forest by 'BNP supporters'. BBC NEWS teams and gullible PC politicians were all fawning over this man, as he bravely told of his 'ordeal'. Following the media frenzy however, and a hugely expensive police investigation, Mr NR, a member of South Woodford's notorious Mulberry Way Mosque, has been arrested and charged with attempting to pervert the course of justice. The trial is expected next year. We will let you know how he gets on."

The Sun wrote on Friday 4th 2009: *"Muslim's 'kidnap' in probe".*

Daily Mail wrote on 12th June 2010: *"The 'illegal' community leader who lied about BNP kidnap".*

The Guardian wrote on 17th June 2010: *"Guilty, but liar fled the UK before trial".*

The Recorder wrote on 17th June 2010: *"Muslim Community Leader claimed he was held at knifepoint - 'BNP kidnap' liar is jailed."*

Epping Forest Guardian wrote on 17th June 2010: *"Guilty, But Liar Flees Country".*

The Guardian wrote on 18th June 2010: *"Suspected mosque fraudster on the run".*

I felt so foolish regarding my initial thoughts about Mr NR. I realised, so late, that he appears to be an accomplished criminal who is both a persistent and a consistent liar. Taking into account his actions and stories, I can only believe that he must be suffering from some mental health issues. I think he has acted disgracefully towards both Muslims and non-Muslim communities. Mr NR was the perfect example of a confused Muslim. I hope that he receives the help and if appropriate the punishment he deserves.

The Muslim community at South Woodford Mosque, was not supporting him as an individual, but we were empowering the Muslim community in Loughton to practice their religion without any fear or intimidation as was exhibited by the BNP in their hate campaign. The Trustees of South Woodford Mosque sent a message of support to Loughton Islamic Group stating that we will continue to support them despite the lies and attacks of the BNP on our Mosque at South Woodford.

6) Civic Services

A) To mark the inauguration of Councillor M. Fazlur Rahman as the Worshipful Mayor of the London Borough of Waltham Forest, I was invited to coordinate the Civic Service on Sunday, 6th October 2002. All the Imams of the mosques in Waltham Forest were invited to attend the Civic Service at the Assembly Hall, Walthamstow, London. I chose a set of verses from the Holy Qur'an, to suit the occasion, for each Imam to recite in Arabic. I then read the translation and explained the meanings of the verses they read.

In appreciation of my contribution, I received the following letter, dated 22nd October 2002, from Mr N Hussain, the Mayoral Escort:

"Dear Dr Fahim

Asalaamu Alaikum Wa Rahmatullahe Wa Barakatuhu

It was, indeed, very kind of you to spare your valuable time to attend and participate in the Civic Service for the Mayor, Cllr M Fazlur-Rahman, held on Sunday, 6th October 2002.

The Mayor and I are both extremely appreciative of your active involvement and for the valuable contribution that made the function so unique and invigorating. Many of the guests were impressed by the unusual nature of the Civic Service. Your presentation and the pre-Tilawat commentary on the various Qua'ranic Suras was very informative and even the non-Muslim guests were highly moved by your commentary that proved an excellent aid to their understanding.

The Mayor and I are fully aware that the success of the function was due -in no small part, to your amazing input and the efforts made by you and the other participants.

On behalf of the Mayor, may I take this opportunity to thank you most sincerely.

May Allah Taa'la Sub'hanullah bless you with HIS boundless blessings.

Yours sincerely

Mr N Hussain
Mayoral Escort"

B) I was invited by the Chairman of Epping Forest District Council, Councillor Brian Sandler, to make a presentation on behalf of the Muslim Faith at the 'Celebration of Faith' Civic Service on Sunday 5th February 2006, at Theydon Bois Village Hall. It was the first time ever that a new Council Leader would invite different faith representatives to participate in a Civic Service. The faiths represented were, Jewish, Muslim, Sikh, Baha'i, Hindu and Christian.

C) On Sunday 28th January 2007, Councillor Ann Haigh, became the new Chairman of Epping Forest District Council. She was so happy to repeat what her predecessor had done. My wife and I were invited to represent the Islamic Faith. The topic I spoke about was, 'What Are My Neighbour's Rights?'

These Civic Services which embraced every faith in our communities were a great sign of unity and cohesion between members of our societies. Cllr Ann Haigh formed Epping Forest Multi-Faith Forum and invited me to join. We had regular meetings to discuss any current issues and provide advice on how to deal with them. The Forum was a great opportunity to get to know each other, as God commands us in 49:13.

D) When Councillor Muhammed Javed, was elected to be the Mayor of Redbridge, in the year 2012/13, he was a pioneer in choosing a chaplain from each faith in the Borough. I was the Muslim Chaplain.

In 'The Mayor's Annual Awards'- 2012/13, I was awarded the following certificate of recognition:

"This certificate is awarded to Dr Mohammed Fahim, Mayor's Chaplain.
Thank you for your services to the community on behalf of the people of Redbridge and for Giving Time for Others.

Councillor Muhammed Javed

Mayor of Redbridge 2012-2013"

I was also a Chaplain to other Mayors in Redbridge. I supported their fund-raising campaigns to help many charities of their choice, by inviting them to our mosque at South Woodford to raise funds from the congregation, as well as donating from our trust. In addition to this, I donated to their cause from my Greenmantle Care Home business.

7) Do British Muslims Support the Army?

I received an invitation from "The Army Presentation Team" (APT) dated 4th June 2010, to attend their presentation on the 21st July at Forest School, College Place, Snaresbrook, London. The invitation started like this:

"Dear Imam,

Whether or not you are supportive of the British Army, we would like to take the opportunity to inform you about our organisation and our current challenges and enable you to tackle us with your views. Please join us at the Army Presentation on Wednesday 21st July 2010..."

I was so sad to read the first sentence. I felt that this invitation referred to an inherent misunderstanding that Muslims as a group might not be supportive of the army. It is for this reason I took the initiative to invite the APT to give a presentation in the London Borough of Redbridge, to clear the misperceptions and also to provide an opportunity for a dialogue with the Muslim community in Redbridge.

On the day of the presentation, I approached the top army officer who was in charge of the event. I voiced to him my disappointment and asked him if he is willing to give a presentation in a mosque? He was so supportive and informed me that members of his team will contact me.

I did not have to wait long. I was invited for a meeting with members of the APT at their headquarters London District, Horse Guards, Whitehall, London. I was so impressed and felt very honoured for the wonderful reception I was given. We had a very positive meeting and the APT kindly enough, accepted my invitation to give a presentation on Saturday 2nd April 2011 at the Islamic Community Centre in Ilford, London Borough of Redbridge.

In my welcoming speech on the day of the event, I said: *"...I believe that every British citizen, irrespective of his ethnicity or religion, must be supportive to the army as a defender of the State. As a practicing Muslim, this is not just a national duty, but it is a religious obligation.*

"However, for an individual or group to support a war or not, is a completely different matter. There are many people in Britain, mainly non-Muslims, who objected to the war in

Iraq and Afghanistan. The pre-war rallies in London were clear evidence of this fact and ever since the Anti-War Movements periodic protests are a clear sign of this.

"The protestors sincerely believe that by opposing an illegal war, they were in fact supporting the troops. Why? Because this would lead to their safe return and avoid the killing of innocent civilians in those lands with whom Britain has no direct war.

"During the last election campaign some Muslims decided to boycott it, claiming that it was un-Islamic to take part in secular elections. At South Woodford Muslim Community Centre and in Ilford Islamic Centre we conducted a series of hustings with many politicians from different parties to create greater political awareness among our community and to prove that it is permissible in Islam to participate in elections by either going out to vote or by becoming a candidate.

"Unfortunately, some Muslims have a similar view regarding joining the British Army. Imagine if Britain is under attack, who would defend us? Isn't it the brave men and women of our army who would carry their lives in their hands and go out willingly to protect all of us? However, if the enemy occupies the country, it becomes an Islamic obligation for every civilian, including women, to go out to defend our beloved Britain.

"When Saddam Hussain, the late president of Iraq, attacked and occupied Kuwait and annexed it to Iraq, the entire International community, including Muslim countries, applied verse 9:49 of the Qur'an:
'If two parties of the believers fight with each other, make peace between them; but if one of them acts wrongfully towards the other, fight that which acts wrongfully until it returns to God's command; then if it returns, make peace between them with justice and act equitably; surely God loves those who act equitably.'

"The world tried to make peace between the two countries, but when it failed to convince Saddam to withdraw, they all fought him, as commanded by God in the same verse.

"However, the world refused to accept the annexation of Kuwait, but unfortunately, accepted the annexation of Jerusalem following the 1967 war between the Arabs and Israel. This shows the double standards of the world we live in.

"According to the Qur'an, God clearly states when a war should be waged:
'And fight in the Way of God, those who fight you, and don't transgress, surely God doesn't love the transgressors.' 2:190

"The British troops played a major role in defending and protecting the Muslims in Kosovo, who were subject to ethnic cleansing by the Serbs. They also acted as part of the peacekeeping force in Bosnia.

"Last week, our army took the initiative to defend the civilian population in Libya. This act was in accordance with verse 4:75: 'And what reason have you that you should not fight in the Way of God to support the oppressed among the men, the women and the children whose cry is: "Our Lord! Take us out of this town, whose people are oppressors, and give us from You, a guardian and give us from You, a helper." '

"As Muslims, our loyalty is to God. This means we have to abide by all His Commandments. One of these Commandments is to be loyal to the country we live in. This means we have to honour each and every agreement or covenant and respect and obey the law of the land.

"The army is not only here to participate in wars. The army ensures our safety and security at all times, so we can enjoy a peaceful and prosperous life.

"May God save our Army, our Queen and our Country. May God bless you all."
My welcoming speech went down very well. The event was a great success as it was attended by many Muslims from different ethnicities who never had such an opportunity to have a direct dialogue with very senior members from the Armed Forces. They participated very positively during the Questions & Answer session. The audience were very impressed with the presentation. They were very pleased to hear about the different roles played by the army during times of conflict and peace. It was a very highly informative and educational opportunity for all of us.

In response to this successful event, I received the following letter, dated 19th April 2011, from the Deputy Commander, Brigadier Matthew P Lowe:

"Dear Doctor Fahim,

ARMY PRESENTATION TEAM SPECIAL EVENT ILFORD SATURDAY 2 APRIL 11

I would like to pass on my thanks to you for hosting the Army Presentation Team at the Islamic Community Centre in Ilford on Saturday 2 April. Events like these really help to strengthen the understanding that all local communities have with regard to the purpose and remit of our Armed Forces and crucially reinforce the mutual benefit that can be gained from this greater awareness.

It was very good to see the range of backgrounds and positions of audience members on the day, especially with the degree of influence that those who attended have over their local community and surroundings. I was very pleased to hear the types of questions that were posed to the Presentation Team as these serve to confirm the usefulness of these occasions and I hope that your audience members found the event interesting as well as informative. I would welcome any feedback that you have gained from those who attended.

Thank you for your kind words prior to the presentation itself. We relish these opportunities to integrate with members of the public at the very heart of the community and my thanks to you and Mr Qaiser Malik for all the arrangements you made with the handling of the audience generation and especially with the provision of refreshments which add to a more satisfying experience for those guests who make the effort to attend.

Once again, my thanks to you for a successful event and I hope you found a positive experience for the team to be in Borough of Redbridge.

Your sincerely

Matthew"

Armed Forces Day 30th June 2013

I was invited to offer prayers for the armed forces alongside the Chaplain to the Mayor and a Rabbi from the army. I was so honoured and proud to show my support to our Armed Forces. I said the following prayer:

"In The Name of God, The Most Merciful, The Most Compassionate.

O God! The Lord of the Seven Heavens and the Magnificent Throne.
The God of Abraham, Moses, Jesus and Mohammed.

On behalf of our armed forces, we invoke You as Saul and his army did when they faced Goliath, they said: 'Our Lord! Pour out constancy on us and make our steps firm; help us against those who reject faith.' By God's will they defeated them and David slew Goliath.

Our Lord! Strengthen our Army with the Holy Spirit as You strengthened Jesus.

Our Lord! We invoke You to empower our troops to only participate in just wars and support them with Your angels and return them safe to their families and their country.

Our Lord! Forgive the dead who fought in Your cause and admit them to Your Gardens of Bliss.

Our Lord! Give patience and perseverance to those who lost their loved ones, shower them with Your Mercy and reward them for their calamity.

As victory is only from God, our Lord, Make our troops victorious so none can overcome them.

May God save our Queen, our armed forces and protect our country.

May God's Peace prevail.

May God's Peace be upon all of you."

In response to my participation, I received the following message, dated 1st July 2013, from Cllr Ian Bond, Deputy Leader of the Council:

"Dear Dr Fahim,

After yesterday's ceremony at the Town Hall I just wanted to drop you a note to thank you for your support for the event, and particularly for your very well chosen contribution. As you probably know, I was standing in for the Leader of the Council in his absence, and several *people spoke to me afterwards to say how much they appreciated particularly your involvement and your words.*

Kind regards

Ian"

The above event was reported in the local London paper the "Ilford Recorder" on Thursday July 4th, 2013, *"...Prayers were given by a priest, rabbi and imam to mark the occasion. In his prayer, Dr Mohammed Fahim, of the Qur'an Murkuz Trust, Mulberry Way, South Woodford, said: 'Oh Lord, we invoke You to empower our troops to only participate in just wars and support them with Your angels and return them safe to their families and their country.' ..."*

World War I Centenary

I received the following letter, dated 28th May 2014, from Cllr Ashley Kissin, the Mayor of London Borough of Redbridge:

"Dear Dr Fahim,

World War One Centenary

As part of the Council's arrangements to commemorate the centenary of World War 1, two corporate events have been arranged. The first will be an informative event held at Ilford War Memorial Gardens on Saturday, 2nd August between 1pm and 4pm.

The second event will be a service that will be held on Sunday 3rd August commencing at 12 noon at the front of the Town Hall, Ilford.

I would be delighted if you were able to join me."

And on 11th July 2014, I received the following request from the Mayor's Office,

"Dear Dr Fahim

World War One Centenary

If you are attending on the Sunday (Drumhead service) would you be prepared to say a few words during the service?

Yours sincerely

Alan Patterson

Mayor's Officer"

I was very delighted to attend and participate in the service as part of **"Prayers by multi faith leaders"**.

Following this event, I was further invited as the Muslim Police Chaplain (Volunteer) and Chairman & Head Imam of South Woodford Mosque, to participate in the Remembrance Service on Monday 28th July 2014. The Service was to honour the 23 officers of the Metropolitan Police Service, 'K' Division, and all those who gave their lives during the Great War, 1914-1918.

Chief Superintendent Tony Nash, Borough Commander - Newham, Operation Valour, ended his invitation letter dated 20th February 2014, by saying:

"...We would be honoured by your presence at both occasions. Formal invitations will follow in due course. I look forward to a reply confirming your attendance at your earliest convenience to the above address."

I was very honoured to attend both occasions. In the Remembrance Service held at Barking Abbey, I read "The Exhortation" from "For the fallen" (Laurence Binyon, 1914). It was a very moving experience. My participation as the Muslim Chaplain and Imam was very highly appreciated.

The Commandant's Parade

My wife and I attended the Commandant's Parade on Wednesday 10th April 2019, at the Royal Military Academy, Sandhurst, Camberley, England. We were invited by Officer Saheed Khan in appreciation of my community work. Following is the letter of invitation:

"Dear Sir,

I have received your kind donation of the Season's Greetings Card for which I am very grateful. Thank you!

I would like to invite you to attend the Commandant's Parade on Wednesday 10th of April 19 at the Royal Military Academy Sandhurst (RMAS).

The Commandant's Parade is the full dress rehearsal of the graduation parade for all the British and foreign officers after a year of training at the Home of Army Leadership at RMAS. Some of them would become world leaders. It is a spectacular event that is full of pomp and ceremony and personally I think this is an opportunity not to be missed.

Please keep this date free in your diary. Timings are from 0930 to approximately 15:00 hours.

Would you kindly accept this invitation until a more formal invitation will be sent in due course. I look forward to hosting you InshaAllah.

Yours Kindly

Mr Saheed Khan
Warrant Officer 2
Army Engagement Group"

What a great honour and wonderful experience to be there. We met so many professionals from different disciplines working with the army, e.g. engineers, doctors, IT consultants, and scientists. I wished if I was much younger, I would have definitely joined the Armed Forces. When my wife was introduced to a number of medical doctors, her comment was: "I wish I had spent my medical career serving with the Army." We as Muslims should all be proud of our Army and encourage our children to join.

3.2.14 Christmas and Easter as Inter-Faiths Opportunities Between Muslims and Christians

1) Introduction

I'm giving below my personal experience and future vision regarding Christmas and Easter celebrations by British Muslims in the UK as a form of Inter-Faith and Inter-Religious dialogue to promote reconciliation and building peace.

Every year, British Muslims are missing two golden opportunities to propagate the message of Islam, a message of peace, tolerance and justice, and to show how they integrate into the British society without losing their religion or watering down their faith.

The two occasions are Christmas and Easter celebrations.
The literal meaning of "Merry Christmas" is that "I wish you a happy celebration of Jesus' birthday". Unfortunately, many Muslims respond in an aggressive, rude or impolite way if someone wishes them a "Merry Christmas". Instead of saying "thank you" or "I also wish you the same" they say "No thanks, I don't celebrate Christmas." Although God commands them in verse 4:86 of the Qur'an that they should return the greeting in a more courteous way or at least just return it

The two occasions are Christmas and Easter celebrations. The literal meaning of "*Merry Christmas*" is that "I wish you a happy celebration of Jesus' birthday". Unfortunately, many Muslims respond in an aggressive, rude or impolite way if someone wishes them "Merry Christmas". Instead of saying "thank you" or "I also wish you the same" they say, "No thanks, I don't celebrate Christmas." Although God commands them in verse 4:86 of the Qur'an that they should return the greeting in a more courteous way or at least just return it.

Muslims are commanded by God to believe in all His Prophets and Messengers, without making any distinction between any of them, as stated by God in 2:136, 2:285, 3:84 and 4:150-152.

So, if Muslims believe in Mohammed and Jesus, why do many of them celebrate the birth of Mohammed and not the birth of Jesus? To celebrate, I mean to emulate, to study the Message they delivered, the lifestyle they lived, the great sacrifices they made and the legacy they left behind.

Let the members of each Muslim family get together during the Christmas holiday and forget about their differences. Let them talk about the purity and chastity of Mary, the role model to each and every Muslim girl, who must remain pure and chaste until she gets married. Let them reflect on how kind Jesus was to his mother who faced her angry people who accused her of committing adultery. Let them study the miracles of Jesus who gave life to the dead and healed the lepers and the blind, all by God's Decree. And despite all this, he remained to be a man, not God or the son of God.

When Prophet Mohammed (pbuh) was asked: "Why do you fast every Monday?" He replied: "A day I was born on and a day on which I received the first revelation ". So, he was celebrating the two occasions by fasting every Monday.

When he arrived in Madina, he noticed that the Jewish community were fasting. He asked them, 'Why are you fasting?". They answered, "It is a great day!" "Why is it a great day?" asked Prophet Mohammed (pbuh). They replied, "It is the day God saved Moses and the Israelites and drowned Pharaoh and his army. Hence, Moses decided to fast on this day (as a form of recognising the favour of God and giving thanks)". So, Mohammed (pbuh) said: "I have more to do with Moses than you" and he declared it a fasting day for the Muslims as well. This is the 10th day in the first month, Moharram, in the Islamic calendar. Regrettably, there are many Muslims who are not aware of this.

Mohammed (pbuh) did not ask the Jews to prove what the correct date was when Moses and the Israelites crossed the Red Sea, because it was something which had already happened, so the exact date was irrelevant.

The same with Christmas. whether Jesus was born on 25th December or 7th January, or any other date is irrelevant as Jesus was born already. The day he was born, was full of Peace as stated in the Qur'an in 19:33. The Qur'an tells us that he was born in the season of fresh, ripe dates, which could, in the Middle East be in the month of September. But it does not give the exact date because it is irrelevant.

Muslims have two feasts which they celebrate every year. The Arabic word for a feast is Eid. These two feasts are the feast of ending the fast of the month of Ramadhan and the feast of sacrifice, following the annual pilgrimage to Makkah.

However, there are certain days in our lives and our history, which we should remember and celebrate. In verse 5:24, God commands that we must remember "His Days".
In Arabic it is called "Ayyam" and the singular is "Yawm". The words "Eid" and "Yawm" have completely different meanings in Arabic. The days of God are the days when He showered us with His Mercy, Blessings and Favours and examples of these days are:
* the days when His prophets were born
* the day when He saved prophet Abraham from the fire
* the day He saved Ismael from being sacrificed
* the day He saved Moses and the children of Israel from Pharaoh
* the day He saved Jonah from the tummy of the whale
* the day He saved Jesus from his enemies and raised him alive onto Himself
* the day He saved Mohammed (pbuh) from his enemies when he emigrated from Makkah to Madina
* the day He took Mohammed (pbuh) on a journey by night from Makkah to Jerusalem and then into the heavens

- the day He started the Revelation to Mohammed (pbuh) in one of the last ten nights of the Holy month of Ramadhan

There are many other 'Days of God' in addition to the above which we should remember.

2) How do I celebrate Christmas?

I do celebrate Christmas by exchanging cards and gifts with my Christian brothers and sisters in humanity, and delivering talks about Mary and Jesus in the Qur'an, and getting my family together to study what God says about the virgin birth in the Qur'an. Also, by remembering and helping the poor, the needy and the lonely people. I do not celebrate Christmas by consuming alcohol or clubbing as this is against the teachings of Islam.

The BBC calls me *"The Imam who wears a tie and sends Christmas cards"*. I'm happy to be called that! Let me explain in more details my personal interaction with Christmas:

2. A) My Islamic Christmas Cards

In 2005 I decided to design a set of special Islamic Christmas cards talking about Mary and Jesus from the Qur'an. I print about 4,000 cards every year. I send them to members of the Royal family, members of the Houses of Parliament and Lords, churches, neighbours, colleagues at work, the Pope, all European leaders, etc... Amazingly I receive so many positive responses and interesting comments. I am pleasantly surprised and honoured that HM the Queen, the Prime Minister and the Pope respond to my cards every year.

On Tuesday 19th December 2017, Sky News reported: *"Pope and Queen among thousands sent Islamic Christmas cards by London Imam. Dr Mohammed Fahim hopes his cards will help dispel misconceptions about Islam and encourage more Muslims to celebrate Christmas."*

"Every Christmas London Imam sends Cards to Pope, Queen. A London Imam has sent thousands of Islamic Christmas cards around the world for ten years in his effort to highlight the significance of Jesus (peace be upon him) for Muslims and to share the festive season with his community..." Reported by "About Islam & News Agencies" on 19th December 2017.

Asian-Image wrote on 21st December 2017, *"Meet the Imam who sends out 4,000 Christmas cards every year..."*

"The imam who sends Christmas cards to the Pope. Every year, thousands of people from the Pope to Queen Elizabeth receive Christmas cards from an unlikely sender: a British Imam seeking to highlight the significance of Jesus for Muslims..." Reported by Free-Malaysia-today on 20th December 2017.

"London Imam uses Christmas opportunity to spread positive messages about Islam - Muslim Engagement and Development..." Wrote mend.org.uk on 21st December 2017.

I give below a few responses I received for my Islamic Christmas Cards:

1) The first ever response I received from her Majesty The Queen was dated 4th January 2006 and came from Sandringham House, where Her Majesty was spending Christmas:

"Dear Dr Fahim

The Queen wishes me to thank you so much for the message you have sent her for Christmas and the New Year.

Your good wishes are greatly appreciated by Her Majesty who hopes that you too have had a very happy Christmas.

Yours Sincerely

Lady-in-Waiting"

2) And the first response I received from His Holiness Pope Benedict XVI was dated 11th January 2007, from the Vatican:

"Dear Doctor Fahim

His Holiness Pope Benedict XVI has received the kind message of seasonal greetings that you sent to him and he has asked me to thank you. He joins all men and women of good will in the hope that the New Year will bring ever greater respect and understanding among the people of the world.

His Holiness invokes an abundance of divine blessings upon your loved ones in the coming year.

Yours sincerely

Monsignor Gabriel Caccia
Assessor"

3) From the "Direct Communications Unit" at 10 Downing Street, I received the following response dated 7th January 2008:

"Dear Dr Fahim

The Prime Minister has asked me to thank you for your recent Christmas card.

Yours sincerely

G Edwards"

4) Another response from the office of Prime Minister Rt Hon David Cameron dated 10th December 2015:

"Dear Dr Fahim

I am writing on behalf of the Prime Minister to thank you for your recent correspondence and Christmas card.

Mr Cameron very much appreciates your taking the time and trouble to share your views with him.

Yours sincerely

Correspondence Officer"

5) The following is the response received from Prime Minster Mrs May, dated 20th December 2016:

"Dear Dr Fahim

I am writing on behalf of the Prime Minister to thank you for your correspondence.

Mrs May appreciates the time you have taken to get in touch and share your thoughts.

Thank you, once again, for writing to the Prime Minister.

Yours sincerely

Correspondence Officer"

6) On 3rd January 2008, the following response was received from The Office of TRH The Prince of Wales and The Duchess of Cornwall, at Clarence House:

"Dear Dr. Fahim,

The Prince of Wales and The Duchess of Cornwall have asked me to thank you for the card you so kindly sent to them this Christmas.

Their Royal Highnesses greatly appreciated your kind thought and have asked me to send you their warmest thanks and their best wishes for the New Year.

Yours sincerely

Mrs Claudia Holloway"

7) The following response was received from Revered Kevin McDonald, Archbishop of Southwark, London, dated 16th December 2008:

"Dear Dr Fahim,

Thank you very much for your Christmas greetings. I also much appreciate the collection of texts from the Holy Qur'an which I find very helpful.

With every good wish.

Yours sincerely

Kevin McDonald
Archbishop of Southwark"

8) The next response dated 18th December 2008, was received from Rt. Rev. William Kenney C.P., Auxiliary Bishop of Birmingham:

"Dear Dr Fahim

Many thanks for the wonderfully photographed Christmas card you recently sent me. I have never seen one quite in that format before and I fully appreciate the beautiful quotes you have supplied.

With an assurance of my prayers and best wishes to you and all in your community.

Yours sincerely

Rt. Rev. William Kenney C.P.
Auxiliary Bishop of Birmingham"

9) Cllr Irfan Mustafa, London Borough of Redbridge, wrote on 20th December 2006:

"Respected Dr Fahim

Assalamualikum

Thank you for the beautiful card. This is the best ever card I have received with such a good message and information to our non-Muslim brothers and sisters. As always you are doing a wonderful work of real Dawah by propagating information about very peaceful religion of Islam to everyone. May Allah bless you and reward you for this.

Please convey my regards to your wife and accept my good wishes for a happy and prosperous New Year.

Yours sincerely

Irfan Mustafa"

10) Lord Hylton, House of Lords, sent the following message on 7th January 2009:

"Dear Dr Fahim

Thank you for the Christmas card you kindly sent me. Despite the profound doctrinal differences, there is a certain degree of overlap between Islam and Christianity. I respond warmly to the way in which you promote Islam as a religion of peace, justice and tolerance. This is so much needed when the Deobandi and Wahhabi factions, and the violent jihadists present such a stark alternative.

May I mention a few practical areas for cooperation

The Ammerdown Centre near Bath is committed to develop inter-faith and inter-religious dialogue and to promoting reconciliation and peace-building. Every two years it runs a Jewish/Christian/Muslim Summer School. Its email and website are:

The Ammerdown Conference and Retreat Centre
Ammerdown Park
Radstock
BA3 5SW
Tel: 01761 433709
Fax: 01761 433094
Email: centre@ammerdown.org
Website: www.ammerdown.org, www.ammerdown-conference.o.uk

Forward Thinking *is working through Muslims to help local Muslim communities with positive community relations and with connections to all kinds of British Institutions. Ask for Huda or Jusuf; I am a Trustee.*

Forward Thinking

84-86 Regent Street

London

W1B 5DD

Tel: +44 (0) 20 7734 2303

Fax: +44 (0) 20 7494 2570

Website: http://www.forwardthinking.org

Lastly, there is the appalling situation in Gaza and the West Bank. I am working on this in Parliament and indirectly on the ground. Even if we cannot do much to influence things, it is essential to prevent the current tragedies from spilling over into hatred and divisions in Britain.

Yours sincerely

Hylton
House of Lords"

In response to Lord Hylton's email I wrote on 7th January 2009:

"Dear Lord Hylton

Many thanks for your kind response. Also I am so grateful regarding the information you provided for future cooperation.

Being an executive member of the Three Faiths Forum in East London, I lead, with a Rabbi and a Priest a group of 23 Muslims, two Christians and one Jew to visit the Holy Land in October last year. This was the first ever trip by a group of British Muslims lead by a British Imam to Israel. The main objective was to achieve peace and reconciliation. The trip gained a lot of publicity in the Jewish press and local press in East London.

May God bless you for your efforts to help to reduce the suffering of the people in Gaza. Wishing you a very happy and peaceful new year.

Best regards

Yours sincerely

Dr Mohammed Fahim
Ph.D., M.Sc., B.Eng., MBCS, CITP, FCMI, C.Eng."

11) In Dec 2014, I received a very interesting response from the Rt Hon Desmond Swayne, the Minister of State for International Development, comparing my card to a paper written by a Muslim called Abdul Hurriyah condemning Islam, which he received just before Christmas.

Mr Swayne wrote:

"Dear Dr Mohammed
Thank you for your excellent card. See below the article it inspired me to write for the Salisbury Journal, and published on Thursday 1st January 2015, just as the events in Paris began to unfold.
Yours sincerely
Desmond Swayne"

At the end of his article to the Salisbury Journal, Mr Swayne said: *"In the days before Christmas I also received a Christmas card from Dr Mohammed Fahim, the head Imam at the Woodford Muslim Community Centre, wishing me God's peace, mercy and blessings. The card pointed out, something of which I was unaware: that over 1.5 billion Muslims worldwide believe in Jesus Christ, his virgin birth, his message, all his miracles, his ascension into heaven, and his second coming. On the reverse of the card is the following statement: 'Islam is a religion of peace, justice and tolerance. It rejects violence and condemns the killing of civilians anywhere in the world irrespective of their race or religion even if Islam is Insulted or ridiculed'. Abdul Hurriyah may think that Dr Fahim is deluded or dishonest, but I think we need to hear a great deal more from Dr Mohammed Fahim, and millions like him."*

12) The constituency office of the Rt Hon Steve Baker, Conservative MP for Wycombe, requested more cards to be sent to his office to show them to other people in his constituency.

13) Claudia Spens M.V.O. from The Office of TRH The Duke and Duchess of Cambridge and HRH Prince Henry of Wales, wrote on 26th January 2017 from Kensington Palace:

"Private and Confidential

Dear Dr. Fahim,

I am writing to thank you for your card and enclosure of 8th December (2016) to The Duke and Duchess of Cambridge and I must apologise for the delay in replying to you.

It was so kind of you to take the trouble to write as you did and Their Royal Highnesses would have me send you their warmest thanks and very best wishes.

Yours sincerely
Claudia Spens"

14) The following is the response of the Army Engagement Group, dated 5th December 2018:

"Dear Dr Fahim

Assalamu Alaikum

I hope you are in the best of health and Iman.

Thank you for your lovey Season's Greetings Card to the Army Engagement Group. As a Muslim serviceman it is a real pleasure to read and appreciate the effort you have gone to in creating it. It is a serious and festive way of building bridges between our faith and Christianity. It is the best card I have seen and is a very powerful message!

I see that you designed and produced it. I would be most appreciative if I could purchase some cards from yourself!?

Kind regards

Sid Khan

Warrant Officer 2
Saheed Khan (Intelligence Corps)
Army Engagement Group"

15) Responses from Our Neighbours at South Woodford, Christmas 2001:

A) *"To Islamic Community Centre*
South Woodford

Dear Islamic Community,

We would like to express our appreciation for your thoughtful Christmas card. We know that you are a peaceful community and are happy to have you as our neighbours.

Thank you once again.

Yours sincerely

Mr and Mrs B. M
Mulberry Way South Woodford
27/12/01"

B) *"To the Muslim Community, Mulberry Way*

Merry Christmas and a Happy New Year.

Thank you for your card.

From
Your Neighbours
X Violet Road
Christmas 2001"

C) *"To the worshippers at 12-14 Mulberry Way*

Happy Christmas

Season's greetings from your neighbours at XX Primrose Road and a peaceful New Year throughout the world."

D) The following response was the funniest one:

"DO NOT Put Such Rubbish Thro our door again - Try going to classes + learn some grammar + punctuation. I find this Very Offensive"

16) Jerry Crowley, the Advertising Manager, for the 'In Touch' magazine wrote on 7th January 2016:

"Dear Dr. Fahim,

This is a very belated e-mail, to thank you for the Christmas card you kindly sent me. I'm afraid this only reached me at the Church on the verge of Christmas, hence this slow acknowledgment.

I also want to thank you for the sentiments the card expressed, regarding your religion's belief in Jesus and all his works; for its clear and unambiguous statement that Islam is a religion of peace, justice and tolerance; and for its various excerpts from the Qur'an.

As someone who perhaps spends too much time writing about Middle East politics, and not enough time studying what true Islam stands for, I have been only vaguely aware of much of this, and have therefore found the Qur'an quotations very illuminating. It is also really gratifying, at this difficult time for relations between Islam and Christianity, to learn that our two faiths have so much in common.

*I wish you and the South Woodford Muslim Community well, and also thank you for your cheque to cover the **In Touch** adverts."*

The above responses are examples of many replies I received from Kings, Queens, Presidents, Prime Ministers and Religious Leaders all over the world.

On the other hand, when I shared these cards with some Imams from other mosques, they were so critical: *"How dare you say peace be upon you to these Christian Kafers (unbelievers)?"* they asked. So I responded by saying: *"Don't you know that my parents could be Christians, or Jews or even pagans, and God commands me to keep their good company and honour them. Don't you know that God allows me to marry a Christian or a Jewish woman and she can continue to practice her religion? Don't you know that our food is lawful to them and theirs is lawful to us? Don't you know that God commands us to have a good relation and deal equitably with everyone, except those who fight us for our religion or force us to leave our homes?".* I supported each statement by verses from the Qur'an but unfortunately it fell on deaf ears. I wonder what message these radical imams, or maybe confused Muslims, would deliver to their congregations, especially the young ones?!

2. B) The Christmas Tree - an Islamic Perspective

The Catholic Church of St Thomas of Canterbury, in Woodford Green, published my article "The Christmas Tree", in ISSUE 1 2006 of their magazine **"In Touch"**.

The editor Leon Menzies wrote: **"An Imam living and working in our parish writes poetically of his personal celebration of the birth of Jesus."**

"As a man of faith who believes in all God's Divine Revelations, and in all His Prophets from Adam to Mohammed without making any distinction between any of them, I find the Christmas tree gives me a lot of inspiration.

"Each year when I see the tree glowing with its decoration of tinsel and baubles, I'm reminded of the many trees described in the Qur'an, which speak to me of God.

"I'm reminded of the creation story when Adam and Eve fell into temptation and ate from the forbidden Tree of Eternity in the Garden of Eden. They repented and God forgave them.

"It reminds me of the Gofa trees with their tall, straight trunks which Noah had to plant so that he could build the Ark and save the righteous from the floods that covered the earth.

"It reminds me of the tree which grew up to shelter Jonah, its leaves soothing his ulcerated skin after he had been spewed out of the belly of the whale.

"It reminds me of the burning bush where God spoke to a fearful Moses asking him to return to Egypt to bring the Children of Israel out of slavery.

"It reminds me of the palm tree beneath which Mary delivered Jesus.

"It reminds me of the tree under which the disciples from Madina promised Mohammed they would adhere to the absolute unity of God, neither would they steal, commit adultery, kill their children, nor knowingly commit any evil and always obey God's commandments.

"It reminds me of the parable of the goodly Word. A goodly word is like a goodly tree whose roots are firmly fixed and its branches reach to the heavens. It brings forth its fruit at all times by the decree of its Lord. This goodly tree is known for its beauty, giving pleasure to all who see it; its stability remains firm and unshaken in storms, because its roots are firmly fixed in the earth. Its branches reach high and wide, catching all the sunlight from the heavens. It gives shade to countless birds in its branches and provides shelter for man and animals beneath. It provides fruit in abundance year after year. So also is the good Word, the word of truth, goodness and justice. It is as beautiful as it is true and is found in all the ups and downs of this life and even beyond. Deeply rooted in the soul of the man who has faith in God, it is never shaken by sorrow, or what seems a calamity.
The Word spreads above, around and below and because a divine light illuminates it, its consolation reaches countless numbers of people of whatever race or culture. To the man who carries the Word, he knows that he is only a channel, attributing all that he is and has to God who provides all things.

"In contrast to the goodly Word, the evil word is like the evil tree of Zaqqum, the bitter tree that has its roots in the very bottom of Hell. Its stalks produce bitter fruit likened to the heads of devils and those who fill themselves with its fruit find themselves in a vicious spiral of corruption. The evil word spreads out into our environment.

"Man destroys the beautiful tree of life by polluting the earth and poisoning the roots. Vast acres of rain forest are cut down to satisfy the insatiable demands of those countries that already have so much.

"Our hearts are hardened against the God who loves us. Our ears are deaf to warnings; our eyes are blind to suffering. In our arrogance we believe we can use the earth and its resources for our own selfish ends, caring little for the damage inflicted, the fertile plains turning to deserts, the seas choked with sewage, the skies obscured by the clouds of pollution. Today God has no need to unleash destruction on His people; we have chosen to unleash the destruction on ourselves.

"So as Christmas comes round once more, I am reminded of the two contrasts of good and evil. I am saddened that we forget the message that God entrusted to Jesus to bring to the world and only remember the non-stop consumerism, commercialization and the over-indulgence in alcohol and food.

"Let us not waste the opportunity this year of remembering the wider implications of our *greed and selfishness. Let us remember that there is a God who loves us."*

3) How Do I Celebrate Easter?

I dedicate Good Friday every year to talk to my congregation about what Islam says regarding what happened to Prophet Jesus on this day and how God saved him and raised him unto Himself?

I also organise a lecture to the children and their parents to talk about the same topic. Non-Muslim neighbours and church representatives are also invited. The lecture has a Q&A session to enable everyone to participate.

4) My Vision

Another way for me to celebrate Christmas is to exchange gifts with my Christian friends, colleagues and neighbours. According to Islamic history, the Prophet Muhammad (pbuh) exchanged gifts with non-Muslims. Whenever I explain this to Muslims at large, the radicals among them would object violently to my suggestions. I find it extremely difficult to even talk to radical Muslims as they do not know how to debate or respect the views of others. I always say to the confused Muslims who condemn Britain and call it "a land of blasphemy", that they should leave, stop claiming benefits, stop using the NHS or even stop sending their children to state schools.

Since the year 2000, I dedicate every Friday in December to talk to my congregation at South Woodford mosque about Mary and Jesus in the Qur'an. During the school Christmas holidays, I arrange a lecture for the Muslim children and their parents as well as the non-Muslim neighbours and church representatives, who are also invited. At the end we have a Q&A session which is usually very exciting.

I would like to have a nativity play from an Islamic perspective, performed by the Muslim children of our mosque's school. I will direct it myself and ensure that it will be on social media, as well as national and international news.

I would like to see every mosque and Muslim school in the UK emulating the above strategy to educate Muslim children and the public about Jesus and Mary in the Qur'an. I want them to participate and celebrate the two occasions, namely Christmas and Easter, in the way I described above. I want them to show the world that Muslims are integrating without losing their religion or watering down their faith, whilst embracing British values which do not contradict with Islamic values.

Surely, with measured and respectful discussion and allowances made for differences, through shared education and understanding, we can begin to see the common grounds and the fertile area, ready to sow the seeds of true brotherhood. This is what a connected, multi-faith and cohesive society needs to flourish.

3.2.15 Her Majesty's Diamond Jubilee

Following my Christmas card to her Majesty, in December 2011, I received a response dated 5th January 2012 from Sandringham House:

"Dear Dr Mohammed
The Queen wishes me to write and thank you very much for the message which you sent for Christmas.

Her Majesty greatly appreciated your kind thoughts in what was a particularly historic year for The Queen and her family, and I am to thank you once again for your continuing loyalty and support.

Yours sincerely,
Lady-in-Waiting"

And I received the following invitation from the Greater London Lieutenancy dated 26th January 2012:

"Dear Dr Fahim,

HER MAJESTY'S DIAMOND JUBILEE NORTH LONDON LUNCHTIME RECEPTION

Your name has been recommended to Her Majesty's Lord Lieutenant of Greater London, Sir David Brewer CMG, JP, as a north London resident who is recognised as an 'Achiever'. Consequently, he would like to invite you to attend Her Majesty's Diamond Jubilee North London Lunchtime Reception at Waltham Forest Assembly Hall, Forest Road, Walthamstow, E17 4JA, on Thursday 29th March 2012.

This is an unaccompanied invitation.
This is an unaccompanied invitation.

Please confirm your wish to attend by completing and signing the enclosed form, and return it to this office as soon as possible and certainly not later than Wednesday 29th February.

You will receive an official invitation from this office approximately one month before the date of the Reception together with Guidance Notes detailing the arrangements for the event.

Sir David Brewer hopes you will be able to accept this invitation and share in this enjoyable and memorable day.

Yours sincerely,

Ed Partridge

Wing Commander Ed Patridge

Clerk to the Greater London Lieutenancy"

On 10th February 2012, I wrote to Her Majesty congratulating her on her sixty year Diamond Jubilee:

"Your Majesty

On behalf of the Muslim Community in South Woodford, Woodford, Snaresbrook and Loughton and in my capacity as the Head Imam and Chairman of South Woodford Muslim Community Centre and Mosque, I would like to wish Your Majesty congratulations on reaching this momentous sixty year Diamond Jubilee Anniversary as Sovereign of the Realm.

The stability, security, prosperity and respect we have enjoyed as your subjects over your Reign is truly magnificent and very highly appreciated by the Muslim Community.

God says in the Holy Qur'an: "O ye who believe! Obey God, and obey the Messenger and those of you who are in Authority." 4:59

I remember your Majesty in my prayers every day.

I thank God and your Majesty, for the Civil Liberties and Equal Opportunities we enjoy, for the security we experience in both Domestic and National Capacity, for the Health Service, Education and Social Security and the true democracy your governments have practiced in clear transparency and accountability.

We, as British Muslims feel indebted to your Majesty that we can practice our religion without fear or intimidation in such a Great Tolerant Country.

Muslims are commanded by God to respect and obey the law of the country they live in, to respect other religions and uphold human rights. Islam condemns violence and aggression in all its forms, and the killing of any innocent people anywhere in the world.

I would also like to thank your Majesty for the invitation I received from Your Majesty's Lord Lieutenant of Greater London, Sir David Brewer, to attend Your Majesty's Diamond Jubilee North London Lunchtime Reception at Waltham Forest Assembly Hall, on Thursday 29th March 2012. This is a great honour.

The Muslim Community and I wish Your Majesty many more years to Reign with good health and happiness.

May God Almighty Bless Your Majesty and the Royal family

God save our Glorious Queen.

I have the honour to be your Majesty's humble and obedient servant.

Dr Mohammed Essam El-Din Fahim Ph.D., M.Sc., B.Eng., C.Eng. M.B.C.S., C.I.T.P."

I received the following response from Her Majesty dated 23rd February 2012, from **Buckingham Palace:**

"Dear Dr Fahim

I have been asked to thank you for your letter of 10th February containing a message from South Woodford Muslim Community Centre and Mosque.

This has been shown to Her Majesty and I now have pleasure in enclosing her reply.

Yours sincerely,

David Ryan
Director, Private Secretary's Office"

"I my grateful thanks to the members of the Muslim community of South Woodford, Snaresbrook and Loughton for their kind message of congratulations, sent on the occasion of the Sixtieth Anniversary of my Accession to the Throne.

In return, please accept my good wishes for a most memorable and enjoyable Diamond Jubilee year.

ELIZABETH R."

3.2.16 The Passing of Prince Philip and Our Sincere Condolences to the Royal Family

Upon the sad death of Prince Philip, I sent the following message of condolences to HM the Queen:

"

Dr Mohammed Fahim
10/14 Mulberry Way
South Woodford
London
E18 1ED

Her Majesty The Queen

Buckingham Palace

London SW1A 1AA

Friday 9th April 2021

Your Majesty, The Queen,

It is so sad to hear about the death of His Royal Highness The Prince Philip, Duke of Edinburgh.

Please accept the sincere condolences of the Muslim communities in South Woodford, Snaresbrook, Woodford, Buckhurst Hill and Loughton.

I was honoured to have met with Prince Philip on two occasions. First, when my Redbridge Rotary Club invited him to the Royal Festival Hall in the Rotary year 2004/05 to receive the highest honour in Rotary in recognition of the great community work which Prince Philip was doing. The second, was when I was invited to attend your Majesty's Diamond Jubilee, North London Lunchtime Reception at Waltham Forest Assembly Hall, Walthamstow, on 29th March 2012.

May God shower Prince Philip with His Mercy and admit him to His Gardens of Bliss. May God give your Majesty and all members of the Royal family patience and perseverance. May God and the Holy Spirit be with your Majesty and comfort you at this very difficult time. Our thoughts and prayers are with your Majesty. Please do let us know if there is anything else that we can do at this very sad time.

Kindest regards,

Dr. Mohammed Fahim
Ph.D., M.Sc, B.Eng, MBCS, CITP, FCMI, C.ENG
Chairman and Head Imam
South Woodford Mosque & Muslim Community Centre
Muslim Chaplain to the Met (Volunteer)

10/14 Mulberry Way, South Woodford, London, E18 1ED.
drmohammed.fahim@gmail.com"

I also shared the above message of condolences with members of the congregation at our mosque. Unfortunately, I received two very disappointing responses from two individuals.

A) The first response was from Mr K. A. MBE.

Disappointed Dr Sahib

"Dear Dr Fahim PhD, MSc, BEng, MBCS, CITP, FCMI, CENG,

Assalamu 'Alaikum,

I pray this email finds you in good and faith. Many in the Muslim community were astonished to read your letter to the Queen, in which you stated ' May God shower Prince Philip with Mercy and admit him to His Gardens of Bliss'.

There is no harm in sending a letter of condolence and respect but why is it that community leaders like yourself have to cross the red lines with such remarks. Clearly contravening the Book & Hukam of Allah (swt), whose Masjid/House you claim to represent. You have all these titles/degrees and you are undoubtedly a man who considers himself learned and scholarly, so what part of this verse do you not understand 'It is not (permissible) for the Prophet and the believers to seek forgiveness for the idolaters, even if they are kinsmen, after it became clear to them that they are the people of hell.' [Al Qur'an 9:113]

Please reflect and admit your error and refrain from such actions in the future. Sharm aur hayya di gali yaar, appa Queen da ihtram ta kardi an, likin audi chamche ta na baniye. Khuda di wasti.

Ma'Salaam,

K. A. MBE"

I found the above response to be very rude, aggressive, and baseless. Another example of confused, ignorant and aggressive Muslims. I remembered when God sent two of His messengers, Moses and Aron, to a tyrant Pharaoh, He commanded them in 20:44, to speak to him gently and mildly, perhaps he may heed or fear God. I also found his response was lacking any form of respect, or loyalty or indeed showing any real sympathy to the Royal family. I felt much hurt by his aggressive confusion and communication with me.

I'm glad I have included in Part I (page 31) of this book a section on "Special Consideration for the People of the Book", to educate those who are ill informed, like Mr K. A. MBE.

I immediately sent the following reply to him, while adhering to God's command in 25:63: "The (true) Servants of the Most Gracious are those who walk on earth in humility and when the ignorant (the foolish) address them (aggressively), they say 'Peace'."

My Response ....

"Dear Mr K. A. MBE
Salam
Many thanks for your email.

The verse you referred to, 9:113, talks about Pagans, idol worshippers المشركين
Prince Philip was not an idol worshipper. He was from the People of the Book اهل الكتاب.
So before attacking me, you need to understand the Arabic of the Qur'an.

The Qur'an makes clear distinctions between the idol worshippers and the People of the Book. For example, verse 5:5, makes their food lawful to us and our food lawful to them. It also allows a Muslim man to marry a chaste Christian or a Jewish woman, and she can continue to practice her religion and will enjoy equal rights like a Muslim wife.

Allah tells us in 5:116-119, that on the Day of Judgment Jesus would respond to Allah's question in 5:116, "O Jesus the son of Mary! Did you say to people 'take me and my mother for two gods beside Allah?' Jesus would respond by asking Allah to either punish them or forgive them, 5:117-118:
"I said to them only what You commanded me to say, (saying): 'Worship Allah, my Lord and your Lord.' I was a witness over them while I remained among them, and when You took me away, You were the Watcher over them, and You are the Witnesses over all things. If You punish them, they are Your servants. If You forgive them, You are the Exalted in power, the Wise."

"This is the limit of intercession that men of God can make on behalf of sinners," Footnote 832, A.Y.Aly.

Jesus would have not asked Allah to forgive them if they were idol worshippers.

It is entirely up to God to forgive or to punish. My prayer for Prince Philip was following what Jesus said.

As mentioned above, it is entirely up to God only, to forgive or to punish as stated in many verses in the Qur'an. Few examples are given below:

"To God belongs the sovereignty of the heavens and the earth. He forgives whom He wills and punishes whom He wills. And God is All-Forgiving, All-Merciful." 48:14

"That God may reward the truthful for their truth, and punish the hypocrites if He wills, or turn mercifully to them. God is indeed All-Forgiving, All-Merciful." 33:24

"To God belongs all that is in the heavens and all that is in the earth. He forgives whom He wills, and punishes whom He wills. God is All-Forgiving, All-Merciful." 3:129

"To God belong all that is in the heavens and all that is in the earth. Whether you disclose what is in your minds or you conceal it, God will call you to account for it. He will forgive whom He wills and punish whom He wills; and God has power over everything." 2:284

"He (God) punishes whom He wills, and shows mercy to whom He wills, and to Him you will be returned." 29:21

"Do you not know that to God belongs the kingdom of the Heavens and the earth? He punishes whom He wills and forgives whom He wills. And God has power over all things." 5:40

Kindest regards

Dr. Mohammed Fahim
Ph.D., M.Sc, B.Eng, MBCS, CITP, FCMI, C.ENG"

Upon sharing the above communications with several members of the congregation, I received many messages of support:

Some messages of support ....

"An excellent reply that shows knowledge and patience for the less well informed." Saleem Malik

And I received the following from Dr Qadir Bakhsh MBE:

"Assalammoalaikum Dr Fahim,

Your answer was succinct and spot-on.

May Allah سبحانه و تعالى *guide us all to be polite and courteous in engaging in any discussion and try to be respectful.*

I found the tone of Mr K.A a bit condescending and contemptuous, particularly the last two lines in roman Punjabi. I am sure he knows that you would not understand that: how rude and inappropriate.

If he understands and concurs with your explanation, then he should apologise. That will be a great gesture for a Muslim.

Wasalaam

Dr Qadir Bakhsh MBE"

The following is the response I received from Muarrij Ahmad:

"I'm so sorry you had to receive such a pathetic and insulting message. He obviously is very high up on his "MBE" horse.

Also if he sent you this message, he comes across as very insecure. Why would anyone say "Dear Dr Fahim PhD, MSc etc." If you are genuine, you would not take anything personal and

309

you would address the facts. Clearly, he has some sort of deficit which he is trying to make up for.

The worst thing is he can't even speak Punjabi properly and what did he write? I understand Punjabi very well, as well as Urdu. But this does not make sense. He clearly has no limits and wants to be abusive. Any professional person would not stoop to such levels.

Personally I would not furnish him with your precious time and bother sending him a response. He can say what he likes. It does not make it true.

I don't think he is even who he says he is. I could not find anything on the internet for someone with this name with an MBE. Unless he has reversed his name as there is one person, who comes from Punjab, working in Iraq with this name Abdul A. K who has an MBE. There is no way to be sure."

B) **The following is the second response I received:**

"Asalaamu Alaikum Warahmatullahi Wabaraqatahu,

I pray my message finds you in the best of health and imaan.

On the authority of Abi Ruqayyah Tamim ibn Aws ad-Dariyy (RA) that verily the Prophet (peace be upon him) said: "The religion is naseeha (good advice)". The people said: "To whom?" The Prophet (peace be upon him) replied: "To Allah and to His book and to His Messenger and to the leaders of the Muslims and to the common folk of Muslims. [Reported by Muslim]

I was writing in regards to your recent letter to the Queen (dated 9th April 2021). As Muslims, we must be compassionate and empathetic to all people, especially through times of difficulty. We should do this with respect and sincerity but not compromise our own values or beliefs. I feel your letter compromised this position and as a leader of the community it important that we are clear in our communications to avoid raising doubt.

May Allah SWT guide us and keep us steadfast.

Jazak'Allahu khair
A. Abu Maryam"

My Response ………………….

"Salam my dear brother
Many thanks for your message.
Could you please explain what did I say which compromised our values or beliefs?"

He responded by saying:

"Walaykum Asalaam,

Jazak'Allahu khair for your prompt response.

The invocation of the Holy Spirit."

I further responded ………………..

"Salam my dear brother
Many thanks for your response.
The Holy Spirit in the Qur'an i.e. in Islam, refers to Arch Angel Gabriel, pbuh. I have been a preacher for the last 52 years and I will never compromise my religion or water down my faith."
And I referred him to verses 2:87, 2:253, 5:110 and 16:102.

His response was………………..

"I am aware of Jibreel being referred to as Ar-Ruh but in our tradition we don't supplicate to him nor associate him with the Christian understanding of the Holy Spirit. I think in the context of addressing a Christian with reference to the Holy Spirit, it blurs this difference amongst our two faiths. This is especially true for those who don't appreciate this difference and cannot determine your intention.

I hope my feedback is clear and I pray we both gain some benefit from this conversation."

My response to above ………………..

"In my message I'm not supplicating to Gabriel pbuh, and no one should do that. I can ask Allah to support you with the Holy Spirit and send His
Angels of mercy on you. There is nothing wrong in that. However, it is our duty as Muslims to explain to others what the Islamic meaning is of روح القدس , the Holy Spirit as stated in the Qur'an.

To the Jews, as Allah states in 2:97-98, Gabriel is an enemy! To the Christians the Holy Spirit is one of the three coeternal and consubstantial persons in the Trinity. Which is totally rejected in Islam.

My dear brother, Her Majesty the Queen is the Head of the Church of England, and she knows exactly what I mean by the Holy Spirit. If I'm talking to an average Christian, then we need to be more specific, to minimise the confusion, as you were saying.

This is a very positive and healthy dialogue, and I'm so grateful to you for it. May Allah always unite our hearts, increase our knowledge and accept our prayers."
Some further messages of support from congregation members ………..

"Please don't worry about these people, you have educated them in your responses الحمد لله"
Bilal Nawaz

"Salaam thanks for sharing your thoughtful and referenced email responses to the two aggrieved individuals. I also feel as Brother Bilal states that you have educated them from your stance and clarified specifically the "Holy Spirit". It may be that they still are aggrieved and for that you are not responsible 👍Take care" Tallat Bhatti

3.3 Conclusion

Many British Muslims are either born in this great country or they are immigrants like me. One of the main challenges I faced when I came to England in July 1970, was how to engage effectively with people who did not share my religion or culture. I was excited to build new connections and friendships within my new networks, such as my colleagues at work, my neighbours where I lived or my university acquaintances. To overcome this concern, I relied entirely on the Qur'an and the tradition of Prophet Mohammed (pbuh), who sought to build relationships and trust by clearly defining and practicing the rights of neighbours, irrespective of their religion or ethnicity. He showed kindness and affection towards his non-Muslim neighbours. When he immigrated from Makkah to Madina after thirteen years of persecution by his own people, he formed the Madina Charter, which allowed Muslims, Jews and pagans to live together in peace and harmony under his leadership.

In this Chapter, I have detailed my involvement with different communities, organisations, schools, government departments, religious forums, and dignitaries. I have not wasted a single opportunity in delivering God's Message using wisdom and good preaching. My motto is: "The human race is one family, hence we are all brothers and sisters in humanity, irrespective of our ethnicities or religions".

Whilst delivering God's Message, some people have been hostile towards me, not only from the non-Muslim communities, but also from within the Muslim community. I had to exercise extreme patience and consideration in my response to them and continue to do so. However, the insults and the disappointments I have experienced were nothing compared to the insults and challenges faced by God's Messengers and this has given me strength and resolve to continue in my journey towards building community cohesion, tolerance and shared understanding.

It is the responsibility of all Muslims to not waste an opportunity of conveying the Message of Islam, only if they have adequate knowledge themselves and their conduct reflects the true teachings of Islam. Therefore, a Muslim's responsibility is to, first and foremost, educate themselves in the Qur'an and Prophetic teachings. This will enable them to respond to people in the correct manner, and to train themselves to debate with knowledge and courtesy, whilst being good listeners and not to condemn others or claim purity for themselves.

Indeed, it is only when people feel truly heard that they begin to fully comprehend that there may be another viewpoint and perhaps in time will be ready to listen. This does not mean they will automatically change their viewpoint and of course we have no right to demand this but when people are ready to listen, this in my experience is when those precious bridges of tolerance and understanding begin to be constructed. It is the investment of time and understanding in building these bridges that can help us all safely cross the many trials and challenges that can arise over time when religion is debated.

As Muslims, our loyalty is to God. This means we must abide by all His Commandments. One of these Commandments is to be loyal to the country we live in. Subsequently, we must honour all agreements and pledges and respect and obey the law of the land.

I believe that every British citizen, irrespective of his ethnicity or religion, must be supportive to the police and the army as defenders of the State. As a practicing Muslim, this is not just a national duty, but it is a religious obligation.

I mentioned earlier that Christmas and Easter are two golden opportunities for Muslims to deliver God's Message. I would like to see every mosque and Muslim school in the UK emulating the above strategy to educate Muslim children and the public about Jesus and Mary in the Qur'an. I want them to participate and celebrate the two occasions, in the way I described in this Chapter. I want them to show the world that Muslims are integrating without losing their religion or watering down their faith, whilst embracing British values which do not contradict with Islamic values.

If you want to see my Islamic Christmas cards and some of the responses received, please refer to the following Instagram and Facebook links below:

http://instagram.com/swic.uk
http://facebook.com/swic.uk
http://twitter.com/ukswic
https://www.youtube.com/c/swicsouthwoodfordislamiccentre
https://swic.uk

Bibliography

A) Qur'anic Sources, Translations, Tafasir, Etc.

Ali, Abdullah Yusuf. The Meaning of The Holy Qur'an. Beltsville, Maryland: Amana Publications, 2001.

Al-Ghazaly, Mohammed. Nahwa Tafsir Mawdo'ee Le-Sewar Al-Qur'an Al-Karim. Cairo, Egypt: Dar Ash-Shorouq, 1st Edition, 1995.

Al-Mahalli, Jalal Al-Din and Al-Suyuti, Jalal Al-Din. Tafsir Al-Imamain Al-Jalalayn. Beirut, Lebanon: 1974.

Al-Nasafi, Abdullah Ibn Ahmad. Tafsir Al-Qur'an Al-Jalil. Cairo, Egypt: Al-America Press, 1936.

Al-Sha'rawi, Mohammed Metwalli. Tafsir Al-Sha'rawi. Cairo, Egypt: Akhbar El-Yom Press, 1975.

Barlas, Asma. Believing Women in Islam: Unreading Patriachal Interpretations of the Qur'an. Austin, USA: University of Texas Press, 2002.

Ibn-Kathir, Emaduldin Ismail. Tafsir Al-Qur'an Al-Azim. Cairo, Egypt: Dar Ehiaulkutub Al-Arabia, Esa Al-Baby Al-Halaby Press, 1946.

Ismael, Mohammed Bakr. Kholasat At-Tafsir. Cairo, Egypt: Dar Almanar, 1995.

Kassam, Zayn. The Hermeneutics of Problematic Gender Verses in the Qur'an. London and New Jersey: Zed Books, 1996.

Tantawy, Moammed Said. Banu-Israel fi Al-Qur'an wa As-Sunna. Cairo, Egypt: Dar Ash-Shorouk, 2nd Edition, 2000.

Wadud-Muhsin, Amina. Qur'an and Woman. Kuala Lumpar: Penerbit Fajar Bakti Sdn.Bhd, 1994.

B) Fatwas Sources

Al-Qaradawi, Yusuf. Fatawi Mu'aasera. Cairo, Egypt: Dar Al- Qalam, 6th Edition, 1996.

Ibn-Taimeia, Abi-Alabbas Taqi Al-Din Ahmad Ibn Abdul-Halim. Al-Fatawi Al-Kubra. Beirut, Lebanon: Dar Al-M'arefa,

Saqr, Ateya. Al-Fatawi. Cairo, Egypt: Al-Maktaba Al-Tawfeqeia

C) Fiqh Sources

Abu-Zohra, Mohammed. Osool Al-Fiqh. Cairo, Egypt: Dar Al-Fikr Al-Araby, 1997.

Al-Gazery, Abdul-Rahman. The Book of Fiqh as per the Four Mazhabs. Cairo, Egypt: Dar Al-Irshad,

Al-Ghazaly, Mohammed. Fiqh As-Serah. Alexandria, Egypt: Dar Al-D'awa 6th Edition, 2000.

Al-Ghazaly, Mohammed. As-Sunnah An-Nabawia bain Ahl Al-Fiqh wa Ahl Al-Hadith. Cairo, Egypt: Dar Ash-Shorouk, 2011.

Al-Qaradawi, Yusuf. Fiqh Al-Awlaweyat. Cairo, Egypt: Maktabet Wahba, 3rd Edition, 1999.

Al-Qaradawi, Yusuf. The Lawful and the Prohibited in Islam. Plainfield, Indiana, USA: American Trust Publications, 1994.

Al-Sha'rawi, Mohammed Metwalli. Al-Fiqh Al-Islami, 100 Questions and Answers. Cairo, Egypt: Maktabat At-Turath Al-Islami,

Darwesh, Hussain Ali. Al-Merath fi Al-Islam as per the Four Mazhabs. Cairo, Egypt: Al-Zahra Lel-Ilam Al-Araby, 5th Edition, 1987.

Ibn-Hazm, Abi Mohammed Ali Bin-Ahmad Bin-Said. Al-Muhalla. Cairo, Egypt: Dar Al-Turath,

Ismael, Dr Mohammed Bakr. Al-Fiqh Al-Wadheh mena Al-Ketab wa Assuna based on the Four Mazhabs. Cairo, Egypt: Dar Al-Manar, 1990.

Sabeq, As'sayed. Fiqh As'sunnah. Beirut, Lebanon: Dar Al-Ketab Al-Araby & Cairo, Egypt: Dar Al-Fath, 2004.

Al-Albany, Mohammed Nasir, Ar-Rad al-Mufhim. Amman Jordan: Al-Maktaba Al-Islamia, 1st Edition, 2000.

D) Scientific Sources

Board of Researchers under the Research Programme of 1985-1990. Scientific Indications in the Holy Qur'an. Dhaka, Bangladesh: Islamic Foundation Bangladesh, 2nd Edition, 1995.

Bucaille, Maurice. What is the Origin of Man? Urdu Nagar, LHR: Al-Falah Islamic Books, 5th Edition, 1989.

E) Other Islamic Sources

Abdel Haleem, Harfiyah; Ramsbotham, Oliver; Risaluddin, Saba and Wicker, Brian. The Crescent and the Cross, Muslim and Christian Approach to War and Peace. Great Britain: MacMillan Press Ltd, 1998.

Abu Shuqqa, Abdul Halim Mohammed. Tahreer Al-Maraa fi Asr Ar-Resalah. Cairo, Egypt & Kuwait: Dar Al-Qalam, 8th Edition, 2010.

Ad-Dhahabi, Muhammad Bin Uthman. The Chief Sins (Al-Kaba'r). Beirut, Lebanon: Dar Al-Kotob Al-Ilmiyah, 1st Edition, 1999.

Al-Ghazaly, Mohammed. Kholoq Al-Muslim. Cairo, Egypt: Dar Nahdet Misr, 22nd Edition, 2014.

An-Nawawi, Abu Zakariya Yahya Bin Sharaf. Riyadh-us-Saleheen. Karachi, Pakistan: Dar Ahy'a us-Sunna Al-Nabawiy'a, 1984.

Engineer, Asghar Ali. The Rights of Women in Islam. USA.UK.INDIA: New Dawn Press, Inc., 2nd Revised Edition, 2004.

Confused 💔 Muslims.Qom – Confessions of a London Imam

"An excellent and powerful guidebook to navigate the arena of Islam and no question is taboo, here is the guide you have been waiting for"

So, Islam is the final message from God to mankind, a great religion and the way to peace and prosperity...

But...

- Why the current internal conflicts in many so-called Muslim nations?

- Why is there a rise of Islamophobia?

- Why are Muslims feeling misunderstood and the religion becoming synonymous with terrorism?

- Why does it seem that Muslims cannot live alongside other religions in peace?

This book provides answers to the above issues and more. It challenges and rectifies current misconceptions both for those within the faith and to those outside. Information presented on the basis of extensive research, solid religious understanding and in reference to all Qur'anic text.

A handy guide to all, those engaged in education, community development work, the police, corporate world and indeed anyone who wishes to understand the true Islamic viewpoint on any issues of life or death and gain an insight into the reasons for the decline of Muslim nations.

This book is a refreshing insight into the religion of Islam. A religion that empowers women, condemns violence and advocates for peace.

Dr Mohammed Fahim, PhD, MSc, BEng, MBCS, CITP, FCMI, CEng is the Chairman and Head Imam of South Woodford Islamic Centre. He has dedicated the past 25 years to leading the Centre and Mosque to become an integral part of local life for the Muslim residents, whilst striving to develop the Centre's close and welcoming relations with its immediate neighbours of all faiths and none. As a member of the Three Faiths Forum, he has promoted unity and understanding between the Abrahamic faiths, giving talks, lectures and Holy Land tours. Becoming a member of the London Muslim Communities Forum in 2010, he has been consistently and actively involved in enhancing community relations and cohesion. This book allows you to accompany Dr Fahim as he travels back to recount his first steps on British soil, and also his journey around the globe. His heart ultimately resting in East London, his home for the past 50 years, this book shares some of the challenges he has faced as an Imam. Dr Fahim shines a candid light on radical Muslim teachers, taboo subjects such as FGM, domestic violence, honour killings and suicide etc. Discussing issues in an open way, this book debunks many myths of Islam and allows readers to gain an in depth understanding on the true Islamic perspective.

Printed in Great Britain
by Amazon

39165423R00178